Behavioral Objectives in Curriculum Development

Behavioral Objectives in Curriculum Development

Selected Readings and Bibliography

Miriam B. Kapfer

Educational Technology Publications
Englewood Cliffs, New Jersey 07632

First Printing

Library of Congress Catalog Card Number: 77-122809

International Standard Book Number: 0-87778-001-3

Printed in the United States of America

To my husband Philip, and our children, Paul and Stephanie—whose behavioral objectives helped me complete this book of readings.

Preface

The specification of objectives for education is not new. Neither is concern for the sources, form, and content of such objectives. However, during recent years, and particularly during the decade of the Sixties, the function of behavioral objectives in curriculum development has received renewed emphasis. Educators have become aware of the Taxonomy *in the cognitive and affective domains. Interest in Mager's* Preparing Instructional Objectives *has expanded from almost exclusive use by programmers to extensive use in all areas of curriculum planning. The number of behaviorally oriented articles, monographs, and other media appearing on the professional scene has multiplied rapidly. In sum, behaviorally stated objectives are increasingly accepted as keys which unlock the doors of better instruction and more productive learning.*

Yet, many curriculum leaders, curriculum development teams, programmers, and individual teachers experience difficulty at some point in the preparation and use of behavioral objectives. These difficulties arise from several sources—(1) a presumed paucity of useful materials on the subject; (2) occasionally inappropriate approaches, purposes, and difficulty levels of the materials that are available and known; (3) a lack of conviction in some quarters concerning the genuine importance of behavioral objectives; and (4) the very real difficulty of creating materials which effectively incorporate the behavioral approach.

The first of these problems—the assumed lack of useful materials on behavioral objectives—is more apparent than real, perhaps because much of the practical thought and information on the subject that now is available is only recently available. Most of the material in the present volume, for example, appeared in print during the last three years. Major books on the subject (in addition to the well-known Mager, Bloom, and Krathwohl works) are practically non-existent, and the several smaller but quite useful monographs which deal with the subject, either briefly or in some detail, are widely dispersed in terms of publishers and sponsoring groups. For the first time, in the present volume, an attempt is made to bring together a convenient collection of current thought on the subject, together with references to many other works which provide both historical and contemporary perspective for the field.

Second, the problems stemming from the difficulty levels and purposes of available materials are largely solved in the present volume if one considers both the materials actually reprinted here as well as those suggested in the bibliographies at the end of each section in the book. The materials range considerably with respect to purpose, intended audience, level of sophistication, and medium.

Third, the resistance of people to a popular and compelling, but new (to them), idea can sometimes be re-created in a positive form by exploring similar reservations expressed by leading thinkers. Simply the recognition that problems concerning the new idea do exist, and the realization that the new idea is not being touted as a failure-proof panacea, are sometimes adequate to motivate the "unbeliever" to approach the new idea with an open mind. Thus, it was considered important to include a section in the book which would both raise questions and answer, as well as possible, many of the often expressed reservations concerning the behavioral approach.

The fourth source of problems mentioned above concerns the genuine difficulty of preparing behaviorally oriented curricular materials. Even though some materials of a simple and purely practical nature have been included in this volume, no intention to over-simplify should be assumed. The difficulty of writing objectives which adequately communicate the observable behavior expected of the student, while at the same time avoiding triteness and maintaining educational respectability, is a very real problem. Those who have actually worked with teachers in the development of behaviorally oriented curricular materials will recognize this problem immediately as a persistently difficult one. Therefore, in addition to including a number of selections which emphasize a very straightforward, practical approach, other materials were selected because of their higher level of abstraction. In this way an attempt was made to provide a useful balance of theory and practice.

Specifically, the book is organized into eight sections. Part I is a compilation of practical materials which reinforce and elaborate on a few basic ideas about behavioral objectives. Part II deals with the common ways of analyzing and classifying objectives. In the third section, the adaptability of the behavioral approach to the teaching of values is explored. In Part IV, the use of behavioral objectives in curricular strategies, including independent study and individualized instruction, is described. Part V provides specific ideas and examples of the use of behavioral objectives in various subject matter areas. Part VI deals with behavioral objectives as a part of broadly defined "educational technology," a topic which encompasses systems development, computer assisted instruction, and learning packages. In Part VII, the relationship of objectives and fruitful evaluation is considered. The concluding section, Part VIII, deals with the historical and theoretical background of the behavioral approach as well as with some of its problem areas. Of course, these eight categories are not mutually exclusive. In fact, a single article may touch on several categories. The book was organized, however, to correspond to the needs of users with varied interests and specialties. Articles then were placed based on their primary focus with reference to those needs and interests.

This book of readings is designed for use by educators at all levels of influence and responsibility. Perhaps most importantly, however, it is intended for use by individual teachers and teaching teams who have dedicated themselves to transforming national, state, district, school, teacher, and even student goals into statements which define as precisely as possible the specific objectives for the student's learning. Unless teachers understand and appreciate the value of behavioral objectives, and communicate these ideas to the student, the ultimate goal of the behavioral approach, the improvement and individualization of learning opportunities for the student, will not be realized.

A final word concerning terminology—the reader will notice that the term "behavioral objective" has been used thus far to refer to the type of objective which attempts to define exactly what, how well, *and* under what circumstances *a student will be able to perform. In reading the various authors contained in the book, it will soon become evident that other terms meaning essentially the same thing are often substituted for "behavioral objective." These include "instructional objective," "learning objective," "operational objective," "performance objective," "performance criterion," and possibly others. The particular term used is more often representative of author preferences than of basic differences in meaning among the terms.*

Miriam B. Kapfer

Contents

Behavioral Objectives in Curriculum Development

Part I

Behavioral Objectives— An Overview of What, Why, and How

Each of the selections in Part I is included because of its pertinence to one or more of the following questions: "What are behavioral objectives?" "Why are behavioral objectives important?" and "How are objectives written in behavioral terms?"

Practical answers to these three questions are urgently needed when teachers, programmers, or curriculum development teams are initially faced with the problem of stating specific objectives for a given educational course, experience, or task. Once these questions are answered, even if somewhat hastily or superficially, then the curriculum worker is freed to proceed with his immediate writing task. At the same time he is being prepared to pursue further the more complicated levels and applications of educational objectives. Thus, Part I serves as an overview, while subsequent sections focus in greater depth on several other aspects of behavioral objectives.

As the reader proceeds through Part I, he will note that the various writers who have been included are often saying essentially the same thing, but in different ways. Thus, the answers given to the what, why, and how questions should provide an "in-tune channel" for most readers; explanations and examples used by one writer may reach a certain group of readers, while another writer's style and material may be more meaningful to a different group.

The Deterline article heads this section because in it the problems relating to insufficient use of objectives are pointed up in ways that have an amusing but serious ring of familiarity. The selections by Esbensen and Craik delineate the basic elements of the behavioral approach. The Cohen article provides supplementary ideas concerning sources, levels, and sequences of objectives. In the final article, Rahmlow provides a practical procedure for developing well-stated and meaningful instructional objectives, test items, and learning activities.

In an era in which people are accustomed to thinking in terms of the "games people play," Deterline amusingly describes what he calls the "Big Game" of education. He believes that students spend too much time guessing the teacher's rules for getting through the "murk of overabundant disorganized information." New ground rules are proposed for a trauma-free education game by providing students with course objectives in the form of minimum performance requirements and sample test items.

The Secrets We Keep from Students*

WILLIAM A. DETERLINE

Teachers spend most of their time presenting information to students— as much information as possible, in as many ways as possible.

Students listen to lectures, watch demonstrations, work in laboratories, read textbooks, consult supplementary references, look at illustrations, sit through audiovisual presentations, take part in discussions with teachers and fellow students, and confer privately with teachers.

Unfortunately, they are all too often overwhelmed by the bounty heaped upon them.

They carry out activities called *studying, reviewing, note taking,* and *outlining*—all as part of an attempt to process a mass of information and "learn it." By "learn it" we mean that their behavioral repertoires are

*Reprinted from *Educational Technology, 8,* February 15, 1968, pp. 7-10, by permission of the publisher and the author.

to change so that they can then produce equivalent forms of the information, apply it, explain it, make decisions on the basis of it, solve problems, or do something that indicates that the content of the course has been assimilated.

Supposedly, the student's task is to learn the course content; in reality, it is *not* intended that he learn *all* of it. For example, it is not difficult to imagine a dialogue like this taking place between a student and his teacher:

Scene: A classroom. The teacher has just given the students their graded essay examination papers, and a student has asked why one of his answers received zero credit.

Teacher: Because I asked you to explain the general principle, and you only discussed a specific example.

Student: But you taught us all about that example.

Teacher: Yes, and we discussed many other examples, but only to make the principle easier to understand. That's what you were *really* supposed to learn—the principle. Don't you remember our going over the principle several times?

Student: Vaguely, but I remember the examples better. We spent more time on them and they were easier to understand.

The teacher and the student have become ensnared in an almost universal educational problem. And here is another dialogue that illustrates the same problem in another form:

Student: I don't think this question is fair.

Teacher: Why not?

Student: Because it is about something that doesn't seem to be very important. You spent only a short time on it, and the book covers it in only a half a page. I concentrated on this other topic because it seems to me to be so much more important. You spent three class periods on it, and it fills almost eight pages in the book, but you only asked two questions about it. What should I do before the next test in order to study the right things?

What can the teacher say? Study everything?

These examples are only two possible manifestations of a problem encountered by all students and all teachers—and we can probably add, a problem encountered all of the time: students cannot discriminate the exact composition and form of the behavior that makes up the instructional objectives of most courses. They cannot discriminate because no one tells them exactly what they should be able to do at the end of instruction; they are not told the objectives of a 50-minute class period, a homework assignment, or a complete course. We inundate them with information of all kinds and in all forms, but we do *not* tell them what to do with it or exactly what performance is expected of them. How is the student to discriminate, select, and attend appropriately? He can't.

Consequently, he is left with the chilling prospect of either trying to learn everything or concentrating on a manageable portion—hopefully the correct portion—and ignoring the rest. If he tries to learn everything, there is a better than even chance that he will know a little bit about everything, but not enough about anything. If he tries to "pick his spots," he runs the risk of choosing the irrelevant portions for his study in depth.

Providing Guidelines

If we neglect to provide the necessary guidelines prior to starting the course of instruction, we could still salvage something by providing that guidance after presenting the information but *before* testing the student's learning. But do we?

When anxious students press us for information about a forthcoming examination, we generally refuse to provide specific answers to specific questions. We guard our test with an enthusiasm and vigor that would impress the CIA! We make examinations a dandy surprise and a traumatic experience.

Students, at least by the time they get to college, learn something about the game called "Try to figure out the teacher's test building strategies." The first examination given by a teacher usually furnishes information to the students that they should have been given long before the examination period, on the day that they first encountered the material later covered by the examination.

In addition to outraged indignation by students who do not play the strategy guessing game very well, another frequent response to the first examination, usually by students who have become fairly skillful players, is "So this is the way the cagey old rascal plays the game!" This is how we compound our first error: we heap secrets upon secrets! Ten teachers presenting the same course content would probably construct ten different types of tests. The first likes essay questions. The second is a true-and-false devotee. The third formulates questions requiring concrete, factual answers. The fourth expects extrapolation from practical examples to abstract concepts. And so it goes.

All of these test items are valid, and every teacher probably makes use of all of them. That, however, is not the point. Admitted or not, almost every teacher has a *preference* for a particular type of question, and his tests will usually contain more items of that type. This, of course, is only a temporary secret since the first test gives it away. While it lasts, however, it adds to the general confusion created by the Big Game.

"Ground Rules" Needed

Students have enough problems without having to try to learn to play games without ground rules but with penalties that always go against the same team. Bill Cosby, the comedian, does a brief skit about football referees and their explanations of the pre-game toss of the coin that determines who kicks off and who defends which goal. He extrapolates to several other conflict settings and describes the referee's telling Washington and Cornwallis that Washington had called the toss of the coin correctly: "All right, the colonists won the toss so they can wear whatever they like and hide behind trees. You British have to wear red coats and march in straight lines." Students preparing for tests have apparently also lost the toss of the coin.

And any father, preparing to assemble a child's wagon, car, or more complex unassembled toy, with all of the poles and tubes and boards and chains and hooks and nuts and bolts and washers in vast and awesome confusion on the floor at his feet, can readily identify with the student, particularly when he finds that the assembly directions are missing.

Down with Guessing Games

Course examinations do not have to be traumatic. Students should not have to play guessing games about objectives; students should not have difficulty discriminating objectives from instructional clarification content, irrelevant content, or enrichment and interest-only content. The game should be designed with better odds for the student, and we should always provide concise directions with every set of parts.

Most teachers do attempt to provide some specific guidance in some form, some of the time, but there should be a better basis for doing it with precision, without fail, all of the time. ("Without fail" was not intended as a pun, but who knows what the consequences might be!)

Too many proposed "solutions" or "improvements" in instructional methodology begin: "The teacher should . . ." I am sure that teachers appreciate suggestions of this sort, since the additional activities will help fill up all that free time that they have available during the school day! We should have objectives for every course and for every instructional event, presentation, or class period. We should *not,* however, assume that the identification and specification of objectives can be done on a part-time, additional-duty basis by teachers who have direct instructional responsibilities.

Recommendations

Textbooks should include specifications of the objectives they were designed to achieve, cross-referenced to content presentations, and they should also contain sample criterion test items, problems, and activities. Unfortunately, textbook authors keep secrets from everybody: students, teachers, school systems, and even their publishers! What I am recommending, obviously, is that *all* textbooks meet the exacting standards set for *programmed* textbooks by the joint committee of the American Educational Research Association, the American Psychological Association, and the Department of Audiovisual Instruction of the National Educational Association.

Specification of additional objectives or deletion of certain objectives could be done by curriculum specialists or by local or national curriculum study groups, but objectives should come to the classroom from "somewhere." The teachers and the students can proceed from there.

Robert Mager's book, *Preparing Instructional Objectives,* was at one time entitled, *Preparing Objectives for Programmed Instruction,* and it was considered to be an "in-group" item by the people involved in programmed instruction.

Today, however, neither behaviorally defined objectives nor Mager's book belong exclusively to programmed instruction; teachers, schools, entire school systems, curriculum committees, and people concerned with instruction in many settings are seriously attempting to follow Mager's guidelines. But using objectives as a basis for the design of instruction and as guides for the teacher or writer is using only part of the potential of the objectives. And Mager commented on that too:

> *"If you give each learner a copy of your objectives, you may not have to do much else."*

What Would Happen?

What would happen if objectives could be given to students? We already have considerable evidence from many sources, including experimental settings and a few operational school systems, that a new game with good ground rules suddenly appears—one that is more exciting to watch and more fun to play.

If students are told precisely what the objectives are, in the form of descriptions of at least minimum performance requirements, and are given sample criterion questions, the entire learning task suddenly breaks through the murk of overabundant, disorganized information so that definable goals and directions for student activity are clearly visible.

This does not mean that studying will be any easier or that the subject matter concepts or study materials will be learned without difficulty. It does mean that the studying will be more relevant, time will be more fruitfully spent on appropriate content, and each student will have a basis for discriminating his own progress, obstacles, and any need for assistance.

Teaching would benefit and so would learning. Examinations would become something quite different and less threatening. A student entering a classroom to take an examination should feel as smug and secure as an individual who has somehow gotten a copy of the examination in advance, but without the guilt. We should have no secrets from our students—if we, the leaders, know where we are leading our students. Is *that* the secret we are zealously guarding?

In a concise and Magerian approach to learning objectives, Esbensen answers the question, "What are the characteristics of a well-written instructional objective?" Using a wealth of examples, he focuses on the writing of statements which describe the student's performance, the conditions under which the performance occurs, and the extent of the performance. Esbensen's final comment concerning the elimination of the "traditional fuzziness of classroom assignments" alludes to perhaps the most important reason for using the behavioral approach—so that each student can be given the objectives needed to motivate and guide him in his own learning.

Writing Instructional Objectives*

THORWALD ESBENSEN

For many years, educators have talked about the importance of instructional objectives. The purpose of an instructional objective is to make clear to teachers, students, and other interested persons *what it is that needs to be taught—or what it is that has been taught.*

A well-written instructional objective should say three things: 1) what it is that a student who has mastered the objective will be able to *do,* 2) under what *conditions* he will be able to do it, and 3) to what *extent* he will be able to do it. To put the matter in a single sentence, a well-written instructional objective should specify under what conditions and

*Reprinted from the *Phi Delta Kappan, 48,* January, 1967, pp. 246-247, by permission of the publisher and the author.

to what extent a certain kind of student performance can be expected to take place.

Performance—conditions—extent. Let us consider first the word *performance.* Performing means doing. A student who performs something does something.

Here are two statements. Which one is expressed in terms of student performance?

A. *The student will have a good understanding of the letters of the alphabet,. A through Z.*

B. *The student will be able to pronounce the names of the letters of the alphabet, A through Z.*

Statement B tells what it is that the student will be able to *do.* He will be able to *pronounce* the names of the letters of the alphabet, A through Z.

Statement A tells us that the student will have a good *understanding* of the letters of the alphabet. But this is not very clear. We cannot tell what it is that the student is supposed to be able to *do* as a result of this understanding.

Let's try another pair of statements. Which one is expressed in terms of student performance?

A. *The student will have an adequate comprehension of the mechanics of punctuation.*

B. *Given a sentence containing an error in punctuation, the student will correct the mistake.*

Statement B tells what it is that the student will *do.* Statement A, which says that the student will have an adequate *comprehension* of the mechanics of punctuation, is pretty vague. We cannot tell what it is that the student is supposed to be able to *do* as a result of his comprehension.

At this point, an objection may be raised. Isn't the person who is comprehending something doing something? Isn't intellectual performance an acceptable kind of student performance?

Certainly. The difficulty is that mental activity, as such, is not directly observable. We cannot literally open up a person's head and see the thinking that is going on inside. If it is to be of use to us, a statement of performance must specify some sort of behavior that can be observed.

This does not mean that we are not concerned about intellectual performance. It does mean that since mental activity, as such, is not directly observable, some sort of behavior that is observable will have to stand for or represent the intellectual performance we have in mind.

For example, suppose that we are interested in having students know something about the writing style of Ernest Hemingway. Whatever may be intellectually involved in the attainment of this goal, it should be apparent that the language of our aim as stated leaves much to be desired.

What is the student who *knows* able to do that the student who does *not know* is not able to do? This is the important question, because we cannot measure the accomplishment of our instructional purpose until we have worked out a clear answer to it. Although there is no single answer (our objective of "knowing something" is too vague for that), here is a possible statement of desired performance: *Given 10 pairs of short prose passages—each pair having one selection by Ernest Heming-way and one by a different author—the student is able, with at least 90 percent accuracy, to choose the selections written by Hemingway.*

Performance—conditions—extent. We have been talking about *performance*. Let us now consider *conditions*.

Here is one of our earlier statements concerning the alphabet: *The student will be able to pronounce the names of the letters of the alphabet, A through Z.* We have said that this statement is expressed in terms of student performance. Does this statement also set forth the *conditions* under which the performance is to take place?

It does not. For one thing, we cannot tell from our statement whether the student is to pronounce the names of the letters *at sight or from memory.* If the letters are to be shown, we do not know whether the student is to work with capital letters, small letters, or both. Nor do we know whether the student is to work with these letters in regular sequence or in random order. Obviously, each set of conditions is substantially different from the rest, and will make its own special demands upon the student who attempts to accomplish the objective.

Let's examine two more statements. Which one sets forth the *conditions* under which a certain kind of performance is to take place?

A. *Given the Dolch list of the 95 most common nouns, the student will be able to pronounce correctly all the words on this list.*

B. *The student will be able to pronounce correctly at least 90 percent of all words found in most beginning reading books.*

Statement A, which tells us that the Dolch list will be used, sets the conditions for the demonstration for student mastery. We are told that these particular words, and no others, are the ones at issue for this objective.

Statement B, offering us only the dubious clue of "words found in most beginning reading books," does not tell us enough. Our conditions need to be defined more precisely than this.

We come now to the matter of the *extent* and *level* of performance. A well-written instructional objective will establish an acceptable minimum standard of achievement.

Look at this objective: *Given 20 sentences containing both common and proper nouns, the student will be able to identify with very few mistakes both kinds of nouns.* Does this objective establish a minimum standard of achievement?

It does not. It leaves open to question the number of mistakes which are considered "a very few."

Here is the Hemingway objective we looked at earlier: *Given 10 pairs of short prose passages—each pair having one selection by Ernest Hemingway and one by a different author—the student is able, with at least 90 percent accuracy, to choose the selections written by Hemingway.* Does this objective establish a minimum standard of achievement?

It does. The student is expected to be able to make at least nine correct choices out of the 10. This constitutes a minimum standard of achievement.

Let's try one more objective: *The student should be able to pronounce from memory, and in sequence, the names of the letters of the alphabet, A through Z.* Does this objective establish a minimum standard of achievement?

It does. The objective implies that we are looking for 100 percent mastery. However, we could, if we wanted to be explicit, restate our objective in this way: *The student should be able to pronounce from memory, in sequence, and with 100 percent accuracy, the names of the letters of the alphabet, A through Z.*

An instructional objective should not ordinarily be limited to specific *means* (particular materials or methods), but should be stated in terms that permit the use of various procedures. Look at this statement of an objective: *Given the California Test Bureau's E-F level programmed booklet on capitalization, the student is able to work through the exercises in this booklet with at least 90 percent accuracy.* Is this objective limited to the use of a particular instructional item or procedure?

It is. The objective is expressed exclusively in terms of performance with a specific booklet. Although the particular kind of skill development that is promoted by this booklet is presumably also fostered by other instructional materials and methods, no such options are available under the terms of our objective as it is now written.

Look at this statement of an objective: *Given 20 sentences containing a variety of mistakes in capitalization, the student is able, with at least 90 percent accuracy, to identify and rewrite correctly each word that has a mistake in capitalization.* Is this objective limited to the use of a particular instructional item or procedure?

It is not. The objective as expressly stated permits us to use a number of instructional items that show promise of being able to help students attain the desired performance. Among these items are not only the California Test Bureau's E-F level material but the somewhat simpler

C-D level presentation, a programmed booklet by D. C. Heath, Unit 11 of English 2200, Unit 9 of English 2600, Lessons 87 and 88 of English 3200, several filmstrips on capital letters, and so on.

Finally, a well-written instructional objective will suggest how its accomplishment can be measured. This follows from our view that a well-written objective specifies under what *conditions* and to what *extent* a certain kind of student *performance* can be expected to take place.

Look at this objective: *The student should know the alphabet.* Does this objective suggest how its accomplishment can be measured?

It does not. The reason for this judgment is that *knowing the alphabet* can mean different things to different people. Therefore, depending upon what is meant, the measuring of this knowing will take different forms.

Suppose we elaborate upon our objective so that it reads: *Shown the letters of the alphabet in random order (in both upper and lower case form), the student is able to say the name of each letter with 100 percent accuracy.* Does our objective now suggest how its accomplishment can be measured?

It does. The objective as stated makes plain how its accomplishment can be measured.

If teachers at all levels of schooling would be this explicit in writing instructional objectives, they might reasonably hope to eliminate almost immediately one major cause of learning failure among students: the traditional fuzziness of classroom assignments.

Craik emphasizes the value of behaviorally stated objectives for both the programmer and the classroom teacher. The author "practices what she preaches," first of all, by establishing three behavioral objectives for the reader of the article, and then by constructing what is essentially a brief program to enable the reader to reach those objectives. A learner self-test and test key conclude the article.

Writing Objectives for Programmed Instruction— or Any Instruction*

MARY B. CRAIK

Since its entrance on the scene, programmed instruction has been praised, condemned, misunderstood, or ignored. Some have greeted it with open arms and have seen it as a panacea for all educational problems. Some have viewed it as a threat to the teacher's role. They have visions of the teacher being replaced by a gigantic machine which will make robots of students.

Some have given programming a brief glance and have seen only the format *without understanding the underlying principles,* and, with false superiority, have shrugged it off as just another workbook or test. Still others, especially those older teachers who have settled into a comfortable routine, have simply ignored it.

It will be some time before the real value of programming as a method can be ascertained. Many more programs need to be developed and used before any judgments can be made regarding its value as an instructional

*Reprinted from *Educational Technology, 6,* February 28, 1966, pp. 15-21, by permission of the publisher and the author.

tool. If programming fails in its original purpose, it still will have made some contributions to the instructional field. One major contribution is its emphasis upon task analysis and specific definition of objectives.

Before a programmer can begin to write, he must be able to state specifically what the behavior of the learner will be when the learner has completed the program. In order to do this the programmer conducts an analysis of the area concerned and determines in detail what skills, knowledge, and understandings are necessary for the learner to possess if he is to successfully perform the given job. The programmer then works directly from this set of objectives in determining what subject matter to include and exclude, what important skills are necessary, and the proper sequencing of instruction.

Too often the classroom teacher has beautiful but vague ideas about the purposes of his course, units, or day's lesson plan, and has not forced himself to go through the tedious task of setting these down on paper. He chooses his subject matter, methods, and details according to many criteria, very seldom calling on the "non-existent" objectives he is supposedly carrying around in his head. He then wonders why the students fail to learn what he wanted them to learn.

The techniques outlined in this paper are of interest to educators who will write their own programs, to those who desire to use programs successfully in their teaching experience and, especially, to the classroom teacher who desires a practical method of defining more precisely the specific objectives of a course. The general ideas are based on approaches first presented by Robert Mager in *Preparing Objectives for Programmed Instruction*.

The specific objectives of this paper are as follows:

1. The learner is to develop knowledge of the five important parts of a specific objective and will demonstrate this knowledge by being able to state them in writing from memory.
2. The learner is to develop an understanding of preparing specific objectives and will be able to pick out from a given list of ten objectives those objectives which meet the criteria of a good objective, with no more than three mistakes.
3. The learner is to develop skill in writing specific objectives and will be able to write ten specific objectives in one hour with no more than three mistakes.

Five Basic Steps

Before going into the details of the five steps involved in writing specific objectives, there are some general considerations to be made.

1. Objectives should be clear and concise. The teacher should not be concerned with writing something beautiful and flowery. He is not producing a work that the literature critic will judge. He should be interested in writing his objectives so that anyone who is knowledgeable in the subject can read and know precisely what is meant. There should be no room for misinterpretation.
2. The objectives should be realistic and fit the grade level for which they are written. If the reader thinks this is unworthy of comment, all he needs to do is to examine critically almost any published list of objectives for a unit or course. He will find that most sound good but there are too many and they are too difficult for the given grade level and amount of learning time.
3. Objectives should be attainable by instruction and capable of being measured. Many teachers say they are teaching such things as honesty, leadership, and creativity to name but a few. In reality, they have done very little to foster these ideas, let alone actually provided instruction to develop and then measure them. For example, many lists of objectives make some reference to fostering the democratic way of life. If the courses of study are examined it will be found quite often that there is nothing pertaining to democratic living, and in addition the teacher is using authoritarian methods. Such things may and probably should be stated as general ideals for education but they have no place in the list of working objectives for a subject matter—unless leadership, honesty, etc., are the subjects of the unit.
4. Specific objectives listed for a particular unit or course should be claimed *only* if the course develops them entirely, or more so than any other course, or to a significant degree.
5. And last of the general considerations, there should be as many objectives as are necessary or appropriate for the course or unit.

The details of writing a specific objective can be simplified or divided into five basic steps, each of which is a necessary part. First, they should be stated from the learner's point of view. Second, the category describing the type of learning should be stated. The third step is one of stating what is expected of the learner in behavioral terms. Fourth, the conditions under which this behavior is to occur should be described, and fifth, the level of proficiency is to be stated. It should be pointed out at this stage that there is a close relationship between the category chosen and the behavior and that these must be compatible with each other.

Now look at each step in detail. At first glance it may seem unnecessary to say that an objective should be stated from the learner's point of view. If you will look at objectives as commonly written you will see that this is a crucial point. Many teachers are thinking in terms of what *they* will do, and so write statements such as, "encourage the student to," or "stimulate the student to." This type of objective is stated from the teacher's point of view and can lead into unnecessary pitfalls. An instructional objective should always start with the learner or the student and go on from there.

All instructional goals should be divided into a selection of categories which will include all types of behavior. The six categories used here are arbitrarily chosen, but this is necessary in order to define the terms and make sure that each individual interprets them in the same way. The author feels that practically all behavioral goals can be classified into six categories, which are: (1) knowledges, (2) understandings, (3) skills, (4) attitudes, (5) appreciations, and (6) interests. The writer recommends that the novice restrict himself to the first three listed, as he is on pretty shaky ground when he claims he can measure an attitude, an appreciation, or an interest in a testing situation in the conventional classroom. This does not mean to say that it cannot be done, but that it is a very difficult task which the average classroom teacher is not likely to do successfully.

Now let us look at the three most frequently used terms (knowledges, understandings, and skills) and define them as they are used here. How would we describe or be able to tell that a person knows or has some *knowledge* about a thing? If he could name it, we could say that he has some knowledge concerning it. If he can point it out, describe it, recognize it, or define it, he has some knowledge of it. For purposes of writing specific objectives we will use knowledge to mean that the learner knows something about the thing with which we are concerned. For example, we could say that a person who can name the different parts of a car engine has some knowledge about car engines. This does not necessarily mean that he can repair it, but if he can point out or name its parts he does have knowledge concerning it. It may be or may not be, depending on your point of view, a sad commentary, but many and possibly most of the learnings in our schools fall into this category.

Now let us define the second category, *understanding*. This is where most teachers would like to place the emphasis in our schools. Here we are going beyond knowledges and are expecting a terminal behavior that is more complex. The previous example may serve to clarify the difference between knowledges and understandings. If the learner can not only name and point out the parts of the car engine but can also tell you the function of each part, the relationship between these functions, and can explain how the engine operates, we can then say that he has an understanding of how a car engine works. Other types of behaviors which could demonstrate understandings are such things as: explaining cause and effect relationships, evaluating a specific objective, applying the understanding to a new situation, and solving a new problem.

To explain the third category, *skill,* let us again go back to the car engine. If the student can examine a defective engine and repair it, we can say he has developed *skill.* If a student can write correct sentences, we can say that he has skill in writing correct sentences. If he can write specific objectives that meet the criteria for a good objective, we can say that he has developed skill in writing objectives. It is possible that the student could repair the engine, work a math problem or write a correct sentence, thus demonstrating skill and still not have an understanding of what he is doing. For this reason it is necessary to separate the two if an understanding is required in relation to the objectives set by the teacher.

The third important part in writing an objective is stating it as a terminal behavior. When it is said that an objective should be stated as a terminal behavior, we are talking about the behavior the learner is to exhibit in order to demonstrate that he has attained the correct behavior. When writing an objective one must be as specific as possible in the choice of words describing the behavior. A good rule of thumb to follow is one of trying to visualize the behavior as stated. For example, "The student is to develop an appreciation for the democratic way of life."

If we ask five people to write down exactly what the student is doing when he is demonstrating the attainment of this objective, it is suspected that we would get several different answers. In this example it is difficult to picture or visualize the behavior. If there is considerable difficulty in describing, or if each description is different, then we know that the statement has not been specific enough and is open to misinterpretation. After writing the terminal behavior it is a good idea to close our eyes and see if we get a picture of the student's activity. If not, then the steps should be retraced and the objective rewritten.

In addition to stating the behavior in an objective, a fourth important part is specifying the conditions under which the behavior will be performed. Will the learner be able to use notes and references or must he rely on his memory alone? Will there be a time limit and specific place where he is to perform? If so, this should be included in the objective. If no time limits, use of references, etc., are stated, we can assume that they are not conditions which have to be met. If this cannot be assumed, then make sure the pertinent conditions are included. Since the attainment or measurement of many objectives in our schools is based on examinations of some kind, the testing situation will probably best describe the conditions.

The fifth step is one of stating the degree of proficiency with which the behavior is to be demonstrated so that we can determine success or a failure. Just how well is the learner to perform to be able to say he has succeeded? In the example concerning the repairing of a car engine, would we say that the learner was successful if he makes the engine run? If the objective is one of having knowledge of the parts of a flower and demonstrating this knowledge by pointing out and naming each part, with how many different kinds of flowers should the learner be able to do this? One? Two? Ten? Does he have to know all of the parts or just some of them? Can he get along by being able to name half of them? This will be a subjective determination made rather arbitrarily by the teacher, but it should be based, as much as possible, upon the knowledge the teacher has concerning the particular group of learners and the difficulty of the task. If the teacher's expectations are too high or too low some alteration may be needed. The best advice that can be offered at this point is to be as realistic as possible. Even though the teacher may have limited experience, he should set some level of proficiency.

In summary we can say that the five important steps in writing a specific objective are found in the answers to the following questions:

1. Who is to perform?
2. What category of learning is involved?
3. What is the terminal behavior?
4. Under what conditions will it be demonstrated?
5. What degree or level of proficiency is to be met in order to succeed?

One other important point should be made concerning the relationship between the parts of an objective. If the objective states that "the student is to develop skill in writing objectives" and the evaluation is based on ability to state the five steps in writing objectives, then there is no agreement between the category and the terminal behavior. The objective has stated *skill* and measured *knowledge*. In order to find out whether the learner has developed *skill in writing,* the evaluation must be based on a demonstration of writing objectives.

In order to determine whether you have met the objectives of this paper, try the following:

I. Name in writing five important steps or parts of a specific objective.
II. Which of the listed objectives meet all of the requirements of a good specific objective:
1. The student is to develop a working knowledge and a basic understanding of the history of electricity and magnetism in

order that he will better understand the many forms of electricity.

2. The student is to develop understanding of the structure of the novel as applied to *Silas Marner* by tracing the structure of the novel in a paper written outside of class with no more than three errors.
3. The student is to develop knowledge of repairing an automotive generator so that he can describe correctly in writing all repair procedures when given a hypothetical situation concerning a defective generator.
4. The student will be expected to gain a basic knowledge of the three major causes of World War II. The three causes are expansionism, imperialism, and militarism. The student will be expected to understand the influences of the causes at the 70% level of accuracy.
5. The purpose of the unit on vocabulary development is to increase the vocabulary of the student by five new words each week by having him write the five new words and their definitions to be turned in on Friday of each week.
6. The student is to develop knowledge of the story pertaining to the Mexican independence. He will demonstrate this knowledge by being able to state the eight important points in writing from memory in 15 minutes with no more than three mistakes.
7. The student is to develop skill in writing a biography of Cervantes in Spanish without the use of notes, in 50 minutes.
8. The student is to develop an understanding of the history of drama so that he can write a paper describing the life of one playwright with no more than four mistakes.
9. To encourage the student to understand the writings of Shakespeare by giving lectures and leading discussions of the history and the customs of the times.
10. The student is to develop knowledge of the vocabulary used in *The Merchant of Venice* so that he can write the definitions of 50 words chosen from the play without the use of any aids in 60 minutes with no more than 15 errors.

III. Write 10 specific objectives for a unit in your subject matter.
IV. Now check your performance with the following key and see whether you have succeeded or failed according to the level of proficiency set in the objectives for the paper.

Key to questions:
I.
1. Written from the student's point of view.
2. Name the category.

3. Describe the terminal behavior.
4. State the conditions.
5. Set the level of proficiency.

II.

1. No terminal behavior, no conditions, and no level of proficiency.
2. Acceptable.
3. Acceptable.
4. No terminal behavior and no conditions.
5. Teacher's point of view rather than the student's, no category, and no level of proficiency.
6. Acceptable.
7. Unrealistic under given conditions, and no level of proficiency.
8. Category and terminal behavior not compatible; writing a biography of a playwright is no indication of an understanding of the history of drama.
9. Teacher's point of view, no terminal behavior, no conditions, and no level of proficiency.
10. Acceptable.

III. Check each of your objectives according to the criteria set up by the check list given in the paragraph beginning: "In summary we can say . . . ."

Although Cohen's frame of reference is college teaching and learning, his comments concerning defining instructional objectives are also of value to curriculum developers at other levels of education. He explains how measurable objectives can be generated from non-specific statements of educational purpose. Especially useful are a number of sample objectives in varying stages of specification.

Teach Toward Measurable Objectives*

ARTHUR M. COHEN

Although the relationship may be implicitly felt rather than explicitly demonstrated, there is a direct connection between institutional goals and faculty purposes. This tie stretches from the lofty and general goals usually stated in college catalogs to the direct objectives toward which students strive within their courses. For a college to achieve its purposes effectively, the instructor must be aware of both his own specific aims and the more generalized directions of the institution.

The connection is readily apparent to teachers in some types of institutions. In purely vocational schools, for example, where the aim is to prepare students for trades employment, faculty find their classroom purposes relatively clear. In comprehensive junior colleges, liberal arts colleges, and universities, however, the instructor may find it more difficult to establish a direct line between the multi-faceted purposes of the institution and his own specific practice.

The manner in which the purposes of a college or university relate to each classroom can and should be operationally traced. Goals are

*Reprinted from *Improving College and University Teaching, 14,* Autumn, 1966, pp. 246-248, by permission of the publisher and the author.

typically stated broadly: "It is the function of the college to help its students meet their needs as members of our democratic society," "The college desires to make the student aware of his physical environment," "It is expected of all students that they develop an appreciation of the unique values of our cultural heritage." Subject matter in the curriculum is drawn from several bodies of organized thought. It is assumed that the student, having mastered each subject, will become "aware of his environment" and "appreciative of the values of our culture."

Indeed, a logical relationship may be traced between curricular aims and institutional purposes. This can be found in catalog descriptions where courses typically carry subtitles such as "A study of American institutions with emphasis on the political system at all levels," "Physical, economic, and social factors related to the production and distribution of the world's major resources," "A survey of literature since the Romantic Era." It is easy to draw a fairly direct line from these designations to specified institutional purposes.

The teacher, taking cues from the subject of his course, narrows the scope a step further. He expects his students "to have a clear understanding of the economic, social, and political forces which shaped America," "to know how climate and topography relate to the production of certain crops," or "to recognize the types of poetry common to various periods in English literature." He assumes that when students have achieved these understandings and recognitions, they are on their way toward meeting the general standard set by the college. Thus the school program is built like an inverted pyramid, with broad institutional goals drawn from social and human needs at the top and narrow directions based on student learning at the bottom of the figure.

Despite the presumed influence of environment and co-curriculars, the tenable portion of student change in desired directions is to be found in the curriculum and, in fact, within each course. It is difficult for an instructor to say (and almost impossible for him to justify) that he has been instrumental in moving a group of students directly toward becoming "members of our democratic society." He can, however, state with assuredness that his course relates to this broad goal. If he can demonstrate that his students have moved toward the course objectives, he can safely say they have come closer to the evinced goals of the college.

But how to substantiate this? How to state with confidence that one's students have made specific gains within a single course? It is likely that much of what an individual teacher does to stimulate student learning cannot be determined. But it is quite evident that college teachers can employ objective measures more widely than they presently do. Each instructor, whatever his field, can build a set of specific measurable objectives toward which his students can strive and through which he may assess his own contribution to the purposes of his institution. This set fits at the very point of the pyramid, the point where each student labors to gain the bits of knowledge which, when incorporated into his store of learning, will affect his general behavior.

As a first step in finding suitable objectives, the instructor may want to use a cross-sectional chart with desired abilities and aptitudes running along one axis and subject matter clustering along the other. Algo Henderson has recommended use of such a matrix.[1]

Plotting the axes should be a fairly routine process for the college teacher. Subject matter can usually be arranged according to certain natural divisions. Textbook chapters are often prepared in this manner. These sections are placed along one axis. Along the other are listed the specific abilities which the teacher sets as eventual student accomplishments. "Recall of facts," "application of formulae," and "analysis of communications" are commonly stated proficiencies; "acceptance" and "appreciation" are others. The *Taxonomy of Educational Objectives* refines these terms and explains their application,[2] but the teacher may wish to create his own list. In any case, the work of building objectives begins at the point where the axes of subject matter and thinking abilities intersect.

To qualify as being specific and measurable, an objective must meet certain criteria. These may be broadly stated in the form of two questions: "What will the student be able to do?" and 'How will I know when he is able to do it?" Restating the questions, the teacher needs to ask himself: "What particular skill, knowledge, or quality of appreciation do I expect the student to possess when he has completed the course unit?" and "What evidence can I gather to show that he has gained this objective?"

The objective itself will specify these variables: (1) the type of behavior the student is to exhibit, (2) the criterion of performance, and (3) the conditions under which the performance will occur. Answering questions on a test is a type of behavior commonly expected of students. Other behavioral evidence could include such diverse activities as voluntary reading, political activism, or, if the course is prerequisite to another, attaining a certain grade in the sequential course. The main point is that the activity be observable.

Criteria of performance may include such measures as the percent of correct responses on an examination, the number of books read, number of hours spent in a particular activity, or the grade to be achieved. And if it is to be considered a factor in the criterion performance, time allotted to the representative task must also be specified.

Spelling out the conditions under which the performance will occur completes the specific objectives. Here the type of examination is noted, whether it will be open or closed book, oral or written, multiple choice or matching. If it is to be an essay examination, it is well to specify approximate length, format, and grading standard. If the performance involves an outside activity, its mandatory or voluntary condition should be noted.

A few examples will serve to illustrate the above points. An objective often found in political science courses is, "The students will be stimulated to take an active part in local and national politics." This objective can readily be related to institutional goals and, as such, is worthy of inclusion in the course. It goes beyond classroom performance and implies that the student's long-range behavior has been affected. However, the objective as stated is vague and does not meet the criteria for specific measurable objectives. What is the student doing when he "takes an active part?" Is he voting, campaigning for a candidate, or running for office himself? What evidence will the teacher gather to determine if he has succeeded in stimulating his students to "become politically active"? Will he poll them to see how many voted or campaigned? What percent of the class must "become active" if he is to consider himself successful in stimulating them to positive performance? The teacher may be well aware of his general aim but, if his objective does not include the specific type of behavior, criterion of performance, and conditions under which the performance will occur, he falls short in meeting the demands of his task.

Consider the same general aim when it is followed by one or more specific objectives:

> By the end of the course, 90% of the students eligible to register to vote will have done so.
>
> In the next election campaign, 25% of the students will participate by distributing handbills or working in a candidate's office for at least forty hours.
>
> Within five years at least one student will himself campaign for a public office.

Here we see that the teacher can readily gather evidence to determine whether he has achieved these specific objectives.

A general goal commonly designated by teachers of literature courses is, "The students will gain an appreciation for Twentieth Century American literature." This, too, is vague. What must the student do to give evidence that he has gained this appreciation? Will he voluntarily read contemporary poetry? Will he buy a certain number of novels per year? Will he take several more literature courses? Add a set of measurable objectives and the goal is made clear:

> Although poetry is not "covered" in the course, 75% of the students shall voluntarily read at least five poems by contemporary Americans before the end of the term.
>
> Fifty percent of the students shall elect to take a second course in American literature within one year after completing this course.
>
> Each student shall voluntarily buy and read an average of four novels per year for the next three years.

Thus the type of behavior expected, the criterion of performance, and the conditions under which it will occur are specified. Here the gathering of specific evidence to demonstrate behavioral gain in the desired direction is made possible.

The measurable objectives specified above are offered merely as examples of use of the technique. Each teacher will want to build a group to fit his conception of his course's contribution in moving students toward educational goals.

Examination of the little manual, *Preparing Instructional Objectives,*[3] might prove worthwhile for each teacher wishing to look further into this method.

There are several real advantages accruing to the instructor who builds measurable objectives for his class:

1. Students know what is expected of them and can plan their studies accordingly. The game of "I'm the teacher and I know a secret; guess what you have to do to pass this course" is eliminated.
2. Grading is facilitated when course objectives include specific performance criteria.
3. Clear direction is provided in the selection of materials and methods.
4. The teacher can try various techniques with his different classes in order to decide upon those which lead to the most effective learning situation.
5. The teacher can justify to outsiders his use of certain methods or materials if he is able to submit evidence that his students have gained in particular directions.
6. Comparisons of effectiveness can be made between class and class and between teacher and teacher.

In many instances, it is necessary to apply certain measures at the beginning of each course unit so that determination of actual gain can be made at the end of the unit. This is particularly important for courses in which all students will have some prior knowledge of the subject to be taught. Often examinations which test learning achieved in one unit can serve as pretests for subsequent units.

It is important to emphasize that each instructor be encouraged to build his own set of objectives within the limits of his subject field and the goals of his institution. In some cases the members of a department may wish to use a common group of objectives, but this is for them to determine. Most important, in any case, is that each teacher be able to say, "My objectives stem from these institutional purposes. I arranged a situation in which my students moved from this measured point to that measured point; they are thus closer to the goals of the college." Only then will he know that he has had an effect, that he has indeed taught. Not until teachers take a lead in this type of self-evaluation will they be able to view themselves as integral parts of the total educational process.

REFERENCES

1. Algo Henderson. The Design of Superior Courses. *Improving College and University Teaching, 8,* 2, Spring 1965, pp. 106-109.
2. Benjamin Bloom (Ed.). *Taxonomy of Educational Objectives, I: Cognitive Domain.* New York: David McKay Co., 1956; David R. Krathwohl, *et al., Taxonomy of Educational Objectives, II: Affective Domain.* New York: David McKay Co., 1964.
3. Robert Mager. *Preparing Instructional Objectives.* San Francisco: Fearon, 1963.

Rahmlow attacks the problem of triviality in objectives by presenting a four-step iterative procedure for developing well-stated but, at the same time, meaningful behavioral objectives. His method includes the preparation of sample test items and suggested learning activities to accompany each instructional objective. Useable by both the novice and the experienced instructional planner, the suggested procedure is designed for practicality as well as efficiency and quality of product.

Specifying Useful Instructional Objectives[*]

Harold F. Rahmlow

It has often been stated that it is easy to develop precisely stated instructional objectives for trivial and mechanistic situations, whereas it is extremely difficult or impossible to develop precisely stated instructional objectives for meaningful situations. In this paper a method for developing well-stated instructional objectives for meaningful content is presented. This method brings together all that the specifier of the objective knows about developing drafts of an objective, developing criterion measures for the objective, defining the principal performance called for in the objective, and specifying learning activities for achieving the objective, and focuses these components on the development of a well-stated instructional objective.

It has been stated by Mager[1] that there are five major activities related to objectives. The five related activities are derivation, specification, selection, implementation, and assessment of objectives. These

*Reprinted from *NSPI Journal, 7,* September, 1968, pp. 10-13, 15, by permission of the publisher and the author.

aspects of objectives can be dealt with independently; however, if one is eventually to derive any benefit from objectives, one must consider all of the activities. Therefore, although this paper deals only with the specification of objectives, it is well to have clearly in mind the other four aspects of dealing with objectives.

The method for developing instructional objectives described here not only helps clarify the instructional objective but also assists in specifying the type of learning activities which would be useful in attempting to obtain the behavior called for in the objective. The steps in developing meaningful instructional objectives are:

1. Quickly draft a rough objective.
2. Write sample test items which illustrate the behavior called for by the objective.
3. Specify the principal performance called for in the objective.
4. Specify learning activities which are useful in attaining the objective.

As the writer proceeds through these steps, his real intent in writing the objective becomes clear, and each step contributes to refinement or redefinition of the instructional objective and the previous steps.

Let us examine the rationale behind this method and then look at an example of its application. The greatest benefit of the first step is that it helps you get started. It is very difficult and time consuming to sit around thinking of precisely how to state an objective before one puts anything down on paper. Once something is down, it is then easier to look at and correct; it is the initial giant step that often consumes an inordinate amount of time. This initial draft of the objective should be considered a very crude beginning which will probably undergo many changes before it is in final form.

After something that roughly resembles a good instructional objective has been dashed off, the next order of business is to write a sample evaluation item for the objective. Often in developing tests for objectives we are forced to reveal the real intent of our instructional objectives. By trying to write a sample test item as soon as a draft of the instructional objective has been completed, the writer is forced to clarify the instructional objective and square it with what will eventually become some evaluative instrument. Writing a sample test item also serves a further purpose. By calling it a sample test item, the objective writer is indicating that this is the type of evaluation he considers appropriate for assessing the objective. This sort of inside information will be very useful for the objective writer if he later becomes a test writer, or will be invaluable to the test item writer who was not in on the development of the objective. Further, if presented to the student, the sample test item provides a self-evaluation activity to assist him in deciding whether he can achieve the objective.

The third step in the proposed schema for developing instructional objectives is to specify the principal performance called for in the objective. The state of the art is not at a point where one can always be successful in specifying the principal performance to his own satisfaction, but the mere exercise of trying to do so has the benefit of helping further clarify the intent of the objective and at the same time revealing inadequacies in our knowledge of the principal performance associated with various types of objectives. Often we attempt to determine the principal performance before we see that our objective may be misleading. The objective may have words in it which we do not really mean; and, when we come to specify the principal performance, this becomes obvious. We know very little today about classifying the principal performances called for in many of our instructional objectives.

The specification of the principal performance called for by an objective is often the most difficult part of the entire sequence. Although there is no comprehensive list of principal performances available, the list suggested by Mager and Beach[2] could serve as a useful starting point. They recommend the principal performances of recall, speech, discrimination, manipulation, and problem-solving. These performances were developed for vocational situations and have certain limitations with respect to traditional academic areas. Probably the area of problem-solving is the weakest link in this list of performances. The list, however, does provide a useful starting point upon which to build.

Having reached the point of revising our objective based upon, first, the initial draft, second, the writing of a sample test item, and third, the identification of the principal performance in the objective, let us now turn to the specification of the learning activities useful in assisting a student to attain the behavior specified in the objective. Specifying the learning activities serves a dual role. Obviously, if we can specify the type of learning activity that is most useful in attaining the objective, we are well along the road to either selecting or developing instructional materials and experiences which will aid students in achieving the objectives. The main item under consideration here, however, is the clarification of the objective itself and not the specifying of learning activities. The reason for specifying learning activities here is to help clarify the objective. Many objective writers, especially those who are also experienced teachers, are more familiar with learning activities than with the results of those activities. Therefore, an experienced teacher will often be able to clarify the intent of his instructional objective much better after he has considered the learning activities which he feels are appropriate for achieving the behavior required in the objective. In fact, if one examines the present-day public school curriculum, one might conclude that it would be best to start deriving instructional objectives by listing learning activities and then working back from there. The present-day curriculum in most, if not all, areas is based on instructional activities and materials and not on behavioral objectives. Instructors speak of books completed and of lectures presented rather than of objectives attained by students.

Because the present-day curriculum is so highly oriented toward learning materials and activities, it is best to begin with an objective and then ultimately check this objective against the learning activities rather than vice versa. If objective writers continue to begin with the learning activities, they are apt to restrict the curriculum to what is available rather than to have the materials expand to meet the needs of students and the intent of the instructors.

The brief explanation presented above specified the role of each of the four steps in developing instructional objectives and illustrated how each contributes to a more refined statement of an instructional objective. Now let us look at an example of this method put into practice. Let us assume that we are working in the science area and wish to have the students know something about things which are living and those which aren't. Our quick initial statement of an instructional objective might be, "Understand what is meant by the term, 'living object.'" By putting this objective down, we have a start, but we obviously do not have a good instructional objective.

A sample test item for this objective might be, "Is a cat living?" As we can see from this sample test item, what we may mean by "understand" is "answer questions," since our sample test item calls for the student to answer questions on whether something is living or not. Therefore, we revise our objective to read, "Answer questions on whether an object is living or non-living." Already we are moving toward a better instructional objective.

Now let us put down the principal performance called for in the objective. After a little reflection, one will note that the principal performance called for in this objective is discrimination. If a student is to answer questions on whether something is living or not, he must be able to make the decision on whether that object is living. Therefore, the principal performance is discrimination. The principal performance is not answering questions. Now, if we revise our objective, it would read, "Discriminate between living and non-living objects."

Now let us next move to the specification of some learning activities for achieving this objective. A couple of learning objectives might be, "Look at some photographs of objects and state whether the objects in the photographs are living or non-living." Another learning activity might be, "Make a list of five things in your back yard that are living and five that are non-living." The specification of these learning activities reveals a further element of the objective. Until this time we have not specified whether the objects to be classified are the objects themselves (such as a real cat), merely picture representations of the objects, or verbal representations of the objects. Now, if we revise our objective, we come up with the form, "Given an object, a picture of the object, or the name of an object, classify it as living or non-living." Thus we can see that going through the successive stages of *drafting the objective, writing the sample test item, identifying the principal performance,* and *specifying learning activities,* we have come up with better successive approximations of our real intent in the instructional objective. Now the sample test item is not compatible with the objective; we need to give more information about our cat. Some better test items would be, "Is a sleeping cat alive?" or "Is the stuffed cat in this box alive?" The principal performance and the learning activities still hold up well, so our cycle is complete.

It is worth noting, as an aside, that if one has gone through the exercise of developing an objective in this manner, one is forced to be honest about specifying learning activities for the student and about specifying the type of question to be asked of the student. For example, in the objective as stated above, "Given an object, a picture of an object, or the name of an object, classify it as living or non-living," it would be far better and more honest to ask the student to classify something or to discriminate between living and non-living things rather than to ask him some tangential question which may or may not reveal the information desired; e.g., "Does the mechanistic theory of life propose that there is no fundamental difference between living and non-living things?" Likewise, after one has specified the principal performance and learning activities, one can check the consistency of these two. For example, in this case every learning activity should focus on providing the student with practice or information useful in classifying objects as living or non-living. If the student does not receive such practice as a result of a learning activity, it should be reconsidered. It is at this point, however, that another weakness in the state of the art is revealed. We do not at this time know what learning activities are most effective for achieving particular types of principal performance. By attempting such an exercise, however, we begin to attack the problem and can collect data on the relative usefulness of different types of learning activities for different types of students in achieving various performance categories.

Consider another example. Suppose a student is studying income tax.

STEP 1.

First Draft Objective: Know about income tax.

First Draft Test Item: If a man with no dependents earns $16,000 per year, how much federal tax must he pay?

Looking at the sample test item, it is obvious that the objective should say something about figuring the tax.

STEP 2.

Second Draft Objective: Given a person's income and number of dependents, compute his federal income tax.

Second Draft Test Item: If a man with no dependents earns $16,000 per year, how much federal tax must he pay?

First Draft Performance: Computation.

The principal performance now is computation, but the objective we had in mind included more than doing the arithmetic computation. We want him to read the instructions, select appropriate information, and apply that information to determine his tax.

STEP 3.

Third Draft Objective: Given a person's income and number of dependents, determine his federal income tax.

Third Draft Test Item: If a man with no dependents earns $16,000 per year, how much federal tax must he pay?

Second Draft Performance: Problem solving.

First Draft Learning Activity: Read "Teaching Taxes," IRS Publication Number 21. Practice filling in a tax form.

STEP 4.

Fourth Draft Objective: Given a person's income, filing status, and tax credit information, determine his federal income tax.

Fourth Draft Test Item: If a man with no dependents earns $16,000 per year, how much federal tax must he pay?

Third Draft Performance: Problem solving.

Second Draft Learning Activity: Read "Teaching Taxes," IRS Publication Number 21. Practice filling in a tax form.

The prime product of the four-step procedure described above is to produce a clearly specified instructional objective. Once objectives have been clearly specified, the way is clear for the selection, implementation, and assessment of these objectives. A clearly specified instructional objective may or may not be worth selecting for further use. However, because the objective is clearly specified, the task of making the selection is now a great deal easier. If the objective is selected and it is decided to implement and proceed with its assessment, the other steps involved in the specifying of the objective become useful in themselves. To assist in implementing the objective, one may wish to give the student not only the objective but also the sample test item and the list of appropriate learning activities. For some students, this may be all the instruction necessary. The sample test item helps the student to evaluate his progress in achieving the objective, and the learning activities assist the student in deciding the type of activity in which he can appropriately engage. For any person charged with responsibility of selecting or developing instructional materials, the specifying of the type of learning activity appropriate for the achievement of a given objective is worthwhile.

Summary

A four-step iterative procedure for clearly specifying instructional objectives has been developed. These four steps are 1) drafting the objective, 2) writing a sample test item for the objective, 3) specifying the principal performance called for in the objective, and 4) specifying appropriate learning activities for the objective. This iterative process produces a well specified objective useful in helping to make decisions about selection, implementation, and assessment of objectives.

REFERENCES

1. Robert F. Mager. Deriving Objectives for the High School Curriculum. *NSPI Journal, 7,* 3, March, 1968, p. 7.
2. Robert F. Mager & Kenneth M. Beach, Jr. *Developing Vocational Instruction.* Palo Alto, California: Fearon, 1967.

Part I

Additional Media

Bernabei, Raymond. *Behavioral Objectives: An Annotated Resource File.* Harrisburg, Pennsylvania: Bureau of Curriculum Development and Evaluation, Department of Public Instruction, 1968, 55 pp.

Brackenbury, Robert L. Guidelines to Help Schools Formulate and Validate Objectives. *Rational Planning in Curriculum and Instruction.* Washington, D. C.: National Education Association Center for the Study of Instruction, 1967, pp. 89-108.

Burns, Richard W. Behavioral Objectives: A Selected Bibliography. *Educational Technology, 9,* April, 1969, pp. 57-58.

————. Objectives and Classroom Instruction. *Educational Technology, 7,* September 15, 1967, pp. 1-3.

————. The Theory of Expressing Objectives. *Educational Technology, 7,* October 30, 1967, pp. 1-3.

Canfield, Albert A. A Rationale for Performance Objectives. *Audiovisual Instruction, 13,* February, 1968, pp. 127-129.

Cohen, Arthur M. Defining Instructional Objectives. B. Lamar Johnson (Ed.) *Systems Approaches to Curriculum and Instruction in the Open-Door College.* Los Angeles, California: School of Education, University of California, Los Angeles, 1967, pp. 25-33.

Deno, Stanley R. & Joseph R. Jenkins. *Evaluating Pre-Planned Curriculum Objectives.* Philadelphia, Pennsylvania: Research for Better Schools, 1967, 25 pp. plus appendices.

Edling, Jack V. Educational Objectives and Educational Media. *Review of Educational Research, 38,* April, 1968, pp. 177-194.

Eiss, Albert F. Performance Objectives. *Bulletin of the National Association of Secondary School Principals, 54,* January, 1970, pp. 51-57.

Esbensen, Thorwald. *Performance Objectives.* Duluth, Minnesota: Duluth Public Schools, 1967.

Harbeck, Mary B. Questions and Answers on Behavioral Objectives. *Croft*

Professional Growth for Teachers: Science, Junior High School Edition.
Second Quarter Issue, 1969-1970, pp. 7-8.

Mager, Robert F. The Need to State Our Educational Intents. *Technology and Innovation in Education.* New York: Frederick A. Praeger, Publishers, 1968, pp. 35-40.

———. *Preparing Instructional Objectives.* Palo Alto, California: Fearon Publishers, 1962, 60 pp.

——— & K. Zinn. *Objectives.* Ann Arbor, Michigan: The University of Michigan, Center for Research on Learning and Teaching, 1967. (This is a computer-assisted course on the identification of written objectives for programmed instruction. Designed for the IBM 7010 computer, it consists of 506 statements and is 60 minutes in length.)

——— & H. F. Rahmlow. *Goofing Off with Objectives.* Los Altos Hills, California: Mager Associates, 1969. 14½ minutes, 16mm, sound, color.

Plowman, Paul. Behavioral Objectives and Teacher Success. *Behavioral Objectives Extension Service.* Chicago, Illinois: Science Research Associates, Inc., 1968-69, 32 pp.

Popham, W. James. *The Teacher-Empiricist: A Curriculum and Instruction Supplement.* Los Angeles, California: Aegeus Publishing Company, 1965. 76 pp.

Slack, Charles W. The Politics of Educational Objectives. *Educational Technology, 7,* July 30, 1967, pp. 1-6.

Stasiewski, Anne. Setting a Course for Yourself and Your Students. *Grade Teacher, 84,* April, 1967, pp. 96-97.

Summers, Frances L. Watch Your Objectives! *The Instructor, 74,* September, 1964, p. 55.

SWRL materials:

    Stating Educational Outcomes. Inglewood, California: Southwest Regional Laboratory for Educational Research and Development, 1968. 19 pp.

    Baker, Robert L., Vernon S. Gerlach & Howard J. Sullivan. *Constructing Behavioral Objectives.* Inglewood, California: Southwest Regional Laboratory for Educational Research and Development, 1968, 44 pp.

    Baker, Robert L., Vernon S. Gerlach, Richard E. Schutz & Howard J. Sullivan. *Developing Instructional Specifications.* Inglewood, California: Southwest Regional Laboratory for Educational Research and Development, 1968, 54 pp.

    Popham, W. James. *Educational Criterion Measures.* Inglewood, California: Southwest Regional Laboratory for Educational Research and Development, 1968, 34 pp.

    Michael, Jack L., Carole S. Waina & Robert L. Baker. *Managing Classroom Contingencies.* Inglewood, California: Southwest Regional Laboratory for Educational Research and Development, 1968, 50 pp.

Talmage, Harriet, & Susan M. Markle. Objectivity and Subjectivity on the Subject of Objectives: A Research and Reactive Review of the Popham Program. *NSPI Journal, 7,* November, 1968, pp. 14-19.

Trow, Clark. Behavioral Objectives in Education. *Educational Technology, 7,* December 30, 1967, pp. 6-10.

Vimcet Series: illustrated filmstrips, accompanying audio-taped narrations, and instructor's manuals.

    Popham W. James, & Eva L. Baker. *Educational Objectives.* Los Angeles, California: Vimcet Associates, 1967, 37 frames, 25 minutes.

————. *Systematic Instructional Decision-Making.* Los Angeles, California: Vimcet Associates, 1967, 27 frames, 20 minutes.

————. *Selecting Appropriate Educational Objectives.* Los Angeles, California: Vimcet Associates, 1967, 44 frames, 26 minutes.

————. *Establishing Performance Standards.* Los Angeles, California: Vimcet Associates, 1967, 46 frames, 22 minutes.

————. *Appropriate Practice.* Los Angeles, California: Vimcet Associates, 1967, 30 frames, 31 minutes.

————. *Perceived Purpose.* Los Angeles, California: Vimcet Associates, 1967, 37 frames, 31 minutes.

————. *Evaluation.* Los Angeles, California: Vimcet Associates, 1967, 43 frames, 29 minutes.

Walbesser, Henry H. *Constructing Behavioral Objectives.* College Park, Maryland: The Bureau of Educational Research and Field Services, College of Education, University of Maryland, 1968, 90 pp.

Part II

Classifying Objectives to Improve Instruction

In the initial article in Part II, Krathwohl provides a rationale for classifying objectives according to frameworks or taxonomies. He states:

> *The need for objectives at various levels of abstraction has given rise to frameworks or structures that assist in the analysis and development of these objectives. One of these frameworks [is] the* Taxonomy of Educational Objectives *. . .*
>
> *Basically the taxonomy grew out of an attempt to resolve some of the confusion in communication which resulted from the translation of such general terms as "to understand" into more specific behaviors . . .*

The second article, by Simpson, includes more recently developed taxonomical and theoretical work in the psychomotor domain.

In the final two selections, Loree and Williams relate various objective classification schemes to education for creativity, thus answering the potential criticism that highly specified objectives impede creative teaching and learning behaviors.

Krathwohl served as primary author of the 1964 affective portion of the Taxonomy of Educational Objectives *and was a leading participant in the formulation of the 1956 cognitive domain. Thus, he is an undisputed authority on the development, classification, and use of objectives in education. In the article presented below, Krathwohl identifies and explains the need for three specificity levels in the development of objectives—general goals for initial program planning, goal statements for instructional units or courses, and objectives for specific lesson plans. He examines the cognitive and affective domains of the* Taxonomy *as well as Gagné's classification of capabilities for potential implications for curriculum building and instructional materials development.*

Stating Objectives Appropriately for Program, for Curriculum, and for Instructional Materials Development[*]

David R. Krathwohl

The frontiers of knowledge retreat before many kinds of research. The research usually reported is experimental or empirical in nature. But we also learn about education when we find means to name and organize the phenomena of education more precisely. Such conceptual research, based on previous findings and thinking, is the kind described here.

This article is concerned with the use of educational objectives at several levels of detail in the educational process. The most general levels

[*]Reprinted from *The Journal of Teacher Education, 16,* March, 1965, pp. 83-92, by permission of the publisher and the author.

of objectives are most relevant to program planning, the intermediate level to curriculum development, and the most specific level to instructional materials development. The article makes two basic points:

1. Objectives at several levels of generality and specificity are needed to facilitate the process of curriculum building and instructional development.
2. A framework or taxonomy currently exists which can facilitate the development and analysis of objectives at the intermediate level, and one is at present being developed at the more detailed level.

Analysis of Objectives—A Powerful Tool for Educational Improvement

The emphasis upon making educational objectives specific by defining the goals of an instructional course or program has gone through many cycles since Ralph Tyler gave the topic considerable prominence in the late thirties. For some educators, careful attention to spelling out in detail the objectives of a course has become a kind of religion. Others, interestingly enough, seem to have heard of the practice of delineating objectives but, somehow or other, have been early inoculated against the notion and have so become immune. Those of us who work as advisers to various fields of higher education, particularly with our colleagues in liberal arts, home economics, etc., are impressed with the power of this simple tool to help people structure courses and view their own process of teaching with a renewed interest and from a new perspective.

Viewed both in retrospect and contemporaneously, specifying educational objectives as student behaviors seems to be a useful and powerful approach to the analysis of the instructional process. Granted it implies a particular view of the educational process. In it, "education" means changing the behavior of a student so that he is able, when encountering a particular problem or situation, to display a behavior which he did not previously exhibit. The task of the teacher is to help the student learn new or changed behaviors and determine where and when they are appropriate.

A major contribution of this approach to curriculum building is that it forces the instructor to spell out his instructional goals in terms of overt behavior. This gives new detail; indeed it yields an operational definition of many previously general and often fuzzy and ill-defined objectives. Such goals as "the student should become a good citizen" are spelled out in terms of the kinds of behaviors which a good citizen displays. There are then statements, such as, "the student shall be able to identify and appraise judgments and values involved in the choice of a course of political action," "he shall display skill in identifying different appropriate roles in a democratic group," or "he will be able to relate principles in civil liberties and civil rights to current events." Thus the instructor knows what kinds of behavior he is to try to develop in the classroom. In addition, the problem of assessing the extent to which he has achieved his goals becomes markedly simplified. He needs only to provide the student with a situation in which the kind of behavior he is seeking to instill should be evoked and then observe to see whether indeed it appears. Spelling out the behaviors involved in an objective such as the above frequently means specifying several pages of concrete behaviors. Such specification often gives teachers a fresh perspective on their courses and new insights into ways to teach and to evaluate their teaching. This kind of analysis of objectives is clearly a step forward.

This approach to instruction fits in very well with the behaviorist school of psychology, the well-spring from which came the recent emphasis on teaching machines and programmed instruction. It is not surprising, then, that a renewed emphasis on educational objectives resulted from the development of programmed learning. The careful specification of a step-by-step procedure for the learner calls for clearly understood objectives specified at a level of detail far beyond that usually attempted. In programmed learning, such objectives have come to bear the name of "terminal behaviors." As psychologists, physicists, systems development specialists, and others have attempted instructional programming, they have turned to education for a greater understanding of how adequately to specify educational objectives so that they concretely describe a "terminal behavior."

The Need for Objectives at Several Levels of Analysis

The renewed emphasis has given new insight into and perspective on the whole problem of the level of specificity needed in objectives. It is now clear that we need to analyze objectives to several levels of specificity depending upon how we intend to use them. At the first and most abstract level are the quite broad and general statements most helpful in the development of programs of instruction, for the laying out of types of courses and areas to be covered, and for the general goals toward which several years of education might be aimed or for which an entire unit such as an elementary, junior, or senior high school might strive.

At a second and more concrete level, a *behavioral* objectives orientation helps to analyze broad goals into more specific ones which are useful as the building blocks for curricular instruction. These behaviorally stated objectives are helpful in specifying the goals of an instructional unit, a course, or a sequence of courses.

Third, and finally, there is the level needed to create instructional materials—materials which are the operational embodiment of one particular route (rarely are multiple routes included) to the achievement of a curriculum planned at the second and more abstract level, the level of detailed analysis involved in the programmed instruction movement. Just as the second level of analysis brought into concrete, detailed form the ideas of goals and purposes that were in the mind of the good teacher as he planned at the first and more abstract level, so this kind of detailed analysis brings into focus the objectives of specific lesson plans, the sequence of goals in these plans, and the level of achievement required for each goal or objective if successful accomplishment of the next goal in this sequence is to be achieved.

In realization of this, we find Gagné, Mager, and Miller[1] all writing about the analysis of objectives for programmed instruction with a plea that objectives be given a great deal more specificity so that they may be more easily turned into instructional materials. They call for a description of the situation which ought to initiate the behavior in question, a complete description of the behavior, the object or goal of the behavior, and a description of the level of performance of the behavior which permits us to recognize a successful performance.

We may note in passing that even this may not be enough specification for the development of instructional materials. There is no mention in this of the characteristics of the learner and his relation to the learning situation. Thus, not all objectives or terminal behaviors will be appropriate for all kinds and types of students. Neither will the same level of proficiency be appropriate for, nor expected of, different levels of ability. Thus a successful performance cannot have a single definition. Further, those planning instructional materials need to know where the student starts, what he brings to the situation (the "entry behaviors"). We may also need to know something about the motivation for learning (or lack of it if, for example, we are dealing with the culturally disadvantaged), and the pattern of problem solving available to us (for example, in teaching the social studies, one approach for those with rigid value patterns, another for those more flexible). While this is not a complete list, it clearly indicates that a great deal more specification is required in developing instructional materials than in laying out curricular goals.

But to return to our main theme, if we make our goals specific enough to prepare instructional materials, why use the other levels at all? Should we not, for example, discard at least the second level? Not at all! Four points need to be made.

First of all, curriculum construction requires a process of moving through descending abstractions from very general and global statements of desirable behaviors for a program, to intermediate level statements that indicate the blocks from which the program will be constructed, and finally to quite detailed statements which spell out the sub-goals, their relation to one another, and the level of achievement which results in the successful attainment of the intermediate-level behavioral descriptions. All levels of specification of objectives are needed to guide the planning of the educational process. Only as each level is completed can the next be begun. The first level guides the development of the second, the second guides the third.

To return to our example of the development of citizenship, we earlier noted three objectives at the intermediate level. Once these are specified, we can begin to think at the third level of very specific goals and their teaching sequence. For example, one would specify the different possible desirable roles in a democratic group, how these roles would build on one another, to what situations each was appropriate, and how successfully each should be displayed before passing on to the next. Each level thus permits and guides the development of the next level of specification.

Second, not all objectives lend themselves to the *complete* specification at the third level. In some instances, the universe of behaviors is completely circumscribed. For example, there are only 45 sums of two numbers 0 through 9 which need be learned, and we can specify that these must be mastered with perfect accuracy. But in many instances we cannot specify all the instances of behavior. Gagné's contrasting terminology of "mastery" objective to apply to the former and "transfer" objectives to the latter helps to illumine this difference. We cannot predict all situations the student will encounter or all the situations to which he should be able to transfer the behaviors, but we can specify a currently known sample. Nearly all our complex ability and skill objectives—application, analysis, evaluation, etc.—are "transfer" objectives. Their specification will be inexact and confined to a known sample of relevant and typical kinds of behaviors.[2] Transfer objectives seem to constitute the major *ultimate* goals for the bulk of the educational process. More exact specification of mastery goals may be possible in industrial or vocational training for specific occupations than in general education. Thus the level of detail with which educational goals can be usefully specified will depend somewhat on their nature. Again we see that several levels of specificity are needed to handle different kinds of objectives.

Third, we need to have objectives at several levels of abstraction so that we can continually examine their interrelation to one another. When developing a curriculum, we try to get those involved to agree at as detailed a level as possible. But complete agreement can probably be reached only at the more abstract levels. Thus we can get general agreement that students should be good citizens, but we may get some disagreement as to what this means operationally or in behavioral terms. For some teachers this may mean that all students are taught to engage in some political action—ringing doorbells at election time, writing congressmen, etc. To others this may be confined to voting and attempting to understand and to discuss issues with others. Further, such definitions will change as society and its pressures and fads change. It helps to have agreed-upon general and global objectives to which all curricula can relate. These objectives can then be redefined at the less abstract level in relation to the overall goals.

Fourth, and finally, there are many routes from the intermediate level objective to the specification of instructional materials. For example, take the objective: "The student shall be able to recognize form and pattern in literary works as a means to understanding their meaning." This is a useful objective at the intermediate or curricular-building level of abstraction, but how does the teacher translate this into a choice of instructional materials? Does he choose those literary forms and patterns which are likely to have a maximum transfer to all kinds of literary materials and teach them, or does he choose those forms and patterns that will permit the deepest penetration of meaning, and concentrate on them, assuming the other forms and patterns will be picked up in the course of reading? Both approaches might be acceptable. It helps to have the objective in its original abstract form to serve as a basis for judging the routes to its achievement. The routes might be thought of as sub-objectives needing evaluation to help in learning which route best achieves the intermediate-level objective.

We do not have enough psychological knowledge for the teacher and the developer of instructional materials to move with certainty from an intermediate-level objective to a single set of very detailed and concrete objectives. In the example given above, for instance, we have little theoretical basis for judging the language forms and patterns that will permit the most complete understanding of literary material. Both the instructional materials specialist and the teacher precede the psychologist into an area of most-needed research. They must make choices while the psychologist is still developing the knowledge to help them.

Thus there are at least four reasons why objectives at various levels of analysis are useful and needed in the instructional processes:

1. Each level of analysis permits the development of the next more specific level.

2. Mastery objectives can be analyzed to greater specificity than transfer objectives.
3. Curricula gain adoption by consensus that what is taught is of value. Consensus is more easily gained at the more abstract levels of analysis.
4. There are usually several alternative ways of analyzing objectives at the most specific level. Objectives at the more abstract level provide a referent for evaluating these alternatives.

It seems clear then that objectives at several levels of abstraction are useful and important in the educational process. Let us turn now to some of the structures that have been constructed to aid exploration at these levels.

I.   The Taxonomy of Educational Objectives— Framework for Curriculum Building

The need for objectives at various levels of abstraction has given rise to frameworks or structures that assist in the analysis and development of these objectives. One of these frameworks, the *Taxonomy of Educational Objectives*,[3] appears to have proven useful in the analysis of objectives at the intermediate curriculum-building level.

Basically the taxonomy grew out of an attempt to resolve some of the confusion in communication which resulted from the translation of such general terms as "to understand" into more specific behaviors. Thus the "understanding" of Boyle's laws might mean that the student could recall the formula, tell what it meant, interpret the particular meaning of the law in an article about it, use the formula in a new problem situation he had never met, or think up new implications of its relationships.

The problem of precisely identifying what is meant by particular terms plagues the evaluator as well as the curriculum builder. For one thing, these two must communicate with each other since the test constructor seeks accurately to translate the curriculum builder's objectives into situations where the student can display the behavior if he knows it. Accuracy in this translation is essential. Further, evaluators working at different institutions on similar curricula know they have something in common but frequently find it difficult to communicate accurately about it. Given precise communication, they could share and compare the effectiveness of learning devices, materials, and curricula organization. It was with this in mind that a group of college and university examiners, under the leadership of Dr. Benjamin S. Bloom of the University of Chicago, attempted to devise a framework or taxonomy that would help to hold terms in place, provide a structure which would relate one term to another, and thus provide additional meaning for a given term through this interrelationship.

The taxonomy of educational objectives is basically a classification scheme just as biological taxonomy is a scheme for classifying animals into class, order, family, genus, and species. In the educational objectives taxonomy, the kinds of behavior we seek to have students display as a result of the learning process are classified. Every behavioral objective is composed of two parts—the behavior the student is to display and the subject matter or content that is then used in the display. The taxonomy deals only with the behavioral part of the objective; the content or subject matter classification is left to the Library of Congress, the Dewey Decimal System, and such other similar classifications.

For purposes of convenience the taxonomy was divided into three domains, the cognitive, affective, and psychomotor. Handbook I, *The Cognitive Domain,*[4] has been available since 1956. It deals with objectives having to do with thinking, knowing, and problem solving. Handbook II, *The Affective Domain,*[5] was published in 1964. It includes objectives dealing with attitudes, values, interests, appreciations, and social-emotional adjustments. The psychomotor domain covers objectives having to do with manual and motor skills. The feasibility of developing it is being studied by a group at the University of Illinois under Dr. Elizabeth Simpson.

I have described the taxonomy as follows:

"Basically the taxonomy is an educational-logical-psychological classification system. The terms in this order reflect the emphasis given to the organizing principles upon which it is built. It makes educational distinctions in the sense that the boundaries between categories reflect the decisions that teachers make among student behaviors in their development of curricula, and in choosing learning situations. It is a logical system in the sense that its terms are defined precisely and are used consistently. In addition, each category permits logical subdivisions which can be clearly defined and further subdivided as necessary and useful. Finally the taxonomy seems to be consistent with our present understanding of psychological phenomena, though it does not rest on any single theory.

"The scheme is intended to be purely descriptive so that every type of educational goal can be represented. It does not indicate the value or quality of one class as compared to another. It is impartial with respect to views of education. One of the tests of the taxonomy has been that of inclusiveness—could all kinds of educational objectives (if stated as student behaviors) be classified in the framework. In general, it seems to have met this test."[6]

The Cognitive Domain of the Taxonomy

Similar to the distinctions most teachers make, the cognitive domain is divided into the acquisition of knowledge and the development of those skills and abilities necessary to use knowledge. Under the heading "Knowledge," which is the first major category of the cognitive domain, one finds a series of subcategories, each describing the recall of a different category of knowledge. Each of the subheadings is accompanied by a definition of the behavior classified there and by illustrative objectives taken from the educational literature. In addition, there is a summary of the kinds of test items that may be used to test for each category, a discussion of the problems which beset the individual attempting to evaluate behavior in the category, and a large number of examples of test items—mainly multiple choice but some essay type. These illustrate how items may be built to measure each of the categories.

The taxonomy is hierarchical in nature, that is, each category is assumed to involve behavior more complex and abstract than the previous category. Thus the categories are arranged from simple to complex behavior, and from concrete to abstract behavior.

Perhaps the idea of the continuum is most easily gained from looking at the major headings of the cognitive domain, which include *knowledge* (recall of facts, principles, etc.), *comprehension* (ability to restate knowledge in new words), *application* (the ability to use abstractions in particular and concrete situations), *analysis* (the ability to break down material into its constituent parts and to detect relationships among the parts), *synthesis* (the ability to produce wholes from parts, to produce a plan of operation, to derive a set of abstract relations), and *evaluation* (the ability to judge the value of material for given purposes).

Since the cognitive domain has been available for some time, perhaps this brief summary will suffice to remind the reader of its nature or to intrigue him to look into it if it has not previously come to his attention. Since the affective domain is newer, let us examine it in more detail.

The Affective Domain of the Taxonomy

Though there is confusion in communication with respect to terms in the cognitive domain, those who worked on the taxonomy found the confusion much greater when they began work on the affective domain. The state of communication with respect to a term like "really understand" is nothing compared to the confusion that surrounds objectives dealing with attitudes, interests, and appreciations. When we say that we want a child to "appreciate" art, do we mean that he should be aware of art work? Should he be willing to give it some attention when it is around? Do we mean that he should seek it out—go to the museum on his own, for instance? Do we mean that he should regard art work as having positive values? Should he experience an emotional kick or thrill when he sees art work? Should he be able to evaluate it and to know why and how it is effective? Should he be able to compare its esthetic impact with that of other art forms?

This list could be extended, but it is enough to suggest that the term "appreciation" covers a wide variety of meanings. And worse, not all of these are distinct from the terms "attitude" and "interest." Thus, if appreciation has the meaning that the student should like art work well enough to seek it out, how would we distinguish such behavior from an interest in art—or are interests and appreciations, as we use these words, the same thing? If the student *values* art, does he have a favorable *attitude* toward it? Are our appreciation objectives the same as, overlapping with, or in some respects distinct from, our attitude objectives?

In addition to the greater confusion of terms, the affective domain presented some special problems. For example, the hierarchical structure was most difficult to find in the affective part of the taxonomy. The principles of simple to complex and concrete to abstract were not sufficient for developing the affective domain. Something additional was needed.

By seeking the unique characteristics of the affective domain, it was hoped that the additional principles needed to structure an affective continuum would be discovered. Analysis of affective objectives showed the following characteristics which the continuum should embody: the emotional quality which is an important distinguishing feature of an affective response at certain levels of the continuum, the increasing automaticity as one progresses up the continuum, the increasing willingness to attend to a specified stimulus or stimulus type as one ascends the continuum, and the developing integration of a value pattern at the upper levels of the continuum.

A structure was first attempted by attaching certain meanings to the terms "attitude," "value," "appreciation," and "interest." But the multitude of meanings which these terms encompassed in educational objectives showed that this was impossible. After trying a number of schemes and organizing principles, the one which appeared best to account for the affective phenomena and which best described the process of learning and growth in the affective field was the process of internalization.

Internalization refers to the inner growth that occurs as the individual becomes aware of and then adopts attitudes, principles, codes, and sanctions which become inherent in forming value judgements and in guiding his conduct. It has many elements in common with the term socialization. Internalization may be best understood, by looking at the categories in the taxonomy structure, as explained in our book:

"We begin with the individuals being aware of the stimuli which initiate the affective behavior and which form the context in which the affective behavior occurs. Thus, the lowest category is 1.0 *Receiving*. It is subdivided into three categories. At the 1.1 *Awareness* level, the individual merely has his attention attracted to the stimuli (e.g., he develops some consciousness of the use of shading to portray depth and lighting in a picture). The second sub-category, 1.2 *Willingness to Receive,* describes the state in which he has differentiated the stimuli from others and is willing to give it his attention (e.g., he develops a tolerance for bizarre uses of shading in modern art). At 1.3 *Controlled or Selected Attention,* the student looks for the stimuli (e.g., he is on the alert for instances where shading has been used both to create a sense of three-dimensional depth and to indicate the lighting of the picture; or he looks for picturesque words in reading).

"At the next level, 2.0 *Responding,* the individual is perceived as responding regularly to the affective stimuli. At the lowest level of responding, 2.1 *Acquiescence in Responding,* he is merely complying with expectations (e.g., at the request of his teacher, he hangs reproductions of famous paintings in his dormitory rooms; he is obedient to traffic rules). At the next higher level, 2.2 *Willingness to Respond,* he responds increasingly to an inner compulsion (e.g., voluntarily looks for instances of good art where shading, perspective, color, and design have been well used, or has an interest in social problems broader than those of the local community). At 2.3 *Satisfaction in Response,* he responds emotionally as well (e.g., works with clay, especially in making pottery for personal pleasure). Up to this point he has differentiated the affective stimuli; he has begun to seek them out and to attach emotional significance and value to them.

"As the process unfolds, the next levels of 3.0 *Valuing* describe increasing internalization, as the person's behavior is sufficiently consistent that he comes to hold a value: 3.1 *Acceptance of a Value* (e.g., continuing desire to develop the ability to write effectively and hold it more strongly), 3.2 *Preference for a Value* (e.g., seeks out examples of good art for enjoyment of them to the level where he behaves so as to further this impression actively); and 3.3 *Commitment* (e.g., faith in the power of reason and the method of experimentation).

"As the learner successively internalizes values, he encounters situations for which more than one value is relevant. This necessitates organizing the values into a system, 4.0 *Organization*. And since a prerequisite to interrelating values is their conceptualization in a form which permits organization, this level is divided in two: 4.1 *Conceptualization of a Value* (e.g., desires to evaluate works of art which are appreciated, or to find out and crystallize the basic assumptions which underlie codes of ethics) and 4.2 *Organization of a Value System* (e.g., acceptance of the place of art in one's life as one of dominant value, or weighs alternative social policies and practices against the standards of public welfare).

"Finally, the internalization and the organization processes reach a point where the individual responds very consistently to value-laden situations with an interrelated set of values, a structure, a view of the world. The taxonomy category that describes this behavior is 5.0 *Characterization by a Value or Value Complex,* and it includes the categories 5.1 *Generalized Set* (e.g., views all problems in terms of their esthetic aspects, or readiness to revise judgments and to change behavior in the light of evidence) and 5.2 *Characterization* (e.g., develops a consistent philosophy of life).

"Stripped of their definitions, the category and sub-category titles appear in sequence as follows:

1.0 Receiving (attending)
    1.1 Awareness
    1.2 Willingness to receive
    1.3 Controlled or selected attention
2.0 Responding
    2.1 Acquiescence in responding
    2.2 Willingness to respond
    2.3 Satisfaction in response
3.0 Valuing
    3.1 Acceptance of a value
    3.2 Preference for a value
    3.3 Commitment (conviction)
4.0 Organization
    4.1 Conceptualization of a value
    4.2 Organization of a value system
5.0 Characterization by a value or value complex
    5.1 Generalized set
    5.2 Characterization" [7]

Uses of the Taxonomy

The nature of the taxonomy should now be clear. What, however, are its uses? We have indicated that a prime use is in the analysis and classification of objectives.

No longer should a teacher be faced with an objective like "the student should understand the taxonomy of educational objectives," or "he should appreciate the value of taxonomic frameworks." Rather the teacher can now specify whether the first of these objectives would be at the lowest level of comprehension where he would at least expect the student to be able to translate the term "taxonomy" into something like "a classification system of educational goals," or perhaps at a deeper level of understanding, classified as interpretation, where the student could restate the ideas of the taxonomy in his own words. In short, the taxonomy is a relatively concise model for the analysis of education objectives.

The taxonomy, like the periodic table of elements or a check-off shopping list, provides the panorama of objectives. Comparing the range of the present curriculum with the range of possible outcomes may suggest additional goals that might be included. Further, the illustrative objectives may suggest wordings that might be adapted to the area being explored.

Frequently, when searching for ideas in building a curriculum, the work of others is most helpful. Where one's own work and that of others are built in terms of the taxonomy categories, comparison is markedly facilitated. Translation of objectives into the taxonomy framework can provide a basis for precise comparison. Further, where similarities exist, it becomes possible to trade experiences regarding the values of certain learning experiences with confidence that there is a firm basis for comparison and that the other person's experience will be truly relevant.

It is perhaps also important to note the implication of the hierarchical nature of the taxonomy for curriculum building. If the analysis of the cognitive and affective areas is correct, then a hierarchy of objectives dealing with the same subject matter concepts suggests a readiness relationship that exists between those objectives lower in the hierarchy and those higher.

The development of the affective domain has pointed up the problems of achieving objectives in this domain. For instance, a study of the relation of the cognitive and affective domains made it apparent that achievement in the affective domain is markedly underemphasized. Thus, the garden variety of objectives concentrates on specifying behavior in only one domain at a time. No doubt this results from the typical analytic approaches to building curricula. Only occasionally do we find a statement like 'the student should learn to analyze a good argument with pleasure." Such a statement suggests not only the cognitive behavior but also the affective aspect that accompanies it.

In spite of the lack of explicit formulation, however, nearly all cognitive objectives have an affective component if we search for it. Most instructors hope that their students will develop a continuing interest in the subject matter taught. They hope they will have learned certain attitudes toward the phenomena dealt with or toward the way in which problems are approached. But they leave these goals unspecified. This means that many of the objectives which are classified in the cognitive domain have an implicit but unspecified affective component that could be concurrently classified in the affective domain. Where such an attitude or interest objective refers, as it most often does, to the content of the course as a whole or at least to a sizeable segment of it, it may be most convenient to specify it as a separate objective. Many such affective objectives—the interest objectives, for example—become the affective components of all or most of the cognitive objectives in the course.

The affective domain is useful in emphasizing the fact that affective components exist and in analyzing their nature. Perhaps by its very existence it will encourage greater development of affective components of cognitive objectives.

Further, in the cognitive domain, we are concerned that the student shall be able to do a task when requested. In the affective domain, we are more concerned that he *does do* it when it is appropriate after he has learned that he *can do it*. Even though the whole school system rewards the student more on a *can do* than on a *does do* basis, it is the latter which every instructor seeks. By emphasizing this aspect of the affective components, the affective domain brings to light an extremely important and often missing element in cognitive objectives.

Another aspect which came to light was the extremely slow growth of some of the affective behaviors. We saw this as having implications for both the cognitive and affective domains. Thus, every teacher attempts to evaluate the changes that he has made in his students, and it is clear that it is entirely possible for him to do so successfully at the lower levels of the taxonomy. But a teacher will rarely have the same students over a sufficient period of time to make measurable changes in certain affective behaviors. Some objectives, particularly the complex ones at the top of the affective continuum, are probably attained as the product of all or at least a major portion of a student's years in school. Thus, measures of a semester's or year's growth would reveal little change. This suggests that an evaluation plan covering at least several grades and involving the coordinated efforts of several teachers is probably a necessity. A plan involving all the grades in a system is likely to be even more effective. Such efforts would permit gathering longitudinal data on the same students so that gains in complex objectives would be measurable. Patterns of growth in relation to various school efforts would be revealed. Planned evaluation efforts to measure certain cognitive objectives on a longitudinal basis are to be found in some school systems, particularly where they use achievement test batteries designed to facilitate this. Similar efforts with respect to affective objectives are quite rare. If we are serious about attaining complex affective objectives, we shall have to build coordinated evaluation programs that trace the successes and failures of our efforts to achieve them.

In particular, we noted that there was a great deal of "erosion" with respect to the affective domain objectives. When a curriculum is first conceived, affective objectives play an important part in the conceptual structure of the courses. But as time goes on, they cease to have influence on the direction of the courses or in the choice of instructional activities. In part, this results from the fact that rarely are affective objectives reflected in the grading process. Students tend to concentrate on what counts, and affective objectives rarely appear to do so. Since a part of this lack of emphasis on affective objectives in grading is due to the inadequacy of measures and ways of relating measures to objectives, it is possible that the sections of the taxonomy dealing with measurement in the affective domain may help to make these objectives more realistic parts of those courses in which affective objectives are important.

II.   A Framework to Facilitate Construction of Instructional Materials

Perhaps this is enough to indicate the existence and potential usefulness of the taxonomy structure as a means of working with objectives at the curriculum-building level. What about the specification of objectives at the instructional material-building level? Gagné writes:

> Is it in fact possible to divide objectives into categories which differ in their implications for learning? To do this, one has to put together a selected set of learning conditions on the one hand, and an abstracted set of characteristics of human tasks on the other. This is the kind of effort which has been called *task analysis*. Its objective is to distinguish, not the tasks themselves (which are infinitely variable), but the *inferred behaviors* which presumably require different conditions of learning. Such behavior categories can be distinguished by means of several different kinds of criteria, which in an ultimate sense should be completely compatible with each other. What I should like to try to do here, however, is to use one

particular set of criteria, which pertain to the question of "What is learned?" [8]

Gagné's categories are a blending of behavioristic psychology and cognitive theory; the lowest four are related to the former, the upper four to the latter.

His categories also are hierarchical in the sense that having any one capability usually depends upon the previous learning of some other simpler one. Thus, his two top categories of problem solving and strategy-using "require the pre-learning of:

Principles
    which require the pre-learning of:
Concepts
    which require the pre-learning of:
Associations
    which require the pre-learning of:
Chains
    which require the pre-learning of:
Identifications
    which require the pre-learning of:
Responses." [9]

In more detail his categories are:

Response learning. A very basic form of behavior is called response learning, or is sometimes given other names, such as "echoic behavior." The individual learns to respond to a stimulus which is essentially the same as that produced by the response itself. . . .

Identification learning (multiple discrimination). In this form of behavior, the individual acquires the capability of making different responses to a number of different stimuli. Of course, he does this when he identifies colors, or late model cars, or numerals, or any of a great variety of specific stimuli. . . .

Chains or sequences. Long chains of responses can most readily be identified in motor acts of various sorts. But there are many kinds of *short* sequences which are very important to the individual's performance. One of the most prominent is a chain of two acts the first of which is an *observing response*. If one is concerned, for example, with getting someone to put 17 in the numerator, this act has two main parts: (1) finding the location of the numerator (an observing response), and (2) writing in that place the numeral 17. In establishing such behavior as part of the larger and more complex performance like simplifying fractions, one has to see to it that such a chain is learned. . . .

Association. For many years, psychologists appeared to be considering this the most basic form of learning, but such is no longer the case. It is now fairly generally agreed, and supported by a good deal of evidence, that the learning of associations involves more than a S-R connection. Instead, an association is perhaps best considered as a three-step chain, containing in order (1) an observing response which distinguishes the stimulus, (2) a *coding* response which usually is implicit, and (3) the response which is to be expected as the outcome of the association. . . .

Concepts. A concept is acquired when a set of objectives or events *differing* in physical appearance is identified as a class. The class names for common objects like chairs, houses, hats, are the most familiar examples. . . . If one can assume these more basic forms as having been acquired, then the procedure of concept learning is fairly simple. It consists mainly in establishing associations in which the variety of specific stimuli that make up the class to be acquired are represented. . . .

Principles. The next more complex form of learning pertains to the acquisition of principles. One can consider these, in their basic form, as a chain of concepts of the form If A, then B. . . . Again it is evident that the important set of conditions necessary for principle learning is previous learning, this time of the concepts which make up the principle. One either assumes that the learner already knows the concepts liquid, heating, and gas, in acquiring the principle, or else they must first be learned. . . . But when one can truly assume that concept learning has previously been completed, the conditions for principle learning become clear. The proposed chain of events is presented by means of particular objects representing the concepts making up the chain. . . .

Problem solving. Problem solving is a kind of learning by means of which principles are put together in chains to form what may be called higher-order principles. . . . Typically, the higher-order principles are induced from sets of events presented to the learner in instruction. If carried out properly, these become the generalizations which enable the student to think about an ever-broadening set of new problems. . . .

Strategies. Are there forms of behavior which are more complex than principles, or than the higher-order principles acquired in problem solving? Some authors seem to imply another *form* of learned organization in the strategies with which an individual approaches a problem. There can be little doubt as to the existence of such strategies in problem solving. It may be that strategies are *mediating principles* which do not appear directly in the performance of the task set to the individual, but which may nevertheless affect the speed or excellence of that performance. . . . But it is possible to conceive of strategies as being principles in their fundamental nature, and of being made up of chains of concepts. . . .[10]

(This framework is developed in further detail in Gagné's *Conditions of Learning,* Holt, Rinehart and Winston, 1965.)

Important Needed Research—How to Relate the Frameworks

One may question whether either or both of these frameworks are adequate to the tasks that they have set for themselves. If nothing else, however, perhaps they have heuristic value. In fact, by their very existence, they immediately raise the question, How are the two frameworks related? and its derivative question, What instructional methods are of most value in achieving certain categories in either framework? For example, how does Gagné's strategy development relate to the skills of the cognitive domain in applying, analyzing, synthesizing, evaluating? What instructional methods most efficiently and effectively permit achievement of these goals? These are questions that should be the focus of considerable educational research.

Summary

To sum up, we have explored the necessity for developing objectives at several levels of generality and abstraction as appropriate for different stages in the process of course and instructional materials development. Increasingly, the means are becoming available to do a more thorough and precise job of working with objectives at these different levels. We have explored several frameworks: the Cognitive and Affective Domains of the Taxonomy of Educational Objectives and the classification of capabilities developed by Gagné. We have especially examined some of the implications of the former. Hopefully, as these come to the attention of those actively concerned with course and instructional materials building, their heuristic value will be tested and they may be revised to the point where the process of curriculum building and instructional materials development is better structured and more researchable. As this comes about, perhaps the growth we all seek in the science of education will be at least somewhat accelerated.

REFERENCES

1. Gagné, Robert M. The Analysis of Instructional Objectives. A paper prepared for the National Symposium on Research in Programmed Instruction, Department of Audiovisual Instruction, National Education Association, 1963.

   Mager, Robert R. *Preparing Objectives for Programmed Instruction.* San Francisco, California: Fearon Publishers, 1962.

   Miller, R. B. The Newer Role of the Industrial Psychologist. *Industrial Psychology.* B. von H. Gelmer (Ed.), New York: McGraw-Hill Book Co., 1961.

2. Mager and others suggest that criterion performance for a successful completion be specified, e.g., "given a human skeleton, the student must be able to identify correctly by labeling at least 40 of the following bones," or "the student must be able to reply in grammatically correct French to 95% of the questions put to him in an examination." (*Op. cit.*, p. 50.) It is worth noting that such levels have one meaning for mastery objectives. (e.g., he should be able to give the capital and lower case letters for the entire alphabet) when the universe of behaviors is known and specified. They have a different meaning when test questions of different complexity are constructed to an indeterminate universe of behaviors in a French quiz. In the latter instance, judgment of both the level of difficulty of the problems and the matter of adequacy of sampling enter the evaluation process, and both must be taken into consideration in judging a successful performance.

3. Bloom, Benjamin S. (Ed.) *et al. Taxonomy of Educational Objectives: The Classification Of Educational Goals. Handbook I: Cognitive Domain.* New York: David McKay Co., 1956.

   Krathwohl, David R., Benjamin S. Bloom & Bertram B. Masia. *Taxonomy of Educational Objectives: The Classification of Educational Objectives. Handbook II: Affective Domain.* New York: David McKay, 1964.

4. Bloom *et al., op. cit.*

5. Krathwohl, Bloom & Masia, *op. cit.*

6. Krathwohl, David R. Taxonomy of Educational Objectives—Its Use in Curriculum Building. *Defining Educational Objectives.* C. M. Lindvall (Ed.), Pittsburgh, Pennsylvania: Regional Commission on Educational Coordination and Learning, Research and Development Center, University of Pittsburgh, 1964, p. 21.

7. Krathwohl, Bloom & Masia, *op. cit.*, pp. 34-35.

8. Gagné, Robert M. The Implications of Instructional Objectives for Learning. *Defining Educational Objectives.* Lindvall, *op. cit.*, p. 38.

9. *Ibid.*, p. 45.

10. *Ibid.*, pp. 39-44.

A group at the University of Illinois under the leadership of Dr. Elizabeth Simpson began in 1964 to develop and refine an exploratory taxonomy of educational objectives in the psychomotor domain. Information concerning the project was submitted to the U.S. Office of Education in 1966 and is available from the ERIC Document Reproduction Service (ED 010-368). The project report also appeared in the Winter 1966-67 issue of the Illinois Teacher of Home Economics. *In the excerpt reprinted below, Simpson offers a comprehensive view of the psychomotor classification scheme.*

Educational Objectives in the Psychomotor Domain*

ELIZABETH SIMPSON

Many who made use of the two sections of the taxonomy of educational objectives, in the cognitive and affective domains (Bloom, 1956; Krathwohl *et al.*, 1964), felt a serious lack in not having a classification system for educational objectives in the psychomotor domain. Such a system would be useful for the development of curriculum materials and as a basis for evaluation of educational outcomes. The psychomotor domain has relevance for education in general as well as for such areas of specialization as industrial education, agriculture, home economics, music, art and physical education.

*Reprinted from Calvin J. Cotrell & Edward F. Hauck (Eds.), *Educational Media in Vocational and Technical Education: A Report of a National Seminar,* The Center for Research and Leadership Development in Vocational and Technical Education, The Ohio State University, 1967, pp. 38-47, by permission of the publisher and the author.

Out of the investigations that my co-workers and I carried out over a two-year period has emerged a classification system for educational objectives in the psychomotor domain. Whereas I do not believe that this system is "on the wrong track," I believe that it is in need of further development and of trial in a variety of test situations.

Preliminary investigations with respect to the development of the classification system for educational objectives in the psychomotor domain led to the conclusion that there is a hierarchy among the three domains. The cognitive domain, though certainly very complex, is, in a sense, somewhat "purer" than the other two domains. That is, cognition can take place with a minimum of motor activity. Also, feeling may not be greatly involved—although it would seem reasonable to assume some degree of affect. The affective domain necessarily involves considerable cognition as well as feeling. And, the psychomotor domain, as implied in the very name, involves cognition and motor activity, as well as affective components involved in the willingness to act. The increasingly strong involvement of all three domains, from the cognitive to the affective to the psychomotor, resulted in a special problem of complexity in developing a classification system for this third domain.

The approach taken in developing the classification system for the psychomotor domain was an exploratory one. General procedures to guide the investigators were outlined, but these were deliberately left flexible, accommodative, and "open."

The disadvantage of such an approach is the possibility of some loss of time and energy in pursuing the objective; that is, this approach may be somewhat lacking in efficiency. On the other hand, it avoids the narrow restrictiveness of a more cut-and-dried approach. It opens the way for the possibilities of greater creativity.

General procedures included the following:

1. A comprehensive review of related literature, especially of any that described ways of classifying psychomotor activities, and, hence, suggested possibilities for classifying the educational objectives of this domain.

2. Collecting and analyzing the behavioral objectives of this domain as one way of gaining insight regarding a possible classification system.

3. Laboratory analyses of certain tasks to discover by observation and introspection the nature of the psychomotor activity involved. These analyses were carried out by the research assistants on the project who had read widely in the area before attempting the analyses.

4. Conferences with scholars who have specialized knowledge of the nature of psychomotor activity, development of classification systems for educational objectives, and of the areas of

study where educational objectives in the psychomotor domain are of paramount concern.

From the beginning, it was readily apparent that, if the classification system were to be taxonomic in form, an "organizing principle" would have to be found. This question was kept in mind as work progressed.

Ascertaining what objectives "fit" in this domain was an early concern. The definition given in the *Taxonomy of Educational Objectives, Affective Domain* (Krathwohl, 1964) served as a guide: Psychomotor objectives are those which "emphasize some muscular or motor skill, some manipulation of material and objects, or some act which requires a neuromuscular coordination."

It was not always an easy task to ascertain whether a given objective was primarily of one type or another. One problem was related to *type of performance* called for in the objective. The concern of this project is performance of a particular sort, that involving motor activity. But, performance may be almost wholly of a cognitive type and, although at this point of time with reference to the project, it seems a bit strange, confusion sometimes resulted from uncertainty regarding the primary nature of the activity involved in an objective.

Another problem, one that is frequently encountered in analyzing educational objectives in all three domains, had to do with the lack of specificity of the objectives. That is, many that certainly involved a great deal of motor activity, almost equally also involved the other domains. These were broad objectives, such as: ability to give a successful party, ability to conduct a meeting, and ability to conduct a play period for small children. The investigator finally concluded that those were in the "action-pattern" domain,* hence beyond the other three domains.

The Classification System, Psychomotor Domain

With the foregoing brief introduction to the psychomotor domain, I would like to present the schema in its present form. The major organizational principle operative is that of complexity, with attention to the sequence involved in the performance of a motor act.

1.0 Perception—This is an essential first step in performing a motor act. It is the process of becoming aware of objects, qualities, or relations by way of the sense organs. It is the central portion of the situation-interpretation-action chain leading to purposeful motor activity.

*The term "action pattern" was used in *Elementary School Objectives,* by Nolan C. Kearney, Russell Sage, 1953.

The category of perception has been divided into three sub-categories indicating three different levels with respect to the perception process. It seems to the investigator that this level is a parallel of the first category, receiving or attending, in the affective domain.

1.1 *Sensory stimulation*—Impingement of a stimulus(i) upon one or more of the sense organs.

    1.11 *Auditory*—Hearing or the sense or organs of hearing.

    1.12 *Visual*—Concerned with the mental pictures or images obtained through the eyes.

    1.13 *Tactile*—Pertaining to the sense of touch.

    1.14 *Taste*—To ascertain the relish or flavor of by taking a portion into the mouth.

    1.15 *Smell*—To perceive by excitation of the olfactory nerves.

    1.16 *Kinesthetic*—The muscle sense; pertaining to sensitivity from activation of receptors in muscles, tendons, and joints.

The preceding categories are not presented in any special order of importance, although, in Western cultures, the visual cues are said to have dominance, whereas in some cultures, the auditory and tactile cues may preempt the high position we give the visual. Probably no sensible ordering of these is possible at this time. It should also be pointed out that "the cues that guide action may change for a particular motor activity as learning progresses (e.g., kinesthetic cues replacing visual cues)." (Loree, June 1965.)

1.1 *Sensory stimulation*—Illustrative educational objectives:

    "Sensitivity to auditory cues in playing a musical instrument as a member of a group."

    "Awareness of difference in 'hand' of various fabrics."

    "Sensitivity to flavors in seasoning food."

1.2 *Cue selection*—Deciding to what cues one must respond in order to satisfy the particular requirements of task performance.

    This involves identification of the cue or cues and associating them with the task to be performed. It may involve grouping of cues in terms of past experience and knowledge. Cues relevant to the situation are selected as a guide to action; irrelevant cues are ignored or discarded.

    1.21 Illustrative educational objectives:

        "Recognition of operating difficulties with machinery through the sound of the machine in operation."

"Sensing where the needle should be set in beginning machine stitching."

"Recognizing factors to take into account in batting in a softball game."

1.3   *Translation*—Relating of perception to action in performing a motor act. This is the mental process of determining the meaning of the received cues for action. It involves symbolic translation, that is, having an image or being reminded of something, "having an idea," as a result of cues received. It may involve insight which is essential in solving a problem through perceiving the relationships essential to solution. Sensory translation is an aspect of this level. It involves "feedback," that is, knowledge of the effects of the process; translation is a continuous part of the motor act being performed.

1.31   *Translation*—Illustrative educational objectives:

"Ability to relate music to dance form."

"Ability to follow a recipe in preparing food."

"Knowledge of the 'feel' of operating a sewing machine successfully and use of this knowledge as a guide in stitching."

2.0   *Set*—Set is a preparatory adjustment or readiness for a particular kind of action or experience.

Three aspects of set have been identified: mental, physical, and emotional.

2.1   *Mental set*—Readiness, in the mental sense, to perform a certain motor act. This involves, as prerequisite, the level of perception and its sub-categories which have already been identified. Discrimination, that is, using judgement in making distinctions, is an aspect.

2.11   *Mental set*—Illustrative educational objectives:

"Knowledge of steps in setting the table."

"Knowledge of tools appropriate to performance of various sewing operations."

2.2   *Physical set*—Readiness in the sense of having made the anatomical adjustments necessary for a motor act to be performed. Readiness, in the physical sense, involves receptor set, that is, sensory attending, or focusing the attention of the needed sensory organs and postural set, or positioning of the body.

2.21   *Physical set*—Illustrative educational objectives:

"Achievement of bodily stance preparatory to bowling."

"Positioning of hands preparatory to typing."

2.3 *Emotional set*—Readiness in terms of attitudes favorable to the motor act's taking place. Willingness to respond is implied.

2.31 *Emotional set*—Illustrative educational objectives:

"Disposition to perform sewing machine operation to best of ability."

"Desire to operate a production drill press with skill."

3.0 *Guided response*—This is an early step in the development of skill. Emphasis here is upon the abilities which are components of the more complex skill. Guided response is the overt behavioral act of an individual under the guidance of the instructor. Prerequisite to performance of the act are readiness to respond, in terms of set to produce the overt behavioral act, and selection of the appropriate response. Selection of response may be defined as deciding what response must be made in order to satisfy the particular requirements of task performance. There appear to be two major sub-categories, imitation and trial and error.

3.1 *Imitation*—Imitation is the execution of an act as a direct response to the perception of another person performing the act.

3.11 *Imitation*—Illustrative educational objectives:

"Imitation of the process of stay-stitching the curved neck edge of a bodice."

"Performing a dance step as demonstrated."

"Debeaking a chick in the manner demonstrated."

3.2 *Trial and error*—Trying various responses, usually with some rationale for each response, until an appropriate response is achieved. The appropriate response is one which meets the requirements of task performance, that is, "gets the job done" or does it more efficiently. This level may be defined as multiple response learning in which the proper response is selected out of varied behavior, possible through the influence of reward and punishment.

3.21 *Trial and error*—Illustrative educational objectives:

"Discovering the most efficient methods of ironing a blouse through trial of various procedures."

"Ascertaining the sequence for cleaning a room through trial of several patterns."

4.0 *Mechanism*—Learned response has become habitual. At this level, the learner has achieved a certain confidence and degree of skill in the performance of the act. The act is a part of his repertoire of possible responses to stimuli and the demands of situations where the response is an appropriate one. The response may be more complex than at the preceding level; it may involve some patterning of response in carrying out the task. That is, abilities are combined in action of a skill nature.

4.1   *Mechanism*—Illustrative educational objectives:
     "Ability to perform a hand-seaming operation."
     "Ability to mix ingredients for a butter cake."
     "Ability to pollinate an oat flower."

5.0   *Complex overt response*—At this level, the individual can perform a motor act that is considered complex because of the movement pattern required. At this level, a high degree of skill has been attained. The act can be carried out smoothly and efficiently, that is, with minimum expenditure of time and energy. There are two sub-categories: resolution of uncertainty and automatic performance.

    5.1   *Resolution of uncertainty*—The act is performed without hesitation of the individual to get a mental picture of task sequence. That is, he knows the sequence required and so proceeds with confidence. The act is here defined as complex in nature.

        5.11   *Resolution of uncertainty*—Illustrative educational objectives:
         "Skill in operating a milling machine."
         "Skill in setting up and operating a production band saw."
         "Skill in laying a pattern on fabric and cutting out a garment."

    5.2   *Automatic Performance*—At this level, the individual can perform a finely coordinated motor skill with a great deal of ease and muscle control.

        5.21   *Automatic performance*—Illustrative educational objectives:
         "Skill in performing basic steps of national folk dances."
         "Skill in tailoring a suit."
         "Skill in performing on the violin."

We believe that the schema in its present form is useful. Whether there is sufficient distinction between one category and another, however, may still be in question. Perhaps additional sub-categories to increase the discrimination quality are needed for some of the major sections.

Another question that needs further investigation is the following: Is there perhaps a sixth major category which might be designated as *adapting* and *originating*? Probably such a level is needed. At this level, the individual might be so skilled that he can adapt the action in terms of the specific requirements of the individual performer and the situation. He might originate new patterns of action in solving a specific problem. Or, do these activities take place at all levels? Must the individual have attained a high degree of skill in order to adapt and originate?

One next major step is that of providing for trial of the schema in many situations and revising it in light of the trials. Another important step that should be taken is that of looking critically at the relationships among the three domains. It is readily apparent that they are closely related and that a single educational objective might have a particular significance in one domain and another in another domain. For example, at the *mental set* level in performing a motor act, knowledge is required; hence, an objective that "fits" this level would also fit into the cognitive domain and could be classified there.

Much work is needed in studying the psychomotor domain and its relationships to the other two. Serious consideration needs to be given the "action-pattern" domain suggested by Loree (1965, 1966). The roles of sub-objectives and the interplay of "domains" in such broad objectives as the following is a matter requiring investigation: 1) to develop the ability to manage a farm, 2) to express ideas in a clear manner before a group, and 3) to manage a home.

The magnitude of the tasks ahead is readily apparent. Direction is somewhat obscure. That, however, is part of the fascination of working on an essentially creative task.

REFERENCES

Bloom, Benjamin S. *et al. Taxonomy of Educational Objectives, Handbook I, Cognitive Domain.* New York: David McKay Co., 1956.

Carlson, Nancy and Mildred Griggs. *The Psychomotor Domain, A Selected Bibliography with Annotations.* Division of Home Economics Education, Department of Vocational and Technical Education, University of Illinois, Urbana, 1966.

Krathwohl, David R., Benjamin S. Bloom, and Bertram B. Masia. *Taxonomy of Educational Objectives, Handbook II, Affective Domain.* New York: David McKay Co., 1964.

Loree, M. Ray. Correspondence with Elizabeth Simpson, June, 1965.

———. Creativity and the Taxonomies of Educational Objectives. Speech given at Home Economics Division, AVA Convention, Denver, Colorado, 1966, p. 1.

———. Relationships Among Three Domains of Educational Objectives. *Contemporary Issues in Home Economics,* A Conference Report. National Education Association, Washington, D. C., 1965, p. 75.

Simpson, Elizabeth J. The Classification of Educational Objectives, Psychomotor Domain. *Illinois Teacher of Home Economics, 10,* 4, pp. 121-126.

Loree examines each of the categories in the cognitive and affective domains of the Taxonomy *of Educational Objectives for relevance to education for creativity. He accepts the definition of creativity as behavior which is characterized by originality (novelty), adaptiveness, and realization. Although the illustrations used by Loree throughout the paper relate most closely to the field of home economics education, his comments are useful for other fields as well. In addition, he provides insight into the nature of the* Taxonomy, *and describes possible techniques of educating for creativity.*

Creativity and the Taxonomies of Educational Objectives[*]

M. Ray Loree

The two taxonomies of educational objectives—one in the cognitive domain (Bloom, 1956) and a second in the affective domain (Krathwohl, Bloom, and Masia, 1964)—represent efforts to analyze and impose some form of organization upon the multitude of educational objectives found in present day schools. One danger in fragmenting the educational venture into specific educational objectives is that important global objectives may be lost in the process. For example, a global objective for a home economics program may be the development of

*Paper originally presented at Home Economics Division, AVA Convention, Denver, Colorado, 1966; reprinted by permission of the author.

the "good homemaker." It is legitimate, therefore, in evaluating a set of educational objectives for a home economics program, to raise the question: "Does this set of objectives add up to the production of a good homemaker?" Or we might select some characteristic deemed to be of great importance to the educated man. We might raise the question of what sub-objectives should be included in a program designed to help students to become more creative so that their education results in a way of living that ensures growth and, with this growth, an ever increasing freedom.

In this paper I will try to make an initial exploration of the meaning of the two taxonomies of educational objectives when emphasis is placed upon education to develop creativity. First, some consideration of what is meant by the term "creativity" is in order.

Creativity Defined

What are the essential characteristics of creative behavior? Researchers on creativity are not in full agreement on this question. For some students of creativity, *novelty* is *the* one distinguishing characteristic of creativity. Guilford (1965, p. 6), for example, states: "Creative thinking is distinguished by the fact that there is something novel about it—that is, to the thinking individual. The degree of creativity shown is directly proportional to the degree of novelty." Other students are not satisfied with this definition. The high school home economics student who plans a meal consisting of bread, potatoes, and ice cream as a first course may have a rather novel meal plan. However, most home economists probably would be critical of this combination of foods as one course in a meal.

MacKinnon (1965) considers novelty as a necessary but not sufficient aspect of creativity. In addition to novelty MacKinnon (1965, p. 160) adds: "If a response is to lay claim to being a part of the creative process, it must to some extent be adaptive to, or of, reality. It must serve to solve a problem, fit a situation, or accomplish some recognizable goal. And, thirdly, true creativeness involves a sustaining of the original insight, an evaluation and elaboration of it, a developing of it to the full. Creativity, from this point of view, is a process extended in time and characterized by originality [novelty], adaptiveness, and realization." MacKinnon's third essential characteristic of creativity—sustaining the original insight—is not usually considered as part of the essence of creativity. However, it was a characteristic of the group of creative professional people who were selected by MacKinnon for study. This group included creative writers, painters, architects, mathematicians, research workers, inventors, and senior college women.

For purposes of this paper, MacKinnon's definition of creativity will be accepted. Our problem now is twofold: first, to examine the implications of the definition within the field of home economics; and second, to elaborate the definition in terms of the categories of the two taxonomies of educational objectives.

Creativity and Home Economics Education

One way we can start our exploration is by examining an educational objective that is found in many home economics education programs. The objective, "The ability to plan menus," will serve our purposes. The home economics teacher who values creativity will encourage her students to search for novel menus (MacKinnon's first characteristic) that are appropriate to the situation (MacKinnon's second characteristic) and will encourage her students to elaborate or work through their plans with sufficient attention to detail (MacKinnon's third criterion). Usually the *appropriateness* of a menu is judged in terms of criteria such as (1) nutritionally adequate for the family, (2) meets individual needs, (3) attractiveness, (4) achievable for the situation, and (5) reasonable in cost.

The interior decorator is creative when (1) she plans a unique arrangement of furniture in a room, (2) *providing* her plan is practical, functional, artistic, and appropriate for the individuals who will live in the room, and (3) *providing* she works out the many sub-problems involved in her initial plan. The interior decorator, then, is creative when her work is characterized by originality, adaptiveness, and realization.

Perhaps I do not need to belabor the point. Within all areas of a home economics program, the teacher can provide students with many opportunities to be creative. The teacher who values creativity certainly will provide such opportunities and will reward with commendations creative behavior when it appears. But can the teacher do more than provide opportunities for creativity and encourage creativity? Can the teacher help the non-creative student to become creative? Let us see whether an examination of the concept of creativity in terms of the taxonomies can help to answer these questions.

Creativity and Cognitive Domain

In the *Taxonomy of Educational Objectives, Cognitive Domain* (Bloom, 1956), educational objectives are classified into six categories. These are knowledge, comprehension, application, analysis, synthesis, and evaluation. These major categories are ordered on the basis of complexity, with knowledge being the least complex category and evaluation the most complex. Each succeeding category subsumes the behaviors described in the preceding categories. Thus, knowledge is included within comprehension, knowledge and comprehension are subsumed within application, and so on.

Let us first describe briefly the behaviors subsumed within each category in the taxonomy; second, explore the relationship of each category to creativity; and finally, consider some implications for home economics education.

Knowledge

From a learning standpoint, knowledge objectives involve the acquisition of information, the learning of the sequence of steps required to perform a complex process, and the learning of abstractions, principles, generalizations, and theories. From a testing standpoint, knowledge objectives entail remembering, either by recognition or recall, previously learned facts, concepts, events, principles, and theories. Thus, knowledge objectives involve the acquisition and retention of materials. "Knowledge of the principles and facts of food preparation" is an example of a knowledge objective. The teaching job for this objective is, first, to identify the principles and the multitude of facts subsumed by the objective; and, second, to arrange learning experiences through which the principles and facts are easily acquired and readily retrieved from memory storage. The testing job requires sampling from the population of principles and facts in order to estimate the extent to which the student has attained the objective.

It seems fairly clear that the student does not have to be creative in order to attain a knowledge objective. The student merely memorizes, and this is not creativity. But it would be wrong to conclude that knowledge objectives are irrelevant to education for creativity. To be creative in any field of endeavor it is necessary to know something about the field. Mary Henle (1962), in a stimulating chapter in the book *Contemporary Approaches to Creative Thinking,* has pointed out an interesting paradox in this connection. The paradox is that immersion in one's subject is a prerequisite to creative thought, yet our knowledge of current ideas in a field may blind us to new ones. Thus, while you do not have to be creative to attain knowledge, it is difficult if not impossible to be creative in a field unless you do attain knowledge. To illustrate, it would be very difficult for me to be creative in preparing a five course dinner for a party of eight. It would be difficult simply because I do not know enough about food preparation. I might be able to satisfy the first criteria of creativity, i.e., "originality," but I would earn an F grade on the criteria of "adaptiveness," particularly if adapativeness included the palatability and attractiveness of the food served.

Keeping Mary Henle's paradox in mind, the challenge to the home economics teacher who wishes to foster creativity is to help students to attain knowledge objectives without blinding them to new ideas. What we want to develop is the student with a thorough knowledge in his field who is also open and receptive to new knowledge, new ideas, and new experiences.

Retrieval of knowledge also may be a creativity variable. Guilford's battery of creativity tests (Guilford, 1959) includes a set on "fluency." For example, the person tested is asked to write down as many words as he can that are suggested by the word "soft." A comparable item for a home economics student would require the student to write down as many words as she can that are suggested by the word "carbohydrates." Another of Guilford's tests requires the student to list as many uses as he can for a common brick. In these tests, the number of responses produced is a function of the adequacy of a person's retrieval system as well as a function of knowledge he possesses. Possibly the adequacy of a person's retrieval system is the more important variable in accounting for individual differences in creativity among students. Bloom and Broder (1950), in their monograph on *Problem-Solving Processes of College Students,* found that the unsuccessful problem solver often had sufficient information to solve a problem and yet failed because he did not retrieve the required information. Perhaps the memory storage of a person may be like a filing system—either well-organized or messy. The home economist who plans a meal figuratively may refer to files in her memory storage—files like carbohydrates, proteins, color, texture, etc. The rank amateur is more likely to proceed in a much more disorganized fashion as he refers to an unclassified series of his past experiences with foods. However, even among home economics students there will be a considerable variability in the number of bits of relevant information they are able to retrieve for a given home economics problem. Unfortunately we have much to learn on how to improve a student's information retrieval system. One possible teaching implication may be that we should present information to students in a structured or organized form so as to facilitate the retrieval process. Another prosible teaching implication is that we should give students practice in structuring or organizing the information they possess.

Comprehension

The comprehension category of the cognitive domain includes those objectives, behaviors, or responses which represent an understanding of concepts, principles, and ideas, and the ability to glean the meaning from materials communicated. Test items in the comprehension category must have some element of novelty so as to guarantee that the student arrives at an answer to a question because he comprehends the material, not merely because he recalls it. Three types of comprehension behavior are considered in the taxonomy. The first is *translation*. In this type of comprehension, the individual puts a communication into other language. Mathematical symbols into verbal language, French into English, musical notes into sounds—all are examples of translation. A second type is *interpretation*. In this type of comprehension, the learner is able to group the meanings of communication containing numerous ideas, see the interrelationships between the parts, and recognize implied generalizations that are implicit within the communication. The third type of comprehension is *extrapolation*. Here, the individual is able to go beyond data presented on the basis of trends present in the data.

How are educational objectives in the comprehension category related to education for creativity? Two points can be made. Objectives in the comprehension category encompass behaviors that enable the individual to be effectively creative but do not insure the development of creative behavior. In other words, the attaining of comprehension objectives is a necessary but not a sufficient condition for the development of creative behavior. As we have noted, this was also true for knowledge objectives, and it is equally true for the remaining categories within the cognitive domain. The second point that can be made concerns the teaching procedures used to promote comprehension objectives. To illustrate this point, let us explore the way in which concepts are learned. Parenthetically, we may note that in testing a student's mastery of a concept, we usually would want to go beyond mere memorization, and test for a student's understanding of a concept.

A concept may be defined as a generalization formed by abstracting some characteristics or critical attributes from a class of objects or events. A person demonstrates that he has formed a concept when he is able to discriminate between instances and non-instances of a concept, on the basis of the abstracted characteristics. "Fruit" is a concept. Oranges, bananas, apples, and peaches are instances of the concept "fruit." We are able to discriminate between fruits and non-fruits on the basis of certain critical attributes that we abstract from fruits. For example, "a product of plant growth," would be one critical attribute through which we discriminate between fruits and non-fruits. The concept "citrus fruits" represents a sub-classification of fruits and the critical attribute, "rich in vitamin C," enables us to discriminate between citrus and non-citrus fruits. The more accurately we identify the critical attributes that define a concept, the finer discriminations we can make between instances and non-instances of a concept.

We have defined a concept. Let us now examine how concepts are taught. Remember, the basic point that I am attempting to establish is that the extent to which concept learning contributes to the development of creativity depends upon the process through which a student learns a concept. In general we may teach concepts deductively or inductively. Usually we teach concepts deductively. We first define the concept to be taught; then we give the student practice in recognizing instances. For example, in dress designing, the teacher may define the concept of "formal balance" and then give the student practice in recognizing instances or illustrations of formal balance. The teacher may define and organize other concepts related to dress design, such as form, color, pattern, and texture, and concepts related to the effects created, such as rhythm, balance, harmony, and subordination. From concepts such as these, as I understand it, principles of design have been generated. Then, from a variety of illustrations, the student can be given practice in recognizing the principle of design illustrated. This is deductive teaching. The definition of a concept is the starting point. Students then are called upon to recognize illustrations of defined concepts.

To teach concepts inductively, the teacher begins with the presentation of instances of the concept. The task of the student is to discover the critical attributes that discriminate exemplars of the concept from non-exemplars. For example, in generating concepts, the teacher may present four instances of designs that illustrate opposition of color, along with one design with repetition of color. The task of the student is to find the one instance that is different from the other four and give some name to the characteristic or critical attribute that permits the discrimination. Or the whole host of designs (thirty or forty) may be presented to students. The teacher selects designs which exemplify concepts that the student is expected to discover. The task given the student is to classify the designs into groups and to give names to the attributes that serve as a basis for classification. This process of searching for attributes that serve to discriminate one set of objects from another is itself an exercise in creativity. Students may come up with a quite different classification system for the objects or events they are called upon to classify. This procedure, known as "learning by discovery," is being tried out currently by a number of different teaching fields. It is a time consuming process. In fact, one of the advocates of learning by discovery has wryly commented that it is a method of teaching children in two weeks what you can tell him in two minutes. But the important outcome is not mastery of the concept itself. The value, rather, rests in the process through which the children learn to create new concepts or discover old ones.

Probably, children in school learn some concepts inductively and some deductively. While learning concepts inductively is more time consuming, children enjoy discovering concepts even at a very early age. I remember my efforts to teach the concept "daughter" to a four-year-old, and his searching behavior to discover the concept when he did not understand my explanation. I was working one summer afternoon in a flower bed. The four-year-old noticed my daughter going back and forth from a room that adjoined the back porch of my home and the kitchen that also adjoined the back porch. She was getting ready for a date. My little friend asked me, "Are you going some place?" I could not at the time understand why he asked this question because I was working in old clothes. In retrospect I believe that, for my little friend, one person in your family getting dressed up meant that you might be expected soon to be called upon to get dressed up too. When I told my friend that I was not going out he asked me, "Then why is your mommy getting all dressed up for?" I, of course, was immensely flattered to be considered so young but felt duty bound to try to explain that the young lady who was getting all dressed up was my daughter, not my mother. It was here that I experienced great difficulty. The concepts "mother," "father," and "sister" are not too hard for a four-year-old. He can relate these concepts to his own subjective experience. The concept "daughter" is more difficult. My friend listened to my explanation and was puzzled. He thought back in his own experiences and said, "Maybe she's your sister." I tried again to explain without success. Then he said, "Maybe she's a lady you brought home for the night." Let me hasten to add that his sister had brought a little girl home for the night the week before and that this was the source of his idea.

The point I am trying to make with this story is that children at a very early age try to find meaning in the phenomena they encounter. This searching for meaning is often thwarted in the classroom when the teacher feels called upon to tell children the meaning of concepts rather than permit them to discover meanings.

The Remaining Cognitive Categories

We have examined the first two categories of the cognitive domain—knowledge and comprehension—and have explored the relationship of educational objectives in these categories to education for creativity. The following points have been noted:

1. Knowledge and comprehension may be thought of as "enabling objectives" for creativity education. The person who has ac-

quired information and has developed an understanding of concepts, principles, generalizations, ideas, and theories is in a better position to be creative than a person who has not.

2. Retrieval of information is particularly important to the process of creating. Hence, it is of importance that children be aided in structuring or organizing the information they acquire so that it will be more readily available for retrieval. Perhaps the student should be given some practice in restructuring the information he acquires so as to improve his retrieval system. Possibly, also, the student should be given practice in searching his memory for information relevant to solution of problems.

3. The teaching procedure known as "learning by discovery" may be useful for objectives in the comprehension category. Through this procedure the child may learn to create new concepts or discover old concepts.

Points we have made for the knowledge and comprehension categories are equally true for the remaining categories in the cognitive domain taxonomy. Educational objectives within the categories of application, analysis, synthesis, and evaluation may be regarded as descriptions of problem-solving strategies or information-processing strategies. Let us look further at the remaining categories.

Application. Application is the third category in the cognitive domain. Application-type objectives involve applying a principle, generalization, or rule of procedure in solving a problem. The problem must be new to the student and the principle required for its solution must be unstated. Hence, in order to solve the problem, the student must understand the problem asked and select from memory storage the principle that is required for its solution.

Analysis. Analysis objectives involve breaking down a communication into its elements or parts, and seeing the relationships among the parts and the way in which they are organized.

Synthesis. Synthesis is the opposite process to analysis. Synthesis objectives involve putting together elements so as to form a unique whole. This is the category that gives widest scope to creative behavior on the part of the learner.

Objectives in the knowledge, comprehension, application, and analysis categories are necessary to attain synthesis objectives. Synthesis objectives merely add one new requirement, i.e., putting together elements to fashion a new communication or product. When the attainment of a synthesis objective is judged on the basis of the uniqueness as well as the appropriateness of the communication or product, we have what we might term a "creativity objective."

The creative person selects from his memory storage the information, concepts, principles, and techniques for applying principles, ideas, feelings, and past experiences that are essential to the fashioning of something that is both unique and appropriate.

An emphasis upon creativity, in a home economics program, means an emphasis upon synthesis objectives. To foster creativity, then, the teacher would provide students with opportunities to plan as well as opportunities to carry out their plans. Also, the teacher would need to value creative expression.

Evaluation. Evaluation is the sixth and most complex category in the cognitive domain. Evaluation is defined as the making of judgments about the value, for some purpose, of ideas, works, solutions, methods, materials, etc. It involves the use of criteria as well as standards for appraising the extent to which particulars are accurate, effective, economical, or satisfying.

We have seen that creativity objectives correspond to synthesis objectives with an emphasis upon uniqueness or novelty. Evaluation objectives are relevant to creativity objectives if novelty, or uniqueness, in addition to appropriateness, is emphasized in an evaluation objective. For example, the interior decorator would be demonstrating evaluation-type behavior in making judgments concerning the relative merits of alternate furniture arrangements in a room. The interior decorator also would be stressing creativity objectives if she did not insist that the arrangement should be traditional.

Creativity and the Affective Domain

The creative person is more than a person who has developed a set of intellectual skills that enable him to be creative. He is this, plus being a person with additional characteristics. He is a person who is open to new experiences and new ideas. The motives that impel the creative act are many and complex. Crutchfield (1962) differentiates between *intrinsic, task-involved* motivations for creativity and *extrinsic, ego-involved* motivations. When the creative act is performed for its own sake, we have intrinsic, task-involved motivation. Extrinsic, ego-involved motivation is exemplified by the person who tries to be creative in order to obtain material gain, or recognition, or other motives extraneous to the task itself. Crutchfield maintains that this extrinsic, ego-involved-type of motivation is likely to interfere with creative behavior and produce conforming behavior. At any rate, it seems clear that the creative person differs in his motivations from the non-creative person. And the motivation of a person who gets creative ideas must be sufficiently powerful to impel him to work through his ideas.

From the literature of creativity, it seems possible that creativity may be fostered through attaining certain educational objectives within the affective domain. Let us turn, then, to an examination of the *Taxonomy of Educational Objectives—Affective Domain*. The five categories included in the taxonomy are:

1. *Receiving*

In this category we are concerned that the learner be willing to receive or attend to certain phenomena in his environment. Some objectives in this category are:
  (a) Develops an awareness of esthetic factors in dress, furnishings, architecture, city design, good art, and the like.
  (b) Attends carefully when others speak—in direct conversation, on the telephone, or in audiences.
  (c) Listens to music with some discrimination as to its mood and meaning.
  (d) Appreciation (recognition) of family members as persons with needs and interests of their own.

Is there a difference in the receptivity of the creative and the non-creative person? Certainly there is a difference in the degree of openness of the two. It is true that creative ideas do not occur by searching for creative ideas. You do not elicit creative behavior by saying, "Be creative." Yet the student must be receptive to creative ideas when they do occur. The implication for the classroom teacher is that the teacher who encourages the student to express his ideas, who is able to convince the student that she respects his ideas even as she leads the student to examine more closely those ideas, is the teacher who is encouraging receptivity to creative ideas when they do occur.

2. *Responding*

In the responding category we are concerned with responses which go beyond merely attending to a phenomenon. Three subcategories are included under responding:
  (a) Acquiescence in responding. "Willingness to comply with health regulations" and "obeys the playground regulations" are examples.
  (b) Willingness to respond. The key here is voluntary activity. "Voluntarily reads home economics periodicals" would be an example of an objective in this sub-category.
  (c) Satisfaction in response. Here the student evidences some satisfaction derived from an activity. An example of an objective is: "Takes pleasure in conversing with different kinds of people."

MacKinnon (1965), in studying differences between creative and non-creative persons, found that the creative person was more willing to take a chance than the non-creative person, he was flexible, and varied his approaches to problems, attacking problems from different angles and employing a variety of techniques, and he persevered until he arrived at a creative solution. The creative person, MacKinnon found, is especially open to experience, both of the inner self and the outer world, and is free in expressing the conflicts he encounters in life.

3. *Valuing*

In this category emphasis is placed on the development of the values of students. *Acceptance, preference,* or *commitment* to a value represent three sub-categories. The term "value" in this taxonomy is used in its usual sense of considering something of *worth.*

Perhaps the teacher who can best foster creativity is the teacher who values individuality and who respects the individuality of her students. This is not to say that conformity-type objectives have no place in the school curriculum. They do. But the individual can come to terms with the society in which he lives and still become a distinct individual. The creative person is individualistic. The teacher who helps the student to value individuality is helping the student to become more creative.

4. *Organization*

As the learner internalizes values, he encounters situations where more than one value is relevant. In this category the learner organizes his values into a system, determines the interrelationships among his values, and establishes the dominant and pervasive values. For example, the boy or girl who has learned to value both honesty and sensitivity to the feelings of others may encounter situations where these values conflict. "Finding out and crystallizing the basic assumptions which underlie codes of ethics" is an example of an objective in this category.

To grow creatively is not the easiest way to develop. The creative individual values independence of thought and action, and this can lead to difficulties. Openness to new experiences and ideas can lead to the cluttered mind; the adolescent can experience anxiety as he attempts to try to put his ideas and values in order. MacKinnon (1965) states:

> At such times, a parent or a teacher or a friend may be of the greatest help in communicating an empathic understanding of the turmoil going on in the youngster and in conveying to him a quiet, even unspoken, confidence that the anxiety which

he is experiencing will pass. The other way, the non-creative way, is the rigid control of experience—of repressing impulse and imagery, of blinding oneself to great areas of experience, and never coming to know oneself.

Erikson (1959), writing from a psychoanalytic orientation, contends that the central problem facing adolescents is that of developing a sense of ego identity—to answer questions such as "Who am I?" "What do I believe?" "What do I stand for?" Providing adolescents opportunities to explore and develop their own unique value system should be a major responsibility of the school. However a number of educators are critical of the efforts, or lack of effort, of the school to aid youth in exploring their values. Often we find a contradiction between stated objectives and the teaching procedures followed to develop objectives. Dorothy Lee (1963), in a provocative article contained in *Education and Culture*, points out a number of contradictions in home economics programs. Frequently objectives include such statements as "understanding the real values of home life," "appreciating the very real treasure of the family," and "preparing for marriage in order to live fully, richly, and satisfyingly." Yet the means of implementing these objectives emphasize the negative. Home life is pictured as a place full of conflict and restriction as the student is asked to consider "Why do parents 'always' say no?" or "What can a girl do about a 'pesky' brother?" This is the picture presented of "the very real treasure of the family." According to Dorothy Lee the word "enjoy" is rarely mentioned in connection with tasks of the homemaker. Rather, efficiency is the major value, and homemaking tasks are to be performed as rapidly as possible so as to free the homemaker to pursue some worthwhile tasks. Homemaking itself is a "given" that is valueless. And to quote Miss Lee:

> All that the girl can do with the given in family relations is to improve them, adjust to them, correct them so as to make them bearable; or she can use them as an exercise in human relationship, by way of developing her personality. They are not nourishing in themselves or to be enjoyed for themselves. *And she is not expected to find a creative role within the given.*

Educational objectives within the "Organization" category are crucial to creativity education. These objectives are concerned with the organization of values into a system. The teacher can best achieve these objectives if she permits the student to explore alternate value positions. This exploration of value positions can lead the student to the discovery of a creative role for herself. Education for conformity results when the teacher attempts to impose her own values upon the student.

5. *Characterization by a Value or Value Complex*

The various categories in the affective domain are ordered on the basis of the principle of *internalization*. Little internalization characterizes objectives in the receiving category. Maximum internalization characterizes objectives in this final category. The behaviors exemplified by attainment of an objective in this final category are expressions of a person's unique personality characteristics and his philosophy of life. Thus, the person acts consistently in accordance with the values he has internalized at this level. The person develops certain *generalized sets* which influence his behavior in a wide range of situations. The habit of approaching problems objectively, and the readiness to revise judgments and to change behavior in the light of evidence, are examples of this generalized set. The sum total of these generalized sets add up to a development of a philosophy of life—a philosophy of life that influences day-by-day behavior.

Summary

In summary, education for creativity encompasses objectives within both the cognitive and affective domains of the *Taxonomy*.

In the cognitive domain, objectives in the synthesis category give widest scope for creative behavior on the part of the learner. Knowledge, comprehension, application, and analysis objectives may be considered as problem-solving skills that enable the learner to be creative. However, the way these skills are taught is of importance. Creativity is fostered when the learner is required to creatively discover concepts and ways of solving problems. Creativity is stifled when the learner is required merely to passively absorb knowledge.

Creativity, however, is more than a bundle of intellectual skills. It is a way of life. Hence objectives within the affective domain are equally important in education for creativity. Educational objectives within the organization category of the affective domain probably are most pertinent to education for creativity. Adolescence is a period in which a person searches for his own identity. The permissive teacher who maximizes opportunities for students to explore competing value systems at both the verbal and the experiential levels is providing education for individuality and, hence, education for creativity.

References

Bloom, B. S. (Ed.) *Taxonomy of Educational Objectives. Handbook I. Cognitive Domain.* New York: David McKay Co., 1956.
—————— & L. Broder. *Problem Solving Processes of College Students.* Chicago: The University of Chicago Press, 1950.
Crutchfield, R. S. Conformity and Creative Thinking. In H. E. Gruber, G. Terrell & M. Wertheimer (Eds.) *Contemporary Approaches to Creative Thinking.* New York: Atherton Press, 1962, pp. 120-140.
Erikson, E. H. Identity and the Life Cycle. *Psychological Issues, 1,* 1, 1959.
Guilford, J. P. *Personality.* New York: McGraw-Hill, 1959.
——————. Intellectual Factors in Productive Thinking. In Mary Jane Aschner & Charles E. Bish (Eds.) *Productive Thinking in Education.* Washington: National Education Association, 1965, pp. 5-20.
Henle, M. The Birth and Death of Ideas. In H. E. Gruber, G. Terrell & M. Wertheimer (Eds.) *Contemporary Approaches to Creative Thinking.* New York: Atherton Press, 1962, pp. 31-62.
Krathwohl, D. R., B. S. Bloom & B. B. Masia. *Taxonomy of Educational Objectives. Handbook II: Affective Domain.* New York: David McKay Co., 1964.
Lee, Dorothy. Discrepancies in the Teaching of American Culture. In G. D. Spindler (Ed.) *Education and Culture: Anthropological Approaches.* New York: Holt, Rinehart and Winston, 1963, 173-191.
MacKinnon, D. W. Personality Correlates of Creativity. In Mary Jane Aschner & Charles E. Bish (Eds.) *Productive Thinking in Education.* Washington: National Education Association, 1965, pp. 159-171.

Williams utilizes theories and models from Piaget, Bloom, Krathwohl, and Guilford to create a new model for implementing cognitive-affective behaviors in the classroom. Williams' model, designed for use in curriculum planning and inservice training, focuses on the direct encouragement of creative processes through subject matter content.

Models for Encouraging Creativity in the Classroom by Integrating Cognitive-Affective Behaviors*

Frank E. Williams

Recognizing and meeting the intellectual as well as emotional needs of children, leading toward uncovering their creative potential, has become a respectable goal or purpose of education.

As Dr. Donald W. MacKinnon (1969) reports, the characteristics of the creative process and person are distinguished, most generally, by two fundamental sets of traits, one intellective and the other attitudinal or motivational. This paper will discuss a theoretical rationale for several cognitive-affective models from which a new model has been designed for use by the classroom teacher concerned about encouraging creativity through thinking and feeling behaviors among young children.

*Reprinted from *Educational Technology, 9,* December, 1969, pp. 7-13, by permission of the publisher and the author.

Cognitive Domain

The first set of traits, but certainly not first in importance for being or becoming creative, requires a breadth and depth of knowledge and a set of thinking skills for recording, retaining, and processing ones cognized information. Such skills or multi-dimensional talents commonly go under the name of the cognitive domain, and consist of a pupil's logical and rational concerns with what is—algorithmic truths. These are in almost every school's statements of behavioral objectives. Within this set of broad purposes or goals of education, classroom teaching emphasizes academic excellence, subject matter mastery, and the learning of someone else's information. These are played for real with a great deal

---

Figure 1

Piaget's Stage Theory of Intellectual Development

Formal Operations Stage
  Abstract-conceptual thinking
  Reasoning generalized
  Evaluation
  Hypothesizing
  Imagining
  Synthesizing

Concrete Operations Stage
  Analyzing
  Conscious of dynamic variables
  Measures
  Classifies things in groups or series

Pre-Operational Stage
  Symbols and representations
  Acts on perceptive impulses
  Self-centered
  Static-irreversible thinking

Sensory-Motor Stage
  Mute—no use of verbal symbols
  Learns to perceive—discriminate and identify
    objects

---

of time and effort spent on them by the classroom teacher, and regarded as fair game in measuring and assessing a child's intellectual growth.

Most models of the cognitive domain are in the form of a taxonomy consisting of a sequential classification of from low to high order thinking processes. However, those mental processes, such as hypothesizing, synthesizing, inventing, associating, transforming, relating, designing, translating, or combining have been used synonymously by many to define the creative process; yet they are only found within the higher stages or levels of these taxonomy models.

For example, Piaget's (Flavell, 1963) stage theory of intellectual development (see *Figure 1*) places these mental abilities (italicized terms) which define and describe the creative process in the formal

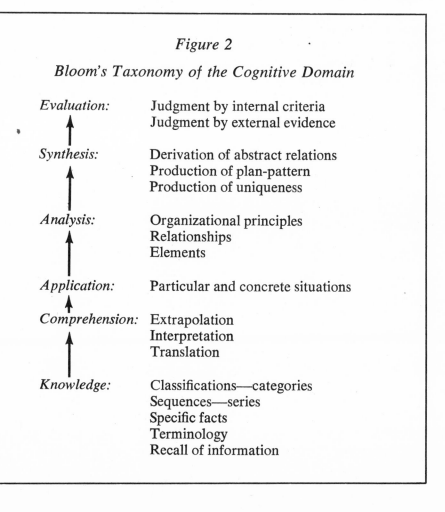

Figure 2

Bloom's Taxonomy of the Cognitive Domain

Evaluation: Judgment by internal criteria
                     Judgment by external evidence

Synthesis: Derivation of abstract relations
                     Production of plan-pattern
                     Production of uniqueness

Analysis: Organizational principles
                     Relationships
                     Elements

Application: Particular and concrete situations

Comprehension: Extrapolation
                     Interpretation
                     Translation

Knowledge: Classifications—categories
                     Sequences—series
                     Specific facts
                     Terminology
                     Recall of information

operations stage, as can be seen appearing at the top level of this taxonomy.

Even in Bloom's taxonomy of the cognitive domain (1956), the processes of synthesis are the most predominant ingredients of creativity, and likewise appear as higher level thought processes at the fifth step of this model (see *Figure 2*).

Those who have developed taxonomy models advocate that later operations are built upon earlier ones, and that intellectual development follows an ordered sequence. They say a child is incapable of learning these higher level thought processes before earlier ones are mastered.

Here is where we get into trouble when teachers want to encourage a young child's creative potential, because these models indicate that creative thinking consists of higher mental processes which may not develop much before middle childhood. Yet, all primary grade teachers are aware of how free and open every young child is to be imaginative, inventive, flexible, and perceptive *at his or her own intellectual level.* That is to say, surely the young child may not be able to break new boundaries, at least in any sophisticated degree, by creating new concepts in the physical sciences; but he or she may be highly original and imaginative in dealing with his or her own discoveries and uses of already existing scientific concepts. Hence, there are some questions raised by classroom teachers when they attempt to apply taxonomical models of cognition for curriculum development or for planning learning experiences which encourage those thinking processes associated with a child's creative potential.

Affective Domain

Another set of traits equally important for being or becoming creative is that broad area of esthetic concerns for feeling, beauty, and form. These make up another important area of educational objectives, which deal with attitudes, values, dispositions, and motivations of the pupil *to want to* do something with information, data, and knowledge which has been cognized.

Such feeling processes include a pupil's inward openness to his own hunches, nudges, guesses, emotions, and intuitive feelings about facts which he has become sensitive to and is curious about. These personal-motivational factors may be most crucial, and make the real difference for the pupil to be willing to appreciate either his own or others' creative productions. These are processes which cause the pupil to operate as much by feeling as by logic, because he is able and willing to deal with fantasy, imagination, and emotion in terms of things that might be—heuristics. This is the insightful person who has the courage to be a bold risk-taker by venturing past the edges of the familiar, who is curious about other possibilities and alternatives rather than dealing with absolutes and permanencies, who uses his imagination to reach beyond artificial or limited boundaries, and who is willing to delve into the complexities of intricate problems, situations, or ideas just to see where they will take him.

Here we are talking about experiences within an educational program that legitimize feelings, offered by teachers who have empathy for intuition and guessing rather than always expecting the child to know. The affective domain has likewise been presented by Krathwohl (1964) as a taxonomical model (see *Figure 3*).

Most teachers would agree that thinking processes really cannot operate without feeling processes. Even as Krathwohl states, "nearly all cognitive behaviors have an affective component." One involves the other, and they cannot be separated. It is possible to attain feeling goals by cognitive means and also to attain thinking goals by affective behaviors. The better the pupil feels about some fact or piece of data, the more curious he becomes, at the conscious level, to want to dig

Figure 3

Krathwohl's Taxonomy of the Affective Domain

Internalizing (automatically characterizes a way of life)

↑

Conceptualizing (organizing a value system)

↑

Valuing (appreciation and commitment)

↑

Responding (willingness and satisfaction)

↑

Receiving (sensitivity and awareness)

in and learn more about it. And vice versa, the more he knows about a subject or area of knowledge, the better he appreciates and values it. Closely related to a pupil's need for knowledge and information is his preference for an internal set of values and personality dispositions which are non-intellective and which comprise the affective domain. I would argue very strongly that a combination of both domains, cognitive and affective, is what makes for *effective* human development and the fully-functioning, creative individual.

Piaget (1967) writes, "There is a close parallel between the development of affectivity and that of the intellectual functions, since these are two indissociable aspects of every action. In all behavior the motives and energizing dynamisms reveal affectivity, while the techniques and adjustment of the means employed constitute the cognitive sensory-motor

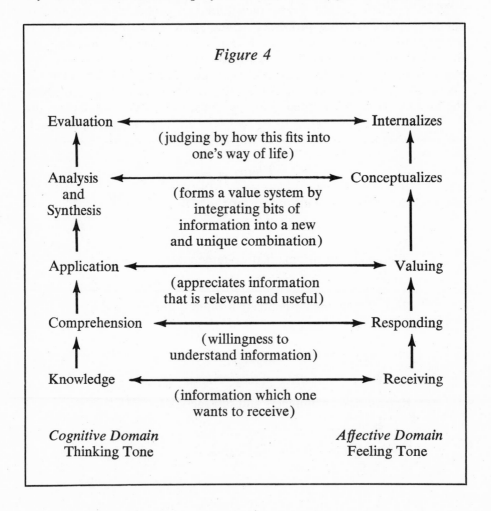

Figure 4

Evaluation ←————————————→ Internalizes
(judging by how this fits into one's way of life)

Analysis and Synthesis ←————————————→ Conceptualizes
(forms a value system by integrating bits of information into a new and unique combination)

Application ←————————————→ Valuing
(appreciates information that is relevant and useful)

Comprehension ←————————————→ Responding
(willingness to understand information)

Knowledge ←————————————→ Receiving
(information which one wants to receive)

Cognitive Domain
Thinking Tone

Affective Domain
Feeling Tone

or rational aspect. There is never a purely intellectual action, and numerous emotions, interests, values, impressions of harmony, etc., intervene, for example, in the solving of a mathematical problem. Likewise, there is never a purely affective act, e.g., love presupposes comprehension. Always and everywhere, in object-related behavior as well as in interpersonal behavior, both elements are involved because the one presupposes the other."

Even though professional educators have for a long time *talked about* motivating the pupil and building positive self-concepts, attitudes, and values, classroom practices for dealing systematically with the promotion of affective behaviors are usually infrequent; and, if they do occur, many teachers really cannot explain what happened or evaluate affective behavioral changes within pupils.

There is a new trend for programs which humanize education; but, when measurement or assessment is called for, the usual cognitive instruments are used, i.e., convergent thinking such as IQ, achievement, or subject matter recall tests. And it should be pointed out that so-called creativity tests, even though their instructions ask the pupil to use his imagination and be curious, are scored solely on four divergent production factors which are cognitive. These are fluent thinking, flexible thinking, elaborative thinking, and original thinking, all identified and operationally defined by Guilford's work and his Structure of Intellect Model (1967). There are no direct measures of affective processes derived from current creative thinking tests which have been used predominantly by researchers and teachers to assess children's creative potential.

Relationship Between the Cognitive and Affective Domains

Attempts to bridge cognitive thinking with affective feeling pupil behaviors or processes have so far been relatively sparse. Michaelis' (1967) book for elementary school teachers discusses evaluating pupil progress in the substantive areas of the curriculum by taxonomical categories across both cognitive and affective domains, according to level of increasing complexity. This book attempts to blend the various stages of the cognitive domain to comparable stages in the affective domain by subject area.

Albert Eiss and Mary Harbeck (1969) have published a book which discusses scientific behavioral objectives in the affective domain. Within this book, Dr. Eiss presents and discusses an instructional systems model consisting of a closed, feed-back loop which relates psychomotor-affective-cognitive domains together. Williams' (1968) Model for Implementing Cognitive-Affective Behaviors in the Classroom attempts to bridge four specific intellective traits with four attitudinal or temperament traits among elementary school pupils.

Figure 4 indicates a hierarchically ordered and interrelated schema between cognitive and affective domain models.

Even though this schema is one attempt to bridge the two domains, it still lacks definitive application when early grade teachers want to foster creativity, because both models are taxonomies with placement of those processes which comprise this human phenomena at higher levels. There are some differing viewpoints among cognitive theorists concerning such categories arranged according to level of increasing complexity, with each category dependent on the preceding ones. Bruner (1960), for instance, has for some time stressed the importance of guiding students to discover how knowledge at any level is related, and indicates that *appropriate method or strategy* to bring this about may be most important. Piaget (Ginsburg and Opper, 1969) likewise indicates that it is possible to accelerate some types of learning by suitable environmental stimuli, and suitable methods may expedite processes of intellectual development. There are some who claim creative processes may only appear later in the life of the child, because before this time he lacks an appropriate cognitive structure in order to make new associations which are novel or unique. Others say that by appropriate teaching conditions and a multitude of different opportunities in a lush environment, any normal child can be creative at his own particular level of creativeness. Thus, different theories about how cognitive and affective processes develop among young children do exist.

What may be one method of alleviating these discrepant viewpoints is a kind of system or model different from a taxonomy. Such a system has been utilized by Dr. J. P. Guilford for his Structure of Intellect Model of cognitive abilities. By means of a three-dimensional, cubical model he adopted a morphological approach to conceptualize intellectual abilities.

A morphology is a way of considering form and structure as an interrelated whole, and differs from a taxonomy in that there is no hierarchical order implied. One very simple example of a morphology is that of forming a chemical compound. When you put two or more chemical elements together, i.e., sodium and chlorine, the relationship of both form a new chemical compound—salt. According to Guilford's model (see *Figure 5*) one up to five operations may be performed upon four types of content to produce six kinds of products resulting in 120 (5 x 4 x 6) possible kinds of intellectual acts.

As Mary Meeker (1969) in her new book states, "The order (of

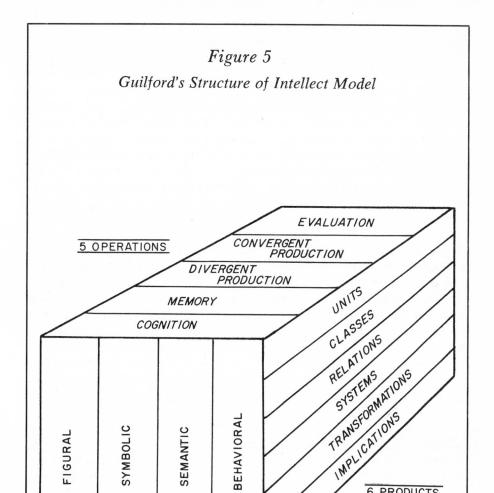

Figure 5

Guilford's Structure of Intellect Model

abilities) is strictly conventional; that is, no priority—logical or psychological, developmental or hierarchical—is intended either within or between the categories of classification." The model, then, implies an interrelated classification of human abilities, many of which contribute to intellectual creativity.

But since Guilford's Structure of Intellect Model was never intended to be used for curriculum planning or for classroom teachers—and it does not include any affective factors—another model or adaptation of existing models was needed. Such a model or morphological structure has been designed by Williams (1966, 1968) as a modification of Guilford's model for the purpose of implementing certain thinking and feeling processes directly related to creativity in the classroom. *Figure 6* shows this three-dimensional cube, much the same as Guilford's cubical model, with each dimension made relevant to an on-going elementary school program (see *Figure 6*). The structure characterizes an interrelationship between one or more strategies employed by the teacher (Dimension 2), across the various subject matter areas of the curriculum (Dimension 1), in order to elicit a set of four cognitive and four affective pupil behaviors (Dimension 3). What the teacher does or what media she or he uses is strategy, but how the pupil thinks or feels is process, and both are related to subject matter content.

Dimension 1 lists subject matter areas of a conventional elementary school curriculum. However, it may be possible to substitute subjects from any other grade level, including high school and college, in this dimension.

Dimension 2 initially listed twenty-three styles or strategies in a prototype model which teachers can employ in their classroom teaching. Upon extensive field testing of the model, this list of strategies has been reduced to eighteen, which avoided a great deal of overlap between some strategies.

These have been devised empirically from many studies of how all good teachers operate implicitly in the classroom. Teaching styles or strategies become a means, through subject matter content, toward an end for fostering eight thinking and feeling pupil behaviors. As one considers these eighteen teaching strategies, which can be appropriately applied across all subject matter areas, a vast number of combinations for learning become apparent.

Dimension 3 consists of eight processes deduced from theoretical studies of how children think and feel divergently. These divergent production factors are certainly most crucial when encouraging a child's creative potential, but have received less attention or have been commonly ignored in the traditional curriculum and classroom. Hence, this dimension of the model is intended to focus upon those cognitive and

Figure 6

A Model for Implementing Cognitive-Affective Behaviors in the Classroom

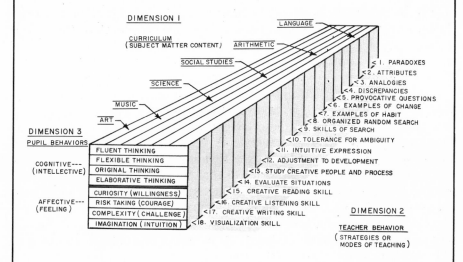

affective processes that undoubtedly are most vital yet have been seriously neglected or at most treated randomly in school classrooms. These pupil behaviors become goals or objectives within themselves, and are regarded as ends to be achieved in classroom teaching.

The model is an applied yet complex structure, based upon theoretical constructs, interrelating a repertoire of eighteen ways for a teacher to cause pupils to think and feel creatively across the substantive areas of the curriculum. Assuming the teacher is able to install it across the six subject matter areas shown, the model indicates there are 864 (8 x 6 x 18) possible interrelated combinations for classroom teaching!

It has been used as a working structure for curriculum planning and as an instructional system to improve teacher competencies through in-service training at project schools across the country. An accompanying training program integrated across the model has been designed to show teachers how it is possible to encourage the eight creative processes directly through subject matter content rather than indirectly or in isolation of the regular school program.

Use of the model likewise has been focused upon classifying instructional media, such as books and films and teacher-developed and field tested lesson ideas designed for use in primary and elementary education (see Williams, 1968, 1970). It is currently being used as a classification system for some of the more recent kits and instructional programs which have concentrated upon a process approach to learning, particularly those relevant to promoting divergent production behaviors in young children. Some of these include the Science Improvement Curriculum Study, the AAAS—Science A Process Approach Program, the EDC—Man A Course of Study, the Reading 360 Program, the Peabody Language Development Kits, the Taba Social Studies Program, and several of the Inquiry Approach Programs. The model is also being adopted by one state department of education program for gifted and talented youth by changing the content dimension, since such children are in need and capable of handling subject areas other than those in the regularly established curriculum.

This model, unlike the others discussed herein, is essentially directed toward and has utility for both pre-service and in-service education programs. It can be used to develop more competent teachers, requiring no radical change in curriculum materials and content. Teachers can be trained to adapt their normal curriculum to the promotion of these important cognitive-affective behaviors among pupils. The model itself specifies terminal behaviors or competencies for which both the pupil and the teacher may aspire. As an interaction model, it specifies performance objectives for both teacher and pupil related to the subject matter curriculum.

In spite of recent emphasis on the necessity for integrating cognitive with affective processes, the gap between what is known about the nature and development of thinking-feeling processes and how this is translated into instructional practice is still enormously wide. This model may serve to somewhat narrow the gap, at least within the area of divergent production.

REFERENCES

Bloom, Benjamin S. (Ed.) *Taxonomy of Educational Objectives, Handbook I: Cognitive Domain.* New York: David McKay Company, Inc., 1956.

Bruner, Jerome S. *The Process of Education.* Cambridge: Harvard University Press, 1960.

Eiss, Albert F. & Mary Blatt Harbeck. *Behavioral Objectives in the Affective Domain.* National Science Teachers Association, 1969.

Flavell, John H. *The Developmental Psychology of Jean Piaget.* Princeton: D. Van Nostrand Co., Inc., 1963.

Ginsburg, Herbert & Sylvia Opper. *Piaget's Theory of Intellectual Development.* Englewood Cliffs, New Jersey: Prentice-Hall, Inc., 1969.

Guilford, J. P. *The Nature of Human Intelligence.* New York: McGraw-Hill Book Co., 1967.

Krathwohl, David R., Benjamin S. Bloom & Bertram B. Masia. *Taxonomy of Educational Objectives, Handbook II: Affective Domain.* New York: David McKay Co., Inc., 1964.

MacKinnon, Donald W. The Courage To Be: Realizing Creative Potential. In Louis J. Rubin (Ed.) *Life Skills in School and Society.* A.S.C.D. Yearbook, Washington, D. C., National Education Association, Association for Supervision and Curriculum Development, 1969.

Meeker, Mary Nacol. *The Structure of Intellect.* Columbus, Ohio: Charles E. Merrill Publishing Co., 1969.

Michaelis, John U., Ruth H. Grossman & Lloyd F. Scott. *New Designs for the Elementary School Curriculum.* New York: McGraw-Hill, Inc., 1967.

Piaget, Jean. *Six Psychological Studies.* New York: Random House, 1967.

Williams, Frank E. Creativity—An Innovation in the Classroom. In Mary Jane Aschner & Charles E. Bish (Eds.) *Productive Thinking in Education.* Washington, D. C.: The National Education Association, 1968.

————. (Ed.) *Seminar on Productive Thinking in Education.* Creativity Project, Macalester College, Saint Paul, Minnesota, 1966.

————. Creativity in the Substantive Fields. Revised paper from a chapter entitled Perspective of a Model for Developing Productive Creative Behaviors in the Classroom in book edited by Frank E. Williams. *Seminar on Productive Thinking in Education,* Macalester Creativity Project, Macalester College, Saint Paul, Minnesota, 1966.

————. *Classroom Ideas for Encouraging Thinking and Feeling.* Buffalo, New York: D. O. K. Publishers, Inc., 1970.

————. *Media for Developing Creative Thinking in Young Children.* Creative Education Foundation, Inc., State University College, Buffalo, New York, 1968.

Part II

Additional Media

Baker, Robert L., Vernon S. Gerlach & Howard J. Sullivan. *Constructing Behavioral Objectives.* Inglewood, California: Southwest Regional Laboratory for Educational Research and Development, 1968, 44 pp.
See also other materials in the SWRL series (Part I).

Bloom, Benjamin S. (Ed.) *Taxonomy of Educational Objectives, Handbook I: Cognitive Domain.* New York: David McKay Company, Inc., 1956, 207 pp.

Burns, Richard W. What Are Learning Products? *Educational Technology, 9,* December, 1969, pp. 72-73.

——— & Gary D. Brooks. Processes, Problem Solving and Curriculum Reform. *Educational Technology, 10,* May, 1970, pp. 10-13.

Carlson, Nancy Wahl & Mildred Barnes Griggs. *The Psychomotor Domain— A Selective Bibliography with Annotations.* Urbana, Illinois: Division of Home Economics Education, University of Illinois, 1966, 17 pp.

Cox, Richard C. & Nancy Jordan Unks. *A Selected and Annotated Bibliography of Studies Concerning the "Taxonomy of Educational Objectives: Cognitive Domain."* Pittsburgh, Pennsylvania: University of Pittsburgh Learning Research and Development Center, 1967, 33 pp.

Espich, James E. Applying Bloom's *Taxonomy of Educational Objectives. NSPI Journal, 3,* November 1964, pp. 6-7.

Franklin, A. David. Ends and Means in Music Education. *Music Educators Journal, 53,* March, 1967, pp. 103-106.

Fromer, Robert. A Basic Difference Between Educational and Training Systems. *Educational Technology, 9,* April, 1969, pp. 51-52.

Gagné, Robert M. The Implications of Instructional Objectives for Learning. *Defining Educational Objectives,* C. M. Lindvall (Ed.) Pittsburgh, Pennsylvania: University of Pittsburgh Press, 1964, pp. 37-46.

———. The Analysis of Instructional Objectives for the Design of Instruction. *Teaching Machines and Programmed Learning, II: Data and Direc-*

tions, Robert Glaser (Ed.) Washington, D. C.: Department of Audiovisual Instruction, National Education Association, 1965, pp. 21-65.

————. Varieties of Learning. *The Conditions of Learning.* New York: Holt, Rinehart and Winston, Inc., 1965, pp. 31-61.

Hodgson, Carol. Taxonomy of Educational Objectives, Psychomotor Domain. *Contemporary Issues in Home Economics: A Conference Report.* Washington, D. C.: National Education Association, 1965, pp. 57-68.

Jarolimek, John. The Taxonomy: Guide to Differentiated Instruction. *Social Education, 26,* December, 1962, pp. 445-447.

Kersh, Bert Y. Programming Classroom Instruction. *Teaching Machines and Programmed Learning, II: Data and Directions,* Robert Glaser (Ed.) Washington, D. C.: Department of Audiovisual Instruction, National Education Association, 1965, pp. 321-368.

Krathwohl, David R. Taxonomy of Educational Objectives—Its Use in Curriculum Building. *Defining Educational Objectives,* C. M. Lindvall (Ed.) Pittsburgh, Pennsylvania: University of Pittsburgh Press, 1964, pp. 19-36.

Krathwohl, David R., Benjamin S. Bloom & Bertram B. Masia. *Taxonomy of Educational Objectives, Handbook II: Affective Domain.* New York: David McKay Company, Inc., 1964, 196 pp.

Loree, M. Ray. Relationship Among Three Domains of Educational Objectives. *Contemporary Issues in Home Economics: A Conference Report.* Washington, D. C.: National Education Association, 1965, pp. 69-80.

Popham, W. James & Eva L. Baker. *Selecting Appropriate Educational Objectives.* Los Angeles, California: Vimcet Associates, 1967. Illustrated filmstrip, accompanying audio-taped narration, and instructor's manual, 44 frames, 26 minutes.

See also other materials in the Vimcet series (Part I).

Simpson, Elizabeth Jane. The Classification of Educational Objectives, Psychomotor Domain. *Illinois Teacher of Home Economics, 10,* Winter, 1966-67, pp. 110-144.

Taba, Hilda. The Objectives of Education. *Curriculum Development: Theory and Practice.* New York: Harcourt, Brace & World, Inc., 1962, pp. 194-230.

Part III

Behavioral Objectives and the Teaching of Values

Today, perhaps as never before, can be identified as a time of pressing social issues. In the face of this fact, should schools engage in the kind of educational tasks which promote values development? Most educators agree not only that schools should participate in values education, but also that it would be difficult to describe a viable curriculum which did not deal with the area of values. This is true for several reasons, including the fact that it is nearly impossible to discuss values in isolation from cognitive and skill learnings. The conditions under which concepts and skills are acquired contribute strongly to values growth.

This is not to say, of course, that the school should be the only social institution responsible for values development, or that the same predetermined set of values should be acquired by all students. Rather, educators should capitalize upon the unique and systematic opportunities inherent within the school framework for examining, interpreting, and clarifying social, ethical, and esthetic issues and values.

In terms of classifications of educational objectives, values fall into the affective domain—those objectives having to do with feelings, interests, attitudes, desires, commitments, and valuations. Does the behavioral approach lend itself to the teaching of values? Critics of this approach have pointed out that cognitive rather than affective areas are more easily behavioralized, and that many cognitive objectives are at once specific, trivial, and nonrepresentative of "really important" affective areas of learning. This observation is perhaps valid as far as it goes, but even so it cannot stand as justification for ignoring either the affective domain or the behavioral approach.

The authors included in Part III provide rationale and techniques for dealing behaviorally with affective goals. The first two articles use social studies as a context for approaches to values education. The third article provides a strategy for clarifying behavioral expressions of affective processes, with an example from the field of music. The latter two articles are not subject matter related, but they also deal directly with the practical problems of operationalizing the affective domain.

Although the following article does not contain actual examples of behaviorally stated objectives, it does illustrate the strong relationship which exists between cognitive and affective learnings. Clegg and Hills observe that the school of today is one of the main value-shaping forces experienced by American youth. The authors urge teachers to establish, as a major teaching objective, a strategy for assisting each student to judge various value positions, to select the individually most acceptable one, and to be able to justify the position selected. The instructional procedures suggested for the valuing process include Taba's cognitive tasks and Raths' work on affective processes. Curricular examples from the social studies, involving both cognitive and affective areas, illustrate the suggested teaching strategy.

A Strategy for Exploring Values and Valuing in the Social Studies*

AMBROSE A. CLEGG, JR.
AND
JAMES L. HILLS

The recent increase in crime rate in the nation and the large number of Americans enrolled in church groups and youth activities suggest an apparent contradiction in the values held by American society.

*Reprinted from *The College of Education Record* (University of Washington), May, 1968, pp. 67-68, by permission of the publisher and the authors.

Crime in the United States increased 17 percent during the first six months of 1967 in a country where the rate of population increase is but 1.15 per cent annually. On the other hand, more than 125 million Americans are affiliated with various church groups, 41 million are enrolled in Sunday and Sabbath Schools; and nearly 32 million young people are members of such groups as the Boy Scouts, Girl Scouts, and 4-H clubs (11: 902, 175, 641, 644).

Each year, similar compilations have contradicted the popular notion that the home, buttressed by the church and related character building agencies, is the most influential in developing sound values in the lives of young people. Nevertheless, newspaper editorials and public forums exhort the home and church to work harder and more effectively to prove their primacy in teaching values. They overlook the questions that should be asked.

Who shapes the attitudes and values of our youth? The school is one of the primary agents for inculcating values, especially those related to the political process, according to recent studies by Hess and Torney (2). They point out that pupil attitudes change markedly over the school years. Important shifts appear to take place beginning in the middle grades. Their evidence reveals clearly that by the eighth grade there is a remarkable similarity between the political values held by pupils and those held by their teachers on a number of variables. They conclude that the schools are one of the major forces responsible for shaping the political values of American youth through the eighth grade.

What value-laden problems must be handled by schools? If the public schools are to provide the type of education that makes intelligent civic participation possible, social studies curricula must be expanded to include a full examination of current value-laden problems. The list should include such topics as civil rights and responsibilities; the myriad problems of minority groups including unemployment, segregation, and quality education; problems of poverty, housing, and health; pollution of air, water, and soil; and problems related to land use, taxation, and augmented social services. All of these pervade every level of the community: local, state, and national.

Which values must be taught? For years educators have been charged with the responsibility of teaching basic democratic values, such as those identified by Hanna *et al.* (1:63-68):

    (1) Respect for the dignity and worth of the individual.

    (2) Concern for the common welfare.

    (3) Faith in the intelligence of common men to rule themselves.

(4) Use of reason and persuasion rather than force for solving problems and settling controversies.

Although the authors reported a number of school practices that evidenced acceptance of these values, the climate found in many classrooms might lead the serious observer to suggest that schools honor these values more often in the breach than in the observance thereof.

What is the problem? While lip service is publicly paid to such basic values as those cited above, private exceptions to these have often been observed in various aspects of American life. Over thirty years ago, Lynd pointed out this problem in his study of Middletown (5:60-62). He reported a number of apparent contradictions, such as:

(1) Individualism, "the survival of the fittest," is the law of nature and the secret of America's greatness; restrictions on individual freedom are un-American and kill initiative.

    But: No man should live for himself alone; for people ought to be loyal and stand together and work for common purposes.

(2) The thing that distinguishes man from the beasts is the fact that he is rational; and therefore man can be trusted, if let alone, to guide his conduct wisely.

    But: Some people are brighter than others; and, as every practical politician and businessman knows, you can't afford simply to sit back and wait for people to make up their minds.

(3) Democracy, as discovered and perfected by the American people, is the ultimate form of living together. All men are created free and equal, and the United States has made this fact a living reality.

    But: You would never get anywhere, of course, if you constantly left things to popular vote. No business could be run that way, and of course no businessman would tolerate it.

Because of the difficulties involved in these contradictory value positions, schools have tended to avoid value-laden problems in the curriculum that would be likely to produce controversy among students or within the community. It is "safer" to present the majority view as though it were the only one. This, in turn, has led to the disillusionment of many students when they became aware of evidence contrary to the majority view such as found in the inconsistencies pointed out by Lynd.

Further evidence of the contradiction in basic values was presented by Keniston in a recent study of alienated youth in American society. As he charted factors in the "alienated outlook," he found the "opposite outlooks" gave a recognizable portrait of the traditional American world view. Some examples, taken from this chart, make this clear:

Alienated Outlook	*Opposite* ("American Culture")
Low view of human nature	Human nature basically good

Futility of civic and
  political activities
	Usefulness, need for civic
	  and political activities

Rejection of American culture	Praise of American culture

Short-range, personally
  centered values
	Long-range, universally
	  grounded values

Intolerance, scorn	Tolerance, respect (3:79-80)

Which value position is "right"? Faced with community and student support for opposing positions on the points cited by Lynd and by Keniston, the teacher needs a validation procedure. He needs a strategy to help students arrive at their own position and be able to justify it. The subtle indoctrination implied in "Teacher says so" is the seed-bed of alienation when pupils are confronted by contrary evidence.

Scriven (7:7-10) has developed an excellent validation procedure based on a reasoned appeal to judgment that could be used along the following lines:

Suppose a class were studying economic conflict and the means to resolve a labor-management dispute. Suppose, further, that the controversy concerned public employees, such as policemen or teachers. Various approaches such as mediation, strike, or compulsory arbitration could be tested against the following questions as suggested by Scriven:

(1) If doing something (e.g., engaging in a strike or compulsory arbitration) will bring about a state of affairs that people value, that is a good reason for doing it.

(2) If there are good reasons for doing something (e.g., engaging in a strike or compulsory arbitration) and none against it, then we should do it.

(3) If there is a conflict of good reasons supporting one or the other proposed actions (e.g., strike or compulsory arbitration), then appeal must be made to a general moral principle such as the equality of rights of both parties, labor and management, to the dispute, as well as an appeal to the common good.

Obviously, many value factors are involved in this example. Children can be encouraged to examine and appraise the many alternatives, their consequences, and the conflicting value positions implicit in each. Ultimately, their choice of position must be based on their judgment of the greatest good for the greatest number of people, recognizing, at the same time, that their judgment may differ from that of other persons. Such a process is often called "valuing."

What instructional procedures are suited to the process of valuing?

Taba's investigations in the cognitive domain have identified specific thinking tasks and appropriate strategies for developing higher thought processes. These have been widely reported (8, 9, 10). Krathwohl *et al.* have pointed up rather clearly the close relationship between the cognitive and affective domains (4:45-62). Looking more toward classroom application, Raths and his colleagues have recently published a collection of promising techniques for helping children deal with values. In their book, *Values and Teaching,* Raths *et al.* identify three basic processes with seven subcategories. (See Figure 1.)

Figure 1

Basic Value Processes

Choosing: (1) freely
                 * (2) from alternatives
                 * (3) after thoughtful consideration of the consequences of each alternative

Prizing: (4) cherishing, being happy with the choice
                 * (5) willing to affirm the choice publicly

Acting: (6) doing something with the choice
                 (7) repeatedly, in some pattern of life
                                          (6:28-30)

If nearly all cognitive objectives have an affective component (4:48), would it be possible to adapt the Taba tasks to accommodate the value dimensions? If Raths' processes are basic, could they be incorporated within the Taba cognitive tasks?

These questions led the writers to undertake an investigation to determine whether the three processes indicated (see asterisks, Fig. 1) could be employed in the classroom setting at the fifth-grade level, and what adaptations might be made to Taba's model of cognitive tasks to get at the values explored. The results of that investigation are presented below.

A Model for Valuing in Social Studies

The Historical Episodes. Classroom materials were designed to present a variety of conflicting views based on historical episodes in the traditional fifth-grade social studies curriculum. For example:

> *Roger Williams*—A tape-recorded narrative portrayed him as being insistent upon preaching his own narrowly conceived and

fundamentalist view of God's covenant with man in the New Zion, even if some of its tenets threatened the social and political order of the New England theocracy. In opposition were John Cotton and the Puritan ministers and Governor John Winthrop, who were determined to maintain religious orthodoxy and the established order.

The Boston Tea Party—This multidimensional episode, with four groups of contending participants, was presented by means of a tape-recorded narrative, accompanied by a series of 35mm colored slides and the leading people and places. King George III and his prime minister, Lord North, were seen as determined to preserve the right of the Crown to rule its colonies and to levy taxes. The merchants of the East India Tea Co. and their consignees here in the colonies were pictured as anxious to protect their financial investments; they viewed the Crown as the best protector of these interests. Sam Adams and the "patriots" were portrayed as zealously determined to preserve the long-established right of local rule and self-determination in taxing. And, finally, Governor Hutchinson, caught in the middle, opposed the King's plan to tax tea, yet was determined to maintain order against the threats of the mob.

A Simple Model. The issue that developed between the Puritans and Roger Williams was investigated by means of a value continuum suggested by Raths. As a preliminary step, an adaptation of Taba's schema (9:73) depicting the formation of generalizations (Cognitive Task II) was made for the formation of value positions (see Figure 2).

Following this, separate continua were made for each position. These became cognitive maps of the discussion. An integral part of the discussion, they provided a visible summary of the alternatives and consequences expressed by the student (see Figures 3 and 4). The continuum depicting the Puritan's alternatives reveals that students offered alternatives, immediate consequences, and subsequent consequences. These "If-then" chains—"If we give him to the Indians, then the Indians might be on his side; if that could happen, we ought to sabotage him to prevent its happening"—provide a pattern which seems to incorporate certain aspects of the cognitive processes identified in both Task II and Task III of Taba's models (8, 9, 10).

A Complex Model. A more complex discussion was undertaken around the issues of the Boston Tea Party. This incident presented problems of scholarship because the text's simplistic stereotype of "good guys" (Patriots) versus "bad buys" (Loyalists) obscured the complexity

Figure 2
Formation of Attitudes and Values

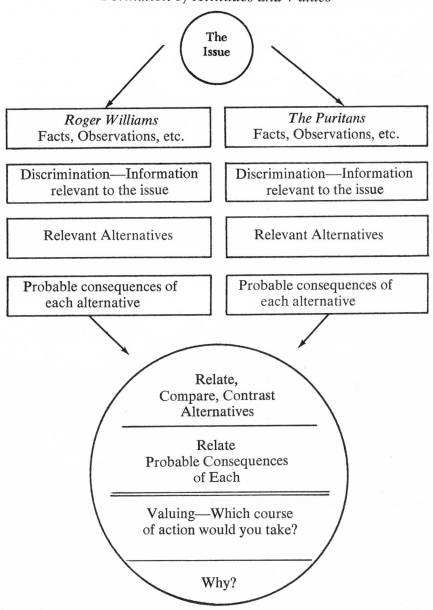

Figure 3

Puritans' Alternatives Regarding Roger Williams

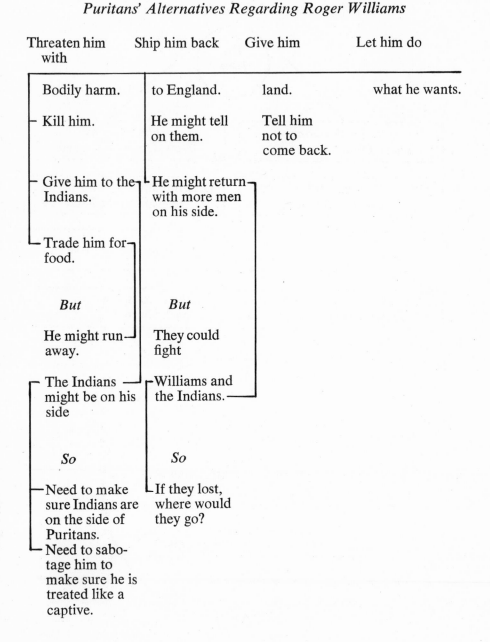

Figure 4

Roger Williams and His Alternatives

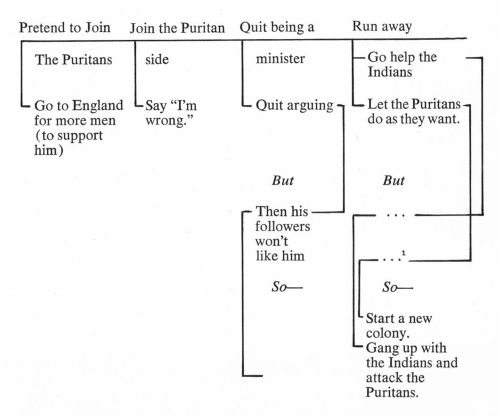

NOTE: [1]Omissions indicate that students jumped directly to long range consequences omitting any plausible intermediate consequences.

of the real issues and the character of the individuals involved. Research revealed at least six positions that could be clearly identified around groups that were involved in the event.

Value continua for four of these were explored in the manner illustrated with Roger Williams and the Puritans. Analysis of the discussion indicated that the handling of these data was much more difficult for the pupils. The post-discussion analysis suggested a strong need for a data retrieval chart to facilitate the higher level cognitive operations necessary as a base for the affective component. A data retrieval chart was devised to facilitate such a discussion (see Figure 5).

Since the data retrieval chart indicates six situations, instead of the two represented by the schema depicting the formation of values and attitudes (Figure 2) discussed earlier, a modification in strategy becomes necessary: The comparison/contrast of "Patriots" and "Loyalists" might be considered a reasonable first step. The comparison/contrast of the positions of Hutchinson versus the "Crown" might be the second step. Depending on the maturity of the class, the time available, and the extent to which the teacher wished to develop understandings of the economic forces underlying the issue, the positions of the colonial merchants versus the tea company could become a third step.

A Sequence of Learning. The order of pursuit for the paired comparisons mentioned may be optional. The crucial points are the following:

(1) Break the task into component parts on which the students can easily focus.

(2) Take up the component parts one at a time.

(3) Tailor the tasks to the ability of the pupils.

(4) Help the pupils organize their data in a form which will facilitate the discussion tasks.

(5) Allow pupils to develop a number of alternatives.

(6) Encourage them to explore the probable consequence of each alternative and its effect on the parties involved.

(7) Urge them to identify the alternative that they would choose under the circumstances.

(8) Express the reason for their choice (get out the underlying value).

The affective sequence differs from that posed by Taba for the cognitive domain (see 9:75).

Such a complex subject should not be attempted during a single period. It could be taken up in segments over successive days. The paired comparisons mentioned above could be a useful basis for dividing the discussion into segments.

Extension of the "If-Then" Questions to Value Positions. One of the important aspects of this exploratory study has been the extension of the "if-then" questions in terms of the value positions evident in the instructional materials. The nature of the eliciting questions dealt specifically with the alternative actions and probable consequences that had to be evaluated in terms of consistency with the expressed attitude and the likelihood of occurrence, given the anticipated action of one or more other participants whose views conflicted. In a sense the kind of intellectual activity involved here is somewhat akin to that of the chess player who learns to anticipate and weigh the multiple consequences of any of several moves open to him.

Eliciting questions such as the following were used:

(1) What courses of action did Roger Williams have, if it were likely that the Ministers (or Governor Winthrop) would . . .?

(2) If you were Roger Williams, what would you choose to do if you expected the Ministers would . . .? Why would you choose such a course?

(3) What are some possible alternatives that Sam Adams might have had, in light of the known views and probable alternatives open to the King, to Governor Hutchinson, and to the tea merchants? What do you expect would have been the probable consequences?

(4) How would you have acted if you were so-and-so? Why?

Figure 5

Data Retrieval Chart for Value Discussion
Focused on Boston Tea Party

	Sam Adams and "Patriots"	"Loyalists"	"Crown" and Lord North	Hutchinson	Tea Company	Colonial Merchants
Who were they?						
What did they say (their opinions)?						
What did they do?						
What effect did it have (on each)?						
What was the final result (to each)?						

Some Tentative Findings. Bearing in mind that this study was an exploratory one (hypothesis-seeking), some tentative findings, nevertheless, can be advanced. Preliminary analysis of the data seems to indicate:

(1) Many of Taba's strategies for forming generalizations and applying principles in the cognitive domain lend themselves to adaptation for use in the affective context.

(2) Children need much more information and time to arrive at value judgments than was available during the experimental

program. This suggests study in depth of a limited number of value issues, rather than a rapid survey of a large number of names, dates, and places.

(3) Eliciting questions need to be sharply defined and must focus clearly on the value element involved.

(4) Children appear to have considerable difficulty in choosing alternative courses of action when several variables are interacting simultaneously. This is especially true when the choice of alternatives is counterbalanced by the anticipated consequences of the alternative actions open to other participants (e.g., as in the Boston Tea Party).

(5) In complex situations, children's choices of alternative courses of action appear to be overly simplistic and tend to resort to stereotyped or even improbable solutions, not unlike those found on Batman or Superman. This is probably due to lack of sufficient background information on which to base more probable choices.

(6) Many textbooks were found to be antiseptically neutral when it came to presenting conflicting value positions. For an approach of this sort a considerable amount of additional materials must be prepared such as slides, tapes, pictures, etc., that will adequately present the topic as a live issue.

Does This Procedure Have Relevance for Current Issues? When the valuing process is linked to historical people and events, the final data are available and the events are removed somewhat from the turmoil of strong emotional involvement in a contemporary issue. The use of historical episodes in the initial experiences, then, has the effect of muting the affective component to an extent sufficient to allow focus on the process. This approach was deliberately chosen by the investigators as a pilot study to permit exploration and mapping out of the process (see Figures 3 and 4), the dimensions of which have not been identified elsewhere.

The writers see this valuing model as having three rather distinct, but closely related, dimensions: (1) learning to use the process described earlier in the paper, (2) learning the necessary content, and (3) developing value identification and commitment.

Since the process cannot be experienced without content, historical content appropriate to the setting was chosen. This would allow the primary focus to be on the *process* during the initial experiences. This is *not* a recommendation that valuing should necessarily start with a historical base. A non-controversial issue, such as fluoridation in a community not strongly divided on the matter, might be fully as useful as a historical event for introducing the process.

It was hypothesized that this reduction of feelings of personal involvement in initial experiences permits the desired processes to be introduced and then reinforced sufficiently to allow subsequent transfer of the process to more emotionally laden topics.* The writers have conjectured that the processes delineated above, tentative though they be, will prove helpful to teachers who wish to deal with "hot" issues in the classroom such as "Black Power," racial violence, Viet Nam, or the draft.

*Krathwohl (4:57-62) has suggested that not only do cognitive factors shape affective learnings, but conversely, affective factors appear to influence cognitive learnings. Thus, the alternate hypothesis, that children can deal directly with current value-laden issues without prior training on historical materials, will be explored in a more rigorously controlled experimental study.

REFERENCES

1. Lavone Hanna, Gladys L. Potter & Neva Hagaman. *Unit Teaching in the Elementary School.* New York: Holt, Rinehart and Winston, 1963.
2. Robert D. Hess & Judith V. Torney. *The Development of Political Attitudes in Children.* Chicago: Aldine, 1967.
3. Kenneth Keniston. *The Uncommitted: Alienated Youth in American Society.* New York: Dell, 1965.
4. David R. Krathwohl, Benjamin S. Bloom & Bertram B. Masia. *Taxonomy of Educational Objectives: Handbook II, Affective Domain.* New York: David McKay, 1964.
5. Robert S. Lynd. *Knowledge for What?* Princeton: Princeton University Press, 1939. For a more extended list, see *Middletown in Transition,* Chapter XII, by Robert S. & Helen Lynd. New York: Harcourt, 1937.
6. Louis E. Raths, Merrill Harmin & Sidney B. Simon. *Values and Teaching.* Columbus: Merrill, 1966.
7. Michael Scriven. *Student Values as Educational Objectives.* Publication No. 124 of the Social Sciences Consortium, Purdue University, Lafayette, Indiana, 1966.
8. Hilda Taba. Implementing Thinking as an Objective in Social Studies. Chapter II in *Effective Thinking in the Social Studies.* Jean Fair & Fannie Shaftel (Eds.) 37th Yearbook for the National Council for the Social Studies. Washington, D. C.: The Council, 1967.
9. ———. *Teachers' Handbook for Elementary Social Studies.* Palo Alto, California: Addison-Wesley, 1967.
10. ———. Teaching Strategies for Cognitive Growth. Chapter 3 in *Conceptual Models in Teacher Education,* John Verduin (Ed.) Washington, D. C.: American Association of Colleges for Teacher Education, 1967.
11. *1968 World Almanac,* Luman H. Long (Ed.) New York: Newspaper Enterprise Association, Inc., 1968.

Using the framework of the social sciences, Fraenkel both asks and answers the questions, "Should values be taught?" and "What values do we want to teach?" He urges greater precision in the description of behaviors which might indicate the acquisition of values. Among possible teaching strategies designed to obtain desired student behaviors, Fraenkel rejects both the moralist and relativistic approaches. Finally, he describes a teaching strategy planned "to encourage students to identify and emphathize with others faced with two or more undesirable and conflicting alternatives."

Value Education
in the Social Studies*

JACK R. FRAENKEL

Value analysis and development cannot be avoided in the social studies. A teacher's actions, sayings, discussion topics, reading assignments, and class activities indicate that he believes certain ideas, events, objects, and people to be important for students to consider. Indications of value are suggested all the time "in the problems that are chosen to be discussed, in the manner in which they are discussed, in the historical documents and events that are emphasized, as well as in the leaders that are chosen to illustrate the important and the worthy and the unimportant and the unworthy in the affairs of man."[1] As Childs has pointed out, the very organization of a system of schools represents a moral enterprise, for it signifies the deliberate attempt of a human society to control the pattern of its own evolution.[2]

*Reprinted from *Phi Delta Kappan, 50,* April, 1969, pp. 457-461, by permission of the publisher and the author.

Nonetheless, it must be admitted that in many instances what value education there is in a particular school or course is not developed through systematic design. As indicated above, the nature of values taught is implicit in the selection and use of materials and assignments. It is important to consider, therefore, whether we want students to develop values accidentally or whether we intend deliberately to influence their value development in directions we consider desirable. I contend that the systematic design of appropriate teaching strategies to bring about desired values is crucially important, and badly needed, in social studies education. We then have at least some control over the kinds of behavioral change we produce.

The question, then, is not "Should values be taught?" but "What values do we want to develop in our students?" and "How can they be developed?"

What Values Do We Want?

The teaching of some kinds of values appears logically and empirically justified if we are to maintain our effectiveness as teachers. As Fenton illustrates, certain behavioral values (e.g., specific rules of order in the classroom) must be established if we are to teach at all. Certain procedural values (e.g., encouraging logical analysis over illogical analysis) are also essential to our pedagogical effectiveness.[3] Indeed, we could not do our jobs if we did not teach such values.

When we come to the question of values which promote a particular point of view (for example, monogamy is a good thing; divorce should not be permitted; money is the root of all evil), however, we are on much more difficult ground. There are individuals (e.g., metaphysical classicists) who will argue that there are a number of "eternal values" existing somewhere in the cosmos that are, by their very nature, "desirable" to possess. These values exist independently of, and are beyond the wishes of, men. "There are certain human acts which are of their very nature, that is, intrinsically, bad and deserving of blame."[4]

The problem, of course, is that what is intrinsically good or bad will be defined differently by different men (or even by the same men) at different times. In a culture as pluralistic as ours, what is sacred to one individual may be anathema to another. Because our culture is so pluralistic, any attempt to develop one set of values as *the* set which all individuals should hold seems doomed to failure from the start.

There are, however, a large number of rather general statements (for example, "promoting the worth and dignity of all individuals") which the majority of Americans hold to be the goals of a democratic society and to which they at least verbally subscribe. For example, the Committee on Concepts and Values of the National Council for the Social Studies identified the following 14 themes, each of which was designated as "a societal goal of American Democracy."

1. The intelligent use of the forces of nature.
2. Recognition and understanding of world interdependence.
3. Recognition of the dignity and worth of the individual.
4. Use of intelligence to improve human living.
5. Vitalization of democracy through the intelligent use of our public educational facilities.
6. Intelligent acceptance, by individuals and groups, of responsibility for achieving democratic social action.
7. Increasing effectiveness of the family as a basic social institution.
8. Effective development of moral and spiritual values.
9. Intelligent and responsible sharing of power in order to attain justice.
10. Intelligent utilization of scarce resources to attain the widest general well-being.
11. Achievement of adequate horizons of loyalty.
12. Cooperation in the interest of peace and welfare.
13. Achieving balance between social stability and social change.
14. Widening and deepening the ability to live more richly.[5]

Any list of such generally stated values (and this list seems as representative of "American" values as any other) would probably be accepted by most people, especially if the statements are not defined any more precisely than these.

One may find it difficult, therefore, to object to any of the goals mentioned above. But, as is usually the case, they are far too general to be of much help when one gets down to designing instructional strategies for value analysis and development. They contain descriptive words like "intelligence," "dignity," "worth," "moral," "loyalty," and "justice," all of which are ambiguous. Our job with such words is to *determine* their meaning. We can do this only "by asking ourselves what, precisely, we are trying to describe or explain by them—what experiences we intend to group together when we use them. For if we do not know what experiences we want to describe or explain when we use descriptive words, then, to put it bluntly, we cannot really know what we are talking about." [6]

We must be much more precise. We need to become conscious of the words we use and *how* we are using them. We must ask ourselves: "What behaviors will we accept as constituting evidence that our students are making progress toward attaining the desired values implicit in generally stated goals like those above?" When we can identify such behaviors, we have at least some idea of what we are looking for. When our students exemplify such behaviors, we have at least some evidence that they are indeed acquiring the values we are trying to develop.

Let us use one of the values listed earlier to illustrate the point more clearly. Theme No. 3 above identifies a "recognition of the dignity and worth of the individual" as a desired societal goal. Most Americans would probably support such a goal as stated. But how can we tell when our students *are recognizing* the dignity and worth of others? As long as our goal remains so generally expressed, we cannot. It is not clear (and thus we do not know) what the students *do* when they recognize individual worth and dignity.

Suppose, however, that we attempt to become more explicit. Can we identify certain behaviors we would accept as *some* evidence that students are recognizing "the dignity and worth of the individual"? We might say that a student:

> • *waits* until others have finished speaking before speaking himself (does not interrupt others);
> • *encourages* everyone involved in a discussion to offer his opinions (does not monopolize the conversation with his arguments);
> • *revises* his own opinions when the opinions of others are more solidly grounded in, and supported by, factual evidence than his own (does not blindly insist on his own point of view);
> • *makes statements* in support of others no matter what their social status (does not put others in embarrassing, humiliating, or subservient positions).

Notice that each of these statements indicates certain behaviors that we desire of students. To the extent that our students display these behaviors in and out of the classroom, we have reason to believe that they are making at least some progress toward attaining the previously identified general goal of recognizing the dignity and worth of other individuals. This is not to imply, however, that such behavioral statements totally capture the essence of the more general goal. No concept as abstract as "the worth and dignity of the individual" can ever be fully and completely identified, let alone put into words. But we can try to describe completely what we believe such a statement means. We can do this by citing examples of student behaviors which we will accept as specific manifestations of the general concept.

Appropriate Teaching Strategies

It is not enough, however, just to break down societal goals into expected student behaviors. We must also plan and develop appropriate teaching strategies* to enable the teacher to reinforce these desired behaviors. Such teaching strategies need to indicate actual procedures for a teacher to use in order to encourage value analysis and the development of desired student values.

The most common means of teaching values employed by teachers in the past has been that of moralistic *telling*. Teachers have used a variety of hortatory and persuasive techniques, emotional pleas, appeals to conscience, slogans, and "good examples" to help students learn to value the "right" objects, persons, or ideas.

A corollary of moralism is the argument for "exposure." According to this argument, the way to help students acquire certain desired values is to expose them continually to the kinds of objects and ideas which possess such values (e.g., a painting by Renoir, a Mozart sonata, *Caesar's Commentaries*—in Latin, of course). In short, if we provide the "right" kind of atmosphere in our classrooms, our students will "catch" the values we desire them to possess. Our job as teachers, then, is to assure that we place our students in the kinds of situations and expose them to the kinds of materials that contain the kinds of values we want "caught." (Should any student not catch these values, naturally something must be wrong with the student!)

The problem with these approaches is that they just haven't worked very well. "If admonition, lecture, sermon, or example were fully effective instruments in gaining compliance with codes of conduct, we would have reformed long ago the criminal, the delinquent, or the sinner."[8] The sad fact is that exhortation rarely produces committed, actively involved individuals. Essentially, it involves one-way communication, and several studies have indicated that one-directional, persuasive communications are relatively ineffective.[9, 10, 11, 12]

A second approach to the teaching of values is that of the moral relativist. Some cultural anthropologists in the last 50 to 75 years have argued that there are seemingly no values that all people endorse. To quote W. T. Stace in *The Concept of Morals:*

*By teaching strategies I mean a variety of general teacher operations that could be used in different contexts. McDonald defines a teaching strategy as "a plan for producing learning, including both the decisions representing the conception of the plan and the actions representing its execution."[7]

The whole notion of progress is a sheer delusion. Progress means an advance from lower to higher, from worse to better. But on the basis of ethical relativity, it has no meaning to say that the standards of this age are better (or worse) than those of the previous age. For there is no common standard by which both can be measured. Thus it is nonsense to say that the morality of the New Testament is higher than that of the Old. And Jesus Christ, if he imagined that he was introducing into the world a higher ethical standard than existed before his time, was merely deluded.

On this view, Jesus Christ can only have been led to the quite absurd belief that his ethical precepts were better than those of Moses by his personal vanity. If only he had read Dewey, he would have understood that so long as people continued to believe in the doctrine of an eye for an eye and a tooth for a tooth, that doctrine was morally right; and that there could not be any point whatever in trying to make them believe in his newfangled theory of loving one's enemies. Too, the new morality would become right as soon as people came to believe in it, for it would then be the accepted standard. And what people think is right is right. But then if only Jesus Christ and persons with similar ideas had kept these ideas to themselves, people might have gone on believing that the old morality was right. And in that case, it would have been right, and would have remained so to this day. And that would have saved a lot of useless trouble. For the change which Jesus Christ actually brought about was merely a change from one set of moral ideas to another.[13]

In short, this position seems to argue that there exists a plurality of value positions that one can take and that one value is as good as any other.

A corollary of this relativistic position is that of the logical positivist who argues that only judgments of fact can be verified. Judgments of value cannot. Judgments of fact refer to present or past realities; they are objective, describe relationships among things, and have assumed referents in nature. They can be tested publicly by anyone through observation or experiment. Judgments of value, on the other hand, cannot be publicly tested, for they deal with feelings and preferences and include value terms that denote a quality of preference which an individual wants to express.[14]

The logical positivist seems to overlook the fact, however, that such statements of value can be submitted to public test, if we can get some agreement on the value terms involved. For example, if I were to say that Nancy is a beautiful girl, this statement is testable enough, if all of those concerned can agree on the meaning of beautiful.* The key question seems to be: "Can the concepts in the proposition be defined in ways that (according to defining criteria) are clear?" Can we agree on the properties of a value concept and state, whenever possible, such properties in behavioral terms?

The central problem of relativism is that it ignores the fact that some values apparently are better than others, and thus worth developing. Whereas moralism encourages an uncritical acceptance on the part of students of the values set forth by teachers (or other adults), relativism provides no guides whatsoever. Neither approach helps students to determine for themselves what it is that they consider to be important.

Thus, either deliberately or by default, students receive their values from a source outside themselves. They acquire what "society" deems to be important rather than determining this for themselves. In a society like ours, however, where many conflicting values exist, students acquire a number of values that are in opposition to each other.** This in turn furthers uncertainty on their part, yet neither moralism nor relativism provides them with any way by which to deal with the conflict which these opposing values produce. As Hunt and Metcalf suggest, to be told that one should always value both honesty and kindness doesn't help much when the two conflict.[15]

Thus, it would seem to make both logical and psychological sense to devise a number of instructional strategies which teachers can use to influence value development in directions which they desire.*** The

*This is not to imply that obtaining such agreement is a simple matter. But we need certainly to make the attempt. Thus, students need to learn various ways of definition (for example, by class and differentia, by stipulation, by example, and by operational analysis) so that they can inform others how they are using value-loaded terms. It is my position that, when and wherever possible, operational (behavioral) analysis is preferable.

**For example, American young people are bombarded from all sides by conflicting slogans. They are urged to be concerned and involved, yet not to interfere in the affairs of others. One should be "genuine" and "authentic," but still not reveal one's true feelings. You may not be able to "keep a good man down," but remember that "it isn't what you know, it's who you know that counts." We may be our "brother's keeper," but "charity begins at home." Though "all men are created equal," don't forget that "blood will tell." Is it any wonder that many students are confused as to what to believe?

***Emphasizing again that what these desired values are will vary considerably from teacher to teacher. I am not arguing for any *one* set of values to be taught. I am arguing for designing clearly thought-out teaching strategies in order to develop predetermined objectives in the area of value education.

strategies described earlier do not appear worthy of endorsement. In the remainder of this article, therefore, let me present one example of a strategy which can serve more effectively to bring about value development in elementary school children.

A Value-Developing Strategy

This teaching strategy is designed to encourage students to identify and empathize with others faced with two or more undesirable and conflicting alternatives.

Festinger has suggested that when individuals are presented with a problem in which two "goods" are in conflict, they will expend effort to study the alternatives open to them.[16] With this in mind, the following strategy was designed:

An Affective Strategy That Develops Empathy for and Identification with Individuals Placed in Conflict Situations

Instructional Objectives: Given the information in the following story, students should be able to :

a. *state* the alternatives open to Willie (the central character in the story);

b. *describe* at least two things that might happen to Willie, depending on what course of action he decides to pursue; and how they think Willie would feel in each instance;

c. *state* what they think they would do if they were Willie, and *explain* why they think they would do this;

d. *describe* how they think they would feel if they did this;

e. *state* what they believe is a warranted generalization about how people feel in situations similar to Willie's.

In this strategy, students are asked to read a story (or have the story read to them, depending on age and grade level) in which an individual, as real-life as possible, is faced with a choice between two (or more) conflicting alternatives. Here is one such story that might be used with first-graders:*

Willie Johnson was in trouble! In school this morning he had thrown his paint water at Sue Nelligan and the teacher

*I am indebted to Cornelius Mahoney of the Raphael Weill Elementary School in San Francisco for preparing the first draft of this story.

had become angry with him. "Why did you do that, Willie?" she had asked. Willie couldn't tell her, because he really didn't know why himself. He knew that Sue had teased him a little, but that wasn't the real reason. He just didn't know! The whole thing put him in a bad mood. From then on, the entire day just went to heck.

In the afternoon he had pushed Tommy Grigsly in the recess line. He also had stamped his foot and yelled at the teacher. The teacher had become angry with him again. But this time she had pinned a note to his mother on his jacket.

That note! He knew it was about his behavior in class during the day. He knew that when he got home his mother would read the note and give him some kind of punishment. Then his father would find out about it and he'd really get it!

On his way home from school Willie was thinking about what his father would do to him.

"Wow!" he thought. "I'll get killed if I take this note home. I'd better take it off and throw it away."

He was just about to do that when he remembered what had happened to Billy Beatty when he was sent home with a note. Billy had thrown his note away and was sent to the principal's office about it. Then Billy was in double trouble!

Wow! He *was* in trouble. He couldn't give it to his mother, he couldn't throw it away. What should he do? He had a problem, all right. He had to make a choice, but how should he choose? No matter what he did, the outcome didn't look too good! What should he do?

Upon completion of the reading, the teacher can ask the class the following questions:

1. What things might Willie do? (What alternatives are open to him?)
2. What might happen to him if he does these things? (Discuss each alternative.)
3. How do you think he'd feel, in each case, if this happened?
4. If you were faced with this situation, what would you do?
5. How do you think you'd feel?
6. Basing your answer on how you've said you would feel and how you think Willie felt, what can you say about how people feel in situations like this?

7. Why do you think people have different feelings about things?

The above question sequence presents one example of a carefully thought-out teaching strategy. Students are asked to determine what alternatives are open to an individual placed in an uncomfortable situation (Question No. 1). No matter what Willie does, the consequences will be rather unpleasant. Thus, the similarity to real life, for who among us has not been at one time or another in a somewhat similar predicament? Students are not only asked to analyze alternatives, however. They are also requested to predict consequences (Question No. 2). In Question No. 3, they are helped to identify the *feelings* of another, and then in Questions No. 4 and 5 to empathize with those feelings and determine how they would feel themselves in such a situation. Questions No. 6 and 7 ask them to try to draw some conclusions about how people in general might feel in such situations. (It is to be emphasized at this point that there are no "right" answers to questions like the ones in this strategy. Nor should there be. For what we are interested in encouraging is a discussion about how people feel—and this is impossible if there is one, and only one, "correct" answer.) The assumption underlying this strategy is that through empathizing with the feelings of another individual faced with unpleasant conflicting alternatives, students will be making affective responses. This makes it possible for affective learning to occur. The reactions of the teacher and other students to what they say would have some effect on what responses are reinforced. Students may also be motivated to change their behavior and become more considerate of others facing conflicts.

This is but one example of the kind of instructional strategy that can be used to further value education in the social studies. It is important for us to develop such strategies. We must first identify and specify behaviorally what our objectives in the affective domain are to be, of course. We must also plan relevant learning activities (e.g., films which represent value conflicts, open-ended filmstrips, panel and class discussions on controversial social issues, guest speakers, student field trips, essays on open-ended topics like "What Makes Me Angry," role-playing, sociodramas, and the like) that will allow students to practice appropriate and varied behaviors. But we cannot leave the accomplishment of affective objectives to chance or to learning activities planned mainly for cognitive goals (no matter how varied and exciting). Teaching strategies identifying specific procedures (such as the questioning sequence presented earlier) that teachers may use must be designed to produce youngsters with desired values.

REFERENCES

1. John L. Childs. *Education and Morals.* New York: Appleton-Century-Crofts, Inc., 1950, pp. 17-19. Quoted in Van Cleve Morris, *Philosophy and the American School.* Boston: Houghton-Mifflin, 1961, p. 289.
2. *Ibid.,* p. 6.
3. Edwin Fenton. *Teaching in the New Social Studies in Secondary Schools: An Inductive Approach.* New York: Holt, Rinehart and Winston, 1966, pp. 41-45.
4. William McGucken. The Philosophy of Catholic Education. In N. B. Henry (Ed.) *Philosophies of Education,* Forty-first Yearbook of the National Society for the Study of Education. Chicago: The Society, 1942, p. 254.
5. Committee on Concepts and Values. *A Guide to Content in the Social Studies.* Washington, D. C.: National Council for the Social Studies, 1957, p. 73.
6. John Wilson. *Language and the Pursuit of Truth.* Cambridge: Cambridge University Press, 1967, pp. 44, 45.
7. Frederick J. McDonald. *Educational Psychology* (Second Edition). Belmont, Calif.: Wadsworth, 1965, p. 690.
8. Solon T. Kimball. Individualism and the Formation of Values. *Journal of Applied Behavioral Science,* No. 2, 1966, p. 481.
9. Leon Festinger. Behavioral Support for Opinion Change. *Public Opinion Quarterly,* Fall, 1964, pp. 404-17.
10. Gordon W. Allport. *The Nature of Prejudice.* Reading, Mass.: Addison-Wesley, 1954.
11. Elliott McGinnies. Cross-Cultural Studies in Persuasion: 1. An Attempt to Induce Both Direct and Generalized Attitude Change in Japanese Students. *Journal of Social Psychology, 70,* 1966, pp. 69-75.
12. A. J. Sykes. A Study in Attitude Change. *Occupational Psychology, 40,* 1966, pp. 31-41.
13. W. T. Stace. *The Concept of Morals.* New York: Braziller, 1937, p. 28.
14. Maurice P. Hunt & Lawrence E. Metcalf. *Teaching High School Social Studies.* New York: Harper and Row, 1968.
15. *Ibid.,* p. 124.
16. Leon Festinger. *A Theory of Cognitive Dissonance.* Evanston, Ill.: Row, Peterson, 1957.

Yelon provides a flowchart for formulating instructional objectives which includes a means of determining students' attitudes and feelings about a given subject area. The author points out the need for estimating whether or not students will be motivated to utilize their in-school learning in out-of-school situations.

A Strategy for Estimating Student Interest*

STEPHEN L. YELON

Most teachers want to have their students use the knowledge, the principles, and the skills learned, not only to pass their final exams, but after their class is completed. Most teachers hope that a student will become so fascinated and curious about a subject that he will immerse himself in related activities after the course. We should not conclude that a student's skilled performance on a final exam reveals a willingness to delve into associated matters later on. At the end of a course, teachers should search for ways to measure a student's attitudes and feelings about a subject in order to get some indication of his future behavior.

Many teachers and psychologists have found relative success in categorizing some expressions of internal processes. For instance, many teachers might agree upon what reading comprehension means, or what behavior indicates knowledge of a concept. Yet most teachers and psychologists have had relatively little success at clarifying expressions of affective processes. For instance, we might have considerable disagreement if we each tried to translate the phrase "an appreciation of music" into a statement describing behavior that we can measure. Therefore, the question we expect our strategy to answer is: How can we

*Reprinted from *Audiovisual Instruction, 15,* January, 1970, pp. 34-35, by permission of the publisher and the author.

formulate a statement of an instructional objective that will include a valid estimate of students' interest and observable, related behavior that we can measure?

The strategy we will employ to answer this question is similar to one used to determine whether a student has learned a concept. There are five major steps in this strategy: specify behaviors, state common attributes, test working definitions, choose school related behaviors, and test objectives.

Figure 1 depicts a flowchart that indicates in detail how to go through these steps.

The first step (Box 1 on flowchart) is to list behaviors which are believed to be expressions of student interest. For example, behaviors that express an appreciation of music might be: going to concerts, buying records, talking about music with friends, subscribing to magazines dealing with music, or a combination of these.

The second major step (Boxes 4-7) is to state the attributes common to these behaviors, which will serve as a working definition of student interest. These attributes are common to the above behaviors: (1) one activity or a combination of activities dealing with music, (2) persistence, (3) expenditure. "Persistence" implies that these acts are continual. Time, energy, or money may be expended. To calculate the intensity of expenditure, one would compare the expense with the resources of the particular person observed. Notice that persistence and expenditure may be cloaked in several garments; the approach to music may be expressed in different ways by the same person. We will retain this statement as a working definition: *Music appreciation is a persistent expenditure in a number of different ways directed toward some activity or object which can be categorized as musical.*

The next step (Boxes 8-12) is to have the definition examined by other teachers. To do this the working definition would be presented, as well as some examples of behavior that conformed to the definition, and some examples that did not. The teachers would be asked to choose those examples of behavior which they believe fit the definition. Their responses would be analyzed by how many true examples were left out and how many false examples were picked. When zero is the answer to both questions, the definition is ready for the next stage. The definition is refined until there is agreement. For example, if we proposed that the following behavior were an example of our definition of music appreciation—"A student consistently purchases books dealing with music from a book program in school"—it might be argued that the student may be coerced to do so. Thus, we might refine our definition to include the characteristic, "without overt coercion," or, "without a reward or punishment administered by another person."

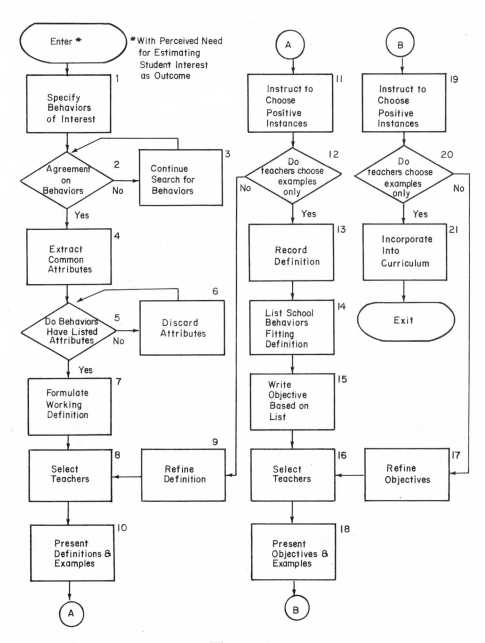

Figure 1

Flowchart: A Strategy for Estimating Student Interest

Next we ask: Can samples be found of behaviors in school which conform to the definition (Box 14)? The list of such behaviors would be used to create objectives in the particular subject matters in which they are found (Box 15). For example, from a list of school activities that are illustrations of our definition, we may create this objective: The learner will express appreciation of music in at least two or more of these ways:

- Writing an English theme about music without having been assigned a topic,
- Playing in the school band over one semester,
- Taking unassigned records out of the music library,
- Going to free school concerts after school,
- Joining the music club and remaining a member.

The fifth step would be to verify the objective in the same way that we refined the working definition (Boxes 16-20).

The reader should remain constantly aware that the goal of this strategy is to get an indication of an important instructional outcome. This strategy is to be followed when one perceives the need for an estimate of whether a student is motivated enough to apply his learning when the course is over.

*Gall briefly describes eight impor-
tant learning intangibles which were
identified during the Norwalk, Con-
necticut, "behavioral outcomes" program. Subsequently he illustrates a
means for behavioralizing and evaluating one of these areas through the
use of a rating scale—a technique
which shows promise for increasing
the observability of affective domain
objectives.*

They Learn More
Than You Teach Them*

Morris Gall

Tests for determining the degree to which children achieve basic
understandings, skills, and competencies have long been available. They
range from the teacher-made class test to the National Standardized
Achievement test. Evaluation of the less tangible goals of instruction
is still an unsolved problem, despite the fact that less tangible objectives,
such as respect for others, ability to work in cooperation with others,
self-evaluation, etc., are at least as important instructional goals as are
the more tangible.

The reason why, we believe, the major emphasis is placed on skills
and understandings is that adequate tests for the less tangible objectives
of instruction have not been developed. Small wonder. Measuring
attitudes, interests, and personal-social adaptability is not easy. Nevertheless, new approaches to education demand new methods of evaluation.
Until such methods are developed, unfortunately, teaching continues
to be herded in the direction of facts and skills, in part because testing
leans that way.

*Reprinted from *Grade Teacher Magazine* by permission of the publisher
and the author. Copyright © April, 1967, by *Teachers Publishing Corpora-
tion.*

A few years ago, I began working with the staffs of Jefferson School and Tracey School in Norwalk on the isolation and definition of some less tangible goals. We ended up with eight . . .

1. *Self-reliance, self-confidence, and independence* (the self-image). Quality of personality. A child has a sense of psychological security and a disposition to stand by his convictions.

2. *Respect for others.* An appreciation of differences, and a tolerance and acceptance of the ways of others.

3. *Group cooperation.* The ability to work in groups, to share, to lead and follow.

4. *Ability to evaluate one's self.* The development of increasingly refined and accurate standards of personal evaluation.

5. *Critical thinking and judgment.* The process, when confronted with a practical problem, of making a choice, a decision, a judgment or a policy.

6. *Concern for truth.* A disposition to keep an open mind and to raise questions about seemingly established authority.

7. *Self-direction.* Increasing competence in formulating problems and in finding solutions independently.

8. *Ability to communicate.* Development of competence in conveying information, ideas, skills, and attitudes to others through the various media of the written and spoken word, the arts, and the sciences.

The next step was to develop evaluative instruments (tests) for these goals. We worked over a period of two years on this problem. An additional group of teachers and administrators from Benjamin Franklin Junior High School and from Fox Run, Brookside, and Columbus Elementary Schools, and Cranbury School also participated actively in the program. We worked out a series of scales, expressed in behavioral terms, for use in rating the children. Typical is the scale for measuring *Respect for Others . . .*

1. Is completely unconcerned with the welfare of others (defaces school property, strikes others, shoves in line, takes personal property of others, uses abusive language).

2. Is beginning to demonstrate some awareness that others have rights.

3. Cooperates in small groups in which only his friends are involved.

4. Is beginning to show some acceptance of others—new children or non-members of his group.

5. Will work cooperatively with children of different backgrounds when directed.

6. Listens to and judges opinions of others without bias.

7. Respects race, creed, color or national origin of others.

8. Treats everyone equally and participates readily in democratic procedures.

9. Has warm regard for the ways and contributions of others regardless of class, color, religion, or other differences from himself.

10. Actively fosters harmonious inter-group relations.

The implications of this program for ethical development and character education are unmistakeable. Each of the eight selected goals has definite implications for character building and ethical growth.

It is difficult at this stage to assess the impact on instruction. However, teachers have testified almost unanimously that the use of the rating scales forces them to look at a child more perceptively. Anecdotes like the following are common:

"Bill, who is two years below grade level, has found it exciting to help our new boy from Canada. They read together with my supervision."

"Dave, who becomes emotional and cries as soon as he can't do something, came to me four times this week for help—without tears. I have been telling him there is no need to cry when he can tell me what is wrong and I can help him to solve the situation."

"Jim said 'no' for the first time to Fred. Jim is Fred's shadow. At last he is gaining some self-confidence and is very eager for his turn in show and tell. In February he wouldn't speak to the class in group discussions. He's not a leader—but he's moving ahead."

"We kept a set of our papers and gave them back to the class near the end of the year. The pupils wrote evaluations of the progress they had made (or lack of progress). Responses showed wide variation in self-evaluation."

"In art, people brought in assorted objects and materials for a collage project. Children shopped at each other's desks to see if they could use or trade materials. Children were happy to donate materials they were not going to use."

"Each child has an individual checklist for language. Before handing in their papers, they use the checklist to find their errors and correct them."

Teachers in the program have enriched their backgrounds by reading specific titles that stimulate thinking about this new curriculum emphasis. Among the works recommended are: *Perceiving, Behaving, Becoming;* The 1962 Yearbook of the Association for Supervision and Curriculum Development; *The Process of Education* by Jerome S. Bruner; *Creative Power* by Hughes Mearns; *The Language and Thought of the Child* by Jean Piaget; and *Evaluation in Social Studies,* Harry D. Berg, editor, the 1965 Yearbook of the National Council for the Social Studies.

Kapfer deals with the affective areas of learning by means of a continuum of observable behaviors. His continuum technique resembles Gall's rating scale for intangible goals (described in the preceding article), but is somewhat more refined.

Behavioral Objectives in the Affective Domain*

PHILIP G. KAPFER

The necessary delimitation and segmentation which commonly occur when writing measurable objectives alienates many teachers. Part of the alienation results from the degree of specificity required in writing behavioral objectives. Such specificity can result in seeming, if not real, triviality. Much of the danger of triviality, however, can be overcome by relating the behaviorally stated objective to its more broadly stated non-behavioral goal.

The purpose of this article is to report approaches to the affective domain currently being developed and used with students as part of a Title III PACE project at Ruby S. Thomas Elementary School in Las Vegas, Nevada. The approach reported in this article should prove useful to teachers and curriculum developers as an initial step in assisting a student to learn a behavior and to evaluate his own attainment of that behavior.

An Approach to the Affective Domain

An initial attempt was made to write behavioral objectives in the affective domain by patterning them after Mager[1] and by beginning at the lowest levels in the *Taxonomy of Educational Objectives.*[2] However,

*Excerpts reprinted from *Educational Technology, 8,* June 15, 1968, pp. 11-13, by permission of the publisher and the author.

it was necessary to modify this approach for these reasons: (1) the *Taxonomy* levels overlap and do not seem to lend themselves to a linear progression of behaviors; (2) behavioral objectives frequently appear to stand on their own in isolation from other objectives, thus, confusing the idea of a related linear progression; and (3) problems of validity of teacher measurement continually thwart efforts at specifying the several components of a behavioral objective.

Hence, an approach was devised which appears to lend itself to any affective area. The approach is a simple one, and involves (1) stating the affective domain objective as an *unobservable* behavior (e.g., receiving, responding, valuing, organizing, characterizing) and then stating the related observable *area* of behavior, and (2) stating finite linear steps in a continuum of behaviors beginning at the "negative" or "neutral" end and progressing to the "positive" end of the continuum.

One such objective and its continuum of behaviors is given below.

Affective Domain Objective and Behavioral Continuum

The student increasingly values independent learning, as observed in his self-initiating and self-directing behaviors.

Continuum
of Behaviors

1. Given a teacher-assigned delimited topic with assigned specified resources, the student follows directions.
2. Given a teacher-assigned delimited topic and assigned alternative resources, the student selects from alternative resources.
3. Given a teacher-assigned delimited topic, the student seeks his own resources.
4. Given a teacher-assigned broad topic, the student delimits the topic and seeks his own resources.
5. Given a student-initiated broad or delimited topic (in or out of school), the student delimits the topic as necessary and seeks his own resources.

The most important function of behavioral objectives, whether affective, cognitive, or psychomotor, is in the direct use of these objectives by the student (1) to learn the expected behavior and (2) to evaluate his own progress in learning the behavior. With reference to the sample continuum above, students might be told:

Here is an objective and a continuum of statements describing the behaviors of people who have achieved this objective at varying levels.

The objective and the continuum of behaviors (assuming that each of these alternative behaviors is actually open to you) relate to your attitude toward independent learning. We do not know very much about changing people's attitudes, but we do think that if you practice behaviors that relate to a given attitude level, the attitude itself might form.

What you have to do is decide what kind of person you would like to be, how independently you would like to function, what kinds and levels of attitudes you would like to hold, and how you would like other people to perceive you so that your self-concept might grow.

Then, you will need to practice the behaviors of people who hold the levels of attitude to which you aspire. You will have to begin by evaluating yourself. Decide where you are on the continuum, and then decide if you are satisfied with the level where you are or if you want to be at a higher level.

We will discuss with you where we think you are on the continuum, and if our evaluation differs from your self-evaluation, then we will want to see why it does.

The behaviors given in the above continuum, when taken individually, seem to relate more closely to the skills area than to the attitude area. However, the *whole,* in this case is greater than the sum of its parts. Continua of skill behaviors with affective implications provide the learner with attainable stepwise models which he can practice. As a result, he possibly will come to hold the related level of attitudes.

By providing the student with continua of behaviors based on reasonably spaced steps, unattainable expectations in the area of attitudes may be avoided.

Further, by capitalizing on the built-in opportunity for dialogue between students and teachers which this approach provides, failure and frustration in the affective domain are unnecessary.

Education can become more human if, for no other reason, in the attempt to make it so we come to grips with the problems of *how to* rather than just *need to*.

References

1. Mager, Robert F. *Preparing Instructional Objectives.* Palo Alto, California: Fearon Publishers, 1962.
2. Krathwohl, David R.; Benjamin S. Bloom & Bertram B. Masia. *Taxonomy of Educational Objectives, Handbook II: Affective Domain.* New York: David McKay Company, Inc., 1964, pp. 95-175.

Part III

Additional Media

Broudy, Harry S. Science, Art and Human Values. *The Science Teacher,* *36,* March, 1969, pp. 23-28.

Burns, Richard W. Objectives Involving Attitudes, Interests and Apprecia-tions. *Educational Technology, 8,* April 30, 1968, pp. 14-15.

Darling, David W. Why a Taxonomy of Affective Learning? *Educational Leadership, 22,* April, 1965, pp. 473-475, 522.

Dowd, Donald J. & Sarah C. West. An Inventory of Measures of Affective Behavior. *Improving Educational Assessment and An Inventory of Meas-ures of Affective Behavior.* Walcott H. Beatty (Ed.) Washington, D. C.: Association for Supervision and Curriculum Development, National Edu-cation Association, 1969, pp. 89-163.

Eiss, Albert F. & Mary Blatt Harbeck. *Behavioral Objectives in the Affective Domain.* Washington, D. C.: National Science Teachers Association, 1969, 42 pp.

Harbeck, Mary B. Instructional Objectives in the Affective Domain, *Educa-tional Technology, 10,* January, 1970, pp. 49-52.

Mager, Robert F. *Developing Attitude Toward Learning.* Palo Alto, Cali-fornia: Fearon Publishers, 1968, 104 pp.

Ochoa, Anna. Valuing: A Curriculum Imperative. *The College of Education Record.* University of Washington, *35,* May, 1969, pp. 69-74.

Rooze, Gene E. Empirical Evaluation of Instructional Materials in the Affective Area. *Educational Technology, 9,* April, 1969, pp. 53-56.

West, Earle H. The Affective Domain. *The Journal of Negro Education, 38,* Spring, 1969, pp. 91-93.

Part IV

Behavioral Objectives and the Curriculum Developer

The rational approach to curriculum development which is encouraged through the use of specified behavioral outcomes has much appeal to educators and laymen alike. There is, of course, opposition to the behavioral approach. However, leading thinkers in the field of curriculum development do not see the current emphasis on behavior specification as being merely faddish or ephemeral. Rather, the use of well-defined objectives in curriculum development may well be an extremely significant and lasting educational advance. The writers whose materials are included in Part IV reflect primarily the positive point of view. The opening articles by Tyler, Kapfer, and Markle and Tiemann provide overall perspective for the materials which follow. Lindvall and Kapfer use the framework of specific projects to discuss techniques related to the definition of objectives at several instructional planning levels. The Yarington article describes a teacher education curriculum developed in performance terms. The final two articles, by Bolvin and Esbensen, highlight the role of behavioral objectives in individualized instructional procedures.

Over a span of more than three decades Tyler has addressed himself to the problem of specifying objectives in such a way as to make them of value in teaching and evaluation. In the following selection Tyler applies the perspectives gained as a result of his work to four questions which are often raised concerning educational objectives. These questions involve (1) the importance of clearly defined objectives, (2) the need for including both content and behavior in statements of objectives, (3) the importance of obtaining balance between generality and specificity in objectives, and (4) the need to make value judgments when selecting objectives for a particular program or school.

Some Persistent Questions on the Defining of Objectives*

Ralph W. Tyler

I should like to comment on four questions which are often raised in a discussion of the subject of educational objectives.

*Reprinted from C. M. Lindvall (Ed.) *Defining Educational Objectives: A Report of the Regional Commission on Educational Coordination and the Learning Research and Development Center,* by permission of the University of Pittsburgh Press and the author. Copyright © 1964 by the University of Pittsburgh Press.

The Importance of a Clear Definition of Objectives

One common question is "Why is it now considered important to define objectives clearly when teachers in the past have done excellent work without having a clear statement of goals?" It is certainly true that many teachers have a sense of what is important for students to learn and some of them are able to translate this notion of educational goals into relevant learning experiences for the student without ever having put down on paper what these implicit aims are. However, many others have not carried their thinking beyond the point of selecting the content to be presented. They have not considered carefully what the students are to do with the content. In such cases, students commonly believe that they are to memorize all or important parts of the content, and other objectives involving behavior other than memorization are not developed.

This question can also be examined from the point of view of the student. When the objectives are clearly defined and understood by the student, he can perceive what he is trying to learn. What happens when the students are not informed of the learning aims? I have interviewed more than 100 students at the upper elementary and secondary school levels, asking them what they are expected to learn in each of their courses, and how they found out what they were to learn. Almost all of the students reported that they found out what they were to learn from three sources: the textbooks and work books, what the teacher did in class, and the advice of other students. Unless the exercises in the work books and the textbook assignments clearly reflect the desired objectives, the student is likely to resort to memorization and mechanical completion of exercises rather than to carry on the activities which are really relevant to the desired goals.

Unfortunately, too, the teacher's behavior in the classroom is not an example of the behavior implied by the objectives of the course. For example, in several college history courses the teachers told me that their objectives were to develop understanding on the part of the students of the way in which past events, episodes, and the like influenced later conditions and problems. They also said that they wanted the students to learn to draw on various sources of information about the past and to be able to explain what is happening today partly in terms of this influence of the past. But in spite of mentioning these kinds of objectives, the teachers' performance in class consisted primarily in lecturing on what they knew about the historical period under study, and quizzing students on the lecture and related reading. The result was that the student, watching the performance of the teacher, thought that what was expected of him was to be able to do the same thing. He felt that he should memorize what people knew about this period rather than develop any of the desired abilities and skills. It is this kind of experience that leads me to believe that when objectives are identified and defined only casually, if at all, the students are likely to get the wrong image of what the teacher is trying to teach and what the student is expected to be able to do. He is misguided rather than helpfully steered in his learning efforts.

Two Aspects of a Clear Definition

A second common question is: "What should be included in a clear definition of an educational objective?" The Conference papers have emphasized the requirement that the definition should describe behavior, that is, *what it is that the student should be able to do, or how he should be able to think or feel.* For example, he may be expected to write clearly or he should be able to observe the results of experiments and draw reasonable inferences from them, or he should be able to perceive and respond to esthetic qualities in music. I believe the papers have given less attention to the other aspect of the definition of an objective, and that is the content involved. Using the previous examples, the definition should not only indicate that in this English class the student is expected to learn to write clearly but also there should be an indication of the kinds of things he should be able to write. The statement that he is expected to be able to write a clear letter of application for a job would include the content part as well as the behavior. Correspondingly, in the second example above, the objective should indicate what kinds of experiments he should be able to observe and draw inferences from the results, and in the third example, the definition should state the esthetic qualities and the kinds of music involved. To specify the kind of behavior to be developed is not enough to guide the selection of learning experiences and the appraisal of results. We must also specify the kinds of content involved.

The Level of Specificity of the Definition

Recognizing the importance of being clear about objectives, sometimes we confuse clarity with a high degree of specificity. For example, a teacher of French may state as one objective the ability to read French. Then in an effort to define what is meant, this is broken down into such specific parts as knowledge of the meaning of the most common 2,500 French words, knowledge of the meaning of each of a number of common French idioms, and so on. These efforts sometimes end up with several hundred objectives for one course. This is too specific, just as the ability to read French is too general.

Here I think we need to make a distinction between the objective in terms of what repertoire we are trying to help the pupil to develop and the analysis that we may make of the objective in terms of a learning sequence. For example, in the case of a foreign language, the objective may be to be able to read the kind of material that you find in the Paris newspapers. This could be an objective, but we may have to define reading somewhat further. For example, what type of understanding is required and how far should he be able to go with respect to the possible varieties of content? Now, it may be that in reaching this type of objective our foreign language teachers would use a plan in which they start from a carefully controlled vocabulary (which was the method used in the early '30s and '40s) or they may use patterns of oral pronunciation (as in the present-day audio-lingual methods). But specifying the various teaching procedures or learning activities is not specifying the objective. The objective should be stated at the level of generality of behavior that you are seeking to help the student to acquire.

Now, this level is largely determined by two factors. One is the level required for effective use in life. This is usually implied by a statement of behavior that can be valued in and of itself. One can easily see the value of being able to read a French newspaper, while being able to identify the subjunctive mood appears to be only a means, not an important objective in itself.

The second factor determining the desired level of generality or specificity is the probable effectiveness in teaching the students involved to generalize the learning to the level desired. Children in the primary grades can usually generalize the idea of addition so that they do not have to practice each number combination again and again as a separate objective. Hence, if this is true, it is possible to seek as objectives for these students: (1) understanding of the concept "addition," and (2) ability to add whole numbers.

In general, the first factor leads to objectives which are not highly specific. The second factor requires us to limit the generality to the level which can be learned by the students involved. This emphasizes the importance of actual experience and empirical evidence in deciding whether a given statement of objectives is too specific or too general.

Considerations Involved in Selecting Objectives

A question continually arising in discussions of this sort concerns a step prior to that of definition: "What considerations should be taken into account in the selection of objectives?" Realizing that there is so much to be taught, so much that it would be valuable for people to learn in a complex society such as ours, and so little time to learn, how do we decide what objectives are worth teaching? I have found it useful to keep in mind several different factors. One of these is an analysis of our culture. Other things being equal it is important to teach those kinds of behavior, those ways of thinking, feeling, and acting that have value in our society and that help the person to become an effective human being in it. As an example of this, the question of foreign language instruction might be used. Some schools have been quite successful in teaching a foreign language at a very early age so that we know that this is something that can be done if it is desirable. But the question that faces the curriculum planner is this: How significant is this foreign language as a means for the pupil's further development? It is more important for the Englishman to learn French than it is for the average American because the Englishman usually has many more opportunities to use it. For the same reason it is more important for the people in Texas to learn Spanish than it is for the people in Illinois to learn Spanish. Where a foreign language can be used, it becomes an important tool of communication.

A related question in which the facts of the culture must be considered is one of the proper grade placement for given objectives or subjects. Where possible, instruction should be planned so that the initial stages of learning will be under the supervision of the school but so that continued learning and reinforcement can and will take place outside the school. For example, if a person is going to Venezuela as a member of the Peace Corps in September, it would be most effective if he were taught Spanish in the months prior to his leaving. This would mean that as soon as he has completed some of the initial stages in learning the language he will have the opportunity to use it outside the classroom and continue to learn under the reinforcing conditions provided by this practical application.

A second factor in selecting appropriate objectives is the present status of the student. What has he already learned? What is he ready for? One of the problems here may be illustrated by developments in mathematics where many high schools are now offering advanced courses. For this reason, as reported to me by some of my college colleagues, some of the topics typically taught in college mathematics courses turn out to be "old stuff" for students coming from the better high schools. I encountered another example of this situation in a recent conversation with a friend whose daughter is a freshman at a leading eastern college. This girl has been greatly disappointed in her first college history course. In her high school history classes, use was made of a variety of interesting source materials, but the college course is using only a textbook which is read and commented on, chapter by chapter. For this student, what had been exciting about the study of history is no longer here. So a key problem in selecting objectives is that of determining the "entering behavior" of the student, just where he is in his educational development and what abilities he brings to the given class or learning situation. Only when this is known can we answer the question of whether or not certain objectives are appropriate for his next stage of development. This requires a procedure for finding out about the students, where they are now, and what their capabilities are.

A third factor in selecting objectives is what we know enough about to teach. It might be nice, for example, to teach a person to employ extra-sensory perception, but we don't know enough about this to teach it. On the other hand, we do know enough about the art of writing to have something to teach children. And, new knowledge in the various subjects is being obtained at a rapid rate. These new developments should be continually examined to see if they provide materials that can be of real value to youngsters. But these new ideas and understandings were not available to teachers at the time they were receiving their education so that we have a problem of keeping our objectives, and our ability to teach them, abreast of the most recent developments in a given field. This is a reason for the continuing effort to involve scientists and other scholars in working with teachers in the development of curricula. New subject resources are becoming available continually, and these should be scrutinized by someone or some curriculum center as a basis for making decisions as to whether or not they should be incorporated into classroom content.

Of course, a fourth basic consideration in the selection of objectives is their relevance to the school's philosophy of education. This philosophy outlines our conception of the "good person" we are trying to develop. It is certainly possible to teach a person as though he were an automaton, and some kinds of training programs in industry are operated pretty much in this way. We can teach him to do all the required things. He can run all of the machines without understanding them. But is this the kind of person we are trying to develop?

We have come to place an emphasis on such things as problem solving and open-endedness, that is, helping the learner to become conscious of the fact that he doesn't have the final answers in this area, that a continuing process of inquiry is involved. We also are putting an emphasis upon the values that come from esthetic experiences in such areas as art and music. But we also have problems of conflicting values and often need to clarify our guiding philosophy. We must continuously be asking the question of what kind of young person it is that it is the responsibility of our schools and colleges to help develop. I have my own answer to the question and I suppose that each one of us does. But the clarification of our values is a basic step in curriculum planning and in the selection of objectives because we can teach in such a way that values or ends are helped, or we can teach in such a way that they are denied.

Finally, a fifth factor in selecting and stating our objectives is the consistency of these objectives with our theory of learning. As an illustration of this consideration, the question frequently arises of the possibility of meeting the demands made upon people today through the preparation provided by our present sixteen years of school. Surely, our people are required to meet the problems of such range and complexity that they can't learn enough in their youth. This dilemma has resulted in a variety of suggestions for the school curriculum. One proposal is that we teach most youth to be a "garden-variety" of citizen who will not be expected to understand much but who can be taught the skills of a particular occupation and a respect for leadership. This is the view often expressed in the English elementary schools. This proposal includes the idea that the responsibility for more adequate understanding and competence to deal with the complexities of modern life will be in the hands of the more privileged group that goes on to secondary schools and colleges.

Another proposal is based on the view that the fields of knowledge are getting so large (as the scientific fields, for example) that we can only expect to cover them rather superficially with some kind of survey. This seems to be a rather common approach.

But a proposal which is currently gaining attention is to start the student from the beginning as an inquirer, as a person who is seeking to learn, giving him the skills and the incentives that lead him to dig deeper into some sample of a content area, and then encouraging him to go on independently while he is in school, and in later life. As one example of this, the new social studies material being developed at Harvard begins at the third grade level with a study of the Eskimo and two other primitive cultures. This program says, in effect, that the culture of man is a developing thing and that its basic elements and the procedure for studying it can best be understood by starting with certain simple samples. The Eskimo is selected, not for the usually romantic reasons that have led to his inclusion in elementary school courses, but because he represents a type of culture which can be studied through the methods of the anthropologist. Then the children study a tribe from central Africa and another from Oceana. These offer the third grader the opportunity to become familiar with primitive societies. And the students begin their study, not by reading a textbook, but by bringing together a variety of materials and resources that are pertinent to the understanding of the culture and appropriate for third-graders so that, from the first, they employ the methods that are useful in beginning to understand what another culture is like. The effort is to develop persons who have the ability and the desire to be continuing inquirers.

Projects of this type are trying to attack the problem caused by the ever-increasing mass of material that should be learned by producing students who have the tools and the general ability to proceed on their own. This approach views education not merely as a process of giving answers, but as a process of producing persons who can find answers on their own, can discover additional questions that need to be answered, can come up with answers to these questions, and engage in an intelligent process of continual inquiry. This approach seeks to develop in students a conviction that the world is an interesting and exciting place where there is much to be seen and understood. The students are out to understand the kinds of problems that are found and the modes of inquiry that are used. They should develop an understanding of how one makes an inquiry if one were looking at a topic from the point of view of the geographer, or from the point of view of the chemist, or from the point of view of the writer of a literary document. They learn to inquire into the behavior of people as well as the behavior of things, of plants and of animals. This approach seeks to develop the necessary skills and the mastery of many of the pertinent concepts. The school is not expected to present all of the details or all of the specific facts or examples. The important learning is for the pupil to understand the basic concepts such as that of social mobility in sociology, of motivation in psychology, or of energy transfer in physics. Concepts of this type are basic to continued investigation in a given area. For example, the new high school physics course developed by the Physical Science Study Committee builds its work around 34 concepts. If the pupil masters these, he has the foundation for further investigation of physical phenomena. He can learn how these concepts are related and can discover many important principles. As an example in the arts, the courses are built around concepts of form and of esthetic values such as that of unity in literature, of the illusion of reality, etc.

The hope is, with this approach, that students really become involved in a life-long process of learning in which the school's role is to get them fairly well started. With such a view the problem of defining objectives becomes that of determining the behaviors, appropriate to the given grade level, that the pupil can carry out so that when he has done this he will have a feeling for the open-endedness of the situation, the new questions to be asked, the new knowledge to be gained, and not feel that the learning is finished. For example, the fifth grade pupil in such a program will not feel that now he knows all there is to know about

Egypt, but will begin to see how what he knows about Egypt relates to other countries, will see, for example, the relationships between rigid social structure and economic backwardness.

What I am trying to suggest here is that, when you are formulating your objectives, it is very important that you have clearly in mind your conception of the learning process and the process of education. In this last illustrative approach, this conception included the notion that the learner is active, that he is looking at the world, and is trying to make something out of it. We are trying to guide him in his continued activity rather than trying to close the world for him by giving him all the answers. We don't want to tell him, "You have learned what there is in this course. Everything was here in the textbook and now you have learned it all." The student must see his learning as a constantly continuing process. To achieve this you will have to think of objectives of the sort that lead from the third grade to the fourth grade to the fifth grade and so on. It might be that in studying science in the third grade the pupils are looking at rocks and trying to make sense out of them while in the fourth grade they are looking at plants and growing flowers. But in both cases they are concerned with the same general notion of the world and how it is to be interpreted. The types of science problems involved and the kinds of skills employed can be stepping stones for continued development.

In closing I would re-state something that was touched upon by Bob Glaser in connection with his experience in producing his program. This is that as you work with objectives and with your efforts to teach them you frequently have a basis for the re-definition of your objectives. As you see what really is possible, you may see more clearly the kinds of things the pupils need in addition to those that you thought of in your original planning. The process of clarifying goals, then working toward them, then appraising progress, then re-examining the goals, modifying them and clarifying them in the light of the experience and the data is a never-ending procedure.

Kapfer defines the role of the "curriculum processor" with respect to the use of behavioral objectives in curriculum development. His discussion indicates the importance of such objectives for developing self-direction in learners. Writers of behavioral objectives will find useful the continuum of action terms provided in the article.

Behavioral Objectives and the Curriculum Processor[*]

A new breed of teacher is developing in American education. He cannot be distinguished from other teachers by age, sex, experience, dedication, or level of militancy. He can be distinguished, however, by the type of educational tasks he performs and by the orientation which he brings to those tasks. His role eventually will be recognized by school boards and administrators through some form of differentiated staffing. If he were given a title, it might be "curriculum processor."

He is involved with students in developing a more humanized school atmosphere, one based on mutual trust and respect. He believes in the heretical assumptions that learning is a natural human enterprise, that students want to learn, and that they will learn voluntarily and efficiently when given opportunities to become responsibly involved in determining the character of their learning experiences.

Not every teacher is capable of or interested in being a curriculum processor, although most teachers can be trained by such a person to use

*Reprinted from *Educational Technology, 10,* May, 1970, pp. 14-17, by permission of the publisher and the author.

the products he develops. The teacher functioning as a curriculum processor believes that behavioral objectives are one of the tools which he uses in curriculum development—so that students can be freed from their traditional dependence on teachers. In essence, the role of the curriculum processor involves translating school district curriculum guides or other curricular sources into desired teacher and student behaviors, by developing and implementing individualized learning materials.

The title of this paper indicates a two-fold focus—on behavioral objectives in the curriculum and on the new role of the teacher as curriculum processor. Concentrating on these two facets of the school necessitates distinguishing between *curriculum* theory and *instructional* theory.

Curriculum theory, as the term is used here, relates to the derivation, specification, selection, mediation, and assessment of behavioral objectives. These topics represent the structure around which this paper is built. Skills in these areas are essential if the curriculum processor is to prepare behaviorally oriented learning materials for use by individual students and small learning teams.

Instructional theory, on the other hand, is concerned with the environmental conditions which are necessary both for the student to acquire the desired behaviors and for him to develop positive attitudes toward learning and toward himself as a learner. Instructional theory is discussed herein whenever its inclusion serves to strengthen the case being made for the use of behavioral objectives in the curriculum. Thus, instructional theory is the fabric which covers the framework of curriculum theory and enables the work of the curriculum processor to achieve its fullest potential in the classroom.

Who Needs Behavioral Objectives?

Much of the literature on writing behavioral objectives is focused on the function of such objectives in curriculum construction and instructional sequencing. Similarly, much of the criticism of behavioral objectives deals with limitations of the function they serve in curriculum theory. Although discourse in these two areas is important, it is not nearly as critical to the training of the teacher as curriculum processor as an examination of *who* needs behavioral objectives. Only through such a discussion can behavioral objectives be placed in the proper perspective so that their limitations in curriculum theory can be overcome in instructional theory and practice.

A good example of the limitation of behavioral objectives in curriculum theory can be seen in many school districts. Despite the serious efforts of school district central office curriculum specialists to promote the use of behavioral objectives, few teacher and building administrators take them (either curriculum specialists or behavioral objectives) seriously. For example, curriculum guides containing behavioral objectives at varying levels of specificity are often ignored by teachers and building administrators, rather than used for school-level curriculum construction.

In fact, in a paper pointing out the limitations of behavioral objectives, Eisner went so far as to say that "if educational objectives were really useful tools, teachers, I submit, would use them. If they do not, perhaps it is not because there is something wrong with the teachers but because there might be something wrong with the theory." [1] However, what is "wrong with theory" has more to do with the theory of instruction than with the theory of curriculum. In those cases in which behavioral objectives are not "really useful tools" for teachers, the problems most often relate to undeveloped systems of instructional implementation rather than to the inadequacy of the objectives.

There are many roadblocks to providing students with adequate behavioral objectives. The most critical one has to do with the philosophy and instructional theory undergirding the operations of many of our schools. In too many schools (with the exception of some in which teachers *are* functioning as curriculum processors) "it seems obvious that our traditional curricula—our time-honored notions about the structure and sequence of content; our preference for seated, indoor, verbal learning activities; our defensive notions about control; our limited respect for the human potential; our undemocratic manipulation of other people's choices; our procedures for being helpful; our concept of the teacher's role" [2]—all these represent untenable positions concerning the conditions under which positive attitudes toward learning develop.

To put it bluntly, we do not trust children, adolescents, young adults, or even mature adults whenever they are placed in school-type situations. For this reason, we do not permit them to make choices concerning what, when, how, and where they will learn. If they do not want to learn what *we* want them to learn, we make life so miserable for them that they have only three available choices. They can knuckle under and either lose their own identity or learn how to beat the system; they can become in-school dropouts; or they can become out-of-school dropouts. According to Clark and Beatty,

> At no time in history have we tried wholeheartedly to foster individuality, to open choice-making, to support the uniqueness of becoming effective, to demonstrate real faith in the potential of humanity. We have accomplished something of these all along because the strength of individuals found effec-

tiveness, but development has been haphazard, by chance and good luck, and in spite of many blocks to learning set up by schools. Even now we could not be altogether successful immediately, but we do know enough about the learning process and how to establish helping relations between people to make a good start.[3]

It is only too obvious that in the many decades general (non-behavioral) objectives have been used in curriculum construction, students have not been given many choices—except to *do* or *not to do* what the teacher directed. When students have been given choices while still maintaining the same old curriculum (such as occurred when students were given independent study time and a choice of places to go in "flexibly scheduled" secondary schools), abortive, laissez-faire conditions frequently developed *for which students were unprepared by earlier experiences.* However, teachers functioning as curriculum processors are able to guide students, through properly constructed lessons, into successful choices in the area where it really counts—in the curriculum.

Who needs behavioral objectives? Students. Behavioral objectives are tools which let students know where they are going so that they can then make intelligent choices concerning how they will get there. Curriculum processors who are constructing individualized curricula in the form of *student* lesson plans containing behavioral objectives are opening up one avenue for choice-making by providing media-and-method alternatives from which students can select. In a few curricular areas, notably science and social studies, teachers are even encouraging students to select and sequence the lessons they desire. Thus, the behavioral objectives the students will achieve have been opened to choice. Where such choices have been provided, students are beginning to make the further step of determining their own behavioral objectives.

If we can keep in mind *who* needs behavioral objectives and *why,* in the ultimate sense, as we are involved in preparing teachers to be curriculum processors, we can avoid many of the problems inherent in the behavioral approach. The choice is ours. We can predetermine all of the subject matter content which everyone must learn (because the teacher knows best!) and force everyone through a single sequence designed to result in the desired behaviors. Or, we can encourage curriculum processors to trust in each student's drive for finding his own effectiveness as a human being. As a result of the latter approach, the curriculum processor can provide the student with alternatives (including the student's as well as the teacher's objectives) through which students can exercise their own individuality and uniqueness in the continuous process of becoming effective.

Formulating Behavioral Objectives

The formulation of behavioral objectives can be divided into two distinct stages. The first stage, *derivation,* refers to the data sources which are employed for locating and developing objectives. The second stage, *specification,* deals with the ways in which behavioral objectives are stated for the user.

Derivation

McNeil,[4] in a discussion of forces influencing curriculum, provides a convenient classification of data sources for deriving objectives. The first data source, *subject matter,* has given us a basically verbal curriculum. This source is exemplified in Bruner's *The Process of Education.* Bruner's emphasis on the "structure of the disciplines" has provided much support for developing conceptual and skill verbalizations (typically abstractions) organized in hierarchies, to serve as the basis for writing behavioral objectives.

The second data source, society, is founded on the assumption that what goes on in schools should be directly transferable to the student's behavior in situations remote from the classroom. According to Woodruff, although "the bodies of verbal information that fill our books and lectures are related to the environment," and thus relevant in that sense, verbal information "is almost completely nontransferable" to in-life behavioral problems.[5] For this reason, the use of society as a data source would require the associated development of a "phenomenalized" subject matter as opposed to subject matter based on verbal abstractions.

The third data source is the *learner* himself. It is concerned with his needs, wants, interests, and concerns. Woodruff's model for an in-life internship curriculum takes into account the learner as a data source through the development of "projects for the production of some object or other form of satisfier the learner wants enough to motive him to work for it."[6] Those concepts and skills (in phenomenal rather than verbal forms) which are necessary for accomplishing projects would then be associated with the projects, thus making the projects serve as carriers for concept and skill learnings (hence the term "carrier projects").

Additional comment concerning the use of verbal subject matter as a data source is not necessary. This has traditionally been our most common source for deriving behavioral objectives, and should remain so in those courses (primarily at the university upper division and graduate levels) which are designed to prepare academic scholars to extend the frontiers of a discipline. However, a great deal of work, with massive funding, is needed to develop phenomenalized subject matter sources as well as pervasive societal and learner data sources upon which behavioral objectives can be formulated. But even without such input, the training of curriculum specialists and processors must encourage greater sensitivity toward a creative synthesis of all three of these data sources for the derivation of objectives.

Specification

Many articles have appeared in the professional literature concerning the specification of behavioral objectives since Mager's book, *Preparing Instructional Objectives,* was published. Most of the articles refer to Mager and identify the following three components that should be included in objectives: (1) *an action*—what the student is supposed to be able to do when he is evaluated—which is communicated by means of action words such as identify, write, list, and contrast; (2) *a context or signal*—the conditions under which the student will be evaluated—which might be implied or stated in a phrase frequently beginning with the word "given," and (3) *a criterion*—the level of performance expected of the student—in which quality and/or quantity expectations are stated.

A word of caution is needed, however, in preparing curriculum processors to write behavioral objectives for use by students. When constructing the criterion portion of the objective, care must be taken to avoid specifying quantitative expectations that might be inappropriate for individual students. In fact, such quantitative specifications might well be omitted from such objectives when preparing student lessons. Qualitative criteria against which the student's performance will be evaluated are much less of a problem. Although there is still a danger of overwhelming the student, the potential for student failure is greatly reduced through provision of a qualitative criterion.

The most important structural part of a behavioral objective is the action term. Sullivan's[7] synthesis of basic action terms is a very useful point of departure for the curriculum processor. Sullivan distilled the somewhat overlapping AAAS (*Science—A Process Approach*) action words into the following six terms: identify, name, describe, construct, order, and demonstrate. The six Sullivan terms, together with equivalent terms, in the continuum given below will help the curriculum processor write behavioral objectives in all curriculum areas. The continuum also includes an explanation of the meaning of each behavior.

(1) IDENTIFY (equivalent terms and phrases—choose, compare, discriminate between or among, distinguish between or among, indicate, mark, match, select):

The learner indicates whether or not specified phenomena (objects, events, or behaviors) are members of a class when the name of the class is given.

(2) NAME (equivalent terms—designate, label, list, state):

The learner supplies the correct verbal label (orally or in writing) for one or more phenomena (objects, events, or behaviors) when the name is not given.

(3) DESCRIBE (equivalent terms and phrases—analyze, characterize, define, diagram, explain, replicate, report, represent, reproduce, tell how, tell what happens when):

The learner represents by words (a) the structure and qualities of the objects or (b) the processes and consequences of events and behaviors.

(4) CONSTRUCT (equivalent terms—build, draw, formulate, make, prepare, synthesize):

The learner puts together the parts (objects, events, or behaviors) making up a concept. Thus, he builds or produces a product such as a drawing, article of clothing or furniture, a map, or an essay. The product itself is evaluated.

(5) ORDER (equivalent terms and phrases—arrange in a pattern, arrange in order, catalog, categorize, classify, list in order, outline, rank, relate, sequence):

The learner arranges two or more phenomena (objects, events, or behaviors) in a specified order. He may be given the names of the objects, events, or behaviors which he must order, he may be asked to name them himself as well as order them, or he may be asked to order them without having to provide verbal labels.

(6) DEMONSTRATE (equivalent terms and phrases—perform an experiment, perform the steps, role play, show the procedure, show your work, simulate):

The learner performs a task according to pre-established or given specifications. The task may involve a number of behaviors including identifying, naming, describing, constructing, and ordering (or combinations of these). The procedures the learner follows in performing the task are of greater concern than the product which may result from those procedures.

By using the above terms, variety and increasingly sophisticated levels of performance can be introduced into the lessons being prepared. Students who do not do well at such verbal behaviors as identifying, naming, and describing can still have successful experiences by selecting lessons which focus on the potentially non-verbal behaviors of constructing, ordering, and demonstrating. At the same time, terminal performances so frequently equated with paper-pencil testing can be substituted by the curriculum processor with a larger proportion of en route behavioral expectations.

Implementing Behavioral Objectives

The implementation of behavioral objectives is a three-stage process. The first stage, *selection,* is concerned with how the user (i.e., both the curriculum processor and the student) can be made aware of the alternatives available for choice. The second step, *mediation,* includes both media and methodology choices which are available to assist the student in achieving the behavioral objectives. The third stage, *assessment,* includes both student and curricular evaluation.

Selection

Mager stated that the "selection of objectives may be made in the presence or absence of information or wisdom, in the presence or absence of clearly specified alternatives, and in the presence or absence of information about implications associated with the selection." [8] This statement holds true both for the curriculum processor and for the student. The curriculum processor's work is greatly facilitated when catalogs of behavioral objectives (e.g., curriculum guides) are available which include (1) the data sources from which the objectives were derived, (2) clearly stated behavioral objectives, and (3) media and methodology suggestions and facilities requirements. Even in those cases where the data sources are primarily of the verbal subject matter variety, the curriculum processor can develop lessons which provide many alternatives for students.

Mediation

The key word, again, is choice. The curriculum processor, through his activities in the development of individualized student lessons, can provide the student with alternative media of all types, including book, non-book, and human resources. Library card catalog entry words also can be provided so that students can locate additional multi-media resources which have not been suggested or which become available subsequent to the lesson's development. There is no question but that "given an objective derived and selected by fair means or foul, it is possible to select ways [note the plural] of achieving it." [9]

The problem which remains, of course, has to do with instructional theory. *Schools must be organized so that the alternatives are honestly available to students.* This is difficult to do in schools which are built and organized like prisons, are overcrowded and oversized, and which are managed as though students should be dependent on the teacher for making most, if not all, of the decisions. Elementary schools across the country either do not contain multi-media libraries or do not make such facilities and equipment available for continuous student use. Many secondary school libraries function almost solely as study halls for doing textbook assignments. Getting teachers involved as curriculum processors can be the first giant step toward correcting such conditions.

Assessment

The curriculum processor's first assessment task, upon completion of the student's lesson plans, is to examine those lessons for internal consistency. The following questions should be answered:

(1) Do the objectives describe behaviors which might be expected to result from internalization of what is to be learned?

(2) Is the student able to practice behaviors which are identical, and also perhaps analogous, to those described in the objective by selecting media and methodology alternatives singly and/or in combination?

(3) Is student evaluation strictly congruent with the behaviors and conditions described in the objectives?

Teachers functioning as curriculum processors frequently have the most difficulty with the third question. Part of the problem is the tendency to employ terminal assessment even though an objective may call for en route assessment. The greatest difficulty, at least initially, relates to the need to rework tests in which the specified evaluation behaviors bear little relationship to the behaviors described in the objectives.

The second assessment task for the curriculum processor occurs during pilot testing and full-scale use of the individualized lessons. Were the students able to achieve the objectives? If not, were the lessons at fault? Were the prerequisite behaviors inaccurately specified or assessed? Were indicators of the achievement of the desired terminal behaviors genuinely assessable? Were students interested in the lessons? That is, did students find the lessons appropriate for accomplishing *their own objectives* as well as the teacher's? These and similar questions can be used to guide the curriculum processor in his ongoing assessment tasks.

Conclusions

Behavioral objectives are a potent weapon either for controlling human behavior or for fostering the full human potential to strive for *individual* effectiveness. We will not be successful in promoting teacher use of behavioral objectives unless we are personally committed to and therefore emphasize the *second* of these alternatives. But who knows? The choice may not be ours. "Perhaps this time it could happen to all of us," say Clark and Beatty, "for it may be that we know enough about manipulating learning to destroy the full realization of human potential." [10]

It is for this reason that a concerted effort is long overdue to develop a large number of curriculum processors at the school level. Such teachers can go far in implementing a behaviorally oriented curriculum theory which is imbedded in a humanistically oriented instructional theory.

References

1. Elliot W. Eisner. Educational Objectives: Help or Hindrance? *The School Review, 75,* Autumn, 1967, pp. 250-260.
2. Rodney A. Clark & Walcott H. Beatty. Learning and Evaluation. *Evaluation As Feedback and Guide* (Ed. Fred T. Wilhelms). Washington, D. C.: Association for Supervision and Curriculum Development, 1967, p. 65.
3. *Ibid.,* p. 66.
4. John D. McNeil. Forces Influencing Curriculum. *Review of Educational Research, 39,* June, 1969, pp. 293-318.
5. Asahel D. Woodruff. Untitled manuscript delivered at the tenth Annual Phi Delta Kappa Research Symposium, Salt Lake City, 1969, p. 3. (Mimeo.)
6. *Ibid.,* p. 7.
7. Howard J. Sullivan. Improving Learner Achievement Through Evaluation by Objectives. Inglewood, California: Southwest Regional Laboratory for Educational Research and Development, undated, pp. 15-17. (Mimeo.)
8. Robert F. Mager. Deriving Objectives for the High School Curriculum. *NSPI Journal, 7,* March, 1968, pp. 7-14.
9. *Loc.Cit.*
10. Clark and Beatty, *op. cit.,* p. 66.

Markle and Tiemann provide insight into ways to work with complex subject matter using the behavioral approach. They draw on the work of Skinner, Bruner, and Gagné on concept learning. The authors suggest that the ability to make generalizations and discriminations is behavioral evidence of the ability to "really understand" a specified concept.

"Behavioral" Analysis of "Cognitive" Content[*]

SUSAN M. MARKLE AND PHILIP W. TIEMANN

Psychologists have been studying learning ever since Ebbinghaus went to work on learning lists of nonsense syllables in the 19th century. One might expect that all these years of activity would produce a significant spin-off for education. Yet a surprising number of psychologists assert that all this research has little to do with the problems of teaching and learning in school—and behave accordingly in their own classrooms.

Two prominent psychologists are not so reticent. Both B. F. Skinner and J. S. Bruner have had much to say to educators. Certainly Bruner's cognitive approach (1960, 1966), with its emphasis on concepts and discovery learning, is far more palatable to most teachers than Skinner's (1968) operant conditioning approach, with its emphasis on responses and conditioning. Instructional technologists seem to favor the operant conditioning model as a way of talking about what they are doing. Perhaps if we look at both models of learning, we can construct a "mix" of the two traditions that really has something to say to educational practitioners.

*Reprinted from *Educational Technology, 10,* January, 1970, pp. 41-45, by permission of the publisher and the authors.

Two models—Skinner and Bruner

When Skinner (1954) boldly asserted that "The techniques are known" and should be applied to classroom instruction, a trip to his laboratory would have easily confirmed such a proposition. The operant conditioning formula requires that an analyst of behavior determine the behavior desired and the conditions under which it will occur, and then simply arrange for that behavior to occur and to be reinforced. Given a simple response, such as a bar-press or a key-peck, and a simple stimulus, such as a light or a buzzer, and a simple reinforcer, such as food or water, an animal, such as a rat or a pigeon, rapidly acquires bar-pressing or key-pecking. The effectiveness of the known techniques could easily be demonstrated to any skeptic. But educators objected to a rat psychologist (or a pigeon psychologist) saying that any of this experimental manipulation is relevant to instruction in the classroom. "Are people pigeons?" they wailed.

Perhaps some day a historian will determine why the objections to the operant model center around man's egotistical rejection of his resemblance to other teachable organisms, rather than around the more obvious deficiency of *Light-on—Press-bar* as a model of "real understanding" of a subject matter. The psychologist in the laboratory has an easy time learning how to teach—the principles *are* known—because he has such an easy time deciding what to teach.

The *Light-on — Press-bar* model suggests the formula that many early programs (and some recent ones) put into effect: Question — Answer or Incomplete-sentence — Fill-in-the-blank. In the presence of the stimulus "A molecule is . . ." the student responds with the definition that the preceding instruction had drummed into him with fading techniques. (We should note that drumming-in procedures were not discovered by operant conditioners!) But even when the student can give the correct response to every such "stimulus" presented to him, something appears to be missing. The model is incomplete.

What is missing is the real world. Early techniques of analyzing subject matter in order to determine what to teach emphasized analysis of the verbal repertoire of a subject matter expert (Markle, 1969). Of course, a physicist will give you a verbal answer if asked a verbal question. But this is not the significant part of his behavior that differentiates him from non-physicists. Any reader can verbalize like a physicist by reading *Science* aloud! Given sufficient time, he could appear even more learned by memorizing the passage. Although much of what goes on in the schools and colleges resembles this model to a frightening degree, perceptive educators are not convinced that such students "really understand" the subject matter.

What behavior would we agree upon as an indication of real understanding? Such a question seems almost absurd to a generation of instructional technologists brought up on behavioral objectives, but we insist that it is too important to be drowned in wise-cracks about non-behavioral terminology. The objective "The student will *really* understand . . ." is the only place to start an analysis of what he will be required to do, and must be kept in front of the analyst at all times.

A person who understands physics behaves like a physicist *under the same conditions* as a physicist. Given a novel slice of reality, he sees it as a physicist would and takes the same actions as a physicist would. Some part of the action may be verbalizing—naming or giving a formula, or such. But the understanding shown by this verbal repertoire is a strong function of the situation in which it occurs. Rarely in the physicist's world is this situation a verbal stimulus, such as "Define sub-atomic particle." Given a complex mixture of manipulations, machinery and observations, the key response is deciding whether or not the observed slice of reality is a member of the class which leads him to say "subatomic particle," or to flick a particular switch, or to take any other action relevant to subatomic particles.

Each subject matter is a way of looking at reality in terms of certain classes (concepts) and hierarchies of classes (conceptual structures) and stated relations between classes (principles). Gagné (1965) reasoned that the understanding of principles which state relationships between concepts depends upon understanding the concepts involved. Conceptual hierarchies are much talked of (Bruner, 1960) but seldom experimented with.* We would like to concentrate on the analysis of subject matter concepts as an illustration of what it means to analyze the conditions under which relevant behaviors demonstrating understanding occur.

Psychologists studying concept learning in the laboratory agree on what they mean by "concept." A concept is a class or category consisting of many members which differ in some ways, but which are alike in certain key ways, causing us to treat them alike. Common examples given in the literature are 'dog' and 'chair,' which obviously show that members of the class may vary in many easily observable ways and yet still remain a dog or a chair. Conceptual categories do not have to be

---

*We are not overlooking here the brilliant hierarchical analysis of information-processing skills which resulted in *Science: A Process Approach.* Problems of analyzing such "learner-based" hierarchies differ in significant ways from those for "discipline-based" hierarchies in which concepts would be organized from the higher or more general to the lower or more specific.

things—any Headstart youngster grappling with the complexity of the slice of reality that leads us to say "through" instead of "into" is learning a concept.

Most psychologists studying conceptual learning have the fun of making up their own concepts. Most imitated of all, perhaps, are the sets constructed by Bruner *et al.* (1956). The "universe of discourse" might be all the possible combinations of (a) squares, circles and triangles; (b) colored red, green and blue; and (c) pictured in groups of one, two and three. (These three attributes with three values each yield a small "universe" of 27 members, but most of the typical Bruner-ians sets included at least 81 members.) A "concept" could then be arbitrarily defined as all members of the set of 'blue pairs' or 'triangles' or 'green circles.' In the typical experiment, the student's task was to discover the concept by selecting particular members of the "universe." Upon finding out whether each selection was an instance or a non-instance, the student could determine what the defining properties of the concept were. Many students have been subjected to this game of "what-is-he-thinking-of-this-time," while psychologists fed them spoon-fuls of information in carefully measured doses, and observed how they used or misused it. A lot was learned from the game (by psychologists, that is). But, like the operant conditioner's *Light-on — Press-bar* model, it is a remote approximation of teaching and learning in the classroom.

In the first place, the "teacher" was not teaching. If the concept was 'all triangles' and the student the usual college sophomore, most of us could figure out how to get him to make the correct response the first time and consistently thereafter! In the second place, unlike the slice of reality that confronts a student looking through a microscope, the attributes or properties of each stimulus in the laboratory game were well known to the "learner." He was not learning 'triangularity'! He was merely trying to find out if triangularity was the correct answer. And lastly, the "universe" of all possible instances and non-instances of any concept was laid out in front of the student in a neat matrix. Reality, even in mathematics, is rarely so brutally logical and nice.

The instructional technologist cannot "make up" the concepts he wishes to teach. He must tease these out of the subject matter. Concepts like 'competition' or 'genotype' are, in the final analysis, nothing more (or less) than the total set of situations or slices of reality which, competent biologists agree, belong in these classes. Also, the key attributes shared by all members of the category are not so apparent to students as were 'oneness,' 'blueness' and 'triangularity' to Bruner's students. The biology student cannot look at (or more likely read about) an example of 'competition' with all the complexities the real-life instance would contain and say "Well, it has these five attributes, and one or more of them must be the key properties." Lastly, rarely, if ever, is there a "universe" of possible instances and non-instances available either to the student or to the lesson designer. It is not the same game.

But suppose we combine the two threads of psychological experimentation. There is the operant conditioner's model of effective techniques for leading the student to respond in the presence of a "stimulus." There is the cognitive psychologist's model of conceptual learning as an information-gathering game. A combination of the two might give us a model for effective information *giving*.

The concept learning model

The learner really understands a concept when he can correctly classify previously unmet bits of reality into two piles: either it is or it isn't an x. Psychologists (Gilbert, 1962; Mechner, 1967; Englemann, 1969) use the terms 'generalization' and 'discrimination' to describe what a student does. Given a new example of 'force,' for instance, a student who recognizes that this new example is a force is *generalizing*. Given a bit of reality which a physicist would not classify as a force, the student who rejects it is *discriminating*. To really understand a concept is to be able to generalize to all possible instances that might be presented and to be able to discriminate all possible non-instances, including those that bear a strong resemblance to the members of the class. These are the key behaviors that distinguish an expert, such as a physicist, from non-experts.

It might be possible, in some cases, to treat concept learning as an instance of the *Light-on — Press-bar* model, by having the student memorize the total universe of instances (Tiemann, 1969). More often than we like to think a concept is inadvertently subjected to this kind of treatment when the instructional sequence presents the student with a few examples (which he memorizes) and the criterion test of his grasp of the concept is the identification of one of the already familiar examples. If he has already seen it before, we have no evidence that he can generalize. If we have no evidence that he can generalize, we have no evidence that he "really understands." *

*Taxonomists such as Bloom (1956) have given examples of test items classified on the basis of their surface characteristics, ignoring what went on in instruction. We would insist that such an effort is futile. A long essay answer relating various trends (supposedly "synthesis") can represent rote learning, while a multiple-choice selection of the date of some event (supposedly "knowledge") can represent some high-powered analytical thinking. Generalization, as we define it, is a function of the relation between the criterion test and the instruction, and not of the particular content or wording of the test item.

When we expect a student to generalize to a completely new instance of a concept as a result of instruction, the new instance cannot be a "trick" question of his "ability to generalize." Similarly, in testing for discrimination, the "ability" to see small differences should be a function of the instruction that has taught the student how, not a function of his position as a good student. The burden on the instructional designer can become quite formidable under these circumstances.

Analysis of subject matter concepts appears much easier than it is. The first temptation for the student analyst is to run to a standard textbook and look up the definition. Perhaps in science instruction this first move is not as fraught with disaster as it is in some fields (such as grammars and some social sciences), where the definitions are likely to be useless (A sentence expresses a complete thought) or erroneous (A noun is a name of a person, place, or thing) or both. In traditional texts, definitions have rarely been tested for their effects on student behavior. A good definition *can* assist a student in looking carefully at the right aspects of the slices of reality that confront him. Although a definition may thus have a role in prompting the learning of discriminations and generalizations, the student's ability to state the definition— precisely or in his own words—is not evidence of understanding (Markle and Tiemann, 1969).

Perhaps the greatest oversight in most texts is the selection of the illustrative example. We use the singular advisedly. *No concept can be learned from a single example,* and yet how many texts present only one? A single example "is never consistent with only one concept" (Englemann, 1969). Any instance is a complicated slice of reality, even when presented as an instance of a "simple" concept. A horsefly as an instance of 'insect' is at the same time an instance of 'flying thing,' 'buzzing thing,' 'pestiferous thing,' 'black thing,' 'biting thing,' and dozens of other possible classifications. What makes it an insect? A second example might help. If we now add a bumblebee, we aid the student in determining that pestiferousness and blackness are not essential to insects, but he can still retain a concept of insects as small, buzzing, flying things with varying levels of "bite." If on the criterion test we were to present him—unnamed—with a choice between a picture of a humming-bird and a small red ant, how would he be likely to respond? For the classroom teacher whose students have "mastered" a text, a question like this is not really funny. Understanding what was really being talked about frequently goes wrong when we challenge the student beyond the safe bounds of what he has memorized. Mastery of textbook talk and of what is being talked about (reality) are different outcomes.

The key to producing the kind of generalization and discrimination that we want lies in the selection of a special rational set of examples and non-examples, based on an analysis of the concept in the real world of subject matter experts. The technique is derived from the same rationale that produced Bruner's studies of concept learning (1956), but with the complete reversal of intent, as suggested earlier. For illustrative purposes, we will use 'insect' as an example.

All examples of the class 'insect' will share certain properties in a combination not possessed by members of any other class. One student analyst* identified these properties or critical attributes as (1) three-part body consisting of head, thorax and abdomen; (2) external skeleton; (3) three pairs of legs; (4) all legs connected to the thorax. All true adult insects would share these properties, while members of other classes might have some, but not all, the attributes.

Any particular instance of 'insect' will also have many other properties: it may vary in size, color, style of locomotion and ecological niche; it may live colonially or not and have wings or not. (A more thorough analysis could have included many more "sometimes" properties of some kinds of insects.) The purpose of locating all these irrelevant properties of particular insects is to select a rational set of examples leading the student to generalize across the total set of insects. A student who says "I never saw an insect that couldn't fly" or "I never saw an insect that lived in the water" will not respond to all situations that would lead an experienced entomologist to say "insect." In other words, the novice's understanding would be limited.

A set of examples is rational to the extent that it covers all the possibilities. Our analyst chose the following: (a) bumblebee—a colonial, winged, medium-sized insect with fuzz (and buzz?) living typically in fields; (b) dragon-fly—a non-colonial, fairly large, four-winged insect living near lakes; (c) springtail—a tiny, wingless, tail-snapping insect living on the surface of the water; (d) stick-insect—a large wingless one, living in trees and matching its environment in color. The analyst has, with this selection, covered various values of the attributes he identified as irrelevant. This selection has nothing to do with the amount of practice which might be necessary for some kinds of students to grasp the concept. The analysis of the range of conditions under which expert entomologists will respond "insect" is only the first step in designing instruction.

While a student is mastering the full range of examples that fall within a class, he must simultaneously master the fine discriminations between

*The analysis was performed by a biology teacher-candidate after working through our program *Really Understanding Concepts*. Neither of us is an entomologist, and therefore we cannot verify the "goodness" of the analyst's insights into the real world of true insects. Truth and rationality are different aspects of subject matter analysis!

insects and other animals that resemble them in many ways, but which are not members of the class. If an insect has, as the analyst identified, *four* key properties, then the most difficult discriminations would be between true insects and any animal that shared *all but one* of these properties; and there will be four such key types of non-examples. Nature, of course, may not cooperate with us in the search for such non-examples among known arthropods and other small animals, as more than one analyst has discovered. Some cells in the matrix may be empty.

Bug A, for instance, would have to have something other than a three-part body, though it must have three pairs of legs attached to a middle part, and an external skeleton. Bug B, the least likely to exist, would have an internal skeleton or none at all, but would otherwise resemble a true insect. Bug C, for which an obvious set of examples exists—the arachnids, would be insect-like except for the number of legs. And Bug D must have at least one pair of its six legs attached elsewhere. The search for these non-examples, or close approximations to them, is the test of the analyst's grasp of his subject matter! Since most of these attributes are visual in this case, a creative teacher could draw pictures of all varieties of "humbugs" to test fine discrimination between insects and non-insects. When new animals are still being discovered by naturalists, we cannot be sure that Nature omitted such possibilities. We can be sure that a skillful entomologist will behave consistently, given a new animal. The student who understands will too.

Finally, the analyst is required to select as test items a completely new set of examples and non-examples, the examples representing the same kind of broad sampling of the total range of the concept and the non-examples representing the same fine discriminations taught in the teaching sequence. If the student is successful on this test, we have pretty good evidence that he sees the world as an expert entomologist does—that he really understands what insects are. He can do more than verbalize like an expert, the too-prevalent result of so much instruction. His responses have been brought under the control of the same slices of reality that lead the expert to respond. The behaviors—generalization and discrimination—are ones well known in the laboratory. The problem the instructional designer must solve is the thorough analysis of the real-world situations (the "universe") under which these behaviors occur. The expert, be he literary critic, atomic scientist, biochemist, or whatever, responds to a complex world which he, as expert, sees in a special way. Instruction that leads the student to see it in the same way leads him to really understand.

References

Bloom, Benjamin S. (Ed.) *Taxonomy of Educational Objectives.* New York: David McKay Co., 1956.

Bruner, Jerome S., Góodnow, J. J. & Austin, G. A. *A Study of Thinking.* New York: John Wiley and Sons, 1956.

———. *Toward a Theory of Instruction.* Cambridge: Harvard University Press, 1966.

Englemann, Siegfried. *Conceptual Learning.* San Rafael, Calif.: Dimensions Publishing Co., 1969.

Gagné, Robert M. *The Conditions of Learning.* New York: Holt, Rinehart and Winston, 1965.

Gilbert, Thomas F. *Mathetics: The Technology of Education. Journal of Mathetics.* Vol. I, No. 1, 1962.

Markle, Susan M. *Good Frames and Bad, 2nd Edition.* New York: John Wiley and Sons, Inc., 1969.

——— & Tiemann, Philip W. *Really Understanding Concepts.* Chicago: Tiemann Associates, Inc., 1969.

Mechner, Francis. Behavioral Analysis and Instructional Sequencing. In Lange, P. (Ed.) *Programmed Instruction: 66th Yearbook of the National Society for the Study of Education, Part II.* Chicago: University of Chicago Press, 1967.

Skinner, B. F. The Science of Learning and the Art of Teaching. *Harvard Educational Review, 24,* Spring, 1954.

———. *The Technology of Teaching.* New York: Appleton-Century-Crofts, 1968.

Tiemann, Philip W. Analysis and the Derivation of Valid Objectives. *NSPI Journal, 8, 6,* 1969.

Lindvall describes a curriculum development project in which the exact definition of instructional objectives received major emphasis. Insights provided by the author into (1) the need for writing objectives at varying levels of specificity, and (2) the practical problems encountered while defining objectives behaviorally, should be of considerable transfer value to other projects attempting to make similar curricular changes. The article also provides illustrations of curriculum development in a seventh grade social studies unit.

The Importance of Specific Objectives in Curriculum Development*

C. M. LINDVALL, *et al.*

In any final sense, efforts in curriculum development or revision are of value only if they have an effect on what happens to pupils as a result of their educational experiences. Although curriculum plans must typically describe classroom activities that will be carried out by teachers and pupils, and must describe the subject matter content that provides the basis for lessons, the plans must include more than this. If such plans are to provide the type of direction that will give the greatest assurance that there will be changes in what pupils learn, they should include

*Reprinted from C. M. Lindvall (Ed.) *Defining Educational Objectives: A Report of the Regional Commission on Educational Coordination and the Learning Research and Development Center,* by permission of the University of Pittsburgh Press and the authors. Copyright © 1964 by the University of Pittsburgh Press.

statements that tell what the pupils will be able to do after they have had the suggested learning experiences. Curriculum plans must be centered on the pupil, and they must be developed in such a form as to cause the teacher to center his attention on the pupil. This will probably not be achieved if the plans describe only the teaching activities and the subject matter content. Plans that include only these elements may too often result in a situation where a teacher feels that instruction has taken place if he has carried out certain activities or "covered" the necessary content. An important step to be taken to avoid this type of situation is to center attention on the desired changes in pupils. It is these changes that must be defined very clearly and that must serve as a focus in curriculum planning.

Of course, it is recognized that some educators will state that they are not concerned with specifying instructional objectives because they do not want to tell the student what he is to learn. They want the learner to raise questions, to develop personal interests, and to make his own decisions as to what he is to pursue. But this merely means that they have objectives of a different type. Their objectives are of the form that the pupil "will raise important questions (probably in some given context)," "will give evidence of having developed personal interests in this area," and "will carry out studies that are of interest to him." These teachers are likely to do an effective job of instruction only if they have some clear conceptions of what they expect the pupil to be like after he has experienced it. If they do not have such objectives, they are likely to "talk about" the abilities they want the pupil to have and only hope that this talking results in the general type of thing they have in mind. Also, if they have not spelled out these objectives, they are unlikely to evaluate pupil progress toward them. Instead, they are likely to develop some type of test or final examination (because this is the accepted thing to do) and measure the pupils' knowledge of certain facts and ideas.

The importance of defining behavioral objectives and the practical difficulties encountered in carrying out this aspect of curriculum planning can perhaps best be documented and illustrated by considering an actual example. To provide this type of illustration, the following pages describe certain aspects of a major curriculum development program being carried out by the Pittsburgh Public Schools and the University of Pittsburgh. Since this effort has involved hundreds of persons and includes courses from the kindergarten through graduate school, it would be impossible to look at this problem in connection with the total plan. An examination of the problem involved in developing specific instructional objectives will require that illustrations be drawn from some limited unit at one particular grade level. However, to show some of the reasons why this step is of particular importance in this type of educational planning, it is necessary to provide some general description of the overall project. For these reasons the following sections first present a general description of the CCD project and then go from this to draw illustrative materials from only one unit in seventh grade social studies.

The Curriculum Continuity Demonstration Project

The Curriculum Continuity Demonstration (CCD) project of the Pittsburgh Public Schools and the University of Pittsburgh is a curriculum development effort having certain unique emphases and goals. Its basic purpose is to demonstrate that in a central-city environment and in schools from which only a relatively small percentage of students will go on to college, it is possible to have a curriculum for the college-able student which will provide him with a continuous educational challenge at all stages of his school career. To achieve this purpose a major effort has been made to build the following elements into the program.

1. New and challenging courses of study have been or are being developed at all grade levels. Since this program is for the college-able student, these courses are offered to sections of the more able pupils.

2. Since the program is intended to offer a "continuous challenge" to the pupil, every effort is being made to develop a true "continuum" from the kindergarten through the graduate school. A course experience at any one level is to be related to and integrated with courses above and below that level. To help achieve this goal each curriculum writing team working in a given content area and at a particular school level is made up of representatives from many levels. For example, a team working on a junior high level course is composed of elementary, high school, and college teachers as well as teachers from the junior high level.

3. The provision for a continuous *challenge* not only requires that course work be challenging but also means that provision must be made for permitting pupils to progress at varying speeds. The program therefore provides for this type of flexible progression.

4. Since students involved in the program are to be faced with a more challenging learning experience and since some effort is to be made to permit each pupil to proceed at his own best pace, it is important that use be made of the most effective instructional techniques and equipment available. In doing this, however, every effort has been made to prevent the basing of any curriculum plans on any new media or equipment. That is,

curriculum plans are completely developed first, and then decisions are made as to what techniques and devices may be helpful.

The General Plan for Curriculum Development

In the work being done to carry out the program of the CCD project, there is no attempt to be radically revolutionary in the content covered or in the organizational principles involved. The work is being carried out within the structure of a large city-school system and a large urban university. Furthermore, its efforts have been concentrated in basic content areas: (1) English or Language Arts, (2) Mathematics, (3) Science, (4) Social Studies, and (5) Foreign Languages.

As was stated previously, each curriculum writing team is made up of members representing a variety of levels in the educational continuum. The overall policy in this work has been to select, for each committee, the most competent persons available, some of whom are experienced and practicing teachers and others of whom are able university scholars in the given subject, and then to give each committee almost complete freedom in planning the courses. That is, the choice of the content of the course, the organizing principles involved, and the methods of instruction that are to be suggested are left to the expert judgement of the authorities making up the committee.

Just where a given committee gets its ideas will vary greatly from subject to subject. In some content areas, such as mathematics, the recent development of rather major programs on a relatively nationwide basis has provided an important source of content. In other areas, such as in social studies at the elementary school level, a great deal of local planning has had to be done concerning organizing principles, the sequence of topics, and the exact content to be used. Of course, in all cases much use has been made of the knowledge of the experienced teacher and supervisor concerning what is of interest to pupils and what things they can be expected to be able to do, as well as the subject matter expert's ideas of what content is most worthwhile.

Procedures for Developing Curriculum Guides

Although the committees have been given the freedom and the responsibility of the type suggested above, they have been asked to carry out their work and to prepare other course materials according to certain procedures. This has been deemed necessary in view of the unique purposes of the CCD project and because of the way in which it is planned to use the materials. These procedures include the following.

Establishing a Sequence of Learnings. Since a major emphasis of the total project is on a learning "continuum" extending through all school levels, it is essential that a first step be that of determining a rather exact sequence of the topics or units to be covered throughout the grades. Once this is established, smaller writing committees can work out the details of the curriculum for any particular level or grade, but with the assurance that what they are planning fits into an organized total pattern. This list of the units to be covered over the total range of all grades is referred to as the "sequence of learnings."

Defining Desired Outcomes or Specific Objectives in Behavioral Terms. A first task of a team working on the development of a specific unit is to define exactly what pupils are to be expected to be able to do after they have mastered the unit. The emphasis here is on stating these objectives in terms of definite *pupil behaviors*. They are not to be stated in terms of what the teacher is going to do. They are not to describe learning activities. Each statement is to describe something that the pupil will be able to do after he has had the learning experience. Also, they are not to be stated in such terms as "to understand . . .," "to master . . .," "to appreciate . . .," etc. Rather they are to tell what a pupil will be able *to do* if he understands, masters, or appreciates. That is, they will be stated in terms of such pupil behaviors as "to explain . . .," "to state . . .," "to solve . . .," "to interpret . . .," "to compare . . .," "to list . . .," etc.

Identifying Suggested Activities. For each unit the responsible committee is to develop a list or brief description of learning activities that should be effective in helping pupils to achieve the specific objectives. Note that this list is intended to be suggestive only. It is not intended as a strait jacket which will prevent the teacher from employing those instructional procedures which seem most effective for him with his particular students.

Developing a List of Suggested Materials. Each particular unit is to be developed further through the identification of textbooks, supplementary reading books, other reading materials, audio-visual aids, and any other materials which should be helpful in teaching the unit.

Suggesting Evaluation Procedures. A final step that must be taken in the development of a unit is to suggest some appropriate procedures that a teacher might use in determining the extent to which pupils have mastered the stated specific objectives. Naturally, these suggested evaluation procedures must be related directly to the previously developed objectives. That is, the objectives tell what the pupil is to be able to do, and the evaluation procedures provide a means of determining the extent to which he is able to do it.

In developing the goals, the activities, and other elements of the curriculum guide as indicated in the foregoing, each committee has been asked to make certain that what is developed be directed toward a variety of types of pupil abilities. For example, they should avoid producing units that are centered solely on the acquisition of knowledge. To aid in the achievement of some balance in the abilities emphasized, it has been suggested that some attention might be given to objectives in each of the following general categories:

1. Knowledge—what the pupil will be able to name, to describe, to list, to state, to explain, etc.
2. Skills and Abilities—what the pupil will be able to do, to solve, to interpret, to work, to apply, etc.
3. Attitudes and Appreciation—what the pupil will enjoy, will choose to do, expressions he will manifest, etc.

In addition to using the above rather broad categories, it has been suggested that committees may obtain help in this task by consulting more detailed listings of categories of objectives such as those found in the *Taxonomy of Educational Objectives.*

It is recognized, of course, that in any given unit certain types of objectives or abilities may be given more emphasis than others. The important point here is that a total curriculum must be concerned with a variety of types and goals.

It will be noted that, for the most part, the above procedures are not greatly different from those that might be included in many curriculum development projects. However, it is felt that the emphasis placed on the second point, that of the exact definition of the specific instructional objectives, is somewhat unique in the CCD project. For this reason a further explanation of just what this means and a consideration of some of the practical problems involved in carrying out this step are provided in the illustration presented in the following section.

Defining Specific Objectives for a Unit in Seventh Grade Social Studies

Just what is involved in the development of specific objectives for a given unit can be illustrated by examining the work of a CCD social studies committee concerned with a particular unit for the seventh grade. In its work the committee followed the general procedures described in the preceding section, and among the units in the "sequence of learnings" identified for the seventh grade level was one on Africa. Of course, in defining this particular unit on Africa it was first necessary to do some general thinking about the types of things that were appropriate for this level. Questions of concern at this point included the following. What had the students learned about Africa in preceding units in earlier grades? What abilities or skills which are basic to work in the social studies, such as the ability to read maps, to make use of reference sources, to develop reports, etc., have the pupils acquired prior to this? How can this unit make use of these abilities and develop them further? What basic principles or streams have been used to provide structure and meaningfulness to previous units and how can they be used with this unit? In the light of present and emerging conditions what content is most important for the student to master at this particular point? Are there later units in the social studies sequence for which this unit must provide prerequisite learnings?

After giving careful consideration to the points raised by questions of the foregoing type, the committee formulated certain general statements of desired outcomes for the unit. Among these were the following:

> Determine how geography has affected the politico-socio-economic development.
>
> Recognize past accomplishments and present problems.
>
> Understand, accept, and appreciate differences among people.
>
> Understand the ever-increasing importance of Africa in the world community.
>
> Understand the difficulties faced by the United States in forming African policies.

These represent only a few of the statements of general outcomes but do serve to illustrate the type of statement that must serve as a starting point for more specific objectives. Each of these statements probably suggests several pupil abilities to the person who formulated it. If they were left in this form they would give no exact guidance to the many persons expected to use the curriculum guide. Different teachers could be developing quite different abilities in pupils and still feel that they are teaching for these goals. This, of course, would be a very unsatisfactory situation, particularly in a curriculum sequence where an emphasis is placed on a learning continuum in which what is learned at one level is built on what has been covered at previous levels. Here it is very important that a teacher at any given level have rather exact information concerning the abilities and understandings that were developed at preceding levels. Objectives that will serve this purpose must be quite specific.

The next step to be taken, then, is to look at each of these first general statements of outcomes and ask the question "What would we expect the pupil to be able to do after he has achieved this goal?" For example, examining the preceding set of goals in this way, we would think of what a pupil should be able to do after he has determined "how geography has affected the politico-socio-economic development of Africa." This could lead to such statements of pupil behavior as the following:

> To be able to describe the geography of the various regions of Africa.
>
> To be able to explain how geography has affected the economic development of at least one country from each major geographic division of Africa.
>
> To be able to explain how geography has affected the social and political development of the same selected countries.

In the same way the goal "Recognize past accomplishments and present problems" might be translated into such objectives as:

> To be able to describe, for each African country, its major sources of income and what must be done if income is to be increased.
>
> To be able to describe past and present social conditions and the problems associated with these conditions.

The goal "Understand the ever-increasing importance of Africa in the world community" could lead to such specific objectives as:

> To be able to list the contributions that African countries make to the world community.
>
> To be able to describe some current world problems resulting from recent political changes in Africa.
>
> To be able to compare the influence that certain African nations had in the world community twenty-five years ago with their present influence.

It should be noted, incidentally, that the objectives developed here are not as detailed as those that would have to be defined (either in writing or in the teacher's mind) prior to the production of a test or other evaluation procedure. The listing of such objectives could result in a curriculum document that would be rather unwieldy to work with, to say the least. However, these curriculum objectives must be so specific as to include the pupil behavior or ability involved and the type of content to which this will be applied. This was the goal in writing the objectives used in the illustration.

Some Typical Problems Encountered in Work on Defining Curriculum Objectives

In curriculum development work involving large numbers of persons and many committees, a variety of problems will be encountered in the effort to define goals and objectives. From the work on the CCD project the following observations may be offered concerning a limited number of such problems.

The example of what may be involved in the production of useful objectives that was described in the preceding section should serve to illustrate the point that this more specific definition of objectives is really a step toward making them more meaningful. If such statements are left in a very general form they provide no real basis for communication. This is true not only of communication between the curriculum developers and the teachers who may later use the course but also of communication between members of a curriculum development team. Real meaning and communication can be achieved only if objectives are translated into pupil behaviors; what pupils will be able to explain, to list, to describe, etc.

The need for this can be illustrated by describing an actual happening at a meeting of one of the curriculum writing committees. This was started by someone making the complaint that "Such specificity and amount of detail is unnecessary. Teachers will know what is meant by these more general statements and be able to supply their own specifics." Since this was raised in connection with some actual statements that were under consideration, one of the other members saw fit to raise the question "Well, in this case, just what are some of the specific pupil behaviors that we might look for if the pupil had achieved the abilities suggested by this rather general statement?" The answering of this question led to over an hour of discussion and dispute, but the group was ultimately able to come up with a short list of behavioral objectives. This served to emphasize the point that communication regarding curriculum goals requires careful specification of their meaning. Also, the fact that this was no trivial task even for a group made up of competent public school teachers and supervisors plus college professors should have helped to dispel the idea that this should be no problem whatsoever for the typical teacher.

This actual happening served to reinforce greatly the feeling of the project staff that, if a curriculum committee is to come up with a product that will be really useful to teachers, there probably should be at least one member of the committee who, at appropriate intervals, will raise the question "Now just exactly what would a pupil be able to *do* if he had achieved or made progress toward this objective?" If this person made no other contribution whatsoever, his total impact on the final result would probably be of the greatest importance.

This insistence upon having objectives worded in terms of what a pupil should be expected to be able to do also contributes to a desirable uniformity in such statements. With a uniformity of this type it is possible to compare objectives suggested by one committee member with those suggested by another, and it is possible to combine contributions from the several members into one meaningful list. Without it the objectives submitted by any one member will most likely be worded quite differently from those submitted by others. People typically have such different ideas as to how objectives should be worded that one person, perusing another's work, is likely to make the statement, "But that is not what is meant by an objective." In the work of curriculum development committees, much time will be saved and needless discussion avoided if from the very beginning it is clear to everyone just what form should be followed in stating objectives.

Another aid to communication and to smoother committee work is the careful definition of certain terms that are likely to be used quite regularly. Just as people have different ideas as to what is meant by an objective so they have different ideas as to what is meant by such terms as "concepts" and "principles" and similar frequently used words. This can result in confusion and an unnecessary waste of time. For example, it may be decided that in developing a particular unit each committee member is to bring in a list of "concepts" that pupils might be expected to master. Typically this will result in some members bringing in a list of terms or words while others submit lists of generalizations or principles while still others may bring in a list of a combination of some of the above. This type of confusion and the related waste of effort can be avoided if prior clarification is made of just what it is that is desired. The development of useful objectives must be an exercise in the careful use of language, and time spent in determining the exact meaning of frequently used words will be well invested.

Summary

In summarizing some of the points made in preceding sections it should be said that one key, and somewhat unique, aspect of the curriculum development work of the Curriculum Continuity Demonstration project has been the emphasis placed on the need for including in each unit a careful listing of the behavioral goals to be achieved. The reasons for this emphasis are found in the basic purposes of the CCD project. These reasons may be summarized in the following points.

1. The CCD program is concerned with providing a challenging experience for the able student. The program is pupil-centered. It involves plans for meeting the needs of individual students. This includes both the setting up of sections for able students and the use of flexible progression on an individual basis. This quality of "pupil-centeredness" is an essential aspect of the program and it is important that it be emphasized to all teachers by making certain that the objectives are pupil-centered.

2. With an emphasis on individualizing instruction and on flexible progression it is essential that rather exact information be available concerning the knowledge and abilities that a pupil should possess after he has had the experience provided by a given unit or term. Only when this is available can we make an evaluation of whether or not the fast student has mastered a given unit and should be permitted to move on to the next. This type of information is essential also if flexibility is to involve having pupils skip certain courses in favor of more advanced work. If decisions of this sort are to be made with any validity, some rather exact information on what pupils are to gain from given courses or units is a necessity. In any program where pupil advancement is based on achievement rather than on time spent in a given class, objectives must be carefully and specifically defined.

3. Central to the purpose of the CCD program is the development of a true learning continuum running through all grades and levels of education. If this is to result, it is necessary to know exactly what abilities a pupil should have after a given experience. Only in this way can gaps and duplication be avoided. In a sense this stress on the importance of continuity is only a more precise emphasis on the rather obvious point that learning is cumulative, that what a pupil learns in grade 2, for example, is built on what he learned in grade 1. The effort of the CCD program is to make this continuity more systematic than is typically the case.

Perhaps it should be stressed here that this is not an effort to put a new type of strait jacket on a teacher or a program. Just how a teacher helps pupils to arrive at various levels of ability is still left very much to the individual teacher. He can use his special talents, the students' peculiar aptitudes and interests, and various environmental factors in ways which seem most appropriate and effective. But the idea of an educational "system" demands considerable uniformity in goals for basic courses. This obvious point manifests itself in our nation's schools in such things as the fact that a pupil can transfer from a school in one city to a school in another without major problems and that pupils in the freshman class of any college come from a variety of high schools and all seem quite well prepared for a common college experience. The need for considerable uniformity in abilities developed has long been recognized as basic to the functioning of a broad-scale program of education.

4. Present-day schools have available to them a variety of techniques, materials, and devices that may be effective aids to learning. An aim of the CCD program is to make use of whatever procedures and equipment will prove most useful for accomplishing the given educational tasks. However, every effort has been made to avoid the situation where things that are new are adopted merely because they have become popular or look interesting or exciting. New materials or techniques must be chosen on the basis of their effectiveness in helping pupils achieve established goals. Decisions of this type can be made validly if the goals to be achieved have been clearly and specifically defined.

The following article provides an illustration of educational objectives at two levels of specificity—(1) the most general type of educational goal, and (2) the more specific type of course or unit objective. These levels are comparable to the lower two specificity levels identified in the selection by Krathwohl—"program planning" and "curriculum development." Kapfer provides an example of how district-level behavioral planning can provide guidance for school-level instructional materials development.

Behavioral Objectives and the Gifted*

Miriam B. Kapfer

In current efforts toward curriculum development and program assessment at all levels of education probably no area of educational thought is receiving greater emphasis than the need to prepare functionally useful objectives. The planners responsible for developing and subsequently evaluating educational programs and the teachers and administrators concerned with the day-to-day operation of these programs are finding it increasingly necessary to be more specific, more precise, and more observable in the delineation of their objectives.

This challenge of adding precision and clarity to goal statements was faced early in the development of a pilot program for the talented, which was inaugurated in 1968 by the Clark County School District, Las Vegas, Nevada. The broad goals of the District's instructional program, which serve as a guide for the education of all students in the

*Reprinted from *Educational Technology, 8,* June 15, 1968, pp. 14-16, by permission of the publisher and the author.

county, are outlined in the District's official "Statement of Educational Principles." The Board of School Trustees specifies in this official statement that "the most important educational task assigned to the school is that of *maximum intellectual development of students.*" Consistent with this priority, the Board has identified as desirable other educational goals such as the ability to "think clearly," "draw conclusions," and "take action based on evidence," as well as proficiency in "problem-solving" and in the "acquisition of knowledge."

Based on the premise that any new curriculum in the District should be developed within the philosophy and guidelines just described, the pilot program for the talented was designed with these broad goals in mind. While such goals for the education of the gifted are not unusual, or indeed different from the goals of education for all children, neither are they unimportant.

The central problem, thus, revolved not around the value of the goals, but rather around a means to operationalize them (1) for initial curriculum planning for the gifted, (2) for on-going efforts to individualize instruction in the gifted program, and (3) for later evaluation of the effectiveness of the program.

Initial efforts to operationalize the above broadly stated goals drew heavily on the work of Guilford* with regard to cognition, divergent production or thinking, and convergent production or thinking. According to Guilford, cognition means "discovery or rediscovery or recognition." The two kinds of productive-thinking operations "generate new information from known information and remembered information." In divergent-thinking operations, Guilford points out that we "think in different directions, sometimes searching, sometimes seeking variety." In convergent thinking, by contrast, the information "leads to one right answer or to a recognized best or conventional answer."

Guilford's structure-of-intellect model was particularly useful in selecting and defining classifications of intellectual ability in the area of divergent production. The following five areas were identified:

1. Fluency—the "ready flow of ideas."
2. Flexibility—"readiness to change direction or to modify information."
3. Originality—production of responses that are "statistically rare," "remotely related," and/or "clever."
4. Sensitivity—awareness of problems and ability to adapt quickly to new situations.
5. Elaboration—expanding upon ideas by filling them out with detail.

*Guilford, J. P. *The Nature of Human Intelligence,* McGraw-Hill, 1967.

In working toward an operational statement of convergent production abilities (i.e., "the drawing of fully determined conclusions from given information), efforts were focused on two areas: (1) the research skills of gathering and selecting, and (2) the research skills of assimilating and analyzing.

How can these ideas concerning intellectual abilities be stated behaviorally so that the teacher can plan effectively for materials, methods, and evaluation?

First, this task could undoubtedly be accomplished in a variety of ways; hence, the scheme of behavioral objectives which follows should be considered merely representative rather than rigid or exhaustive.

Secondly, the reader will notice that the format of each of the performance statements is very nearly uniform. This pattern was chosen, again, not because it constituted the only possibility, but rather because it was a useful way to include the important components of (1) the conditions under which the anticipated behaviors will occur (2) the name of the observable behavior(s) which reflects student attainment of each objective, and (3) the means of identifying acceptable levels of performance.

To summarize, the behavioral objectives listed below relate to the broad goals involved in maximum development of a child's intellectual abilities. As an initial step in translating these goals into useful objectives for program development and evaluation, the convergent and divergent thinking abilities associated with problem solving and critical thinking were behavioralized.

At a subsequent stage of development, of course, these objectives must be further amplified in terms of content applications; teachers will need to associate learning media and methodology with the objectives and re-write them at student levels. Thus, the statements which follow represent a behavioral point of departure for classroom teachers in augmenting and communicating district-level goals to students.

I. *Divergent Thinking* (defined as unlimited solutions to problems)

A. *Fluency*

The student will be given an oral or written stimulus in the form of a problem.

He will be able to respond by stating, orally or in writing, a number of solutions to the problem.

The responses (as measured by a choice of checklists, teacher observations, teacher evaluation, and teacher-made exercises) will be rated on the bases of number and of fluency, where fluency is defined as the free flow of ideas.

B. *Flexibility*

The student will be given two or more problems requiring him to change his patterns of thought from one category to another.

He will be able to respond by stating solutions to the problems.

The responses (as measured by a choice of checklists, teacher observations, teacher evaluation, and teacher-made exercises) will be rated on the basis of variety within two or more categories.

C. *Originality*

The student will be given a problem which is totally unfamiliar to him.

He will be able to respond by stating ideas or solutions to the problem.

The responses (as measured by a choice of checklists, teacher observations, teacher evaluation, and teacher-made exercises) will be rated on the bases of newness and uniqueness.

D. *Sensitivity*

The student will be given oral, written, or physical stimuli which affect his environment.

He will be able to respond by identifying problems and by adapting his oral, written, or physical behavior to fit the new situations.

The responses (as measured by a choice of teacher observations and sophisticated checklists) will be rated on the basis of sensitivity (awareness) as indicated by rate and appropriateness of adaptation. The following criteria of "appropriateness" will be used. Can the student . . .

1. Identify inconsistencies or deficiencies in a situation?
2. Formulate and test hypotheses concerning the inconsistencies?
3. Formulate and test hypotheses concerning the deficiencies?
4. Modify hypotheses concerning the problem situation?

E. *Elaboration*

The student will be given a problem involving a body of accumulated information or materials.

He will be able to respond by stating descriptions which

result from his elaboration and expansion of the existing accumulated information or materials.

The responses (as measured by a choice of checklists, teacher observations, teacher evaluation, and teacher-made exercises) will be rated on the bases of the degree of expansion, through attention to detail, of the accumulated information or materials, as well as on the degree of meaningfulness of the descriptions which result from expansion. The following criteria of "meaningfulness" will be used. Can the student . . .

1. Add details to a completed picture?
2. Supply additional harmonic or contrapuntal lines for a completed musical score?
3. Describe additional embellishments to a short story?
4. Contribute additional detailed steps to planning an event?

II. *Convergent Thinking* (defined as leading to a right answer or to a recognized best or conventional answer)

A. *Research Skill: Gathering and Selecting Pertinent Data*

The student will be given a research problem requiring the obtaining of data for its solution.

He will be able to obtain data by using library (organized) resources and other available (non-organized) resources.

The body of data, and therefore the research skills involved in gathering and selecting it (as measured by a choice of checklists, teacher observations, teacher evaluation, and teacher-made exercises), will be rated on the bases of quantity and quality (pertinence) for the given problem.

B. *Research Skill: Assimilating and Analyzing Data*

The student will be given a research problem together with a body of related and unrelated information.

He will be able to respond by producing statements which arrange, reorganize, and manipulate the relevant information.

The responses (as measured by a choice of teacher-made tests and standardized tests) will be rated on the bases of the number and types of units, classes, and systems which result during the arranging, reorganization, and manipulation (assimilation and analysis) process.

*The need to revise and update
teacher preparation programs has
been pointed out repeatedly by educators concerned with meeting the
changes and challenges on today's
educational scene. Yarington describes an experimental, perfor-
mance-oriented program for training
reading specialists at the University
of Massachusetts. Because the program is not based on traditional
standards such as time spent or
courses completed, the students in
the program progress when individually ready along a variety of instructional routes. They are evaluated on
the basis of the quality of their performance on specified criteria.*

A Performance Curriculum for Training Reading Teachers*

DAVID J. YARINGTON

In a recent guest editorial in the *Journal of Reading,* Niles (1969) advised that "The textbook-lecture-examination course in which the participants may never see or work with a child must be reexamined and a more imaginative and practical approach devised."

Similarly, certification standards for reading specialists have been reviewed and attacked many times (Cook & Kolson, 1963; Kinder, 1968; Yarington, 1967). In fact, a majority of the states have no

*Reprinted from the *Journal of Reading, 13,* October, 1969, pp. 21-24, by
permission of the publisher and the author.

certification standards for reading specialists, while the states that do have standards express them in time-in-course terms. It is interesting to note that the recently revised statement of the roles, responsibilities and qualifications of reading specialists, formulated by the Professional Standards and Ethics Committee of the IRA (1968), described qualifications of reading specialists mostly in time-in-course terms, yet the roles and responsibilities were described in *behavioral* terms. Neither teacher preparation nor certification requirements in reading are meeting the needs of the twentieth century.

A logical scheme for preparing teachers or reading specialists for particular roles and responsibilities, or behaviors, is to devise a performance curriculum. Stated simply, trainers of reading specialists must specify behavioral objectives by devising performance criteria with evaluation implicit, and provide appropriate instruction to meet the objectives.

The concept of instructional objectives certainly is not a new one. Bloom (1956), Krathwohl (1964), and Mager (1962) are becoming household words in teacher preparation institutions. Recently, Eisner (1968) has added the concept of the expressive objective:

> An expressive objective does not specify the behavior the student is to acquire after having engaged in one or more learning activities. An expressive objective describes an education encounter. . . . [and] provides both the teacher and the student with an invitation to explore, defer or focus on issues that are of peculiar interest or import to the inquirer. An expressive objective is evocative rather than prescriptive.

If one accepts Eisner's concept, and the subjective evaluation which must accompany it, then the threat of a *totally* behavioral curriculum is allayed. One may include reflective, creative thinking activities and group discussions in a performance curriculum.

At the School of Education, University of Massachusetts, a performance curriculum for training reading personnel at both the undergraduate and graduate levels is in its experimental stages. During the fall semester, 1969, the curriculum will be instituted. No traditional reading courses will be offered. Lists of performance criteria with multiple instructional alternatives will be available. The first few years of the curriculum will require constant evaluation and revision of the performance criteria and program. The curriculum is part of and will be supported by a larger *Model Elementary Teacher Education Program* (1968) for which a large scale feasibility study is underway.

The major components of the performance curriculum are performance criteria, instructional routes, and credit.

Performance Criteria

Over forty specific performance criteria have been developed covering the knowledge and experiences generally specified in traditional reading preparation programs at the undergraduate and graduate levels, with several innovations. The performance criteria are not arranged in a specific hierarchy even though the successful completion of many do depend upon prior completion of others. However, there are no traditional prerequisites. Several criteria may be completed by the completion of one. For example, the completion of a large scale research study may satisfy lesser criteria for research tools, etc.

Since graduate offerings are open to undergraduates at the School of Education, it is conceivable that an undergraduate may complete most of the requirements for reading specialist certification under IRA standards. Providing competent specialists at the B.A. level would help alleviate the great demand across the country for trained personnel.

The major feature of performance criteria is that they are not time oriented. Some candidates, especially inservice candidates, may successfully pass a criterion on a pretest with no instruction, receive the credit, and move on to another. The use of performance criteria, then, provides an individualized program through which candidates may move as quickly or slowly as their needs and abilities allow.

The performance criteria provide a variety of practical experiences and intellectual endeavors. Perhaps the most important criterion is the one labeled "additional individual projects as designed by faculty and students." This criterion allows the flexibility of designing an alternative for a relevant experience not delineated. For example, a student might receive credit for teaching in a summer reading program under supervision of a faculty member.

A sample performance criterion is as follows:

> *General Objective:* Demonstrate skill in conducting a directed reading lesson.
>
> *Performance Criterion:* Given five children, candidate will conduct a directed reading lesson, demonstrating preparation, a teaching skill (e.g., reinforcement), and follow-up activities and be judged satisfactory by a panel of two faculty.
>
> *Instruction:* (Instructions for a procedure to meet the above criterion are listed here.)

Instructional Routes

In order for candidates to meet the various performance criteria, instruction must be provided. We accept the theory that as teachers have different teaching styles, college students have different learning styles. For each performance criterion, then, at least three alternative instructional routes are provided. The instructional routes are in the form of: a) supervised practical experiences, b) lectures, c) reading lists, d) observing demonstrations, e) individually arranged. For example, here are four alternative instructional routes for the directed reading lesson used to illustrate performance criteria in the preceding section:

1. Practice in the micro-teaching clinic
2. Reading in the library (appropriate reading list provided)
3. Attending lecture-demonstration
4. Practicing in public school classroom

The candidate chooses one or more alternative instructional routes and attempts to meet the criterion when he feels he is ready.

Credit

Since the performance curriculum is not course oriented, each performance criterion must be assigned credit. This may be done by assigning modular credit (x modules equal x hours of credit) to the criteria or by assigning portions of hour credit to each criterion.

Summary

The performance curriculum for training reading specialists is not time-based. It provides for individual differences, flexibility, and a significant departure from traditional time-in-course teacher preparation. Ultimately, reading teachers and specialists will emerge from this program having been judged by performance standards. When seeking certification or employment, the candidate will offer a portfolio of experiences and perhaps even video tapes of his teaching performance, rather than a transcript of courses and grades.

REFERENCES

Bloom, B. (Ed.) *Taxonomy of Educational Objectives, Handbook I: Cognitive Domain.* New York: David McKay, 1956.

Cook, C. & C. Kolson. The Certification Dilemma. *Journal of Teacher Education, 14,* 1963, pp. 184-187.

Eisner, E. W. *Instructional and Expressive Educational Objectives: Their Formulation and Use in Curriculum.* Stanford University, unpublished A.E.R.A. monograph, 1968.

Kinder, R. F. State Certification of Reading Teachers and Specialists. *Journal of Reading, 12,* 1968, pp. 9-12.

Krathwohl, D., B. Bloom & B. Masia. *Taxonomy of Educational Objectives, Handbook II: Affective Domain.* New York: David McKay Co., Inc., 1964.

Mager, R. F. *Preparing Objectives for Programmed Instruction.* San Francisco: Fearon Publishers, 1962.

Model Elementary Teacher Education Program. School of Education, University of Massachusetts, U. S. Department of Health, Education and Welfare, Office of Education, Final Report, Cooperative Research Contract OEC-0-8-089023-3312 (010), 1968.

Niles, O. The Essential Need. *Journal of Reading, 12,* 1969, pp. 271-272.

Roles, Responsibilities, and Qualifications of Reading Specialists. *Journal of Reading, 12,* 1968, pp. 60-63.

Yarington, D. J. Certification for Reading Specialists. *The Reading Teacher, 21,* 1967, pp. 126-127.

As a result of working at the University of Pittsburgh's Learning Research and Development Center, Bolvin has been intimately involved with the Center's Individually Prescribed Instruction Project at Oakleaf and other elementary schools. In the article reprinted below, Bolvin identifies the individualization of instruction as a "basic theme" in current curricular reform. He focuses on the importance of clearly defined objectives in a curriculum designed for individualization. Using goal illustrations from the I.P.I. Project, he describes a step-by-step approach to the tasks of objective specification.

Implications of the Individualization of Instruction for Curriculum and Instructional Design*

John O. Bolvin

One of the basic themes permeating the educational reform movement today is the individualization of instruction. Granted this is not a new theme in education; however, the intensity of interest in it is far greater today than ever before. Some of the factors underlying this emphasis would have to include (1) the introduction of programed instruction, (2) the development of nongraded and team-teaching programs,

*Reprinted from *Audiovisual Instruction, 13,* March, 1968, pp. 238-242, by permission of the publisher and the author.

(3) the wider application of the use of computers, (4) the changing technology and its application to educational problems, and (5) the recent involvement by subject matter scholars and behavioral scientists in the more practical problems of education.

One major problem, the discussion of individualization of instruction, centers around the variety of types of school programs that are identified as providing for individualization. Some educators interpret individualization as simply providing tutorial assistance for pupils and/or providing for independent study. At the same time, there are a few interpreting individualization to mean the planning and implementation of an individualized program of studies tailored to each student's learning needs based on his competencies and his characteristics as a learner. It is this latter definition of the term that has more implication for the application of technology in curriculum planning. What then does this definition of the individualization of instruction mean to the curriculum director? Approaching this problem systematically requires the application of task analysis and of systems analysis. This means that one begins by defining the objectives, analyzing the input and output of the system, determining ways of measuring these factors, and defining and describing all the relevant conditions affecting the system. Since individualized instruction involves the interaction of persons, procedures, and materials, the necessary system is quite complex.

For clarity in discussion, a differentiation should be made between curriculum design, instructional design, and instruction. Curriculum design relates to the determination of the behavioral objectives selected on the basis of the philosophy of education and the structure of the subject matter under consideration. Instructional design is that portion of the educational system relating to factors that facilitate the learning of content, processes, etc., as specified in the statement of objectives. Elements of the instructional design would include diagnostic and evaluative instruments, materials, hardware, and environmental conditions necessary in assisting the learner to acquire the desired behaviors. Instruction is the total function of providing an integrated program of learning experiences for each student.

Curriculum Design

Objectives: A point of departure in attempting to individualize instruction is a statement of the philosophy of the educational program. Of particular importance here is the specification of goals as either stated or implied in this philosophy. Generally these goals should reflect the subject matter to be included, the types or kinds of learning desired, and the learner characteristics to be included or emphasized. For the goals to be in agreement with the definition of individualization applied here, they should include such statements as: every pupil makes continuous progress toward mastery of instructional content; every student continues to mastery of content at his own rate; every pupil is engaged in the learning process through active involvement; the pupil views the learning process as primarily self-directed; every pupil is able to evaluate the quality, extent, and rapidity of his progress toward mastery of successive areas of the learning continuum; the pupil develops a favorable attitude toward school and learning in general; the pupil may develop interest in specific academic subjects; the pupil manifests increased motivation toward academic subjects; different pupils work with different learning materials adapted to individual needs and learning styles, etc.[1] It is from these goals that the plan, operation, and eventual assessment of the program must develop.

To implement these goals, the curriculum designer must first determine the content areas to be included in a total educational program. For each of the specific areas noted it is then necessary to analyze the subject matter domain for structure, including competencies desired, conceptual hierarchies, and operating rules. For instance, in mathematics there might be counting, addition, subtraction, multiplication, division, fractions, etc. In science there might be classification, discrimination, biological measurement, inferring, etc. In reading there might be decoding, structural analysis, literal comprehension, interpretive comprehension, etc. -In the social studies there may be social relationships, time relationships, economic relationships, etc.[2] Generally speaking, this is a task that would involve subject matter specialists, teachers, curriculum designers, and social scientists. Whether it is necessary or even desirable for every school or school district to become individually involved in all aspects of this stage of curriculum design is very much open to question.

Once a possible framework for a particular subject area has been selected, the next step is to begin specifying behavioral objectives. The specifying of educational objectives is fundamental in developing an individualized system of instruction since it provides a real basis for (1) determining materials and learning experiences needed, (2) developing diagnostic instruments to measure each learner's competencies, (3) setting up each student's program of studies, and (4) analyzing teacher functions and activities. Precisely stated objectives permit the analysis of the behaviors required as prerequisites to a given objective. This analysis serves as a guide to the curriculum designer in sequencing and ordering the objectives. Regardless of the way a subject matter is structured, there is usually some hierarchy of objectives that indicates certain performances must be present before learning subsequent performances. Clearly stated behavioral objectives are of assistance to the curriculum designer in establishing this hierarchy of sub-objectives. Since the statement of an objective refers to a behavior which is some performance by the student, the more precise the behavioral objective, the more likely the measurement is to be valid and reliable.

In relation to the development of materials and learning experiences in an individualized setting, it is necessary, at least to some degree, to provide self-instructional materials. It is only through the use of self-instructional materials that individualization will be manageable within the context of an operating school situation. This means that when behavioral objectives are clearly stated, then the persons involved in materials development are better able to develop self-instructional materials that can lead the child to the performance of the desired behavior. From the point of view of teacher functions, it is the responsibility of the teacher to determine whether materials and procedures assigned enable the student to reach the desired level of performance for a particular task. To evaluate this, the teacher must know precisely what it is that the child is able to do after he has had this learning experience. It is important to note here the distinction between the behavioral statement and the process to be used in obtaining the behavior. In the first situation, you may have a sequence of objectives relating to "learning to inquire," while in the second situation, you may require the student to attain the behavioral state by inquiry. In either case, it is important that the teacher know what is expected on the part of the learner.

Techniques for writing behavioral statements have been described by Mager,[3] Lindvall,[4] and others, and may be useful to those initiating such a program. The development of any curriculum requires hundreds of such statements reflecting the generic goals of the learning process. The eventual interaction between curriculum design and instructional design provides a basis for a redefinition, reordering, and identification of additional objectives as the curriculum is implemented.

Ordering: The next major task in curriculum design is the ordering process. An essential characteristic of an effective instructional program is that it permits the student to acquire the necessary skills and competencies before moving to a next hierarchical step for which the present learnings are prerequisites. Since the structure of most subject matter does not follow a single linear pattern, it is necessary to make several kinds of ordering decisions based upon the structure of the subject matter and the goals of the program. The technique of task analysis can serve two useful functions at this stage. In the first instance, it serves as a guide to determining what objectives are useful in attaining another objective. For instance, addition is helpful in learning multiplication. A second use of task analysis is related to what critics characterize as a weakness of this procedure—that of cutting the learning experiences into smaller and smaller steps with the possibility of leading to less and less meaningful experiences. An analysis of the separate tasks involved in attaining each objective can provide a basis for establishing sets of objectives that can be organized as a unit. By grouping these related tasks together under general characteristics it is possible for the teacher and the student to focus both on the individual objective and the larger and more integrating experience.

The end product of such an analysis is a scope and sequence chart divided into levels, units, and objectives. A level in this case consists of a set of operational tasks grouped into categories, and represents a level of achievement at the end of a large sequence of work. Each category within a level would be the unit or unifying set of behavioral objectives.

Having established this scope and sequence chart, the next major question related to individualization is whether a different sequence or ordering is necessary for each learner, for groups of learners, or for selected learners, and if the developed sequence can permit such variations. At present, most individualized instruction programs provide for some degree of variation of routes through the curriculum. In the case of the IPI program as operating in the Oakleaf Elementary School, there are a limited number of variations existing which do provide a number of alternate routes for each learner over the period of a year or so. To illustrate this, it is necessary to briefly describe one of the curricula.

Mathematics is divided into subtopics such as numeration, place value, addition, subtraction, multiplication, geometry, etc. The sequencing and ordering of the objectives for the mathematics program was done separately for each of the subtopics, going from the simple to the more complex. Once this was done, rather arbitrary decisions were made as to when to interrupt the pupil's progress in numeration to begin place value, when to move from place value to addition, etc. Each of these subsets of objectives, then, constitutes a unit, and the combination of units constitutes a level, labeled A, B, C, etc. in Figure 1. The numbers in each cell refer to the number of objectives grouped together for the particular unit.

The general procedure for a student to follow in this program is to move vertically through all the objectives in A level, beginning with the nine objectives in numeration, going to the two objectives in addition, then to the two objectives in subtraction, etc., continuing through A-special topics. However, a student having mastered the objectives of A-numeration, which in this case relates to learning to count to ten, could continue to progress by going to B-numeration, which is counting to 100, thus providing one type of variation, vertical or horizontal movement. Student movement in the horizontal direction is usually the result of his own interests and desires in pursuing a topic he has found interesting or challenging.

Figure 1

Number of Objectives in Each Unit
(A Given Topic at a Given Level)
in Individually Prescribed Instruction Mathematics

Subtopic	Level					
	A	B	C	D	E	F
Numeration	9	9	7	5	8	3
Place Value	—	2	5	9	7	5
Addition	2	11	5	8	6	2
Subtraction	1	4	4	5	3	1
Multiplication	—	—	—	8	11	10
Division	—	—	—	7	13	8
Combination of Processes	—	—	6	5	7	4
Fractions	2	4	5	5	6	14
Time	—	3	5	10	9	5
Money	—	4	3	6	3	2
Systems of Measurement	—	4	3	5	7	3
Geometry	—	2	2	3	9	10
Special Topics	—	—	1	3	3	5

Another variation that exists is the assignment of the order of the objectives within a given unit. Generally, the students follow the sequence of objectives within a unit in the numerical order in which they appear. However, there may be situations in which the individual student might move from objective (1) to objective (7), with the materials for the other objectives available to him if and when he desires to use them. In this case, mastery of all the objectives is generally a requirement before going to the next unit.

A third variation is that of selecting certain objectives and ignoring others for a particular student. This differs from the second technique in that the student may or may not be required to return to the omitted objecives as a part of his program. This selective process is the most difficult to operate and should only be instituted after one is thoroughly familiar with the particular curriculum and relevant characteristics of the learner. In this process, the teacher is actually saying that this particular child does not need to know or is not capable of learning some particular content.

These are only a few of the ways that the curriculum can be modified to provide for individual interests, abilities, desires, etc. As more becomes known about the learning process and perhaps as computers become available for providing the teacher with up-to-date data, more and more variations can be built into a given program by the designer. In the early stages of development it is probably wise to consider a limited number of alternate sequences so that information relative to the alternatives can be assessed and additional alternatives can be built empirically into the design. An important consideration here, however, is the implication that this requirement has for instructional design.

Instructional Design

Once the work of the curriculum design has established the scope and sequence of objectives, the tasks of instructional design begin. In the initial stages of development, the tasks to be considered are the development and specification of evaluation and diagnostic instruments, materials, and related instructional techniques.

Evaluation: A key aspect of individualization of instruction is that each student should be permitted to work at the places in the learning sequence most appropriate for him with amounts and kinds of instruction adapted to his individual needs. Implicit in this statement is the necessity for information related to (1) what the student has already mastered; (2) the extent to which he has already acquired some of the things to be learned in his next sequential step; (3) the extent to which he has acquired the necessary prerequisites in the same content field, other content fields, and certain motor, sensory, and other skills required in learning the new behaviors; and (4) the extent to which he has had sufficient experiences related to a behavior to be able to move to the next point in his program.

Instruments to provide this information must be keyed to the sequence of a given set of objectives. Since the primary use of these instruments is to provide information to the teacher and the student for deciding the next instructional step, the information reported will be in terms of criterion-referenced scores rather than norm-referenced scores. This means that the information reported will tell how well Johnny can do a particular task, not how he compares to others in doing the task.

The first type of tests falls under the heading of placement tests. These instruments provide a profile for each student for each of the subject areas, indicating units in which the student has reached the desired criterion and in which he has not. This information can then be used to determine the first unit of study for each student. The second set of instruments provides information as to how much the student already knows about the assigned unit before he actually begins work in it. It is obvious that instructional decisions should differ for those who have little or no information about a topic and those who already know most of what is desired. These instruments are referred to as pretests. Pretests should also provide information relative to needed prerequisites specific to the learning of any desired behaviors which may not have been measured previously.

Once the student begins working in the selected areas, information relative to progress of the student and appropriateness of the prescribed materials and techniques should be available as an integral part of the system. Since one of the goals of individualized instruction is to permit the instruction to be geared to individual learner characteristics, this information as to appropriateness of assigned techniques is a must. In any case, the student should not work for long without assessment being possible. Finally, the student and the teacher need feedback of information for assessing the nature and kind of knowledge achieved in terms of the criterion that has been established. Instruments for this purpose are referred to as post-tests.

The next major set of tasks in instructional design consists of those tasks necessary in assisting the student in going from the preinstructional state (measured by placement tests and pretests) to the desired level of competence of behavior. This requires the availability of instructional materials, instructional devices, and teachers competent to use a variety of tutorial techniques It also requires the availability of information concerning learning styles, interests, and attitudes of the learner that can be used in developing individualized lesson plans.

There are several basic assumptions underlying the implementation of individualized instruction and several goals associated with the individualizing of instruction that have implications for materials development. Examples of these assumptions are as follows: (1) for individualization to be economically and operationally feasible, much of the instructional material must be self-instructional, (2) the student should be actively involved in the learning process, (3) not all students require the same amount or kind of practice to achieve mastery of a given objective, and (4) different styles of learning require different techniques of instruction. The goals of individualized instruction that have implications for materials design are as follows: (1) a pupil can proceed to mastery at his own rate, (2) every pupil is able to evaluate his own progress, (3) different learning materials are available to accommodate different learning styles, and (4) pupils are able to become self-directed and self-initiating learners.

In general, the implications are that self-instructional materials must be available for those students able to use them, the self-instructional materials must accommodate various learner characteristics (e.g., the child that is advanced in math but not in reading must have materials that can be self-instructional without requiring reading skills beyond his competencies), and the materials must provide for varying paths and branchings. Two factors that make this new instructional designer's role possible are (1) the emphasis on the detailed statement of behavioral objectives, and (2) the availability of such aids to individualization as new low-cost, easily operated technical devices such as tape and disc recorders, single-concept film projectors, other combination audio-visual machines, and computers to assist instruction.

Once the specification of the behavioral objective and its placement within the curriculum have been decided, the instructional designer can determine what minimum competencies can be expected of the learner, approximate age level for most of the students working with the materials, and the criterion level expected as a result of the instruction. Information of this kind can assist in the identification and coding of materials that are already available. For instance, in the IPI mathematics curriculum, the first objective at C-fraction reads: "Divides a whole object into halves, thirds, or fourths, and identifies an object divided into halves, thirds or fourths." [5] An analysis of the A and B level fraction units indicates the child can divide an object into halves and can identify an object divided into halves. Next, since this objective appears at the C level, students encountering this task will be primary age children (6-9) with limited reading skills. Finally, since there are no other indications shown, all children are to be vertically 100 percent competent in doing this at the time of being post-tested. Knowing these points and recognizing that this is an individualized program requiring these materials to be self-instructional for many students, the instructional designer would probably begin his search by looking at commercial films or filmstrips which can demonstrate these concepts to the students. He would probably rule out most commercially available textbooks and workbooks as introductory materials since these generally rely on a great deal of teacher explanation and demonstration.

However, having decided upon the techniques to introduce the vocabulary, concept, and manipulations, the instructional designer may wish to identify materials for practice and could then code available workbook-type materials requiring the child to discriminate between objects divided in halves, thirds, or fourths.

When the package of materials for this set of tasks has been assembled, the designer should appraise its appropriateness by how well it meets the criteria of the system.

In the case of C-fractions, Objective 1, the criteria may be:

1. Can it be used by readers and nonreaders alike?
2. Can it accommodate students who cannot readily go to the abstract of pencil-paper?
3. Can it provide varying sequences for those with varying amounts of knowledge of the behavior before beginning; e.g., the student who can identify objects divided into halves, thirds, and fourths, but who cannot divide whole objects into thirds and fourths?
4. Are the materials organized so that students requiring more and less practice can be accommodated?
5. What provisions are made for providing a variety of objects that can be divided or manipulated by the learner?
6. What are the alternative ways that the learner can demonstrate to the teacher that he can perform these tasks, and are they known by the teacher?
7. What provisions for checking the retention of these concepts are built into the curriculum?

The actual evaluation of the effectiveness of the materials of instruction must always await the ultimate test which is that of usage. As more and more schools adopt individualized instructional systems, the technique of developing materials and the design for evaluating the effectiveness of materials will require more vigorous treatment than given in the past.

Summary

The concern of educators for adapting instruction to the needs of individual students is placing more and more demands upon those involved in curriculum and instructional design. The role of the teacher in such a system makes it mandatory that he be provided with well-defined outcomes to be achieved by the learner, information as to what learner characteristics are related to what kinds of learning, sufficient information about each learner in order to assess his abilities, and a well-defined set of alternatives from which to select the means of assisting a learner to attain the goals desired. This would seem to suggest that those responsible for providing the necessary tools and information to the teacher must begin by defining the objectives of the system, then analyzing the inputs in terms of learner characteristics, determining ways of measuring these factors, and defining and describing all the relevant conditions related to the system. Only in this way will we be able to generate information to feed back into the system to assist in its improvement.

REFERENCES

1. Examples taken from goals stated for the Individually Prescribed Instruction Project, Learning Research and Development Center, University of Pittsburgh, Pittsburgh, Pennsylvania.
2. For more information see Glaser, R. The Design of Instruction. *The Changing American School.* Sixty-fifth Yearbook, Part II, National Society for the Study of Education. (Edited by John Goodlad.) Chicago: University of Chicago Press, 1966. Chapter 65, pp. 215-242.
3. Mager, Robert F. *Preparing Objectives for Programmed Instruction.* San Francisco: Fearon Publishers, 1962.
4. Lindvall, C. M. (Ed.) *Defining Educational Objectives.* A Report of the Regional Commission on Educational Coordination and the Learning Research and Development Center. Pittsburgh: University of Pittsburgh Press, 1964.
5. *Individually Prescribed Instruction Project's Mathematics Curriculum.* Experimental edition. Working Paper No. 26. Pittsburgh, Pa.: Learning Research and Development Center, University of Pittsburgh, September 1, 1967.

Esbensen describes the Student Learning Contracts (SLCs) used to individualize instruction and learning in the Duluth (Minnesota) Public Schools. Behavioral objectives play a central role in both the philosophy and design of SLCs. A sample mathematics contract is included.

Student Learning Contracts: the Duluth Model*

Thorwald Esbensen

Across the country, there seems to be a growing feeling that individualized instruction may no longer be a subject fit only for convention oratory while remaining impossible of attainment in the real-life world of formal schooling. The rapidly developing field of educational technology has given rise to the hope that the intricate problems of classroom management posed by individualized instruction can at last be solved, and that learning can proceed humanely on the basis of each pupil's personal inventory of abilities, needs, and interests.

Ideally, this approach to instruction will take the form of increasingly simplified arrangements based on the principle of self-regulation. To paraphrase that great architect and inventor of the geodesic dome, Buckminster Fuller: the proper challenge is to figure out how to do more and more with less and less. (And the history of science is a constant reminder that the most elegant solution to a problem is often the most simple.)

In this spirit, but with no implication that more elaborate models of Learning Activities Packages are less effective, a description is now

*Reprinted from *Educational Screen and Audiovisual Guide, 48,* January, 1969, pp. 16-17, 35, by permission of the publisher and the author.

offered of the Student Learning Contract commonly used for individualized instruction in the Duluth (Minnesota) Public Schools.

Six Basic Contract Components

Duluth's Student Learning Contracts (SLCs) are divided into six parts. These are: (1) Content Classification, (2) Purpose, (3) Criterion Performance, (4) Test Situation, (5) Taxonomy Category, and (6) Resources. From the standpoint of the student, the most important parts of the SLC are criterion performance, test situation, and resources. Criterion performance says exactly what it is that the student will be expected to accomplish; the test situation makes clear how this performance will be evaluated; and the resources suggest the means that may help the student succeed.

Here is an example of a student learning contract. Notice what it is that the student is supposed to accomplish (i.e., the criterion performance): Given a set of geometric plastic or wood circles, rectangles, triangles, and squares, the student is to identify each geometric figure by name with 100% accuracy.

The test situation specifies how this performance will be evaluated. The student will demonstrate his accomplishment of the criterion performance in the presence of the teacher and upon request.[1]

The resources spell out what is currently available to the student to help him achieve the criterion performance.

The other three parts—content classification, purpose, taxonomy category—are primarily for the teacher (although not exclusively so, the *purpose* of a contract presumably being of some interest to students).

Content classification simply refers to the placement of the contract somewhere in the overall scheme or outline of the curriculum. Educators are used to grinding away at this sort of thing, so no more need be said of this.

Purpose answers the question *why*. Why *this* contract rather than another? Of what *value* is it? What are its *general goals*? The category of *purpose* responds to such questions. Here, too, as with *content classification*, school people are comfortable. They are accustomed to this way of writing and thinking. Indeed, they seldom practice any other. It is not the *why* of *purpose*, but the *what* of *criterion performance* that causes the hangup. By comparison, *purpose* is easy.

(1) A clear statement of criterion performance will almost always make the required test situation fairly obvious. Nevertheless, the writer has seen instances where paper-and-pencil tests have been used to measure the accomplishment of objectives that did not call for paper-and-pencil performance. Needless to say, this is highly inappropriate.

Mathematics Contract

Content Classification:
Geometry
Simple Closed Curves
Circles
Polygons

Purpose:
The purpose of this contract is (a) to introduce pupils to simple geometric figures, (b) to present a situation in which pupils can see polygons as a special type of simple closed curve, and (c) to develop the concept that a polygon is formed by the union of line segments.

Criterion Performance:
Given a set of geometric plastic or wood circles, rectangles, triangles, and squares, the student is to identify each geometric figure by name with 100% accuracy.

Test Situation:
The student will demonstrate his accomplishment of the criterion performance in the presence of the teacher and upon request.

Taxonomy Category:
Comprehension

Resources:
A. Teacher-led presentation
B. *Using Space/Time Relations 4 (AAAS, Science A Process Approach), Shapes and Their Components,* Ideal Company
C. *Using Space/Time Relations 1, Recognizing and Using Shapes and Geometric Wire Forms and Patterns,* Ideal Company
D. Flannel board and different shapes, Judy Company
E. Parquetry Blocks, Playskool
F. The 45 Set of Tracing Shapes-TA 55, Phily & Tacy Limited, Fulham, London, England

The *taxonomy category* is used for classifying the contract according to what student skills are mainly involved. In the cognitive area, for example, the Duluth SLC uses the designations *knowledge, comprehension, application,* and *invention.* These closely resemble those found in Bloom's cognitive domain, but are less detailed.[2] The major reason for the *taxonomy category* being included at all in the format of the contract is that it enables the teacher to see, if he wishes, whether most or all of his objectives are "up on top of the water" (that is to say, largely in the realm of simple recall or recognition, e.g., in what year did Columbus discover America), or whether he has a relatively broad spread of contracts.

The SLC is generally no more than *a single page,* and is *given directly to students who are capable of reading it.* Younger, less capable students must receive this information in other ways—from the teacher personally, from other students, perhaps from sources such as pre-recorded tapes. The mathematics contract we have just examined is a case in point. It is normally encountered at the first grade level and so cannot be read by the students for whom it is intended. Other means of communicating its contents must therefore be employed.[3]

For the most part, however, when we speak of using SLCs at grade levels 3 or 4 through 12, we are envisioning their being read and used by the pupils directly concerned. As such, SLCs may be used by students on their own as instructional guides for independent learning.

Each SLC is assigned a due date, depending on what the teacher thinks about the difficulty of the contract, the ability of the student to accomplish the work, and whatever other considerations may be regarded as pertinent.[4]

Is It Really A Contract? Should It Be?

Objection is sometimes made to the use of the word *contract.* The term implies agreement between two or more parties, and it is often difficult to see what rights the learner has in the matter. This criticism

(2) See *Working With Individualized Instruction: The Duluth Experience,* by Thorwald Esbensen (Fearon Publishers, copyright 1968; paperback; $2.75), for a description of the taxonomy used in the Duluth SLCs.

(3) The *Kindergarten Evaluation of Learning Potential* (KELP) materials are based on an individualized approach to instruction, and contain excellent suggestions for working with young children. The KELP materials are published by Webster-McGraw-Hill.

(4) Some recent developments in the field of achievement motivation strongly suggest that when a viable structure of checks and balances has been worked out (including a suitable reward system), the instructional program will be remiss if it does *not* encourage students to assign their own SLC due dates.

has its greatest force in those instances where the SLC is completely teacher-made and teacher-assigned. And this, true enough, represents the overwhelming majority of cases.

However, if the teacher-made and teacher-assigned contract is currently the most prevalent form of the beast, it is also fair to say that alternative ways of using the SLC are gradually pressing for consideration. Three in particular deserve special mention.

The first of these alternatives is the teacher-made but student-assigned SLC. In other words, from the bank of teacher-made contracts, the student has the privilege of selecting those of his own choosing. This option can provide an interesting test of the belief that in matters of scope and sequence, the teacher knows best. It is the feeling of some observers (this writer among them) that the emperor may have on fewer clothes than he imagines.

The second alternative is the *student-made* and student-assigned SLC to take care of whatever the student may identify as being a weakness in his own academic armor. This is a Know Thyself approach to learning based on a procedure that encourages the student to do something about it. Of course, there will be enormous differences among youngsters in their ability and willingness to undertake this kind of analysis and self-prescription. But the basic idea is consistent with the goal of life-long learning, and should be seriously explored.

The third alternative is also a student-made and student-assigned SLC. However, instead of a deficiency orientation, the emphasis now is on leading from strength. Each student writes his own meter, as it were, in keeping with his own predilections. No concern with smooth achievement profiles here. If-I-were-king is the theme, and every student fashions his own verse.

Four Essential Philosophic Requirements

We have now described in some detail the make-up and place of Student Learning Contracts within the Duluth Public Schools. These relatively simple, one-page guides for student learning are not, of course, neutral with respect to educational philosophy. They are designed to function best in those school environments that give credence to these four elements of effective instruction: (1) learning is aided when the objectives of instruction are formulated in terms of observable student performance; (2) learning is aided when instruction takes account of each pupil's particular set of abilities, needs, and interests—including his ways of responding to different *modes* of instruction (books, tapes, films, manipulative devices, teacher-led discussions, etc.); (3) learning is aided when learners have significant opportunities to help choose the goals of instruction; (4) learning is aided when students can make genuine choices concerning *how* the goals of instruction may be accomplished. Such decisions should properly involve not only a determination of which means may achieve which ends, but also how time itself shall be spent in the pursuit of learning.

These points are hardly new. For many years, in one way or another, they have been stated and restated by educators. Is the present situation any different? Is important action any closer to accompanying all the words? We began this article by assuming so. But we must also recognize that only time will tell.

Part IV

Additional Media

Ammons, Margaret. The Definition, Function and Use of Educational Objectives. *The Elementary School Journal, 62,* May, 1962, pp. 432-436.

Baker, Eva L. Effects on Student Achievement of Behavioral and Non-behavioral Objectives. *The Journal of Experimental Education, 37,* Summer, 1969, pp. 5-8.

Baker, Robert L., Vernon S. Gerlach, Richard E. Schutz & Howard J. Sullivan. *Developing Instructional Specifications.* Inglewood, California: Southwest Regional Laboratory for Educational Research and Development, 1968, 54 pp.

Bishop, Leslee J. Technology and the Possible Curriculum. *Audiovisual Instruction, 13,* March 1968, pp. 223-226.

Burns, Richard W. The Process Approach to Software Development. *Educational Technology, 9,* May, 1969, pp. 54-57.

Cyrs, Thomas E., Jr., & Rita Lowenthal. A Model for Curriculum Design Using a Systems Approach. *Audiovisual Instruction, 15,* January, 1970, pp. 16-18.

DeRose, James V. The Independent Study Science Program At Marple Newton High School. *The Science Teacher, 35,* May, 1968, pp. 48-49.

Drumheller, Sidney J. A Model For Applying the Bloom Taxonomy of Educational Objectives in Curriculum Design. *NSPI Journal, 6,* May, 1967, pp. 10-13, 18.

————. *Handbook of Curriculum Design for Individualized Instruction— A Systems Approach.* Englewood Cliffs, New Jersey: Educational Technology Publications (in press).

Elkins, Floyd S., Ewin Gaby & Michael J. Rabalais. An Instructor + Behavioral Objectives + Multimedia = Success. *Audiovisual Instruction, 15,* January, 1970, pp. 19-21.

Esbensen, Thorwald. *Individualizing the Instructional Program.* Duluth, Minnesota: Duluth Public Schools, 1966, 40 pp.

————. *Working with Individualized Instruction: The Duluth Experience.* Palo Alto, California: Fearon Publishers, 1968, 122 pp.

Gagné, Robert M. A Psychologist's Counsel on Curriculum Design. *Journal of Research in Science Teaching, 1,* 1, 1963, pp. 27-32.

————. The Analysis of Instructional Objectives for the Design of Instruction. *Teaching Machines and Programmed Learning, II: Data and Directions.* Robert Glaser (Ed.) Washington, D. C.: Department of Audiovisual Instruction, National Education Association, 1965, pp. 21-65.

Gerhard, Muriel. How to Write a Unit. *Grade Teacher, 84,* April, 1967, pp. 123-124.

Jones, Richard V., Jr. Learning Activity Packages: An Approach to Individualized Instruction. *Journal of Secondary Education, 43,* April, 1968, pp. 178-183.

Kapfer, Philip G. Practical Approaches to Individualizing Instruction. *Educational Screen and Audiovisual Guide, 47,* May, 1968, pp. 14-16.

———— & Gardner Swenson. Individualizing Instruction for Self-Paced Learning. *The Clearing House, 42,* March, 1968, pp. 405-410.

———— & Glen F. Ovard. *Preparing and Using Individualized Learning Packages for Ungraded, Continuous Progress Education.* Englewood Cliffs, New Jersey: Educational Technology Publications (in press).

McClure, Robert M. *Procedures, Processes, and Products in Curriculum Development.* (Unpublished Ed.D. dissertation, University of California, Los Angeles, 1965), 325 pp.

McKeegan, Hugh F. What Individualizing Instruction Means to the Curriculum Director. *Audiovisual Instruction, 13,* March, 1968, pp. 232-237.

McNeil, Jan & James E. Smith. The Multi's at Nova. *Educational Screen and Audiovisual Guide, 47,* January, 1968, pp. 16-19, 43.

Mager, Robert F. Deriving Objectives for the High School Curriculum. *NSPI Journal, 7,* March, 1968, pp. 7-14, 22.

Morgan, Robert M., & David S. Bushnell. Designing an Organic Curriculum. *National Business Education Quarterly, 35,* March, 1967, pp. 5-14.

Neagley, Ross L. & N. Dean Evans. How to Initiate Curriculum Development in a School District. *Handbook for Effective Curriculum Development.* Englewood Cliffs, New Jersey: Prentice-Hall, Inc., 1967, pp. 156-168.

O'Grady, Jeannette. Clip-Out, Ready-To-Use Unit in the Language Arts. *Grade Teacher, 84,* April, 1967, pp. 125-128.

Ogston, Thomas J. Individualized Instruction: Changing the Role of the Teacher. *Audiovisual Instruction, 13,* March, 1968, pp. 243-248.

Popham, W. James. Focus on Outcomes: A Guiding Theme of ES '70 Schools. *Phi Delta Kappan, 51,* December, 1969, pp. 208-210.

———— W. James & Eva L. Baker. *Systematic Instructional Decision-Making.* Los Angeles, California: Vimcet Associates, 1967. Illustrated filmstrip, accompanying audio-taped narration, and instructor's manual, 27 frames, 20 minutes.

Stowe, Richard A. Putting Salt on the Tiger's Tail, or How to Work With Teachers. *Audiovisual Instruction, 13* (April, 1968), pp. 334-337.

Talbert, Ray L. A Learning Activity Package—What Is It? *Educational Screen and Audiovisual Guide, 47* (January, 1968), pp. 20-21.

Tosti, Donald T. & John R. Ball. A Behavioral Approach to Instructional Design and Media Selection. *AV Communication Review, 17,* Spring, 1969, pp. 5-25.

Tuckman, Bruce W. The Student-Centered Curriculum: A Concept in Curriculum Innovation. *Educational Technology, 9,* October, 1969, pp. 26-29.

Tyler, Ralph W. *Basic Principles of Curriculum and Instruction.* Chicago, Illinois: The University of Chicago, 1950, 83 pp.

Wolfe, Arthur B. & James E. Smith. At Nova, Education Comes in Small Packages. *Nation's Schools, 81* (June, 1968), pp. 48-49, 90.

Young, Martin. Instructional Methods in Continuation Education. *Journal of Secondary Education, 44,* November, 1969, pp. 315-317.

Part V

Behavioral Objectives and the Subject Matter Specialist

Part V contains a number of selections in which the need, construction, classification, and use of behavioral objectives are considered from the subject matter point of view. Both the elementary and secondary levels are represented. Illustrative needs and objectives are presented in art, language arts, mathematics, music, science, and several job training areas. Of course, examples of behavioral objectives in these and other fields can also be found in articles which, due to their primary focus, were included in other parts of the book. References to supplementary examples in a variety of subject matter areas are included in the Additional Media section for Part V.

Bullard cites recent developments which illustrate the need for behavioralized educational goals in art. The arts have generally been more reticent than the sciences to adopt the behavioral approach to curriculum development and evaluation. Thus, Bullard's comments regarding the value of behaviorally stated art objectives are of special interest. He sees operationalized art curricula as contributing both to improved teaching and learning situations and to needed redefinition of the role of art in education.

State Your [Art] Objectives Behaviorally*

JOHN R. BULLARD

Prior to the Conference on Curriculum and Instruction Development in Art Education, the project director asked state directors of art and presidents of state art education associations what they considered the chief obstacle to curriculum development in the field.[1] The project report included segments of letters responding to the question. Obstacles listed seemed to fall under about a dozen categories. Four of these barriers were repeated in five or more of the responses printed in the report. These were: 1) the shortage of qualified personnel; 2) the lack of funds; 3) the lack of value of art in the eyes of the general public; and 4) the lack of value of art in the eyes of the school administrators.

The first two of these obstacles, of course, are not unique to art

*Reprinted from *Art Education, 22,* January, 1969, pp. 26-27, by permission of the publisher and the author.

education; other disciplines complain of the same problems. However, the scarcity of funds and good art teachers and art administrators may also be the result of the other two barriers, i.e., the poor image of art education in the eyes of the general public and the school administrators.

During that same conference, each participant was asked to select from a list the obstacles and needs which seemed most critical to art education. Lack of public awareness of the role of art in general education was ranked as the number one obstacle, while better communication was listed as the major need.[2]

The implication is that the lack of a good public image is the result of professional art educators' inability to communicate. The complete validity of such a position is questionable. Although the majority of art teachers may have a difficult time convincing the nonartist of the value of art in education, whether he be administrator, parent, or student, it is probably not because the art educator is too inarticulate to be interpreted, but because he defends his position with generalizations that he is rarely able to support with concrete evidence.

Tumin suggests that in our efforts to effect educational change we can learn from the experience of the nation in its attempts toward racial integration. He proposes that, in the beginning, small changes are more successful than an attempt at ". . . ending racial discrimination by ordering desegregation without even trying to remove prejudicial feelings."[3]

The promising of miracles by art educators will do more harm than good if they cannot show evidence of such success. If the objectives of art education are stated realistically and operationally in such a manner that the "proof of the pudding" is in the demonstration of the desired behavioral change in the student, the image of art education can improve its stature in a surefooted manner. The analogy here might be that of reaching the top of a tree by carefully climbing from the lowest limb to the highest branch, but firmly establishing a good grip and adequately appraising the strength of the present position before proceeding to a higher level; this approach would be in contrast to the method of taking a "flying leap" at the top branch with the hope, first, that it can be grasped, and second, that it is of substantial strength to support the load that it must bear.

In many instances, art educators cannot deliver these promised miracles. Approaching art education in terms of specific goals which can be shown as contributing factors toward the more general goals may be the most effective way for the discipline to demonstrate its worth.

By approaching the problems of art education from this more restricted point of view, the profession could also capitalize on the theory and techniques of programmed instruction.

Programmed instruction could challenge art educators to communicate to the educational policy makers just what they are trying to do. Current statements of objectives found in art lesson plans, textbooks, course descriptions, state curriculum guides, and professional association creeds fail to do this.

Although it is not the purpose of this article to propose that art education adopt the use of programmed instruction in its curriculum, the following research suggests that programs could be valuable tools when properly used by art educators.

Smellie concluded in his doctoral dissertation that photosketching, a graphic technique, could be successfully taught in autotutorial carrels.[4] Diamond tested the effectiveness of programming college humanities students through an instructional learning sequence in an art gallery. He used a 56-page branching program booklet on Renaissance art, which guided the students through the show. The reaction to the program was favorable or enthusiastic by 95% of the students.[5] Quirke concluded from her doctoral study which used a 95-page programmed text with 147 illustrations that programmed instruction can change attitudes and improve creative behavior.[6] Hofer experimented with the problem of teaching manipulative operations to relatively large groups. Programming "how-to-do-it" projects reduced problems of how fast to present a demonstration, when to prepare and present a demonstration, and how to accommodate those who are absent.[7] Beck successfully taught drafting skills by a program designed to teach "accumulated precision iconic responses" with a teaching machine.[8]

Concepts used by the advocates of programmed instruction must be seriously considered by art educators. Behavioral objectives, i.e., objectives stated so that results of a learning experience can be measured, would enable the teacher to demonstrate that he has, in fact, accomplished the task which he originally stated as his goal.

Asahel Woodruff, reporting his evaluation of the Conference on Curriculum and Instruction in Art Education, stated, "The potential contributions [of art education] should be stated in the form of behavioral objectives. This notion appears to provoke some feelings that the essence of an esthetic field might be violated by forcing it into something as highly structured as a behavioral act. The notion is relatively new in this field and not altogether digestible yet."[9]

L. P. Greenhill, in his evaluation summary of the project to study the uses of the newer media in art education, states that, "Art educators need to sharpen up and define their teaching objectives in terms of what the learner should be able to do as a result of a given art experience or series of experiences." [10] Lanier, [11][12] Ecker [13][14] and Quirke [15] have implicitly or explicitly made similar statements in their writings on programmed instruction.

An area of special concern to art educators historically is creative development. What is creativity? Is novelty creativity or trivia? If we cannot define, operationally, the components of creativity, it is questionable whether or not we can teach it. Unfortunately, "creativity" has become a word to hide behind for all too many unskilled and esthetically insensitive artists and art teachers. Most teachers hope to produce creativity and similar outcomes as a result of their instructional strategy; but the majority are typically at a loss to describe what they do to assist the student in being creative aside from being permissive and not imposing too much structure.

Objectives of "developing creativity, awareness, good taste, etc.," are acceptable only if they can be defined in terms of the terminal behavior required of the student. A statement of objectives will communicate the intent of the lesson or unit of instruction to the degree that it describes what the learner will be doing when demonstrating his achievements, states the conditions under which this behavior must be displayed, and defines the ways of knowing when a criterion has been met. It is recommended that all art educators read Mager's book *Preparing Objectives for Programmed Instruction* [16] if they sincerely wish to write useful instructional objectives.

Conscientious teachers try continually to improve their skills by altering their methods, but most art teachers are hampered by goals, aims, and objectives that are far too abstract. Teachers who attempt to write instructional programs could become better teachers because they begin to understand their objectives in terms of behavioral outcomes to be displayed by the learner. The process of becoming more operational, or less abstract, provides added insight into the teaching-learning process.

The old lesson plan, with its vague objectives, has had its day. Our objectives are not "to appreciate design," but "to be able to demonstrate an understanding of good design by writing six reasons why design sample 'A' is functionally and/or aesthetically better than design sample 'B,' etc."

Fleming has developed a useful taxonomy of behavioral objectives. [17] Summarized, the types of objectives are: 1) knowledge, requiring the learner to recall, recognize, reproduce; 2) analysis, requiring the learner to separate, identify, compare; 3) synthesis, requiring the learner to combine, formulate new relationships, generalize; 4) application, requiring the learner to use information or skills; and 5) appreciation, requiring the learner to demonstrate a desirable interest, or favorable attitude. It should be repeated that student behavioral objectives must be stated in terms of observable behavior, requiring the learner to do something to enable the teacher to evaluate his behavioral change.

Once objectives are adequately stated in behavioral terms, it is time to decide upon a method of instruction. There are an extremely large number of 8mm single-concept film loops, 16 mm films, filmstrips, and useful instructional "programs" available to the art educator. Other alternatives include textbooks, videotapes, studio exercises, and teacher prepared study guides, lectures, and demonstrations. Naturally these alternative methods vary in efficiency in terms of fulfilling specific educational objectives.

The discipline of the visual arts is composed of a body of information or facts which is necessary for thinking and talking about art, and a number of skills which are necessary for producing art products. This information and these skills can be defined, and it is possible to evaluate learning on the basis of measured behavior.

By carefully defining the more specific objectives of the art program, i.e., use of specific tools and/or media, development of vocabulary, ability to defend design decisions, and specific cognitive-motor skills such as perspective drawing, the profession will be in a better position to demonstrate that it is accomplishing what it has set as its educational objectives.

If these specific objectives can be shown to make an important contribution to the broader, more abstract objectives of awareness, creativity, problem solving, appreciation, and various other generalizations used by art educators, they can probably be used as a convincing argument for the role of art in education.

REFERENCES

1. A. Baumgarner (Director). *Conference on Curriculum and Instruction Development in Art Education: A Project Report.* Washington, D. C.: National Art Education Association, U.S.O.E. Grant Contract OE-C 2-6-061772-0804, March, 1967.
2. *Ibid.,* p. 122.
3. M. Tumin. Procedures for Effecting Educational Change. In Baumgarner, *op. cit.,* p. 56.
4. D. Smellie. An Experimental Comparison of the Effects of Four Treatments in Audio-tutorial Teaching upon the Factual Recall and Performance of a Graphic Production Skill. Unpublished doctoral dissertation, Indiana University, 1966.
5. R. Diamond. Programmed Instruction in an Art Gallery. *Report No. 27.* Coral Gables, Florida: Office for the Study of Instruction, University of Miami, April, 1966.
6. L. M. Quirke. There is a Place for Programmed Instruction in the Teaching of the Visual Arts. *School Arts,* March 1964.

7. A. Hofer. Teaching Manipulative Operations with Programmed Materials. *Industrial Arts and Vocational Education,* October, 1964.
8. J. Beck. Programmed Instruction Involving Accumulated Precision Iconic Responses in Drafting. Unpublished doctoral dissertation, Indiana University, 1964.
9. A. Woodruff. Report of the Conference Evaluator. In Baumgarner, *op. cit.,* p. 105.
10. L. P. Greenhill. Evaluation Summary. In V. Lanier (Director). *The Uses of Newer Media in Art Education Project.* Final Report of the National Art Education Association and U.S.O.E., N.D.E.A. Project No. 5-16-027, August, 1966, p. 67.
11. *Ibid.*
12. V. Lanier. Instructional Media: Programmed Instruction. *Arts and Activities,* December, 1965.
13. D. Ecker. Programmed Instruction: Challenge or Threat to Art Education. *School Arts,* October, November, and December, 1963.
14. D. Ecker. Teaching Machines and Aesthetic Values. *N.A.E.A. Studies in Art Education,* 3:8-15, Spring, 1962.
15. Quirke, *op. cit.*
16. R. Mager. *Preparing Objectives for Programmed Instruction.* San Francisco: Fearon, 1962.
17. M. Fleming. *Instructional Illustrations: A Survey of Types Occurring in Print Materials for Four Subject Areas.* Bloomington: Indiana University, November, 1966. Project No. N.D.E.A. Title VII A Project 1381, Grant No. OE-7-24-0210-279.

Caffyn suggests the "terminal be-haviors" approach to curriculum de-velopment in the language arts. In other words, the author begins by listing examples of desired adult competencies in the areas of listen-ing, speaking, reading, and writing. She recognizes that day-to-day in-terim objectives in the language arts must be closely tied to desirable long-range behaviors, and also that intangible, affective learnings are often reflected in cognitive and psy-chomotor behaviors.

Behavioral Objectives: English Style*

Lois Caffyn

Those teachers of English language arts who have become involved in curriculum study—either singly or in committee—in an effort to do some local problem solving, often feel themselves mired down at the beginning of the process in an attempt to formulate acceptable philosophy and objectives. They reach in every direction for a ready-made answer, assuming that someone else has already said it better than they could say it; but sometimes they discover that they are clutching only collected driftwood. The logs may be warped from having grown in a prevailing wind or on the half-darkened side of a hill, or they may be smooth and gray with no place to take a hold. At this point some teachers lose the will to go on with the struggle.

One basic difficulty in either accepting or formulating philosophy and objectives is that they are traditionally stated in terms of learnings that are almost impossible to detect, let alone to measure. They are usually

*Reprinted from *Elementary English, 45,* December, 1968, pp. 1073-1074, by permission of the publisher and the author.

dependent on forms of such verbs as know, understand, appreciate, develop, and enjoy. They are worded in much the same way for all levels from the second through the twelfth grades. With goals stated thus, teachers find little or no relationship between the aims and an actual lesson in a room full of students. Even learners cannot be certain of their own accomplishments.

What, then, should the curriculum committee members do to cross the quagmire and get on with constructive curriculum study and planning? They might well bypass the entire slough and come to firmer ground by another way. They could lay aside both philosophy and objectives and formulate desired adult competencies in the four language areas—listening, speaking, reading, writing—in terms of what people do. The following examples, obviously not a complete listing, are accompanied by suggestions for directions in thinking:

They listen (eagerly, courteously)
>   attend (community meetings, clubs, concerts, lectures)
>   participate (in discussion, conversation, government)
>   discuss (issues, beliefs, new knowledge)
>   converse (with poise, imagination)
>   explain (with clarity, patience)
>   seek (unassigned knowledge, interesting side issues)
>   choose (some challenging reading, stimulating dialogue, some
>   drama and poetry)
>   read (variety, for various satisfactions)
>   share (experiences, humor)
>   habitually use (preferred language forms, appropriate degrees
>   of formality)
>   employ (colorful language, interesting vocal and bodily expres-
>   sion)
>   relate (new knowledge to old, different areas of learning)
>   show (language courtesy, curiosity, emotional control)
>   demonstrate (thought through considered language rather than
>   through violence or profanity)
>   respond (to sensitivity, beauty, fine distinctions)

It has been said of reading that the important thing is not whether one can read but whether he does read. So is it with all the language arts.

When the desired long-range competencies have been formulated, more immediate competencies can be identified for primary, upper grade, junior high, and senior high blocks of grade levels. Within these blocks each unit of work and each individual lesson can be checked for validity as it contributes to one or more of the block and long-range desirable competencies. If it does not serve both, it should probably be eliminated. The relationship is usually clear.

Such desired competencies *are* the goals of language arts teaching—behavioral objectives, if one prefers current educational terminology. The understandings and appreciations of the traditional objectives are reflected in these behavioral competencies. They can be stated alongside as summaries of desired behaviors if the teachers wish. A thoughtful consideration, however, of the stated desirable ends will show rather quickly the felt responsibilities and aims of the language arts teachers, the convictions that make them tick as teachers. These, stated briefly and directly, form the philosophy.

Is it possible, one may ask, for a learner to accomplish the behavioral competencies without the less tangible traditional objectives? It seems possible, but only if he is motivated in all his choices and habits by his image in the eyes of other people. It is not probable. Is it possible for one to attain the traditional goals without demonstration of at least some of these desired behaviors? It seems highly unlikely. Are there no silent, intangible learnings and developing sensitivities that cannot be stated in terms of behavior? There are many quiet understandings and pleasures, especially in acquaintance with literature, and there are taciturn and shy people, but some of their habits and choices will indicate their tastes. The behavioral competencies should be stated to include them.

Such behavioral objectives and philosophy are not driftwood. They are rooted in real evidence of language learning; their branches reach every teacher, every student, and every lesson; and they are especially reassuring to the curriculum committee.

*Relationships among the functions
of nongraded education, individualized instruction, and behavioral
objectives are defined by Drumheller. He recognizes that increasingly individualized curricular approaches based on learner behaviors
cannot occur independently of
changes in teacher roles and schoolwide organizational systems. Using
these ideas as background, Drumheller provides a series of charts listing desired learner behaviors with respect to concepts, skills, and attitudes in the language arts.*

Objectives for Language Arts in Nongraded Schools[*]

Sidney Drumheller

This writer is convinced that a nongraded program must have an
individualized orientation. A system where a classroom teacher uses a
variety of groupings in each subject and these groups use conventional
materials in a lock-step fashion remains a graded system.

The vitality of the nongraded school lies in that key concept, "individualized instruction." To be successful, the entire school must first
commit itself to this. It may be necessary, due to lack of funds and
materials, to compromise procedures somewhat by using groups. But
these groups would have as their central characteristic the constant
attention of the teacher to individual differences, and the justification

*Reprinted from *Elementary English, 46,* February, 1969, pp. 119-125, by
  permission of the publisher and the author.

of procedures on that basis. The traditional lock-step orientation dissolves when a school is committed to an ungraded system.

Upon analysis, only two clearly-defined patterns for curriculum organization emerge, which are poles of a continuum—these being the subject-centered approach that has controlled educational practices for 2,000 years, and the child-centered approach which has been discussed

Subject .... Child
Centered   Centered
(Lock-Step)   (Individualized)

for a half century but has made few inroads in actual practice. Other approaches tend to fall somewhere along the continuum, and are defended as an ideal compromise between the extremes. The lock-step point of view is as essential to the traditional approach as the child-centered, individualized view is to the ungraded approach. One would be hard pressed, however, to find a teacher advocating either extreme in its pure form.

A modern ungraded school must have teachers committed to practice at the child-centered (individualized) pole yet willing to postpone, for the sake of a smooth running system, the realization of this dream until adequate materials are available. This contradiction is what makes the defining of precise objectives for the language arts program so difficult. There are clearly three areas where objectives must be developed:

1. objectives defining desirable communications-related behaviors expected of the learners,
2. objectives defining desirable individualized instruction oriented teacher behaviors, and
3. objectives defining the "system" which organizes the schoolwide program into an organic functioning whole. (This system must run smoothly on an austerity budget with a limited amount of materials.)

Pupil Objectives

The major global language arts objectives have been plotted on the following chart.

One must differentiate between terminal and transitional objectives. The following chart is concerned with the terminal. If we were to tailor a language-arts program to an individual, we would consider his past experiences, learning styles, abilities, etc., and select individualized transitional objectives and routes. For instance, Guilford argues that we store our learnings roughly in four forms—images, symbols, words, and gross body movements. Each individual, however, uses his unique combination of these, and so the teacher, to facilitate learning, should identify the learner's profile. If we wanted to teach two beginning readers—one essentially verbal and the other neuro-muscular—we might use the Scott Foresman basal reader with its rule orientation system for the former, and "Words in Color" with its conditioning orientation for the latter. The end (terminal) objectives are the same, but the means (transitional) objectives are different.

Chart I

As a result of his elementary school experiences the child will send and receive communications using each of the following media with a facility appropriate to his background of experiences, abilities, and age:

	Reading	Writing	Listening	Speaking
By Manipulating the Symbols				
By Communicating Information				
By Contriving and Interpreting Persuasive Communications				
By Producing and Receiving Aesthetic Communications				
By Producing and Receiving Social Communications				
By Producing and Receiving Business and Consumer Communications				

It is obvious that reading has much in common with speaking, writing, and listening, and so materials in all four areas can and should have a common core of transitional objectives. For learners with certain style patterns, the rule system in reading might be modified so that it applies equally well to related media. This would make it almost imperative that a single publisher develop a complete set of learning materials for learners with certain characteristics and label them as such.

Charts II-A, II-B, II-C, and II-D present an extensive list of language arts objectives, both terminal and transitional, which might be appropriate for a highly verbal learner. The row labeled Application describes the major categories on Chart I. The Concepts, Skills, and Attitudes appearing in the remaining rows identify more specific responses likely to be essential in the performance of the application response at the appropriate time. There would certainly be a more extensive list of objectives defining the focuses of a comprehensive collection of daily lesson materials for an elementary school language-arts program. Most of these objectives would fall under one of those on the chart.

This chart should be useful as a guide in selecting published materials for an ungraded program for highly verbal learners to insure its comprehensiveness. Another chart would have to be developed for low-verbal learners.

Teacher Objectives

Teaching in an individualized setting requires techniques and skills somewhat alien to those needed in the "taught to the tune of the hickory stick" classroom. Let us examine a few of these.

The teacher must be able to identify learner characteristics which are related to the student's learning abilities, learning styles, and past experiences. This means that she must be able to administer and interpret test scores and cumulative record data, and make inferences from personal observations which are objective and accurate.

The teacher must be able to recognize the pressures which society is presently placing, and will eventually place, on the child. These pressures identify what he needs to know to live up to society's expectations and to be accepted in it.

The teacher must be able to select terminal and transitional language arts objectives appropriate to the individual child. These objectives must consider both the uniqueness of the learner and the society into which he is merging.

The teacher must be able to choose learning materials appropriate to both the learner and the avowed objectives. This implies a much more sophisticated understanding of the relationship between the learner and the learning materials than had formerly been common among teachers.

The teacher must be able to appraise the progress of individual learners and provide guidance where remedial help is indicated. This implies a much more thorough understanding of strategies used in individualized materials than had been needed when a whole class was using the same program.

The transformation of a teacher from one pole to another of the above mentioned continuum can be likened to the trials and tribulations of a student learning a foreign language. Initially he has to think in the old language, translating his every move. It is hoped that sooner or later he will find himself thinking and counting in the new language. This does not always occur. Some never make the transition.

If the movement to initiate an ungraded program comes from the teachers, the transition is likely to be more swift and complete than if initiated by the administrator. In either event, however, a thorough-going training program for teachers is essential.

System Objectives

"System" refers to the structure, rationale, and those procedures which unify the program into an organic whole, yielding functional learners who exhibit the behavior specified in the avowed objectives of the school. The specifications outlined below must be met by an ungraded system.

The average classroom teacher should be able to comfortably plan, conduct, and evaluate the learning activities of her class in a 40-45 hour week. If the teacher has to spend more time than this, there is something wrong with the system. Either more materials and personnel are needed or some individualization has to go.

All classroom learning activities should be planned around the learning characteristics of the individual students. They can still be taught in groups as long as they do not lose their individuality.

The quality of the learner's performance, on application-focused objectives, should be the major criterion used to evaluate progress, with the standard based on a reasonable performance expected of a student with similar characteristics.

Prescribed guidelines should be available to insure that crucial objectives will be mastered at appropriate stages of development, based upon the abilities and backgrounds of the individual learner.

There should be frequently scheduled opportunities for student-teacher conferences, where each learner can get prompt attention with learning problems.

There should be materials and activities scheduled to provide for the educational needs of the learners so they don't have to wait for materials, or suffer boredom through over-exposure to a single program.

These guidelines should define a structure capable of providing a system flexible enough to serve the nongraded school throughout its transition toward complete individualization.

Chart II-A

ATTITUDES	*Listening Attitudes:* The learner will: Use the appropriate concepts and skills in his daily performance of developmental tasks.
SPECIFIC SKILLS	*Skills Related to Informative Communications:* The learner will: Identify main ideas, sequences of ideas, and details, and make two-point outlines when appropriate. Systematically identify and use appropriate references in pursuit of information. *Skills Related to Persuasive and Editorially Biased Communications:* The learner will: Identify the speaker's intent, mood, and attitude toward the subject. Discriminate between relevant and irrelevant ideas. Discriminate between fact and fiction. Draw inferences using cause-effect relationships. Compare two or more speeches for relative reliability on facts, bias, and currency. *Recreational and Aesthetic Skills:* The learner will: Identify a variety of listening areas which interest him. Specify procedures he can take to find interesting listening in each area (above). Identify times in his schedule when he can get recreational materials and use them.
GENERAL SKILLS	The learner will: Produce the 40 basic English sounds when presented with the spoken letter or digraph. Recall and interpret sentences immediately after he has heard them. Identify relationships between ideas he has heard. Discriminate facts from fiction and from opinion in his listening. Summarize what he has heard.

CONCEPTS	Concepts the learner will describe: the importance of communications to the self the importance of communications to society the importance of communications to society's institutions the impact of scientific advancement on the media we use to communicate the ways in which the motives of man affect the communications he sends and receives the techniques of deception in communications the difference between the free and controlled association of ideas and how a good communication requires both.
APPLICATION	*LISTENING:* The learner will translate, interpret, and extrapolate from formal and informal oral statements in the form of: *INFORMATIVE COMMUNICATIONS:* with a degree of proficiency appropriate to his developmental level and seek out such communications when life-problems require it. *PERSUASIVE COMMUNICATIONS:* with a degree of proficiency appropriate to his developmental level. *EDITORIALLY BIASED COMMUNICATIONS:* with a degree of proficiency appropriate to his developmental level. *RECREATIONAL AND AESTHETIC COMMUNICATIONS:* with a degree of proficiency appropriate to his developmental level and seek out such communications when life-problems require it (self realization concerns).

Chart II-B

ATTITUDES	*Reading Attitudes:* The learner will: Use the appropriate concepts and skills in his daily performance of developmental tasks.
SPECIFIC SKILLS	*Skills Related to Informative Communications:* The learner will: Identify main ideas, sequences of ideas, and details, and make two-point outlines when appropriate. Systematically identify and use appropriate references in pursuit of information. *Skills Related to Persuasive and Editorially Biased Communications:* The learner will: Identify the author's intent, mood, and attitude toward the subject. Discriminate between relevant and irrelevant ideas. Discriminate between fact and fiction. Draw inferences, using cause-effect relationships. Compare two or more sources of information for relative reliability on facts, bias, currency. *Recreational and Aesthetic Skills:* The learner will: Identify a variety of reading areas which interest him. Specify procedures he can take to find interesting books in each area (above). Identify times in his schedule when he can get recreational materials and use them.
GENERAL SKILLS	Learner will: Produce the 40 basic English sounds when presented with the printed letter or digraph. Read words using phonics, context clues, and recalled sight words. Recall and interpret sentences immediately after he has read them. Identify relationships between ideas he has read. Discriminate facts from fiction and from opinion in his reading. Summarize what he has read.
CONCEPTS	Concepts the learner will describe: the importance of communications to the self the importance of communications to society the importance of communications to society's institutions the impact of scientific advancement on the media we use to communicate the ways in which the motives of man affect the communications he sends and receives the techniques of deception in communications the difference between the free and controlled association of ideas and how a good communication requires both.

READING: The learner will translate, interpret, and extrapolate from formal and informal written statements in the form of:

INFORMATIVE COMMUNICATIONS:
with a degree of proficiency appropriate to his developmental level and seek out such communications when life-problems require it.

APPLICATION

PERSUASIVE COMMUNICATIONS:
with a degree of proficiency appropriate to his developmental level.

EDITORIALLY BIASED COMMUNICATIONS:
with a degree of proficiency appropriate to his developmental level.

RECREATIONAL AND AESTHETIC COMMUNICATIONS:
with a degree of proficiency appropriate to his developmental level and seek out such communications when life-problems require it (self realization concerns).

Chart II-C

ATTITUDES

Speaking Attitudes:
The learner will:
Use the appropriate skills and concepts in his daily speaking encounters.

SPECIFIC SKILLS

Skills Related to Informative Communications:
The learner will:
Communicate his desires in a socially acceptable manner, to appropriate persons when in need of assistance or information. Communicate appropriate responses to requests from others for information.

Skills Related to Persuasive Communications:
The learner will:
(Within a moral or ethical framework) convince others to modify their behavior to incorporate his needs or the needs of the larger society.

Skills Related to Social Communications:
The learner will:
When the occasion arises, engage in social conversation with both peers and adults in a manner which is mutually satisfying to the participants.

GENERAL SKILLS

The learner will perform the following skills in a manner appropriate to his developmental level. Skills in:
accurately producing language sounds
pronouncing and using words
effectively phrasing ideas
organizing communications
producing effective voice quality
effective delivery

CONCEPTS

Concepts the learner will describe:
the importance of communications to the self
the importance of communications to society
the importance of communications to society's institutions
the impact of scientific advancement on the media we use to communicate
the ways in which the motives of man affect the communications he sends and receives
the techniques of deception in communications
the difference between the free and controlled association of ideas and how a good communication requires both.

SPEAKING: The learner will translate, interpret, and extrapolate his own experiences and observations in:

INFORMATIVE SPOKEN COMMUNICATIONS:
which communicate with a degree of proficiency appropriate to his developmental level
in a culturally appropriate manner commensurate with his developmental level.

APPLICATION

PERSUASIVE SPOKEN COMMUNICATIONS:
which persuade with a degree of proficiency appropriate to his developmental level
in a culturally appropriate manner commensurate with his developmental level.

SOCIAL SPOKEN COMMUNICATIONS:
which communicate with a degree of proficiency appropriate to his developmental level
in a manner which is self-enhancing
in a manner which enhances the speaker's social stimulus value in the eyes of the recipients.

Chart II-D

ATTITUDES	Writing Attitudes: The learner will: Use the appropriate skills and concepts in his daily speaking encounters
SPECIFIC SKILLS	*Skills Related to Informative Communications:* The learner will: Communicate his desires in a socially acceptable manner, to appropriate persons when in need of assistance or information. Communicate appropriate responses to requests from others for information. *Skills Related to Persuasive Communications:* The learner will: (Within a moral or ethical framework) convince others to modify their behavior to incorporate his needs or the needs of the larger society. *Skills Related to Social Communications:* The learner will: When the occasion arises, correspond with friends in a manner which is mutually satisfying to the participants. *Recreational and Aesthetic Skills:* The learner will: Use all of the above writing media in a manner which is self enhancing. Identify and use for creative purposes oral media which are suitable to his abilities and provide for creative expression.
GENERAL SKILLS	The learner will perform the following skills in a manner appropriate to his developmental level. Skills in: Producing legible letters and words rapidly Producing appropriate words Phrasing communications Organizing communications Editing products for public consumption which are free from errors in: spelling format irrelevancies facts redundancies punctuation grammar
CONCEPTS	Concepts the learner will describe: the importance of communications to the self the importance of communications to society the importance of communications to society's institutions the impact of scientific advancement on the media we use to communicate the ways in which the motives of man affect the communications he sends and receives the techniques of deception in communications the difference between the free and controlled association of ideas and how a good communication requires both.

WRITING: The learner will translate, interpret, and extrapolate his own experience and observations in writing through:

INFORMATIVE COMMUNICATIONS:
which communicate with a degree of proficiency appropriate to his developmental level
in a culturally appropriate manner commensurate with his developmental level.

PERSUASIVE COMMUNICATIONS:
which persuade with a degree of proficiency appropriate to his developmental level

APPLICATION   in a culturally appropriate manner commensurate with his developmental level.

SOCIAL COMMUNICATIONS:
which communicate with a degree of proficiency appropriate to his developmental level
in a manner which is self-enhancing
in a manner which enhances the speaker's social stimulus value in the eyes of the recipients.

CREATIVE EXPRESSIONS:
in a manner which is self-enhancing and possibly in a manner which is educational.

Baughman combines Polya's heuristic reasoning method with Bloom's taxonomy of cognitive objectives in order to formulate designs for behavioral objectives in mathematics. According to the author; the resulting "heuristic-cognitive pattern" promotes a process-oriented teaching style, the development of behavioral objectives that combine process and content, and the development of evaluation procedures based both on process and content. Forty-four objectives, adaptable for mathematics as well as other areas, are presented. Although Baughman makes an uncommon distinction between the terms "behavioral objectives" and "instructional objectives," the intent of his terminology is clear.

Preparing for the Next Mathematics Revolution*

GERALD D. BAUGHMAN

The next revolutionary wave to wash over mathematics education, according to Francis J. Mueller, will place less stress on mathematics while applying greater pressure on education. Mueller is convinced that the next revolution is much closer than most educators realize and that revolutionary issues may be centered around such questions as:

(a) How does one learn mathematics?

(b) How can we select mixes of content from the growing body of knowledge to better suit individual aspirations?

(c) How can we optimize the teaching and learning process in mathematics?[1]

*Reprinted from the *Journal of Secondary Education, 44,* April, 1969, pp. 182-186, by permission of the publisher and the author.

233

Mueller's questions pointedly draw attention to a growing concern in education with the process-content issue.

Futurists agree that the coming curriculum needs to be based more upon process and less upon content. This emphasis upon process calls for the development of a frame-of-reference for this term. In general, the futurists include in process these activities which promote problem-solving, discovery, experimentation, and evaluation.

Each of these four process terms contain definite connotations for mathematics education. Problem-solving implies an extremely high-level, if not the highest level, of mental activity that incorporates all other types of learning and thinking. Problem-solving, therefore, places an emphasis upon cognition and away from considering process as content.

The term discovery has received such harsh criticism and has been so widely misrepresented in classroom practice that it is tempting to side-step further comment. However, if discovery can be viewed as being in one-to-one correspondence with heuristic reasoning, we have a model to guide us. George Polya provides us with a sequenced set of questions and suggestions that aid in discovering the solution to a problem.[2] These questions and suggestions carefully enumerate, indirectly, mental operations typically useful for the solution of problems. Once again the emphasis upon discovery points towards a mental or cognitive process.

Experimentation almost carries the plea, "Please, let me do it myself." Uncontrolled experimentation and overly structured experimentation are at opposite ends of the spectrum. Neither approach provides for determining alternatives or problem-solving. Guidelines are needed for situations that will provide minimal, yet adequate, data for experimentation or individual exploration.

The final futuristic term for process, evaluation, is presently centered around behavioral objectives. Behavioral objectives are the statements concerning student actions in terms of having experienced something deemed as a desirable learning outcome. These behavioral statements necessarily involve a verb denoting some sort of action, a connection with an important structural aspect of the content in the discipline, and a connection with the process of the discipline.

What do these futuristic implications relating to process mean for us in mathematics education? First, let us start with the most difficult of these notions, discovery. The discovery techniques in Polya's heuristic reasoning process are enjoying widespread attention in curriculum projects that are inquiry oriented as well as in research projects pointing toward individual inquiry. It is surprising that so little attention has been paid to this outstanding scheme by the mathematics profession. Using

Polya's own abbreviated list in *How To Solve It,* the following is provided as a brief overview of the heuristic reasoning pattern.

Understanding the Problem

First—You have to understand the problem.

Group 1 Activities—What is the unknown? What are the data? What is the condition?

Group 2 Activities—Is it possible to satisfy the condition? Is the condition sufficient to determine the unknown? Or is it insufficient? Or redundant? Or contradictory?

Group 3 Activities—Draw a figure. Introduce suitable notation.

Group 4 Activities—Separate the various parts of the condition. Can you write them down?

Devising a Plan

Second—Find the connection between the data and the unknown. You may be obligated to consider auxiliary problems if an immediate connection cannot be found. You should obtain eventually a plan of the solution.

Group 5 Activities—Have you seen the problem before? Have you seen the same problem in a slightly different form?

Group 6 Activities—Do you know a related problem? Do you know a theorem that could be useful?

Group 7 Activities—Look at the unknown! Try to think of a familiar problem having the same or a similar unknown.

Group 8 Activities—Here is a problem related to yours and solved before. Could you use it? Could you use the result of the related problem? Could you use the method of the related problem? Should you introduce some auxiliary element in order to make use of the related problem?

Group 9 Activities—Could you restate the problem? Could you restate the problem still differently? Go back to definitions!

Group 10 Activities—If you cannot solve the proposed problem try to solve first some related problem. Can you imagine a more accessible related problem? A more general problem? A more special problem? An analogous problem? Could you solve a part of the problem? Keep only a part of the condition, drop the other part? How far is the unknown then determined? How can it vary?

Could you derive something useful from the data? Could you think of other data appropriate to determine the unknown? Could you change the unknown or the data, or both if necessary, so that the new unknown and the data are nearer to each other?

Group 11 Activities—Did you use all the data? Did you use the whole condition? Have you taken into account all essential notions involved in the problem?

Carrying Out the Plan

Third—Carry out your plan.

Group 12 Activities—Carrying out your plan of the solution, check each step. Can you see clearly that the step is correct? Can you prove that the step is correct?

Looking Back

Fourth—Examine the solution obtained.

Group 13 Activities—Can you check the result? Can you check the argument?

Group 14 Activities—Can you derive the result differently? Can you see the different derivation at a glance?

Group 15 Activities—Can you use the result, or the method, for some other problem?

This discovery model also describes a problem-solving and experimentation or individual exploration process, and depicts a learning-teaching style. If the mental operations involved in heuristic reasoning were identified, they would serve to give greater depth of information upon which to derive behavioral and/or instructional objectives.

Using the *Taxonomy of Educational Objectives, Handbook I: Cognitive Domain*[3] to identify the intellectual abilities employed with Polya's heuristic reasoning process, the following relationships are revealed:

This diagram, omitting the obvious connection of knowledge to all the elements of heuristic reasoning, allows the *Taxonomy* and its many examples of objectives classified into various mental levels to be used as a guide in creating behavioral objectives that demonstrate analysis oriented heuristic-cognitive patterns. Such a list of behavioral objectives might include the following:

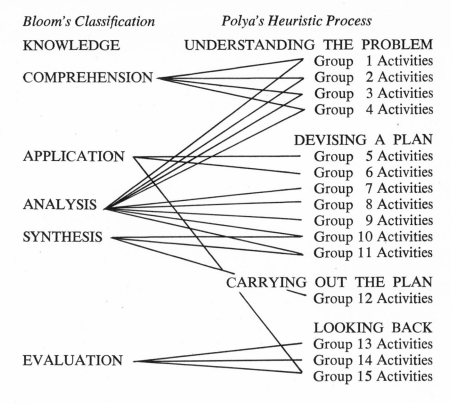

Bloom's Classification	*Polya's Heuristic Process*

KNOWLEDGE   UNDERSTANDING THE PROBLEM
                            Group 1 Activities
COMPREHENSION   Group 2 Activities
                            Group 3 Activities
                            Group 4 Activities

                   DEVISING A PLAN
APPLICATION   Group 5 Activities
                            Group 6 Activities
                            Group 7 Activities
ANALYSIS   Group 8 Activities
                            Group 9 Activities
SYNTHESIS   Group 10 Activities
                            Group 11 Activities

                CARRYING OUT THE PLAN
                            Group 12 Activities

                   LOOKING BACK
                            Group 13 Activities
EVALUATION   Group 14 Activities
                            Group 15 Activities

Understanding the Problem

1. *State* the problem situation in your own words.
2. *Identify* the principal parts of the problem situation.
3. *Describe* various ways that the principal parts of the problem situation can vary.
4. *Distinguish* between the various parts of the condition.
5. *Identify* and *name* the various parts of the condition.
6. *Draw* representations that illustrate different approaches to the problem situation.
7. *Identify* the unknown in the figure or drawing.
8. *Identify* the data in the figure or drawing.
9. *Construct* some sort of notation for the figure or drawing.
10. *Name* the figure parts representing the data.
11. *Name* the figure parts representing the unknown.
12. *Construct* a prediction as to whether it is possible to satisfy the condition.
13. *Construct* a prediction as to whether the condition is sufficient to determine the unknown.

Devising a Plan

14. *Identify* situations where the same problem has been solved previously.
15. *Describe* problem situations previously encountered in which the same problem was used in a slightly different form.
16. *Identify* and *name* a related problem situation.
17. *State* and *demonstrate* a theorem that could be useful in solving the problem situation.
18. *Describe* a familiar problem situation having the same or similar unknown.
19. *Demonstrate* how you can use the method of the familiar problem in solving the given problem situation.
20. *Construct* an inference as to whether the instruction of some auxiliary element will make it possible to use the familiar problem.
21. *State* the problem situation in your own words.
22. *State* the problem situation in as many different ways as possible.
23. *Demonstrate* the solution of some related problem if you cannot solve the proposed problem situation.
24. *Construct* a more accessible related problem situation.
25. *Construct* a more general related problem situation.
26. *Construct* a more special related problem situation.
27. *Construct* an analogous problem situation.
28. *Demonstrate* the solution to a part of the problem situation.
29. *Demonstrate* how far the unknown can be determined by keeping only a part of the condition and dropping the other parts.
30. *Describe* how the unknown can vary when various parts of the condition are used.
31. *Construct* interpolations regarding the usefulness of the given data.
32. *Describe* other data not given that are appropriate for determining the unknown.
33. *Describe* changes in the unknown or the data, or both if necessary, so that the new unknown and the new data are nearer to each other.
34. *Distinguish* between relevant and irrelevant data.
35. *Describe* the use of all the segments of the conditions.
36. *Describe* the use of all essential notions involved in the problem situation.

Carrying Out the Plan

37. *Demonstrate* the checking of each step in carrying out the plan for the solution.
38. *Construct* inferences that clearly indicate the correctness of each step of the solution.
39. *Construct* arguments proving that each step of the solution is correct.

Looking Back

40. *Demonstrate* how to check the result of the problem situation.
41. *Demonstrate* how to check the argument used in solving the problem situation.
42. *Construct* different ways of deriving the result of the problem situation.
43. *Describe* the use of the result of the problem situation for some other problem.
44. *Describe* the use of the method of the problem situation solution for some other problem.

Before these statements can be used in an effective manner for evaluation, the behavioral objectives need to be transformed into instructional objectives. Instructional objectives should convey what it is that a student who has mastered the objective will be able to do or what *performance* is expected, specify under what *conditions* the student is expected to perform his task, and specify the level or *extent* of the acceptable performance that indicates satisfactory attainment of the objective.

In summary, the heuristic-cognitive pattern provides a basis for a teaching style that emphasizes process and for formulating behavioral objectives that combine process and content. It also indicates a model upon which teacher training institutions can develop methods classes in pre-service credentialing programs.

The heuristic-cognitive pattern also allows for the development of evaluation that is based on process-content objectives stated in behavioral terms.

Thus, the heuristic-cognitive pattern provides some basic guidelines by which mathematics educators can prepare themselves for active participation in the next mathematics revolution.

References

1. Mueller, Francis J. The Several Revolutions in Elementary School Mathematics. *NEA Journal; 57,* No. 1, January, 1968, pp. 53-54.
2. Polya, George. *How To Solve It.* 2d. ed. Garden City, New York: Doubleday and Co., 1957.
3. Bloom, Benjamin S. (Ed.) *Taxonomy of Educational Objectives, Handbook I: Cognitive Domain.* New York: David McKay, 1956.

Kapfer uses the context of current trends in education, notably various efforts at individualization, to point out the importance of the behavioral approach to instruction and learning. Applying these ideas to music education, the author provides a logical approach to the development of behavioral objectives in music. The examples illustrate several levels of goal specificity.

The Evolution of a Musical Objective: Practical Examples*

MIRIAM B. KAPFER

What can concerned music educators do about the need to individualize instruction and learning in music? How can behavioral objectives in music be identified and used and how do these activities relate to the process of individualization? Answers to these and similar questions should reflect major innovative curriculum trends and should also be reflected in attempts to develop new curricular guidelines and materials in music.

Current Curricular Trends

A recent widely circulated educational publication[1] listed three "big ideas" that have dominated the world of teaching during recent years. All of these major trends centered around the need to *individualize instruction.* There seems to be little doubt in the minds of many leading

*Copyright © *Music Educators Journal,* 56, February, 1970, pp. 61-63. Reprinted with permission.

educators concerning the direction in which education must move. Both the educational theorists and the developers of technological hardware for education are trying to individualize instruction through whatever processes will bring it about most quickly, including the systems approach, computer assisted instruction, programed instruction, and learning packages.

An important component of each of these approaches to individualization is the formulation of educational objectives in behavioral terms. A quick look at recent issues of a number of professional publications will indicate the current dominance of the behavioral approach in education. For example, in the April, 1968 issue of *Nation's Schools,* Dwight Allen discussed ways in which "badly needed performance criteria" (behavioral objectives) would facilitate the individualization of instruction. In the spring 1968 issue of the *Harvard Educational Review,* Allen pointed to the development and use of behavioral objectives as one of three primary ways in which major current educational problems could be alleviated. In the May 1968 *Bulletin of the National Association of Secondary School Principals,* Henry S. Dyer, vice-president of Educational Testing Service, stated, "It hardly seems likely, after all the discussion during the last ten or fifteen years, that there is anyone even remotely connected with education who remains unaware of the importance of getting educational objectives translated into observable student behavior."

Many other writers have expressed similar views concerning the importance of the behavioral approach in the development and use of educational materials. In fact, educators such as Robert Mager[2] and Castelle Gentry[3] have suggested the preparation, perhaps on a national basis, of catalogs of behavioral objectives in various subject areas. Professional organizations such as the National Science Teachers Association are presently involved in developing extensive lists of specific behaviors that define (in this case) the goal of "scientific literacy" for the generally educated student.[4]

Implications for Music Education

Music educators have not been unaware of these broad educational trends. A similar series of educational priorities incorporating individualized approaches to curriculum development has been suggested for the field of music education. In the Tanglewood Declaration (*Music Educators Journal,* November, 1967), the symposium participants urged that "greater emphasis should be placed on helping the individual student to fulfill his needs, goals, and potentials." Tanglewood recommended, further, that "teachers adopt flexible approaches that will accommodate individual learning differences in students." In the same issue of the *Journal,* Charles Fowler summarized the need for individualizing music instruction: "One fact filters through clearly: no music teacher can be content with presenting a music lesson aimed 'down the middle.'" The need, in the individualization process, for describing and measuring musical behaviors also occupied the thoughts of the Tanglewood participants. They observed that "measurable areas of musical achievement at elementary and secondary school levels have not been determined, nor have criteria for assessment been developed." Charles Leonhard also underlined the need for behaviorized goals in music by stating:

> Closely related to the development of a philosophy of music education is the formulation of a comprehensive statement of objectives clearly in terms of desired behavior. The basis for developing behavioral objectives lies in the analysis and description of the way musicians behave in relation to music. Once these behaviors have been defined, the job of teaching consists of organizing experiences for students which are relevant to learning the behaviors.[5]

The need for providing specific training in the definition of behavioral objectives in music was recognized in the MENC Research Training Project, held in conjunction with each of the six division conventions in 1969. The project's guiding principles were that musical behaviors should be identified and defined operationally, that a substantial number of music educators should be trained to accomplish this task, and that subsequent curricular research and development activities in music would be rendered considerably more productive as a result of the behavioral definition of musical objectives.

Developing a Music Curriculum

It is not necessary, however, to wait for the results of projects having nationwide scope (however desirable these may be) to approach the problem of preparing a music curriculum guide that will encourage individualized and behaviorized implementation at the classroom level. An example of what can be done at the district level is the interim music curriculum guide developed by a small team of educators from the Clark County School District, Las Vegas, Nevada, who were appointed by the southern zone of the Nevada Music Educators Association.[6] In the guide, the familiar activities and performance approach was bypassed in favor of focusing on basic experiences and involvement with the essential elements of music at both the elementary and secondary levels. In preparing the guide, a direct practical approach to behaviorizing the music curriculum involved going only a step or two beyond existing materials.

The curricular guidelines in music that were developed were based on the school district's "Statement of Educational Principles: Objectives of the Instructional Program." These objectives then were considered in light of the desired "musical outcomes" expressed in the MENC publication *Music in General Education*. The "outcomes" statement proved useful at this early point in the curriculum project because it listed general rather than specific long-range goals, stated in nonbehavioral terms. These goals are, in fact, types or categories of behavior, as illustrated in the use of words such as skill, understanding, and knowledge. As such, they form a good starting point for behaviorizing specific music objectives. To the extent that a behaviorally stated objective can be related to a more broadly stated nonbehavioral goal, segmented and sometimes seemingly unrelated musical behaviors can be made more meaningful.

The curricular ideas derived from the school district's general statement of objectives and from the "outcomes" materials were then organized into several sections based on the elements or structure of music. Within each structural area, sample ideas to be learned, behavioral objectives, teaching materials, and teacher or pupil activities were suggested. Significant support for the structural approach to curricular organization in music is evident in statements such as the following by John I. Goodlad:

> There is much work to be done in music education. There is the new math, the new physics, the new biology . . . *all emphasizing the structure of the fields* [italics added]. Music education hasn't reached that point in enough schools. Children should be introduced to the structure of music through a carefully planned, sequential curriculum as rigorous and well-organized as the best math curriculum.[7]

Cognitive and Psychomotor Domains. In the accompanying table, two examples are given showing how specific behavioral objectives in music were derived from general educational goals in the Clark County School District. The worthwhile but very indefinite district-level goals were categorized in terms of long-range behaviors, then were given subject matter "meat," and finally were stated more specifically in terms of desired student behaviors.

HOW BEHAVIORAL OBJECTIVES IN MUSIC ARE DERIVED FROM GENERAL GOALS

1. *General Educational Goal*	2. *Music Education Goal*	3. *Content*	4. *Behavioral Objective*
The District shall be concerned with and assume shared responsibility toward the attainment of the active interest of each student in aesthetic experiences with the skills and attitudes necessary for satisfying self-expression in the creative arts.	*Skills.* He will be able to express himself on a musical instrument.	*Harmony.* Level 3. A triad may be named for the letter name of its root tone; a triad or chord may be indicated in the music by a letter placed with the melody.	Level 3. Given a twelve-bar Autoharp and the score (including chord symbols in the form of letters) of a familiar sixteen-measure melody harmonized with two chords, the student will be able to provide accompaniment to group singing of the melody by locating by letter and playing correctly the required chords ("correctly" being defined as the proper chord sounded with rhythmic accuracy).
The District shall assume primary responsibility for and instruct each student toward his maximum achievement of the following educational goals: Knowledge of man, his nature, his environment, and his relationship to the society in which he lives—including the study of the arts.	*Understandings.* He will understand the relationships existing between music and other areas of human endeavor. The generally educated person integrates his knowledge.	*Harmony.* Level 13. The music of a given period can be related in terms of style (of which harmony is a considerable part) to other types of artistic examples, literary expression, and social customs of that period.	Level 13. Given the stylistic category of Romantic, together with at least one example each of the musical, literary, and architectural achievements of the period, the student will be able within one-half hour, without the use of verbal reference sources, to write a two-hundred-word essay comparing and contrasting in terms of style the given examples.

It is important to understand the relationship between the general goals and the desired student behaviors. The number of behavioral objectives that can be derived from each general goal is theoretically infinite. It is finite in practice only because of the curricular choices that must always be made. The number of teaching and learning materials and methods for each behavioral objective is also virtually unlimited, depending only on financial and human resources and ingenuity. The stated behaviors that relate to the musical content to be learned in this curriculum do not exhaust the possibilities. Curriculum guides should not be used to determine all of the student's in-school contact with music. Rather, the behavioral objectives that define minimum mastery are the foundation upon which divergence and creativity are not only possible but probable.

Affective Domain. It is evident that direct reference to the affective domain was omitted in the preceding examples. Actually, the first general goal in the table contains attitude as well as knowledge and skill components. The behaviorization of attitudes must be handled somewhat differently from the knowledge and skill areas, however, in spite of the close ties that exist between the affective domain and the knowledge and skill areas. For example, an affective objective (stated in nonbehavioral, perhaps even noncontent, terms) such as the following might be used: "The student exhibits increased interest in music as observed in his self-initiating creative behaviors and voluntary response behaviors with regard to music." This objective could then be amplified in terms of a series of behavioral substatements that could be developed either as an accumulation of behaviors or, with more precision, as a continuum of behaviors. The student's achievement of the major affective objective would then be determined on the basis of the number, type, and intensity of the relevant individual behaviors that are evident within the student's total behavior pattern.

The guide developed for the Clark County School District is not considered complete, and the objectives presented here are intended only as examples. The incompleteness of the guide is both its weakness and its strength. It was developed in an open-ended way for two reasons. In the first place, it was intended to be only an interim guide. Secondly, an incomplete type of curricular product resulted naturally from the belief that a guide is important primarily to those who are active at some point in its development, either in the initial stages or at the operational level in the classroom.

During the final phase of development of the music guide—the classroom implementation stage—the teacher will need to rewrite the behavioral objectives in student language if necessary and reorganize and augment the suggested media and methodology into curricular vehicles or packages for use by individual students. These packages should meet requirements of individualization and continuous progress with respect to learning rates, sequences, interests, and styles.

These ideas concerning the formulation and use of behavioral objectives in music curriculum guides represent only one approach. Undoubtedly, this task could be accomplished in a variety of ways, including the establishment of a committee of experts supported by major funding, as was suggested in the Tanglewood report. Yet, until such a task force can develop and disseminate more systematic and comprehensive approaches to the behaviorization of objectives for music education (and rank them in terms of sequence and importance), individual music educators can develop their own guides. Unless music teachers understand and appreciate the value of behavioral objectives in music education, the ultimate goal of the behavioral approach—the improvement and individualization of learning opportunities for the student—will not be realized.

Until a comprehensive catalog of musical behaviors is available, the development of examples such as the ones illustrated in this article is possible in any local school district interested in moving in the direction of translating general music goals into observable student behavior. According to Charles Leonhard, "Accomplishing [this] task represents the next big leap forward in the development of a music program leading to significant achievement, a program that will make a difference in the musical competence of the new generation of Americans."[8] The sum of the best of many local efforts to identify and evaluate musical behaviors might prove to be of substantial value in later, more massive approaches to the task.

REFERENCES

1. *Teacher's Letter* (Croft), *17,* May 15, 1968, p. 4.
2. Robert F. Mager. Deriving Objectives for the High School Curriculum. *NSPI Journal, 7,* March, 1968, pp. 7-14, 22.
3. Castelle G. Gentry. Letters to the Editor. *Educational Technology, 8,* March 30, 1968, p. 16.
4. Albert F. Eiss. The NSTA Conferences on Scientific Literacy. *The Science Teacher, 35,* May, 1968, pp. 30-32.
5. Charles Leonhard. Either We're In Or We're Out. *The Nebraska Music Educator, 26,* April, 1968, pp. A, 22.
6. Miriam B. Kapfer, Duane A. Fuller & Kathleen L. Hogsett. *Interim Curriculum Guide: Music, K-12.* Las Vegas, Nevada: Clark County School District, 1968.
7. John I. Goodlad. Music's Place in Education. *Creative Approaches to School Music.* Chicago: American Music Conference, 1967, p. 2.
8. Charles Leonhard. The Next Ten Years. *Music Educators Journal, 55,* September, 1968, pp. 48-50.

Kurtz uses basically the same straight-forward approach to behavioral objectives as that which characterized several of the articles included in Part I of this book. A principal contribution of the Kurtz article, however, is its illustrative list of behavioral objectives in science and mathematics.

Help Stamp Out Non-Behavioral Objectives [in Science]*

Edwin B. Kurtz, Jr.

About ten years ago a student unwittingly taught me a very valuable lesson. I had prepared a final examination in which 80 percent of the questions were strictly feedback of memorized information. The other 20 percent consisted of questions which required the student to think. No amount of memorization would help answer these questions unless the student could select and integrate certain facts and formulate generalizations. The student who was so helpful to me knew all the memory questions—he regurgitated facts beautifully. But he got a perfect zero on the thought questions. He had memorized the book but didn't know how to use any of that mass of information. He was like a computer with a large memory bank but no program for its use.

This little episode made me resolve to change my teaching behavior so that the behavior of my students would also change as a result of my teaching. It has taken me several years to synthesize my present view that a course should be designed so as to alter the behavior of students. Also it was only recently that I came to understand my objectives well enough to communicate to anyone what I had been thinking about.

*Reprinted from *The Science Teacher, 32,* January, 1965, pp. 31-32, by permission of the publisher and the author.

I should add that others have arrived at ideas similar to the ones I arrived at empirically in my teaching. Indeed, the recent papers of Gagné *et al.* (1-4), describe in detail the behavioral approach to mathematics teaching; they even present experimental evidence in support of behavioral objectives. Of course, it is these studies which have provided the behavioral terms for describing this approach to learning and teaching. To my knowledge there are no comparable studies in science at the college or high school levels. However, the experimental elementary school science program of the American Association for the Advancement of Science is based entirely on a behavioral approach (5, 6). The experimental volumes from that program describe in great detail the objectives, method of instruction, and evaluation procedure. Thus far this program has had a high degree of success.

Let me now describe how you can begin to pattern your own courses along behavioral objectives. First, what behavioral objectives are to be set? And how will you know whether the student has acquired these objectives? The key to these problems is to ask yourself a direct question and then to answer it in unambiguous terms. The key question is: *What do I want my students to be able to do after taking my course that they couldn't do before enrolling in it?* In other words, *don't* ask yourself "What will they know?" but *do* ask "What will they be able to do?" This includes asking whether the student can do or demonstrate ability to carry out both skills and simple to complex thought patterns.

Now, what are some unambiguous answers to the key question? You might state, as many have before you, that the objectives of your course should be to "provide understanding," or "enable a student to be critical," or "educate your students," or "kindle enthusiasm." I grant that these are fine objectives, but they are totally untestable. How would you find out whether your course does "provide understanding," or "enable a student to be critical," or "educate the students," or "kindle enthusiasm"? Such objectives are nebulous and not specific. They do not immediately suggest questions which the student can answer only by demonstrating that he has acquired specific behaviors.

What are some specific behavioral objectives? You need only think of specific tasks or abilities a student should be able to do or demonstrate after taking your course:

> *Classify* a set of objects and *state* the basis of the classification.
> *Distinguish* between an observation and an inference.
> *Construct* a graph from a table of data.
> When given some data, *state* a prediction or inference or *formulate* a hypothesis.
> *Design* an experiment.

Calculate the slope of a curve.

Select proper units for measuring a quantity.

Construct a three-dimensional picture of an object from two-dimensional views of the object.

Describe an object clearly so that another person can draw a picture of the object.

Apply a rule and *calculate* the conversion of a quantity into other units of measurement (e.g., convert milliliters into liters).

Order a group of objects.

Demonstrate how to test a prediction.

State an interpretation of some data.

Formulate an operational definition from some data about something.

Construct a model to fit some data.

Write a concise summary of an experiment in 150 words or less.

Apply a rule to a new situation.

I am sure you can think of many other specific abilities that apply to your own courses. All you need to do is use unambiguous verbs, such as are italicized in the above objectives, and then state an object for the action of the verb.

Now I would not want to suggest or imply that you should stamp out every non-behavioral objective from your courses. Certainly your students should acquire some factual knowledge. But, in my own classroom experience, I have found that students acquire as many, and perhaps even more, facts when the course is designed around behavioral objectives than when factual content is emphasized. Because the students feel they are "doing" and "accomplishing" things when behavioral objectives are set, the number of facts learned per student appears to increase considerably along with the acquired behaviors. Apparently students receive satisfaction from *doing* science rather than *telling* about what science has already done, and this satisfaction somehow stimulates the acquisition of more facts.

There is one final and very important aspect of a behavioral approach to teaching. It is simply that, if you are committed to behavioral objectives in your teaching, you must also test your students in such a way as to find out whether they have acquired the behaviors. But this is the beauty of the behavioral approach I have been describing. Testing for acquired behaviors is easy if you have stated your objectives unambiguously.

Within the subject of your course, you should have no trouble providing the student with a set of objects or their descriptions and asking him to classify them; or presenting the student with a table of data and asking him to construct a graph representing the data; or presenting him a paragraph of information and asking him to list the observations in one column and the inferences in another which are mentioned in that paragraph; and so on for each objective. You may even find that you want to test his acquired behavior in a new context or scientific situation with which the student has had no prior experience. You may even wish to design a hierarchy of behavioral objectives and then teach and test for this sequence of learning, just as Gagné *et al.* have done with certain mathematical knowledges and skills (1, 2). In any event, each test question must require the student to demonstrate a specific behavior; he either can or cannot do it. A student's answer to a test question is correct only in the sense that his answer (a calculation, graph, hypothesis, description, classification, and so on) tells you that he has acquired a certain behavior essential to arriving at the answer.

This brief discussion may not have convinced you to redesign your courses and to stamp out non-behavioral objectives. But if it has made you ask yourself, "What *do* I want the students to be able to do after taking my course that they couldn't do before," the seed of a behavioral approach has been planted. The idea needs only nurturing and time—it took me several years. But I can state with all honesty that this awakening in me of a non-content oriented approach to teaching has stimulated me and my students more than I had ever hoped. It makes little difference what kind of course you are teaching or whether it is for future scientists or nonscientists. The thrill is in seeing your students doing science, not just learning what science has already done, and then measuring quantitatively on an examination how well they have learned to do science.

REFERENCES

1. R. M. Gagné & N. E. Paradise. Abilities and Learning Sets in Knowledge Acquisition. *Psychological Monographs,* 75(14), 1961.
2. ———, J. R. Mayor, H. L. Garstens & N. E. Paradise. Factors in Acquiring Knowledge of a Mathematical Task. *Psychological Monographs,* 76(7), 1962.
3. ———. A Psychologist's Counsel on Curriculum Design." *Journal of Research in Science Teaching,* 1:27-32, 1963.
4. ———. The Learning Requirements for Enquiry. *Journal of Research in Science Teaching,* 1:144-153, 1963.
5. *Science—A Process Approach,* Parts 1 to 6 and Commentary for Teachers. American Association for the Advancement of Science, Washington, D. C., 1964.
6. H. H. Walbesser. Curriculum Evaluation by Means of Behavioral Objectives. *Journal of Research in Science Teaching,* 1:296-301, 1963.

The function of behavioral objectives in the educational programs of the Men's Urban Job Corps Centers is reported. The author classifies learner behaviors as verbal, physical, and attitudinal, and provides a series of sample objectives in each category. The classification system has applicability to other types and levels of education because it facilitates analysis, clarification, and cataloging of types of desired student behavior.

A Classification of Behavioral Objectives in Job Training Programs*

PAUL HARMON

This paper reports work by Cybern Education, Inc. and Xerox Education Division for the Job Corps Men's Urban Centers, resulting in a curriculum system with behavioral objectives as the primary unit.** This paper defines behavioral objectives and then distinguishes 14 types of objectives according to the type of behavioral task the student is being asked to perform. The 14 types of objectives are grouped under three general headings: verbal objectives, physical objectives and attitudinal objectives. Each of the 14 types is described, and the particular considerations for actually writing that type of objectives are given. These 14 type-categories and a few combinations of types have effectively

*Reprinted from *Educational Technology, 9,* January, 1969, pp. 5-12, by permission of the publisher and the author.
**Many of the concepts contained herein were worked out with William Laidlaw and Mary Ann Hammerel, whose contributions are acknowledged by the writer.

allowed for classification of all the objectives prepared during an extensive behavioral objective development effort.

Definition of a Behavioral Objective

For the purposes of Job Corps curricular development, and throughout this paper, an acceptable behavioral objective is defined as a written statement containing:

1. *A Behavioral Objective Title.*
   This title is an abbreviated sentence that is short, descriptive and contains an action verb.
2. A paragraph describing the *Conditions* in which the desired behavior will occur. This paragraph will detail, if relevant:
   a. what tools, equipment and clothing must be used;
   b. what special job aids or manuals may be used (or not used);
   c. what environmental conditions may affect the performance; and
   d. what special physical demands may exist.
3. A paragraph detailing the *Behavior* which the student will perform to show that he has acquired the desired skill. This paragraph will indicate how he is to perform the skill and/or the results of the performance. A step-by-step list may serve this purpose.
4. A paragraph describing the *Success Criteria* by which the student's behavior is to be judged as acceptable or unacceptable. This paragraph will detail, if relevant:
   a. the time allowed to complete the performance;
   b. the number, percentage or proportion of total test items that must be answered correctly to pass;
   c. the actual responses that will be considered acceptable;
   d. the person who will judge or evaluate the performance; and
   e. the distinct point in time at which the performance is considered acceptably completed.

A Classification of Behaviors

Even within the format details above there are many ways that behavioral objectives can be written. In some cases the difference merely represents the style of the author, but in other cases the difference reflects the different types of behavior that the various objectives are attempting to describe.

For convenience, the types of objectives are split into three groups: Verbal Behavioral Objectives, Physical Behavioral Objectives and Attitudinal Behavioral Objectives. Other types of behavior objectives might be added to the list, and some of the types listed might be split into two or more sub-types, but this list can serve as a beginning classification of objectives that vary because they classify different types of behavior.

A Classification of Behavioral Objectives

1.0   *Verbal Behavioral Objectives*
    1.1   Recall a name; list a set of names; state a simple rule or fact.
    1.2   Explain an ordered set of actions (how to do a task).
    1.3   Respond to a series of statements or questions.
    1.4   Solve a specific symbolic problem.
    1.5   Solve a general type of symbolic problem.
2.0   *Physical Behavioral Objectives*
    2.1   Make physical identifications (point to things).
    2.2   Perform simple physical acts.
    2.3   Perform complex actions (with instructions or by rote).
    2.4   Perform physically skilled actions.
    2.5   Perform an appropriate skilled action in a problem solving situation (determine what is to be done and then do it).
    2.6   Determine acceptable quality in physical products.
3.0   *Attitudinal Behavioral Objectives*
    3.1   State or list probable consequences of a given action.
    3.2   Evidence memory of correct social responses over an extended period of time.
    3.3   Respond with limited or controlled responses in given social situations.

Some objectives do not fall into any of these categories. Some objectives involve two or more types of behaviors. For example, often personal/social objectives involve both attitude and physical behaviors. In these cases it is easy to classify a behavioral objective using two numbers.

A detailed review of each type of objective follows:

1.0   The types of behavioral objectives considered in this first section will include numbers with a first digit of 1. This will indicate they are *Verbal Behavioral Objectives*. These objectives are all concerned with the student demonstrating some variation of the behavior of writing or speaking in a given situation.

1.1   *Recall a name; list a set of names; state a simple rule or fact.*

In this type of objective, the student is asked to memorize something and be able to recall it upon demand of the instructor, or in a particular situation. This type of objective is appropriate whenever the situation demands that the student must know some piece of information in order to be prepared for what follows.

In general, the Conditions should include how the student's knowledge (memory) will be tested (by multiple-test, by write-in test, by being asked by the instructor, by showing some other student, etc.).

The behavior will include the exact name, list, set of names, rule, or fact, etc., that the student will be expected to learn.

The Success Criteria will tell what margin of error is allowable. Must the student be literally correct? Must the list be in perfect order? Must it be recalled instantly, in five minutes, etc., In other words, *how* will the student have it memorized?

EXAMPLE

Behavioral Objective Title: State procedure in case of accident

Conditions: Preparatory to a test to be given before the student can enter the Introductory Automotive Shop, without help or aid, and writing out the statement.

Behavior: The student will know the following: In case of an accident in the shop the student should go to the phone and dial security, number .... If an instructor is present, the student should tell the instructor so he can call security. The student should not attempt to give first aid himself.

Success Criteria: The student should be able to write out a near likeness to the above statement. He must state the number of security. He must state that he is not to give first aid himself. He should mention that the instructor should call if he is present. The instructor grading the test will judge if the statement reproduces the essence of the above.

1.2 *Explain an ordered set of actions (how to proceed to do a task).*

In this type of objective, the student is asked to explain how to do a thing. In other words, he is asked to recite or write a step-by-step procedure for the completion of a task.. This type of performance is much like the preceding objective, except in this case the student must know a series of things which happen one after another.

As in the preceding type of objective, the main thing to be sure to include in the Conditions is how the student will be tested. Note: it could be a written or a spoken explanation, but it would not be a demonstration, since that would make it a different type of behavioral objective altogether (type 2.2). Since it is better to have the student demonstrate a thing than to just explain it, consider before writing this objective if a demonstration would be possible instead.

The Behavior should include as exact an explanation as the student is expected to give. If the student will explain it step-by-step, the Behavior will be a list of the steps. The Success Criteria will tell what margin of error is allowable. Must the student include every step? How nearly must his explanation match the behavioral objective? How many times must he explain it to pass? Are there any time limits?

EXAMPLE

Behavioral Objective Title: Describing the events in a firing cycle

Conditions: Upon request of the instructor, and without the use of texts, etc., but with the help of an unlabeled diagram of a piston and cylinder, the student will:

Behavior: State in order the following events:

1. fuel intake valve opens
2. fuel is drawn into cylinder during downward stroke
3. fuel intake valve closes
4. fuel is compressed when piston moves upward
5. spark plug discharge ignites fuel mixture
6. combustion of fuel forces piston down
7. exhaust valve opens
8. piston acts as pump to force exhaust gases out

Success Criteria: The student should be able to run through the above in about two minutes time. He should use the vocabulary stated above and be able to explain the words if asked. The student may miss only one item to pass this objective. No items will be given in the wrong order. The student will be judged by the instructor on this objective.

1.3   *Respond to a series of statements or questions.*

In this type of objective, the student is asked to respond to a series of questions or statements in either written or spoken form.

This type of objective is similar to the preceding two in that the student must respond with a series of answers, which in some structured situations (filling out a job application, for example) could be listed beforehand. Some responses desired in this type of objective, however, require the student to be more flexible and that he choose the most appropriate of many possible responses.

As in the preceding type of objective, the main thing to include in the Conditions is how the student will be tested to assure he can perform correctly. In cases where writing-out is involved, this is not difficult. In situations where it is acted-out or really practiced, it is often difficult to enumerate the circumstances and the success criteria. The Behavior should include as exact a list as possible of what the student is expected to reply to each likely question. This is often hard when many answers are equally acceptable. In these cases, the instructor must be allowed the discretion to determine acceptable behavior. It is sometimes acceptable just to state or attach the questions to which the student must reply (as in the case of a questionnaire he must fill out).

The Success Criteria will tell what margin of error is allowable. Must the student be *literally* correct each time? Must he answer each and every question correctly? In what time must he answer? It is often good to ask the student to perform this type of behavior several times at an acceptable level before passing him.

EXAMPLE

Behavioral Objective Title: Fill out a standard job application
Conditions: In a regular classroom situation, without aid or help.
Behavior: The student will fill out a standard job application form (attach the form to this objective statement).
Success Criteria: The student will fill out the application in 10 minutes or less. The student will have with him, or have memorized, his Social Security number, his draft card number, and the names and addresses of three personal references. The class instructor will check to see that the student has all information with him that is required and that the application form is prepared neatly and correctly as follows: (1) the printing shall be clear and readable, (2) there should be no smudges, and any erasing should be done neatly, and (3) every blank should be filled in with information or with a short dash.

1.4   *Solve a specific symbolic problem.*
This type of objective asks the student to solve a problem. The problem is symbolic (not essentially physical), as in the case of determining the noun of a sentence, or adding a column of numbers, or determining the main idea of a paragraph. It might involve using a catalogue to locate an item or using a dictionary to define a word.

The type of problem referred to in this type of objective is also specific. That means it is a single problem having one answer.

The Conditions should note the situation in which the problem should be solved (as part of a test, as a detailed exercise, etc.). The Behavior should note the specific problem the student is to solve and the answer he should attain. The Success Criteria should include margin of error, time allowed and help available.

EXAMPLE

Behavioral Objective Title: Draw a scale drawing of a landscape
Conditions: With the assistance of one student to help use a tape, and using the blank general map of the entrance road area and drawing

board, drafting equipment, hard lead pencil, and no assistance in the drawing (see attached blank map provided).

Behavior: The student will draw a landscape layout of the present entrance. On the map provided, he will fill in all trees and shrubs in their proper location and sized to scale with the map. See attached map with the trees and shrubs filled in correctly.

Success Criteria: The student's drawing should be like the attached map. The items on the student's map should not be incorrectly drawn or messy. The student may not omit any item. The student's scale may vary by not more than ⅛ inch on any one item. The student must complete the measurements (with assistance) in one day and the drawing within two days after the measurements.

1.5   *Solve a general type of symbolic problem.*

In this type of objective, the student is asked to know how to solve any problem of a general type given to him. The student cannot study a specific problem, but must instead learn the general technique for solving the particular type of problem. The Conditions should note the situation the problem should be solved under (as part of a test, as a detailed exercise, etc.). Give examples of the type of problem to be solved. Give an outline of the procedure to be used in solving the problem if necessary. The Success Criteria should include margin of error, time allowed, help available, etc. Usually, since the student is being asked to be able to solve a general type of problem, he will be given a large number and asked to solve most of them correctly (eight out of ten).

EXAMPLE

Behavioral Objective Title: Adding mixed decimal numbers

Conditions: On a standard entrance exam, or on a quiz after class study, the student will add mixed decimal numbers correctly. The decimal numbers should not be already lined up for addition so that the student is forced to line up the decimal points himself.

Behavior: The student will add decimal problems involving mixed numbers, using one of the standard tests or quizzes.

Example of such a problem:

Add: 23.45, 201.4, 354.001, 234.09, 100.0001

Success Criteria: The student will work at least ten problems of the above type in a period of ten minutes. The student will pass at least eight out of ten, or 80%. The instructor checks the correctness of this addition process.

2.0   The types of behavioral objectives considered in this second section will include all those with a first digit of two. This will denote that they are *Physical Behavioral Objectives.* These types of objectives will be concerned with the student demonstrating behaviors that require him to physically perform a task or job in a given situation.

2.1   *Make physical identifications (point to things).*

This type of objective asks the student to recall the name of a physical object. It is like 1.1 "Recall a name; list a set of names; state a simple rule or fact," except that in the first case the material is to be recalled with purely verbal or paper and pencil work, while in this case the student is expected to actually identify the real object.

In general, the Conditions should explain the test conditions, noting especially what access the student will have to the object to be identified. The Behavior would list the objects, etc., to be identified and will use the names the student will give. The Success Criteria would tell what margin of error is allowable. Must all the objects be correctly named? Must they be recalled instantly? In general, the instructor will judge the success of the student on this task.

EXAMPLE

Behavioral Objective Title: Describe the basic arc welding equipment

Conditions: In the Introduction to Welding Shop, with no help, and using the equipment at the demonstration arc welding bench.

Behavior: The student will point out and name the basic parts of the Arc Welding set-up. He will point to and identify:
1. the source of electricity
2. the electrode cable
3. the electrode holder
4. the electrode
5. the ground clamp
6. the ground cable

Success Criteria. The student must name every item he points to correctly. He may omit one of the six. He must name every item as it is listed above. He does not have to name the items in any particular order. The student must name all the items in less than five minutes to a class instructor.

2.2   *Perform simple physical acts.*

In this type of objective, the student is called upon to perform simple physical acts. This type of performance should be specific and usually is a response to a specific situation of some sort. This type of objective is not too common, since most acts that the student learns that will be written as behavioral objectives will be complex acts (acts where several simple acts are combined). In some cases, however, there are objectives that are important, specific and simple and call for this type of objective. In general the Conditions will simply describe the situation and what tools will be used in the action. The Behavior will include a description of the action to be performed. The Success Criteria will be simple. The student will probably pass or fail the action, as described in the Behavior.

EXAMPLE

Behavioral Objective Title: Shine shoes

Conditions: During the time he is living in the dorm, after being told but without needing to be reminded, and without aid from another student.

Behavior: The student will keep his shoes shined that he uses for evening wear, going to town, etc.

Success Criteria: The student should shine his shoes at least twice in one month's time. He should shine them more often if they are scuffed up or muddy. The student will pass this objective if his staffing committee (dorm counselor, education instructor and vocational instructor) agree that his dress shoes have looked in good shape for one month running.

2.3   *Perform complex actions (with instructions or by rote).*

In this type of objective, the student is asked to perform an act with the aid of instructions, or following instructions as they are verbally given, etc. This type of objective is appropriate when the student does not need to memorize the performance but merely to have had the experience of having done it once, or where he will always be asked to do it with the help of instructions. The level of skill required to perform the task should be minimal.

The Conditions in this type of objective must state what aids the student will have available. It should also tell how much aid he may have. Attach the "aid" if possible.

The Behavior tells the task the student must perform. It gives a description of the task in such detail that any other instructor in the same area will know the task described and how the student is to do it. The "aid" in the Conditions will describe the task, so this section should be kept short.

The Success Criteria tell what will constitute completing the task successfully. If it is a task the student is only doing to be able to say he has done it once, the criteria should be simple. On the other hand, if it is an important task that is demanding in spite of always being done with instructions available, the Success Criteria will be difficult.

EXAMPLE

Behavioral Objective Title: Prepare omelets

Conditions: Given a recipe (from recipe book), skillet, whip with fork, spatula, shortening and range.

Behavior: The student will prepare and cook a plain omelet. He will combine eggs and milk in bowl and whip. He will then place the mixture in a properly heated and greased skillet. The omelet will be folded when coagulation occurs and cooked until ready to serve.

Success Criteria: The finished omelet will be light and fluffy, yellow in color, neatly folded and well heated. The student will prepare at least ten omelets successfully. The class instructor will judge the success.

2.4 *Perform physically skilled actions.*

In this type of objective the student is called upon to perform skilled acts without assistance. It is a complex task, but he knows exactly what he is to do.

Most of the skills taught in vocational programs will fall into this type of behavioral objective. In this objective, the Conditions will include the object to be performed upon, and the tools to be used. It will specify help to be allowed. Manuals may be allowed, but specific instructions are not used (if they were included they would be a type 2.3 objective). Work conditions, place, etc., should be specific.

EXAMPLE

Behavioral Objective Title: Prepare tossed green salads

Conditions: The student will use a knife, wooden chopping block, a large steel kitchen bowl, fresh lettuce, tomatoes, radishes, carrots, celery and without a recipe book.

Behavior: The student will select the appropriate amounts of lettuce, tomatoes, radishes, carrots, celery and onions, taking care to remove discolored and spoiled sections of the vegetables. He will wash and dice ingredients and place them on absorbent paper towels to avoid sogginess. He will then mix all ingredients together in the salad bowl.

Success Criteria: The entire procedure will be judged by the instructor for correct sanitary practices. The instructor will also check on the appearance of the selected ingredients, their freshness and the quantity prepared. Students must prepare two tossed salads in order to pass this objective.

2.5 *Perform an appropriate skilled action in a problem solving situation (determine what is to be done and then do it).*

In this type of objective, the student is asked to do a task that involves two things: (1) determining from many possible problems, the actual problem at hand, and (2) acting to solve the problem. In the Conditions, the situation and limits of the student investigation must be spelled out. Secondly, the tools/assistance that he will use to correct or solve the problem must be stated. This type of performance is complex and is often longer than the preceding types of objectives. The Behavior is also likely to be somewhat lengthy. The response that the student must make to a problem must be spelled out. It may require a second page attached to the Behavioral Objective Statement. The Success Criteria, too, will have two sections. One must establish some criteria for the student's locating the problem and still other criteria for his correcting it. Since he probably has some skill before he attempts an objective like this, the standards should be rigorous. Time limits, standards of performance, etc., should all be at the highest level one wants the student to reach before graduation.

EXAMPLE
Behavioral Objective Title: Repair a flashlight

Conditions: Given a flashlight that does not light and no aid, and being in the basic electronics shop with flashlight batteries, flashlight bulbs and a "tester" available.

Behavior: The student will repair the flashlight and will:
1. check the batteries by removing and replacing them with new ones
2. check the light bulb by removing and replacing it with a new one
3. use a "tester" to determine if switch is working. If the switch is not working, the student should check with the classroom instructor for directions.

Success Criteria: The student will work through the checks in progressive order, stopping whenever the flashlight works. The class instructor will pass on this objective, which the student should do in under three minutes.

2.6 *Determine acceptable quality in physical products.*

In this type of objective the student is expected to display judgment about the quality of a finished product. This is a hard skill to teach or to judge.

A student may be said to be reaching professional attitudes in a vocation (or socially mature levels in everyday life) when he can himself determine if such a thing is acceptable or not, using the standards acceptable to others in the trade. In other words, at this point the student may be said to have internalized the standards of his adopted trade.

The Conditions, in this type of objective, will usually list the sort of things and the circumstances under which the student will be given items to judge. The Behavior will involve the student's selecting or judging items and selecting those of particular quality. In terms understandable to another professional in the field, the quality of items to be selected should be noted.

The Success Criteria should specify how one will know if the student has chosen correctly. In perhaps most cases it will be known because his choice agrees with the instructor's choice. Since this is open to subjective disagreements, it is best if it can be arranged to have two or more judges. If general standards can be stated, they will help.

EXAMPLE

Behavioral Objective Title: Direct planting crew

Conditions: Given a "crew" of three or more other students, and using shovels, tape measures, water cans and hoses.

Behavior: The student will direct (and take part himself) a "crew" in planting trees or shrubs. The crew will demonstrate their skills at:
1. removing plants from nursery
2. bulling and burlaping plants
3. transplanting stock
4. measuring and digging at sight
5. planting stock
6. finishing ground after planting

The "crew leader" will check each task as it is finished to be sure:
1. that the task is done properly, that the stock is not injured, etc.
2. that the task is done neatly, that the nursery and landscape sights are properly cleaned up after the task
3. that all tools are cleaned and returned
4. that all students do their fair shares of the work

Success Criteria: The "crew leader" will be responsible for seeing that the task is performed and that the completed product meets with nursery practices and standards. The class instructor will check the student on this.

3.0   The types of objectives considered in the third section will include all those with a first digit of 3. This will denote that they are *Attitudinal Behavioral Objectives.* These types of objectives will be concerned with the student demonstrating behaviors that indicate he has a desired attitude. Attitudes can be examined directly.

There is, of course, some overlap between verbal, physical and attitudinal objectives. A behavioral objective should be considered attitudinal only when the behavior relates to an attitude, a way of doing a thing, an approach to problems, etc., and not simply the measurement of verbal or physical responses to a situation. In the first two sections (verbal and physical performance objectives) we are concerned with the student's ability to perform given verbal or physical tasks. In the case of attitudinal objectives, we are concerned with the performance of verbal or physical acts that are indicative of mental attitudes or states.

3.1   *State or list probable consequences of a given action*

In this type of objective the student is expected to show that he "understands" the likely results of a given course of action. The action will usually be social, but not always. The Conditions for this type of objective tell the circumstances under which the student proves he can describe, list, name, etc. This will probably be a test, or verbal situation. Does he receive any help, etc.? The Behavior section should describe or list exactly what the student is expected to know or understand. The Success Criteria should tell how often, how fast, and how well the student will respond. If a test item is used, it should be attached to the Behavioral Objective Statement.

EXAMPLE

Behavioral Objective Title: Smoking in bed

Conditions: On a written test, without help.

Behavior: The student will explain that he should not smoke in bed because of the danger he might fall asleep and drop the cigarette and light his bedding. The likelihood of dorms catching on fire and the consequent need for caution should be stressed.

Success Criteria: The student will indicate the above in similar words on the test. The dorm counselor will grade the test. The student must get the whole idea correct to pass.

3.2   *Evidence memory of correct social responses over an extended period of time.*

In this type of objective, one is asking the student to perform in an expected way time after time in one after another example of a situation. The Conditions should specify the situation the student is to respond to. Often this will simply be daily Center life. It should be noted if he is to be aided in the response and how much. The Behavior should spell out how the student is to respond to the situation. It should be in enough detail so that several observers can agree upon the fact that the student is or is not responding correctly. The Success Criteria should state who will observe the student.

It is wise to have as many observers as possible to reduce subjectivity of judgment.

EXAMPLE

Behavioral Objective Title: Demonstrate proper appearance
for vocational class

Conditions: While performing all of the preceding milestones in this module, and without needing to be especially reminded of it.

Behavior: The student will demonstrate that he can appear for class in a way that would help him keep a job later.

Success Criteria: The instructor will sign off on this objective after the student has completed at least two-thirds of the course's objectives while:

1. coming to class in approved clothing (as posted in shop),
2. coming to class with hair of acceptable cleanliness and style, and
3. coming to class with hands and face clean.

3.3 *Respond with limited or controlled responses in given social situations.*

This type of performance situation, as opposed to the previous type of performance in which the student was to respond in one sort of way to a situation, occurs when the student is asked to respond and there is a great variety of ways he could respond that would all be acceptable.

The Conditions for this type of objective should include the situation the student will face.

The Success Criteria in this case merely involves not crossing the limits of behavior in the situation prescribed in the Behavior section. Most often this will be judged by negative instances of behavior rather than positive.

EXAMPLE

Behavioral Objective Title: Behave appropriately during store selling

Conditions: During normal class situations, when the student is "on duty" in the store and selling to other students or staff.

Behavior: The student will use language that will not offend in later job situations. He should not curse or make any obscene remarks or jokes. He should not be insulting to the customer, but rather refer "difficult" customers to his superior.

Success Criteria: The student will not use any inappropriate language for a period of two weeks of selling on the floor. This will be judged by the class instructor.

Summary

Use of this classification system allows the writer of behavioral objectives to clarify his thinking about the type of behavior with which he is really concerned. It allows reviewers and editors a convenient way to catalogue and analyze objectives. It allows one to decide, for example, that a course needs work if, in spite of generally stated intentions, all the objectives turn out to be 1.1 or 1.2 type objectives rather than 2.1 or 2.2 objectives. This classification system has proved helpful in communicating about the many objectives we have reviewed in developing a curriculum system for Men's Urban Job Corps Centers.

REFERENCES

Ammerman, Harry L. & William H. Melching. *The Derivation, Analysis, and Classification of Instructional Objectives.* HumRRO (Human Resources Research Office), Technical Report 66-4, 1966.

Bloom, Benjamin S. (Ed.) *Taxonomy of Educational Objectives. Handbook I, Cognitive Domain.* New York: David McKay Co., 1956.

Crawford, Meredith P. Concepts of Training. In *Psychological Principles in System Development,* Robert M. Gagné (Ed.) New York: Holt, Rinehart and Winston, 1962.

Gagné, Robert M. The Analysis of Instructional Objectives for the Design of Instruction. In *Teaching Machines and Programmed Learning, Vol. II,* Robert Glaser (Ed.) National Education Association, Washington, D. C., 1965.

————. *The Conditions of Learning.* New York: Holt, Rinehart, and Winston, 1966.

Harmon, Paul. Developing Performance Objectives in Job Training Programs. *Educational Technology, 18,* November 30, 1968, pp. 11-16.

Krathwohl, David R., *et al. Taxonomy of Educational Objectives. Handbook II: The Affective Domain.* New York: David McKay Co., 1964.

Lindvall, C. M. (Ed.) *Defining Educational Objectives.* University of Pittsburgh Press, Pittsburgh, Pennsylvania, 1964.

Massey, Carter & John Miller. *How To Write Job Corps Performance Objectives.* Job Corps Center, San Marcos, Texas, 1968.

Mager, Robert F. *Preparing Instructional Objectives* (or *Preparing Objectives for Programmed Instruction*). San Francisco: Fearon Publishers, 1961.

———— & Kenneth Beach, Jr. *Developing Vocational Instruction.* San Francisco: Fearon Publishers, 1967.

Melching, William H. & Harry L. Ammerman. *Deriving, Specifying and Using Instructional Objectives.* HumRRO (Human Resources Research Office), Professional Paper 10-66, 1966.

Office of Economic Opportunity. *Instructional Systems Development Manual.* Office of Economic Opportunity, Washington, D. C., 1968.

Rummler, Geary. *Specifying Terminal Behaviors for Training.* Unpublished paper. Center for Programmed Learning for Business, University of Michigan, 1967.

Smith, Robert G., Jr. *The Development of Training Objectives.* HumRRO (Human Resources Research Office), Research Bulletin 11, 1964.

Part V

Additional Media

Andersen, Hans O. Performance Goals: Where Will They Lead Us? *Croft Professional Growth for Teachers: Science, Senior High School Edition,* Second Quarter Issue, 1969-70, pp. 1-3.

Anderson, Ronald D. Formulating Objectives for Elementary Science. *Science and Children, 5,* September, 1967, pp. 20-23.

————. Has the Objective Been Attained? *Science and Children, 5,* October, 1967, pp. 33-36.

Bartolome, Paz I. Teachers' Objectives and Questions in Primary Reading. *The Reading Teacher, 23,* October, 1969, pp. 27-33.

Bolvin, John O., Billie Hubrig & Ruth Stone. *1967-1968 Reading Curriculum, Experimental Edition with Explanations* (Working Paper Number 28, Individually Prescribed Instruction). Philadelphia, Pennsylvania: Research for Better Schools, 1967, 119 pp.

Brodbeck, May. Logic and Scientific Method in Research on Teaching. *Handbook of Research on Teaching.* N. L. Gage (Ed.) Chicago: Rand McNally & Company, 1963, pp. 48-51.

Burns, Richard W. Objectives in Action. *Educational Technology, 8,* February 15, 1968, pp. 14-15.

Ciancone, Elmer S. New Technique for Instructional Analysis. *Industrial Arts and Vocational Education, 57,* April, 1968, pp. 35-39.

Course Objectives for Industrial Technology I: The World of Construction. Columbus, Ohio: The Ohio State University, Industrial Arts Curriculum Project, 1966, 64 pp.

Criterion Variables for the Evaluation of Guidance Practices: A Taxonomy of Guidance Objectives. Columbia, Missouri: University of Missouri, undated, 31 pp.

DeRose, James V. *The Independent Study Science Program at Marple Newtown Senior High School.* Washington, D. C.: National Science Teachers Association, 1968, 34 pp. (Mimeo.)

Dressel, Paul L. Are Your Objectives Showing? *NEA Journal, 44,* May, 1955, pp. 297-298.

Dunham, Benjamin. MENC Rings a Behavioral Change. *Music Educators Journal, 55,* May, 1969, pp. 65-70.

Dyasi, Hubert Mongameli. *An Exploratory Investigation of Certain Affective Behaviors Associated with the Learning of Science* (unpublished Ph.D. dissertation, University of Illinois, 1966), 127 pp.

Eiss, Albert F. The NSTA Conferences on Scientific Literacy. *The Science Teacher, 35,* May, 1968, pp. 30-32.

————. *Why Behavioral Objectives?* Washington, D. C.: National Science Teachers Association, 1968. An overhead transparency/slide and sound tape sequence.

Fraenkel, Jack R. A Curriculum Model for the Social Studies. *Social Education, 33,* January, 1969, pp. 41-47.

Geisert, Paul. Behavioral Objectives for Biology. *The American Biology Teacher, 31,* April, 1969, pp. 233-235.

Hales, Carma J., Dorothy O. Wardrop & James R. Young. *A Teacher's Guide to Continuous Progress in Reading Instruction.* Salt Lake City, Utah: Continuous Progress Education, Five-District Project, 1967, 82 pp.

Health Education: A Conceptual Approach to Curriculum Design. Washington, D. C.: School Health Education Study, 1967, 141 pp.

Hunter, Madeline C. The Role of Physical Education in Child Development and Learning. *Journal of Health, Physical Education, Recreation, 39,* May, 1968, pp. 56-58.

Kapfer, Miriam B., Duane A. Fuller & Kathleen L. Hogsett. *K-12 Interim Curriculum Guide in Music.* Las Vegas, Nevada: Clark County School District, 1968, 73 pp.

Koran, John J., Jr., Earl J. Montague & Gene E. Hall. *How To Use Behavioral Objectives in Science Instruction.* Washington, D. C.: National Science Teachers Association, 1969, 12 pp.

Learning Research and Development Center, University of Pittsburgh. *Mathematics Continuum—Individually Prescribed Instruction.* Philadelphia, Pennsylvania: Research for Better Schools, Inc., undated.

Lysaught, Jerome P. & Clarence M. Williams. Appropriate Objectives. In *A Guide to Programmed Instruction.* New York: John Wiley and Sons, Inc., 1963, pp. 52-69.

Maffett, James E. *Instructional Performance Objectives for a Course in General Biology.* Bradenton, Florida: Manatee Junior College, undated, 32 pp.

Mathematics Curriculum Guideline, K-6. Las Vegas, Nevada: Clark County School District, 1967. unpaged.

McDermott, John J. Carlisle District Writes Behavioral Objectives. *The Science Teacher, 35,* May 1968, pp. 32-33.

Montague, Earl J. & David P. Butts. Behavioral Objectives. *The Science Teacher, 35,* March, 1968, pp. 33-35.

———— & John J. Koran, Jr. Behavioral Objectives and Instructional Design. An Elaboration. *The Science Teacher, 36,* March, 1969, pp. 10, 77-78.

Oakes, Herbert Irving. Objectives of Mathematics Education in the United States from 1920-1960 (unpublished Ed.D. dissertation, Columbia University, New York, 1965), 246 pp.

Palmer, John R. Does the Study of History Promote Behavioral Change? *Teachers College Record, 67,* November, 1965, pp. 81-89.

Plowman, Paul. *Behavioral Objectives Extension Service.* Chicago, Illinois: Science Research Associates, Inc., 1968-69. See especially the following sections:
>Unit 2: Behavioral Objectives in English and Literature, 28 pp.
>Unit 3: Behavioral Objectives in Social Science, 37 pp.
>Unit 4: Behavioral Objectives in Science, 34 pp.
>Unit 5: Behavioral Objectives in Biology, 29 pp.
>Unit 6: Behavioral Objectives in Mathematics, 29 pp.
>Unit 7: Behavioral Objectives in Art and Music, 32 pp.
>Unit 8: Behavioral Objectives in Reading, 34 pp.

Popham, W. James & Eva L. Baker. *Establishing Performance Standards.* Los Angeles, California: Vimcet Associates, 1967. Illustrated filmstrip, accompanying audio-taped narration, and instructor's manual, 46 frames, 22 minutes.

See also other materials in Vimcet series (Part I).

The Pre-Technology Program: A Descriptive Report. San Francisco: Cogswell Polytechnical College, 1966, 75 pp.

Reading and the Kindergarten Child: Kindergarten Reading Guide and Selected Multi-Media Appendix. Las Vegas, Nevada: Clark County School District, 1968.

Science—A Process Approach: A Guide for Inservice Instruction. Washington, D. C.: American Association for the Advancement of Science, 1967, 128 pp. plus Response Sheets, Process Measures for Teachers, films and in-service "games."

Smith, Robert G., Jr. *An Annotated Bibliography on the Determination of Training Objectives.* Alexandria, Virginia: The George Washington University, 1964, 39 pp.

Social Science Curriculum Guide and Selected Multi-Media, K-6. Las Vegas, Nevada: Clark County School District, 1969, 178 pp.

Vogel, Paul. Battle Creek Physical Education Curriculum Project. *Journal of Health, Physical Education, Recreation, 40,* September, 1969, pp. 25-29.

Woodruff, Asahel D. *Preconference Educational Research Program in Art Education, Final Report.* Washington, D. C.: The National Art Education Association, 1968, 35 pp.

Young, Jay A. Behavioral Definitions of "Understand" and "Think." *The Science Teacher, 36,* November, 1969, pp. 59-60.

Part VI

Behavioral Objectives and the Educational Technologist

The articles included in Part VI have a unifying thread in their direct relationship to the broad field of technology. The term "educational technology" has been variously defined and used throughout recent years. Therefore, an explanation of the way it is used in this volume is in order. Educational technology is used here to refer to both the hardware and the software involved in solving practical and theoretical problems related to learning and instruction. John Kenneth Galbraith, in his book, The New Industrial State, *clearly uses the preceding ideas in the following inclusive definition of technology:*

> *Technology means the systematic application of scientific or other organized knowledge to practical tasks. Its most important consequence . . . is in forcing the division and subdivision of any such task into its component parts. Thus, and only thus, can organized knowledge be brought to bear on performance.*
>
> *. . .*
>
> *. . . the subdivision of tasks to accord with areas of organized knowledge is not confined to, nor has it any special relevance to, mechanical processes. It occurs in medicine, business management, building design, child and dog rearing and every other problem that involves an agglomerate of scientific knowledge.*

*The five articles in Part VI focus on instructional planning and imple-
mentation. Authors included in this section view systems approaches
as the logical "next step" in software—a step which is essential if a
move is to be made from currently prevalent group-paced instruction
to the completely individualized instructional pacing of the future.*

Engman offers a four-phase instructional model or system which assists the educational planner in developing consistent and cohesive teaching strategies, learning materials, and evaluation procedures. Behavioral objectives play a key role in the operation of the system.

Behavioral Objectives: Key to Planning*

BILL D. ENGMAN

The desirability of stating objectives in behavioral terms is hardly debatable. The ability to write behavioral objectives is, however, only Phase I of what should be a four-phase teaching plan. The ability to develop adequately the second and third phases of the sequence determines whether or not the objectives are finally realized. Phase II of this sequence involves the design of appropriate learning experiences, while Phase III involves the construction of evaluative devices which will ascertain the degree to which the desired behaviors have been achieved by the students. Phase IV concerns teacher analysis of the outcomes of a given teaching unit. Regardless of how well a teacher writes statements which satisfy the criteria of a behavioral objective, unless he understands the relationship of the objectives to what follows in the other phases, his teaching may well remain ineffective.

To illustrate this relationship, consider the following objective: "Given a representative sampling of unknown rocks and a testing kit, the student should be able to identify correctly at least one half of the unknown rocks." The implications of this objective include: (1) a sizable collection of rocks of various kinds with which the students can have first-hand experience, (2) an adequate supply of test kits for use in laboratory work and on performance tests, (3) opportunities provided

*Reprinted from *The Science Teacher, 35,* October, 1968, pp. 86-87, by permission of the publisher and the author.

for the actual use of test kits in identification of rocks, (4) relevant content covered by the teacher and grasped by the student, and (5) evaluation in terms of observed ability to use various tests to identify unknown rocks.

If the stated objective is what is wanted as the outcome of our teaching efforts, we must develop our teaching plans accordingly and inform the student of what is expected of him. There are few, if any, valid reasons for not informing a student about what his grade will be based on and how it will be established. More than once teachers have been heard to remark, "If I do this, there will be no curve!" In the first place, this is doubtful; in the second place—so what? Is the role of the teacher to teach in such a way that students master content and skills deemed valuable, or is it to assure that there is always a normal distribution of "A's" and "F's" lest we be accused of being too easy?

There are also psychological factors involved in this approach to teaching which bear favorably on learning. If the teacher defines for the student the objectives of a given unit, the student (1) knows what he is expected to be able to do, and therefore, both his tasks and goals are more definite; (2) is able to identify progress as he moves toward these goals, and is rewarded, thus reinforcing the material; (3) recognizes problems in moving toward the goals, and consequently should seek assistance; (4) realizes when he has arrived at his behavioral destination, thus promoting systems of intrinsic rewards; and (5) more readily accepts evaluation results, assuming the device is appropriate.

There is also a type of security realized by the teacher in this approach. After defining the specific objectives for a unit, the teaching approach is consequently determined. It is relatively easy to identify necessary content coverage, laboratory experiences, materials, and equipment needed to develop a given behavior. Planning is thereby simplified and expedited. In the sample objective above, it is clear that the students must (1) have a workable acquaintance with types of rocks and their characteristics, (2) be given practice in recognizing these characteristics in actual rocks in a laboratory situation, (3) have practice in the use of such materials as streak plates and in the application of various tests to different rock types.

The teacher must also be aware consciously, and constantly, of the final phase—evaluation. He must know at the onset of a unit which materials and content will be deliberately withheld in order that the test is more than simple recall. For example, for the performance test certain rocks must be available which are similar to and in the same categories as the laboratory specimens, but which in a sense are "unknowns." Otherwise identification of the rock may be based on remembering having worked with it, rather than on the ability to discover anew the identification of the "unknown" through the application of laboratory procedures. Thus the teacher must be cognizant in the beginning of at least major items of the evaluation, and gear the learning experiences in such a way that students are moving toward the development of proficiency in these major areas.

Evaluation of Behavioral Objectives

If one believes in the enhancement of teaching effectiveness through the use of behavioral objectives, then one's thinking in terms of testing must shift from measuring mastery of content to measuring achievement of objectives. Content and objectives are not incompatible, however. The point is that content must be tested as it applies to the objectives, rather than as a distinct entity which has no relationship with the activities which precede the test.

The so-called "Law of Effect" tells us that students tend to learn those things for which they are rewarded. If the tests we design to evaluate a given content area are based not on the objectives and supportive activities but rather on the ability to remember unrelated specifics, the purpose of writing behavioral objectives is defeated. Referring back to the sample objective, if instead of giving the students rocks to actually identify on a performance test, we simply ask the student to *list* the characteristics of a given rock, then all the lab experiences could be eliminated without significantly affecting the outcome of the test. They have not been rewarded for what took place in the laboratory; therefore, what happened in the laboratory becomes concomitant learning, if learning at all.

Consistency Keynote

It should be clear now that the key to teaching through the use of behavioral objectives is consistency. The type of activities must be consistent with the statement of outcomes we desire, and the tests or other types of evaluations must be consistent both with the activities and the objectives. There is established, therefore, a logical and orderly developmental sequence from phase to phase. A model of this approach appears below.

Teaching by means of objectives also allows the teacher to evaluate his effectiveness in arriving at the objectives. Failure to realize objectives may lie in: (1) unrealistic objectives for a particular group of students, (2) inappropriate experiences, activities, and/or content, or (3) a poor evaluation device. Analysis of teaching results, reflection on

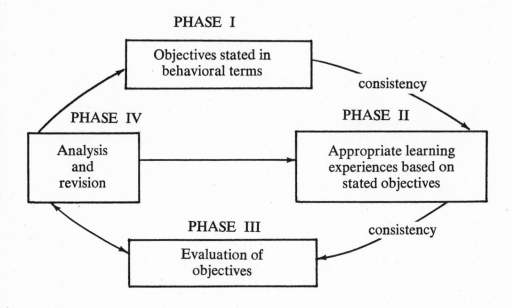

PHASE I

Objectives stated in
behavioral terms

consistency

PHASE IV

Analysis
and
revision

PHASE II

Appropriate learning
experiences based on
stated objectives

PHASE III

Evaluation of
objectives

consistency

what has taken place in the classroom, and subsequent revision should improve teaching effectiveness each time a unit is finished.

Behavioral objectives undoubtedly can be the key to effective teaching in any program. It is vital to remember, however, that the objective requires careful nurture and proper treatment if it is to mature into a realized goal. Whether or not this eventuates depends primarily on appropriate and consistent planning.

*Childs presents a similar but much
more detailed approach to instructional planning than that outlined in
the preceding article. Childs describes a specific series of twelve
activities involved in systematic instructional design, all of which
emanate from the primary activity—
the specification of objectives.*

A Set of Procedures for the Planning of Instruction*

JOHN W. CHILDS

The purpose of this paper is to describe a specific set of procedures for
the planning of instruction. A flow chart is provided in *Figure 1*. This is
intended to aid the reader in following the sequential decisions, activities,
and feedback functions of the proposed set of procedures.

Discussion of Developmental Model

The first activity block in the flow chart is traditional with the education profession. It allows for the inclusion in the developmental process
of a number of significant inputs to the design system.

The basic goals and purposes of education, as drawn from the total
society, must become a part of the educational enterprise. This initial
block suggests that the designer can explicitly recognize the goals of his
particular school, its purposes and aims.

Given a reasonably precise set of statements concerning the general
goals and purposes of the school, the designer moves to the specification
of the behavioral components of each of the goals.

The task of translating the content and experiences of the school into

*Reprinted from *Educational Technology, 8,* August 30, 1968, pp. 7-14, by
permission of the publisher and the author.

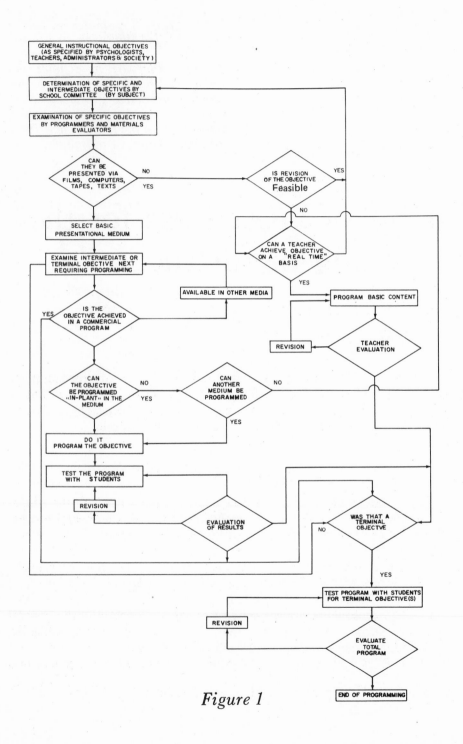

Figure 1

precise statements of behavior is an arduous and lengthy one. In an effort to develop individuals who can do the job of preparing behavioral specifications for something called a course, the author's experience has been that it takes two individuals working together to do a good job. The lone individual is inclined, by the nature of his thinking processes, to miss some significant aspect of the behavior to be learned or the conditions under which it will be learned as he prepares a behavioral specification. When the work is done by a team, the immediacy of feedback concerning missing elements in the specification produces a better behavioral specification in less time.

The meaning of the term "behavioral specification" as used here should be reviewed at this point. The first component of a good behavioral specification is a statement of a learner's observable performance. Examples of some observable performance statements are given below:

> Given a map with a printed compass of the streets and main buildings surrounding a fictitious school building, the student will be able to answer at least six of ten questions based upon the identification of certain main buildings that would be reached if he followed the ten sets of walking directions from the school (like: walk two blocks west and three blocks north from the school) during a twenty minute period with the map and questions.

> At the end of this unit a student will be able to differentiate between the initial sound of "M" and "B."

There are several ways to construct observable performance statements. These statements are only representative of some behavior areas which may be found within a school.

The second component of the complete behavioral specification called for at this point in the flow chart is a statement of the conditions under which the performance will be observed.

The third component of a behaviorally stated objective is a statement of the level of performance, or criterion for the performance.

The third box in our flow chart proposes to submit the specifications developed by the school committee of subject specialists to a team of full-time specialist programmers and materials evaluators. The intent here is to relieve the classroom teacher of the mundane and routine task of searching out or developing new materials with which to implement the objectives. This phase might well be deleted from the chart if one were applying the process to his own personal development behavior;

however, this is the point at which the instructional (1) psychologist, (2) research analyst, (3) curriculum specialist, and (4) media specialist enter the design process with their particular expertise. In the development of instruction, this is the point at which the programmer and materials evaluator must make initial judgments based on experience, knowledge, and learning research about the feasibility of mediating the learning leading to the specific objectives. Here is where input constraints are considered.

If there are limitations in what is available in terms of mediating machinery or mediating software, this is the point in the design process where the limitations can be considered. As a result of the information gathering activity in this block, a decision point is reached concerning the direction of future activity.

The third shows the "go, no-go" decision that must be made concerning the attempt to conduct the instruction in a mediated form. A negative decision at this point will lead to a sequence in the model calling for examination of the objective for possible revision. If a positive decision is reached at this point, then a sequence of development activity follows that selects or produces mediated forms of instruction.

What choices are available if a negative decision chain results from an objective which the design team believes cannot be programmed in a mediated form? It has already been suggested that the first alternative in this situation is the possible revision of the objective; therefore, the first block on the negative chain is one of further decision making on the nature of the objective itself.

Two alternatives are available in the flow chart: first, the positive decision for revision and, second, the negative decision, which leads to additional decision activity. If the design team believes that revision is possible, the proposed revision is fed back to the objective preparation team and a substitute objective is drafted and begins its way through the design process. If the design team ascertains from the objective preparation group that no revision is possible, then the next block in the flow chart raises the question of real-time teacher instruction.

Why, in *this* model, was it decided to put the decision for teacher handling of the objective in real-time after the question of other forms of mediation?

If the decision block for teacher handling of the objectives is placed before the mediation question, teacher handling will frequently occur when some other form might do equally well. It is believed that in the end the teacher *can* do just about any instructional task. But should he? Thus, it seems wise to raise the question of mediated individualized instruction first in the flow chart.

Returning to the teacher decision chain, two alternative decisions again occur. One, the teacher *can* do it on a real-time basis; or two, the teacher *cannot* do it. In the event that the negative decision is made, the model shows a feedback to the objectives determination block. If the first decision is made for teacher handling, then a move is made to a design sequence which produces or secures the content resources the teacher will need to handle the objective.

A return to the main sequence of the developmental flow chart picks up at the mediation decision block. A positive decision at this point results in a task activity labeled "select the basic presentational medium." This particular block implies the full means for the completion of this task.

At this date, the media field knows far too little about the decision structure to use in carrying out this task. Some fairly good specifications of the media characteristics exist, but there is no evidence to tie these characteristics to the learning suggested by the specific objectives. Decisions can be made here by considering such things as logistical requirements, ease of preparation of material, visual or audio nature of the learning experience, or the availability of the medium. What is needed is a classification structure that will allow the designer to *match the medium to the behavioral objective.*

Two efforts at this type of matching have been widely distributed. Robert Gagné, in Chapter XI of his book, *The Conditions of Learning,* (Holt, 1965) supplies a chart relating his eight learning types (into which behavioral objectives may be fitted) to the specific medium of communication that may be appropriate for that type of learning.

Leslie J. Briggs wrote of another procedure for achieving this end in the March, 1967, issue of *Audiovisual Instruction* under the title "A Procedure for the Design of Multimedia Instruction." He drew upon the work of Gagné for his learning-type classifications, but chose to approach the media selection process on an overall basis for a series of objectives rather than on an objective-by-objective base. Both Gagné and Briggs indicate a need for considerable additional research on the media-matching variables.

Once the basic presentational medium is selected, further efforts must be conducted to develop the medium in line with the objectives of the mediated sequence. The next activity block on the flow chart indicates this need by suggesting that each objective be taken on for examination of its implications for the design of the instructional material within the selected medium. It results in a decision block in which the designer must answer the question of programming the objective with the design team or selecting the program from a commercially available source.

This decision block is essential to the function of the media specialist.

Neither the time nor the funds are available to buy time to create the wheel all over again. If an objective is embodied in the material prepared by an outside agency, then we must make use of the material in order to have the energy and time to create the many resources that do *not* exist.

This decision block has three alternatives: first, a positive response that indicates the objective exists in a mediated form, in which case there is a skip ahead to the trial testing of the mediated form; second, the possibility exists that the objective is met in commercially available form but in a medium other than that selected in the previous sequence. In this case, the feedback is to the medium selection activity to check the appropriateness of altering the medium selection. The third alternative here is a new decision block to determine if the objective can be met through the preparation of a mediated unit in the medium selected within the confines of the design team's development resources.

If a positive decision is made here, then the design team turns over the objective and the specifications for the learning material to the programmer for the medium being used. If the decision is negative, then another design team decision is necessary. At this point, other commercially available media have been ruled out. The remaining decision must be to program in another medium or to feed the objective back for revision or reconsideration of teacher handling.

If the decision is to go back to teacher handling, then we enter again our secondary decision chain. Given that the decision is made to have a teacher handle the objective, the basic program content for the teacher must be prepared along with any additional supplementary materials. An addition to this decision chain (that does not occur in regular teaching patterns as we now know them) is the planned teacher tryout and revision cycle for the development of teacher handled objectives.

Returning to the main decision chain and the other alternative decision on programming in another medium, the DO IT activity block appears once again.

Perhaps next to the stress placed on objectives in this model of instructional development is the stress placed on the pretesting of materials for their ability to produce the changes in student behavior called for by the objectives. Thus, the activity block following the act of preparing the mediated material in the selected medium is the testing of the mediated instruction with students.

If this phase of instructional development is treated rigorously, and sufficient tests are conducted to "debug" the instruction, it may be expected that the mediated instruction will be adequately developed for a major trial without damaging results to a large segment of the students for which the instruction is designed. This stage of pilot testing and revision should be an integral part of the design team's activity during the preparation of the material to meet each objective.

Next, the flow chart leads to the activity block of revision. After enough cycles of pilot evaluation followed by revision, two alternative decisions can be made concerning further activity; the design team may reach a decision to completely recycle to consider other instructional strategies, such as teacher handling. The intent is that the evaluation of the mediated instruction will be satisfactory and thus the design effort will move into another decision situation.

The second alternative will be taken if the objective the team has programmed is a terminal one; hence, the developed mediated instruction will move to full scale testing with a large group of students. This test may result in some revision. A cycle for this activity is shown on the flow chart. Following total program review, the instructional planning comes to an end.

In the event that the objective(s) under design consideration is not a terminal objective of the pilot test point, the system recycles to pick up and carry through a new objective(s) until a terminal one is reached.

Summary

The complex description of the functions depicted by the flow chart can be summarized in a set of procedural steps. The procedural steps are, in essence, the decision activities that must go on in the process of instructional design.

1. Determine general objectives.
2. Determine the behavioral objectives.
3. Specify the learning types for each objective.
4. Determine the feasibility of mediated instruction or teacher-handled instruction. If neither, revise objectives.
5. Select the basic presentational medium.
6. Examine each objective and develop programming specifications.
7. Choose between in-house programming and selecting from commercial sources of mediated programs which meet the objectives.
8. Program the objective in-house.
9. Test the program with students.
10. Revise the mediated program.
11. Evaluate the mediated program with a large student population.
12. Revise and conclude the instructional development sequence for any given set of behavioral objectives.

Lehmann reports on the work of Project ARISTOTLE regarding the systems approach to education. He compares the systems approach to the scientific method—"a logical step-by-step approach to problem solving." In applying this approach to education, the ARISTOTLE group defined eight essential steps, one of which was the specification of behavioral objectives.

The Systems Approach to Education*

HENRY LEHMANN

Whenever one is faced with a complex problem these days, someone is bound to suggest that the systems approach should be used, as if this were to guarantee an immediate optimum solution. I wish that there were such a magical panacea to the solution of the complex problems facing our society, whether they relate to Viet Nam, revitalization of our inner cities, public transportation, or the national education system. The systems approach does not provide the ultimate answer by only adding water and shaking vigorously. The systems approach does provide an orderly process for developing a solution, a process which is structured to minimize prejudicial preconceived notions and maximize the objectivity required to arrive at a scientifically correct answer.

Throughout 1967 a group representing government, the educational community, and industry has been meeting to encourage continuing communication of new ideas, developments, and techniques and thereby contribute to the advancement of quality and efficiency of the nation's education and training. To assure that this activity would continue to

*Reprinted from *Audiovisual Instruction, 13,* February, 1968, pp. 144-148, by permission of the publisher and the author.

stimulate an interchange of communication among the governmental-educational-industrial elements of our society, the activity was named Project ARISTOTLE—Annual Review and Information Symposium on the Technology of Training, Learning and Education.

Of the 10 task groups which were active during 1967, one was devoted exclusively to the application of the systems approach to educational problems. The task group devoted the first year to describing the systems approach. The material below is a summary of the approach developed by the entire task group and represents the material presented by the Systems Approach to Education panel at the first ARISTOTLE Symposium held in Washington, D.C., on December 6 and 7, 1967.

The systems approach is nothing new. It is what we have called in the past "the scientific method", and is a logical step-by-step approach to problem solving which we use continually, even though we perform many of the steps unconsciously. Yet it is surprising how often major problems are solved—or are attempted to be solved—by finding politically attractive solutions which are not based on a systematic analysis of the problem and alternate solutions, and therefore end up making the problem worse, rather than solving it.

As developed by Project ARISTOTLE, the systems approach to education consists of eight steps:

1. *Need*—an education/training problem;
2. *Objectives*—measurable learning goals;
3. *Constraints*—restrictions or limitations;
4. *Alternatives*—candidate solutions;
5. *Selection*—choice of best alternative;
6. *Implementation*—pilot operation of the chosen solution;
7. *Evaluation*—measurement of results obtained against originally stated objectives; and
8. *Modification*—the change of the system to correct for the deficiencies noted.

Briefly this list can be restated as:

1. Define the real problem you are trying to solve.
2. Examine many potential solutions and select the one for which an objective analysis has the greatest promise.
3. Measure the results obtained and modify the approach until the problem really is solved.

This may appear to be so self-evident that it is not worthy of discussion. Yet, as in the case with many self-evident "truths," these steps are not always followed properly, resulting in additional confusion rather than solution. The real intent of each step and the manner of application are discussed in the following sections.

Need

The first step is to state the need—the real need of the group under consideration. The real need should address the overall problem to be solved, and not only the educational problem; for the first thing we must recognize is that education, in itself, is only one solution to the problem. A statement of the need should be, for example, "We must provide better medical care," and not, "We need a programmed instruction booklet series for nursing training."

The second statement not only assumes that more nurses will provide better medical care—an action which at best will give only a partial solution to the problem—but also includes the solution; namely, programed instruction in the need statement. This is in complete violation of the systems approach.

The proper way to implement the *need* step, as well as some common pitfalls to be avoided, is shown in Figure 1.

Figure 1

NEED

DEFINITION   A statement of the real problem being faced by the society under consideration—that statement of a problem which initiates consideration of an education/training system as a potential solution.

PROCEDURE   1. Start with an expression of the generalized need; e.g., "we need better medical care."
2. Determine whether education/training constitutes at least a partial satisfaction of the need.
3. Determine in the light of the present state-of-the-art what type of manpower and what skills are needed; e.g., more knowledgeable technologists in the medical and allied sciences.
4. Define more specifically and in greater depth the group of people and skill areas required to satisfy the need.
5. Verify the need and the delineation of the group concerned through the judgment of knowledgeable people in the real world involved.

PITFALLS   1. Have you defined the real need or are you addressing a synthetic sub-problem which may presuppose the answer? (Have you considered the need for updated equipment, rather than more personnel?)
2. Have you based the need too much on assumptions and too little on verified facts?

Objectives

Once the need is properly stated, we can determine what learning objectives must be attained to satisfy the need. In this step we decide what the student should be able to do after having completed the learning experience.

This is the most important step of the systems approach, because all subsequent steps are designed to cause the learning system to meet these objectives. Hence, if the objectives are stated improperly, the systems approach will not lead to the proper solution.

To be useable in the systems approach, the objectives must be stated in terms which can be measured, for otherwise we will never know whether the system as implemented meets the stated objectives. It is this requirement for measurable objectives which makes this step the most difficult in the process.

Most of us can see readily how to write measurable objectives for skill training and for education in mathematics and the physical sciences. For example, it is easy to describe precisely the types of mathematical problems which a fifth-grade student should be able to solve, or which parts of a flower he should be able to identify correctly. The problem becomes more difficult in the language arts, social sciences, and fine arts; yet even there, many behavioral changes expected in the student can be stated in measurable terms. Instead of saying that we expect the fifth-grader to have an understanding of the problems faced by the founders of our country and be able to relate how they affect our current problems, this objective can be stated in more measurable terms as follows: "The student should read the editorial page of the newspaper at least three times a week and should be able to write a 200-word essay on how a similar problem was handled by the fathers of our country."

It is often said that stating educational objectives in measurable terms overemphasizes skills as opposed to education; that it would force the stating of objectives in terms of "The student should be able to list the names of all the Presidents in proper sequential order." As seen from the foregoing example, this need not be the case, but subtle abilities and attitudes can also be stated in measurable terms. This is the greatest challenge to the educational systems designer.

Some guidelines on the preparation of objectives are shown in Figure 2.

Constraints

The universe in which we live does not permit the implementation of just any solution. We are surrounded by constraints. Some of these

Figure 2

OBJECTIVE

DEFINITION   The determination and specification of the terminal capability desired of students after having successfully completed a learning experience.

PROCEDURE   1. Define that portion of the need which can be satisfied by the education/training system.
2. Describe in measurable terms the observable act(s) which will be accepted as evidence of the learner having achieved the objective.
3. Describe the environmental conditions (stress, etc.) under which the desired end behavior must be demonstrated.
4. Define the minimum acceptable criteria for demonstrating terminal behavior objectives.

PITFALLS   1. Are you sure that your objective contributes significantly to satisfying the real need?
2. Are your objectives stated in specific measurable terms (must be able to identify themes from Beethoven and Mozart piano concerti) as opposed to qualitative statements (must develop an understanding and appreciation of romantic music)?
3. Is your definition of the test conditions realistic and valid in light of the true need?
4. Have you confined your statement of objectives to "should be able to do," or have you mixed in references as to how the student will in fact acquire these capabilities?

are permanently inviolate because they represent laws of nature; some are temporarily inviolate because they represent current laws or fiscal limitations, and hence are changeable with time; and others appear to be constraints, but are only the reflection of years of tradition and the status quo.

It is imperative that a comprehensive list of constraints be prepared to guide the selection of alternatives. These constraints should be examined carefully to segregate the inviolate constraints from the assumptions. Too often mediocrity has been perpetuated by an attitude of, "We can't change that, we have always done it that way." Much of the technological progress which has occurred during the current century results from an attitude of scientists and engineers that "there must be a better way" and "unless you can prove that it can't work, I will continue to treat it as a potential solution."

Some guides to the preparation of constraints are listed in Figure 3.

Figure 3

CONSTRAINTS

DEFINITION   Those real-world limiting conditions which must be satisfied by any acceptable system designed to attain the educational objectives.

PROCEDURE 1. Identify the applicable families (initial student behavior, facilities, financial, timing, staff limitations, administrative, political, etc.).
2. List specific constraints within each family and establish source of constraints.
3. Label the constraints by severity (physical law, short term but inviolate, financial or political, psychological or political, subject to change).
4. Rank constraints in order of effect upon the system design.

PITFALLS   1. Have you separated:
. . . facts from assumptions?
. . . constraints from variables?
. . . intuition from bias?
. . . need from pressures?
2. Have "pet solutions" introduced unwarranted constraints?
3. Have you "built in the answer" by seeing non-existing constraints?
4. Have you carefully validated the inviolate constraints?
5. Have you defined the prerequisite or presupposed student entry capability with sufficient accuracy to permit the design of a system to bring about the required change in capability?

Alternatives

You are now ready to generate a list of potential or candidate solutions. This is the step in the process where the much advocated "brainstorm" approach is useful. Since this is not the time to discard or evaluate any solution, and since this is the time to generate all possible solutions so as not to miss the really good one, the development of alternatives should be done in an atmosphere of complete intellectual freedom, with participation from as many different groups of people as possible, as shown in Figure 4.

Figure 4

ALTERNATIVES
  DEFINITION   The generation of candidate systems which could achieve the objectives.

  PROCEDURE   1. Gather data based on current and expected state-of-the-art with respect to potential means toward the specified ends.
2. Solicit ideas from a wide spectrum of sources.
3. Keep written list of all suggested ideas—even if they appear to be impractical or to violate constraints.
4. Gather more data if the ideas are insufficient in quantity or scope.

  PITFALLS   1. Are you soliciting ideas only from the "in-group"?
2. Are you rejecting ideas as being impractical or inappropriate?
3. Do you have enough knowledge of new possibilities to include such solutions?
4. Are you inhibiting individuals from proposing radical solutions?
5. Have you considered selection rather than training as one of your alternatives?

Selection

The time has now come in the systems approach to be critical. This is the step in which we have to select the best candidate solution. This step must also be performed scientifically, otherwise the introduction of bias at this time can make a mockery of the entire systems approach.

The selection criteria must be listed first. By selection criteria we mean those characteristics which a candidate solution possesses which have an impact on the selection. These would include such classical factors as the cost of implementing the solution, the time within which it could be implemented, the degree of risk involved, the impact on other portions of the system, etc.

The next step is to quantify these selection criteria. Professional operations analysts have developed very sophisticated computerized mathematical models to evaluate various alternatives and select the optimum one. Too often, however, the model is much more accurate than the data which can be assembled for a candidate solution. For our purposes, it is probably sufficient to rate each candidate solution against the selection criteria on a $+$, 0, $-$ basis.

After this semi-quantitative evaluation has been completed, look at the picture it presents and apply critical thinking to the answer it appears to give. Don't just add up the pluses and minuses and pick the one with the highest score, because all of the selection criteria should not carry the greatest weight. This is the step in the process where horse sense, experience, and good calm judgment should be introduced. The question to be answered is, "Is this really the best approach?" Many billions of dollars have been wasted by taking the output of a complex mathematical model as the gospel truth because it came out of a computer. There may have been nothing wrong with the computer, only with the data fed into it. On the other hand, numerous executives have wrecked

---

Figure 5

SELECTION

DEFINITION   The systematic evaluation of all alternatives in terms of objectives and constraints to select the one which is considered the most desirable.

PROCEDURE   1. Define the criteria which will be used to select the most promising system.
2. Establish a quantitative method for rating each alternative against the selection criteria.
3. Evaluate the relative importance of the selection criteria.
4. Utilize analytical methods (anything from logical thinking to mathematical models) to select the best alternatives.
5. Review the results of the analysis against mature judgment.
6. Make final selection of alternative(s) for testing.

PITFALLS   1. Have you considered all of the vital selection criteria?
2. Is your scoring system biasing the answer?
3. Do you employ a reasonable balance of analysis and judgment?
4. Are you unintentionally penalizing radical solutions because they will cause you problems?
5. Have you rationalized a predetermined conclusion?
6. Have you objective evidence that the means you are selecting are actually effective?

---

their companies because they failed to rely on objective analyses and made all decisions by "the seat of their pants." A healthy mixture of rigorous analysis (supplying objectivity) and judgment (supplying intangible experience) is necessary to select the best candidate, as described in Figure 5.

Implementation

Once the alternative has been selected—go do it! Nothing will happen until you try it out, and try it in sufficient depth, for a sufficient time, and with sufficient dedication to obtain valuable and accurate results. See Figure 6.

Figure 6

IMPLEMENTATION

DEFINITION   The first adoption of the selected alternative to meet the specified objective.

PROCEDURE
1. Delineate the activity elements, schedule of events, and resource requirements.
2. Plan a program to evaluate the selected alternative(s) in utilizing a pilot program (as a test phase if possible, to minimize the risk).
3. Establish a controlled experiment.
4. Establish machinery to collect data (performance, financial, etc.) to use for evaluation.
5. Implement the program with conviction.

PITFALLS
1. Are you implementing the system in sufficient depth to give it a good chance?
2. Are you prepared to carry on the experiment for a sufficient length of time to gain valid results?
3. Are you considering altering the original plan without sufficient justification?
4. Are you ready to resist those who want you to stop after one of the early faltering steps?
5. Are you able to collect the type of data to prove your numerical rankings of the selection process?
6. Are you prepared to follow through if success is proven or repeat earlier steps if results are unsatisfactory?
7. Above all—do you have enough courage to try something new?

Evaluation

Now that the new educational activity has been implemented the results must be evaluated. Measures must be set up which define exactly the parameters specified in the original statement of objectives. By measuring the behavioral change which the educational experience was designed to bring about we can obtain an objective evaluation of the experience and move away from such subjective values as "the students liked it," "the students appeared happy and inspired."

A list of guides for performing the evaluation is given in Figure 7.

Figure 7

EVALUATION

DEFINITION The determination of the conformance or discrepancy between *all* of the objectives initially specified and the performance that was actually obtained.

PROCEDURE 1. Re-examine the original statement of objectives and collect therefrom the specific measurable end capability statements.
2. Re-examine the original statement of objectives and collect therefrom the statements of the environment within which the capability must be demonstrated.
3. Develop as many reliable and valid tests as may be required to establish whether all the objectives are being met.
4. Incorporate in the tests diagnostic features that provide guides for corrective action.
5. Administer the tests to the experimental system.
6. Interpret the results of the tests both quantitatively and qualitatively.
7. At specified intervals, re-examine and evaluate the need and *all* elements of the system.

PITFALLS 1. Are you testing for the capability originally specified?
2. Are the quantitative measures validated and do they measure the same parameters specified in the objectives?
3. Are the tests reliable (repeatable)?
4. Have you avoided dependence on subjective ("I liked it!") responses?
5. Are you testing for retention of changed behavior?
6. Are the assumptions made during the analysis explicit and tenable?

Modification

You have just completed one iteration of the systems approach. The job is by no means done. It is most unlikely that the evaluation reveals that all objectives were met fully. The nature of the nonsatisfaction of objectives must now be studied, changes must be made in the solution, these changes must be implemented and evaluated. This iterative process must be continued until the objectives are met to the extent desired.

Since the objectives also change with time due to pressures and changes in the external universe, this iterative process probably never ceases; this is not disturbing—man continues to strive for perfection and most probably will never reach it.

Guides for this step are given in Figure 8.

Figure 8

MODIFICATION

DEFINITION   The process of modifying the designed learning system based on deficiencies in meeting the objectives as determined through evaluation.

PROCEDURE   1. Examine discrepancies between specified (objectives) and obtained (evaluation) system performance to determine probable cause for deficiencies.
2. Analyze the entire system to ascertain where the correction can best be made.
3. Develop a specific plan for correction.
4. Make the correction during the next system cycle.
5. Conduct a new evaluation and continue this cycle until the specified performance is attained.

PITFALLS   1. Are you willing to admit that you had discrepancies which need corrective action or are you blaming it on "start up" problems which will go away?
2. Are you sure the system is actually implemented the way you thought?
3. Don't be fooled by initial success, but keep up the evaluation to detect time degradation of system performance, and to evaluate quality of education/training under real-world conditions.

These are the simple steps of the systems approach. This approach is not the answer to the problem, but it does represent an orderly scientific way of finding the answer. As was stated at the outset, this process is not new, it is merely the standard logical scientific approach to problem solving. The important thing is that it works.

We probably use it all the time without realizing it. When we buy a new car, select a new job, or make vacation plans we go through this same process. Or at least we should. When we ignore this process and make our decisions on emotional bases or on inadequate alternatives, we often regret the consequences.

This is the basis of the decision-making process used by industry and government in areas where the penalty of a wrong approach is too costly to conceive. We cannot afford to use less of an approach in structuring our educational systems.

One cannot help but wonder whether the use of such an objective systematic analysis of the educational problems over the last century would have given us our current system of a small school with a teacher for every 25-30 students presenting material in a manner almost identical to thousands of other teachers in similar small schools all across the land.

Is there a better way? I do not know. But we must aggressively search for one, otherwise we cease being creative human beings. And the systems approach will help us find a better way.

Although the authors of the following article have designed their "theoretical construct" for mediating instruction specifically for the social sciences, the ideas involved are not unlike the more general systems approaches described by other authors in Part VI. In all cases, the statement of objectives in behavioral terms is vital. Without performance objectives, sometimes at several levels, the desired monitoring systems can neither be developed nor operated.

A Theoretical Construct for Mediating Instruction in the Social Sciences*

JOSEPH M. CONTE
AND
FENWICK ENGLISH

The conscientious, frustrated educator is confronted with the demanding and seemingly impossible problem of individualizing instruction in an age of sophisticated technology that not only dazzles, but confounds him; the shifting emphasis on new subject matter structures, rather than upon a stable pool of "best" knowledge; and a growing impatience from public school constituencies for higher levels of skilled graduates.

The promise of technology as one way out of the problem has been dimly perceived by some, highly extolled by others. However, as Silberman[16] implied, few teachers or other school personnel have the expertise

*Reprinted from *Audiovisual Instruction, 13,* March, 1968, pp. 249-253, by permission of the publisher and the authors.

to efficiently utilize the new hardware. We have for so long been enmeshed in vague instructional generalities and good intentions (also, we might add, naiveté) and singularly poor application of existing research that we find ourselves unable to do much but dust off our new acquisitions and console ourselves on being "modern."

Recognizing that hardware was the least of the problem, and placed in the practical area where machines, new subject matter, and learning theory had to be reconciled into a meaningful union, the authors attempted to formulate a theoretical construct which would serve to bridge the gap between human insight and competence, new curricula, and new systems of technology.

The criteria used to formulate the construct design also helped in identifying what specific elements would be essential in it. The criteria are as follows:

(1) Educational objectives must be stated in performance terms.

(2) Educational objectives must be translated into specific media sequences (the instructional systems concept). As reviewed by Phillips,[10] the instructional systems concept in curriculum design asks these questions:

> Which resource or combination of resources (people, places, media) is appropriate for teaching what type of subject matter to what type of learning under what conditions (time, place, size of group, and so on) to achieve what purpose?

(3) Evaluation must be an integral part of the model.

In addition, Bruner's[2] key elements in a theory of instruction were helpful in providing guideposts. They are:

> (1) Readiness of the learner to engage in the educational experience. Ryans[12] has indicated that this is "pupil set-establishing." Maccia[6] has described it as one of the four pedagogical moves which can be analyzed. The teacher structures and solicits certain types of specific responses from the students which indicate they are ready for a sequence of instruction.
>
> (2) The body of knowledge should be structured. Bruner[2] states that, "The merit of a structure depends upon its power for simplifying information, for generating new propositions, and for increasing the manipulability of a body of knowledge."
>
> (3) The knowledge should be sequenced. The question to be answered here is how shall the knowledge be presented in a form most meaningful to the learner?

(4) According to Bruner,[2] "A theory of instruction should answer the question as to where 'rewards and punishments' are appropriate." The question of reinforcement, what and when, becomes an important consideration.

The Construct

(1) Unit (parameter) objective(s)
(2) Discipline objective(s)
(3) The parameter objective(s) stated as an hypothesis
(4) Establishment of pupil set
(5) Pre-test (learner entrance performances)
    a. Knowledge as measured by test behavior
    b. Skills as measured by activities or products of learner behavior
(6) Reinforcement/interaction (teacher-learners) for motivation
(7) Sequence (learner enroute performances)
    a. In terms of teacher-directed presentations with media
    b. In terms of learner-oriented behaviors (skills, knowledges, products) as stated in the parameter objectives
(8) Post-test (measurement of parameter performances)
(9) Reinforcement/interaction
(10) Re-cycling (the re-sequencing of production or presentation)
(11) Post-test of re-sequencing (measurement of parameter performance)
(12) Reinforcement/interaction
(13) Unit evaluation of learner parameter performances as stated in original parameter objectives.

Parameter Objectives

The notion of parameter objectives rests on the definition of instruction regnant throughout the construct. It is that of Lumsdaine:[5]

> Instruction . . . refers to any specifiable means of controlling or manipulating a sequence of events to produce modifications of behavior through learning. It is applicable whenever the outcomes of learning can be specified in sufficiently explicit terms to permit their measurement. These outcomes may include changes in attitudes, interests, motivations, beliefs, opinions, as well as in knowledges, skills, and other performance capabilities, so long as they are de-

fined in terms which identify specific, observable behaviors agreed to be manifestations or indications of these outcomes.

The parameter objective(s) attempts to realize the conditions prescribed by Bruner as a requisite for a theory of instruction. In behavioral terms, it states the conditions in which the learner will perform, and also what will be accepted as a standard for achievement. As used in the literature to this point, Mager[7] refers to this type of objective as "terminal." It was felt that this term implied a cessation of learning, whereas "parameter" connotes a framework or the existence of "boundaries" to a given sequence of instruction toward specific objectives. The parameter objectives are the total performance objectives which subsume all sequencing (teacher and media) and/or products, activities, skills, and knowledge (learner behaviors) resulting from instruction.

It has been assumed in the construct design that the parameter objectives are "baseline," i.e., required of all students as the minimum expectation. This does not preclude varying instructional sequencing and variety in teaching strategy as this relates to student abilities, entry behavior, etc. The construct is meant to insure mastery of a deliberately designed body of information and skills. Allen[1] has noted:

> Individualizing the design for a common goal is a matter of pacing, intensity, and repetition of common materials. Too often we neglect to identify a definable standard of achievement which students are expected to master. . . . Without definable and precise standards of achievement, there is no way to diagnose student differences or to develop individualized instruction.

Discipline Objectives

The concept of a discipline objective in the construct is peculiar to the social sciences. Scriven[15] postulates that there are three definitions of the social sciences. The first he calls the "interdisciplinary" view. This rests upon the "false assumption" that there is a common core from which the separate disciplines in the social sciences, i.e., history, geography, anthropology, sociology, psychology, and economics, emerge. Scriven disputes the inter-disciplinary view because there is no evidence of a common core and that "attempts to produce that common core always result in absurdly vague and worthless generalizations about human behavior."

The second view Scriven labels the "multi-disciplinary" approach. This, he feels, is more interesting and productive in the teaching of the social sciences. The idea is to take the case-history method such as the problems of poverty, integration, etc., and trace their development. Another approach would be to view history through the 'eyes of an economist, in which case the course of history is seen "in terms of economic motives." Through the eyes of a sociologist, history would reveal another conceptual scheme. Scriven emphasizes the importance of maintaining the *independence* of these viewpoints.

> The minute that you merge them, you get a smudge from which very little emerges. Also, you lose something that is extremely important—and that is, that if you were to develop the distinct viewpoints further in a particular direction, you might get further research insights.

The third approach mentioned is the "reductionist" viewpoint. Scriven dismisses the reductionist viewpoint as not being productive at this point because the tasks of the sciences are different. It is not possible to reduce the number of sciences by having social sciences attempt to adopt the methodology of the physical sciences, though many have tried.

The approach in developing the construct has been to preserve the dignity of the separate disciplines because their "structure" is basically different. By structure this paper will use the definition of Schwab,[14] i.e., structure refers to the way a discipline is organized, the conceptual frameworks in which it operates, and the methods by which it discovers new evidence and validates that evidence.

The Parameter Objective Stated as a Hypothesis

Recent literature in the soical sciences stresses discovery, inquiry, and process. Price[11] stated:

> Unless we make our students aware that methodology is a part of the social sciences, they cannot later as citizens be blamed for blindly accepting political, social, economic, or religious statements made to them. Every thinking citizen should learn that before he can explain any social activity he must first know how to find the explanation.

The methodology is important in that learners studying history know how to think as historians. It is important that learners understand the role of the historian, evaluate evidence, ponder questions, and be required to explain a period or event in history. Bruner[2] similarly underscored this point.

> . . . a curriculum reflects not only the nature of knowledge itself but also the knowledge-getting process. It is the enterprise par excellence where the line between subject matter and method grows necessarily indistinct. To instruct someone in these disciplines is not a matter of getting him to commit results to mind. Rather, it is to teach him to participate in the process that makes possible the establishment of knowledge. We teach a subject not to produce little living libraries on that subject, but rather to get a student to think mathematically for himself, to consider matters as an historian does, to take part in the process of knowledge-getting. Knowing is a process, not a product.

Michaelis[9] has identified hypothesis testing as a dominant trend in the social sciences:

> The first and predominant objective is to develop an understanding of key concepts, generalizations and themes, and the ability to use them as hypotheses to guide study and as centers around which information can be organized.

Schwab[14] has emphasized that knowledge has a revisionary character which requires that teaching of that knowledge proceed in the light of the inquiry which produced it. Sand[13] noticed that recent work in the individual disciplines in the social sciences stressed not the accumulation of inert information which results in an inventory, but the "transaction which enables the learner to control some part of his environment through the discovery and manipulation of facts and their relationships."

The Scope of Curriculum Content for Social Sciences

The Office of the Los Angeles County Superintendent of Schools, in May 1966, released several position papers which revealed the thinking and concerns of the Statewide Social Sciences Study Committee. If these papers are representative of the concerns of the State Committee, and it is believed they are, the present approach labeled the "cover-all" (chronological) method will be replaced. Keller[4] argues for the "posthole" approach to developing scope in the social science curriculum.

This method involves indepth study of events, periods, and ideas. The prevailing attitude that nothing can be left out of the social science curriculum is impractical in the arena where knowledge is accumulating faster than it can be learned. Keller believes that new materials should be prepared "which will make possible student search and discovery, getting at basic ideas, using the inductive method and use of intelligent post-holing." Far from negating the influence of the chronology, it will increase the necessity for learning chronology, if the question is to be seen in accurate perspective.

In his criticism of present textbooks in the area of history, Metcalf[8] appears to lend further weight to the "post-holing" idea. Since there is more to know, but without increase in textbook space in which to present the information, the practice of "easy familiarity" has emerged. The learner is then confronted with generalizations. Few textbooks provide enough information to allow learners to make meaningful generalizations. Thus, the learner is unable to distinguish between generalizations and accurate historical interpretation.

Learners are exposed to history without ever being required to analyze what they have read or to evaluate it on the basis of scientific criteria, i.e., a methodology of investigation which can be validated. Metcalf[8] summarizes the danger of the practice of easy familiarity.

> . . . he (the learner) will reach wrong conclusions in a straight, chronological, descriptive course rather than in one that emphasizes analysis. In the latter kind of course he may learn to label as pseudo-explanation any explanation whose premises are untestable. These are the explanations that explain "the achievements of a person in terms of his mission in history or his predestined fate, or similar notions that are metaphorical rather than lawlike in their content and language." Such explanations convey pictorial and emotional appeals instead of insight into factual connections.

The approach in developing lessons is aimed at "post-holing," i.e., inquiring in depth to obtain basic information to answer a hypothesis. Chronology is related to the hypothesis and its importance is very relevant.

The construct not only preserves the separateness of the component disciplines of the social sciences, but blends them together to bear upon a problem. The problem then becomes the area in which these disciplines are related and applied. It is thus an example of the "multidisciplinary" approach enumerated previously by Scriven.

Ryans[12] has discussed the notion of pupil set-establishing. This is the place in the construct where the pre-disposition of the learner is established. This predisposition is an awareness or receptivity on the part of the learner. It is the judgment of the teacher in terms of the response and reactions of the pupils when to go ahead into the pre-test. Webster[19] has identified set-establishing as "sensitization."

The Pre-Test

The purpose of a pre-test in the construct is essentially based on the idea of the principle of economy in education as enumerated by Gasset.[3] This principle is that teaching (instruction) exists in proportion to that which the learner is unable to learn. Teaching comes into being when the learner cannot progress by himself without a teacher. Gasset lists the two dimensions important for the student: ". . . first, what he is—a being of limited learning capacity—and second, what he needs to know in order to live his life."

The pre-test attempts to measure the entry behaviors of the student. It attempts to answer the question, "Does the student know what I want to teach him?" If the answer is "yes," an enrichment cycle of instruction is immediately available, providing an alternative to an individual or a group. If "no," the learners proceed through the first sequence of instruction.

Reinforcement

As Bruner[2] stipulates, no theory of instruction can neglect the place of reinforcement.

> Learning depends upon knowledge of results at a time when and at a place where knowledge can be used for correction. Instruction increases the appropriate timing and placing of corrective knowledge.
>
> Knowledge of results should come at that point in a problem-solving episode when the person is comparing the results of his try-out with some criterion of what he seeks to achieve. Knowledge of results given before this point either cannot be understood or must be carried as extra freight in immediate memory.

For this reason, reinforcement has been built into the construct design in the form of learner/teacher interaction after specific performance-testing situations. It does not preclude additional interaction and rein-forcement in shorter sequences of instruction.

Sequence

The idea of predetermined sequence is a definite strength to the con-struct. First, it allows for an accurate diagnosis of the effectiveness of instruction, and second, provides for specific re-sequences of instruc-tion to re-teach groups or individuals. This branching effect, or re-cycling, allows for enrichment and review. It is flexible and repro-ducible, i.e., it may be repeated and/or duplicated as many times as desired by the teacher and/or learner.

As noted by Tanner[17] in his review of research, there may be a conflict between the hypothetical base upon which programmed in-struction theory rests, and methods which are heuristic and aimed at the "eliciting of responses not predetermined by authority."

The point of view of this proposal is that there is room for both in-quiry and sequence within a theoretical structure. First, certain "base-line" information is specified within a hypothetical question aimed at producing inquiry. Learners are then involved in a series of media sequences aimed at changing behavior, i.e., learning. Many of the individual lessons within the construct were purposefully designed to stress the process of learning, research skills, and hypothesis testing. This has been accomplished within the confines of the designated, behavioral-oriented, parameter objectives. Once the learner has partici-pated in the original sequence and mastered the baseline activities, he is not limited in the extent of this personal or private quest. The number of re-cycles as determined by the teacher/learners may be altered or changed as they see fit after the initial teaching sequence is used.

Learners may then practice the desired behaviors as many times as needed within any specified sequence. Stress on the desired behavioral changes may be uniquely tailored to individual learning rates and capacities.

Also, with the use of a specified sequence of stimuli and provisions for re-cycling, it is possible to attain achievement-monitoring and em-ploy diagnostic teaching to a much greater extent than is possible with-out a specified sequence. Sequencing and re-cycling on the basis of achievement, need, and ability are practical and possible in this type of model design.

Ideally, the mediated instruction sequences provide for enroute prac-tice of the skills and knowledge behaviors pertinent to performing the parameter objectives. All sequences are formulated on the parameter performance objectives.

Unit Evaluation

If the parameter performance objectives have been stated in operational terms, the evaluation of the unit is built in. If the students can perform as designated, if the behaviors can be observed, and if the pre- and post-tests are valid, the degree to which learning has occurred can be measured and predicted.

In Conclusion

The major components in the theoretical construct are not new to teachers. It can be observed, for instance, that good teachers will recycle, motivate, establish appropriate set, and reinforce in their classrooms. While the construct cannot guarantee that all teachers will be "good" teachers, it can serve to insure some consistency of sound educational practice.

We envision a howl from some who would assert that teaching is an art and cannot be subjected to precise scrutiny. The authors contend that as long as teaching remains an art, subject to the mysterious peculiarities of the "master artist," it can never be substantially improved. Only when teaching can be subject to the quantifications of science can it be analyzed, evaluated, and improved.

The theoretical construct attempts to blend together elements of change in instruction. It recognizes the teacher as an indispensable and integral element in mediating and individualizing instruction in the social sciences. It is the desire of the authors that the construct will stimulate more discussion and probing in this dimension.

REFERENCES

1. Allen, Dwight W. Individualized Instruction. *CTA Journal,* October, 1965.
2. Bruner, Jerome S. *Toward a Theory of Instruction.* Cambridge, Mass.: Harvard University Press, 1966.
3. Gasset, José Ortega. *Mission of the University.* New York: W. W. Norton & Company, The Norton Library, 1944.
4. Keller, Charles R. *A Folio of Materials Developed Through the Work of the State-wide Social Science Study Committee of California.* Los Angeles: Los Angeles County Superintendent of Schools Office, May 1966.

5. Lumsdaine, A. A. Instruments and Media Instruction. *Handbook of Research on Teaching.* Chicago: Rand McNally, 1963.
6. Maccia, Elizabeth S. Instructor as Influence Toward Rule-Governed Behavior. *Theories of Instruction.* Washington, D. C.: ASCD, Ninth Curriculum Research Institute, 1965.
7. Mager, Robert F. *Preparing Instructional Objectives.* Palo Alto, Calif.: Fearon Publishers, 1962.
8. Metcalf, Lawrence E. Research on Teaching the Social Studies. *Handbook of Research on Teaching.* Chicago: Rand McNally, 1963.
9. Michaelis, John U. Social Studies. *New Curriculum Developments.* Washington, D. C.: A Report of ASCD's Commission on Current Curriculum Developments, 1965.
10. Phillips, Murray G. Learning Materials and Their Implementation. *Review of Educational Research, 36,* No. 3; 1966.
11. Price, Roy H., Warren Hickman & Gerald Smith. *Major Concepts for Social Studies. A Progress Report.* Syracuse, N. Y.: Syracuse University, November 1966.
12. Ryans, David G. A Model of Instruction Based on Information System Concepts. *Theories of Instruction.* Washington, D. C.: ASCD, Ninth Curriculum Research Institute, 1965.
13. Sand, Ole. Basis for Decisions. *Role of Supervisor and Curriculum Director in a Climate of Change.* Washington, D. C.: ASCD, 1965.
14. Schwab, Joseph J. Structure of the Disciplines: Meanings and Significances. *The Structure of Knowledge and the Curriculum.* Chicago: Rand McNally, 1964.
15. Scriven, Michael. The Structure of the Social Studies. *The Structure of Knowledge and the Curriculum.* Chicago: Rand McNally, 1964.
16. Silberman, Charles E. Technology is Knocking at the Schoolhouse Door. *Fortune, 74,* 3, August 1966.
17. Tanner, Daniel. Curriculum Theory: Knowledge and Content. *Review of Educational Research, 36,* 3, 1966.
18. Temple City Unified School District. *Instructional Media System, Phase I.* A Proposal Submitted under Provision of Title III of the Elementary and Secondary Education Act of 1965 (Public Law 89-10), November 1965.
19. Webster, Staten W. Suggested Strategy for Teaching Socially Disadvantaged Learners. *The California Journal of Instructional Improvement,* May 1965.

Eisele identifies behaviorally-stated instructional objectives as one of five essential components in every teaching-learning situation. Subsequently, he outlines the steps involved in preparing computer based instructional resource units and in coding these units to objectives and learner characteristics.

Computers in Curriculum Planning*

JAMES E. EISELE

Very few references are made in the literature to the role of computers in curriculum development. The most recent issue of the *Review of Educational Research*[1] dealing with curriculum planning and development devotes no space to this vital topic. A review of other sources reveals a similar lack of information on this topic.

Similarly, a perusal of notices announcing curriculum conferences, both nationally and in various states, indicates an amazing lack of concern with possible uses of the computer in curriculum development.

Whether, however, this apparent void is indicative of a lack of interest or simply faulty communications is debatable. The purpose of this report is to document one effort to apply computers to curriculum planning** in hopes that others may be stimulated to do likewise. Only in this way can evidence be gathered which will be useful to researchers for continued efforts on this front.

*Reprinted from *Educational Technology, 7,* November 30, 1967, pp. 9-16, by permission of the publisher and the author.

**For purposes of this article, curriculum planning is defined as a systematic effort to improve instruction (the teaching-learning situation).

Background

Harnack[2] began experimenting with a manual card-sort system in 1962 to both isolate and relate variables which were relevant to the teaching-learning situation. Underlying his experimentation was a sound model of curriculum development which provided a comprehensive framework for decision-making about teaching and learning. Basically, this model describes five components of every teaching-learning situation: instructional objectives, content, instructional activities, instructional materials, and evaluation devices. In addition, this model suggests a host of learner characteristics and professional concerns which are considered in instructional decision making.

The "instructional model" is as follows:

Knowing the individual pupil's needs, the teacher selects objectives which are related to his needs. In turn, the teacher identifies content, activities, material, and evaluation devices related to the objectives. Since there are several options (content, activities, materials, and evaluation devices) for any given objective, the teacher must make a further selection and identify those appropriate to the specific learner and which satisfy any particular professional preference. In order to do this, the teacher first examines the learner's characteristics and makes any professional decisions he deems prudent. With these decisions made, the teacher can select the necessary components for an "individually tailored curriculum guide."

Seldom, however, have teachers had the time or facilities to make these highly sophisticated kinds of decisions. Hence, a system was devised, first using a card-sort, to make some preliminary decisions with automated equipment. Units are constructed, consisting of instructional objectives, content, instructional activities and materials, and measuring devices. All items, except objectives, are then coded for three criteria: objectives, learner characteristics, and professional decisions. A more detailed description of how the units are constructed and coded follows.

Identifying Topics and Getting Under Way

The selection of unit topics was as critical as any phase of the project. Unit topics are often called organizing centers. One significant quote is sufficient to illustrate the importance of their selection.

> Perhaps the most critical and central concept related to the teaching operations is the idea of the organizing center. As

"the point where all the important aspects of the teaching act can be related and given focus," its effect on the quality of instruction cannot be denied.[2]

Hence, very careful attention was given to selecting topics which met the criterion of good centers of organizing. This task was accomplished by examining a host of possibilities as suggested by many educators and students of education. Only after careful deliberation was a consensus reached on fifteen topics which met the criteria for good unit topics.

With the topics identified, teachers were sought from throughout the state of New York to develop the chosen units. Five to seven teachers were chosen for each of the fifteen units to work for a period of three to four weeks, depending on the scope of the unit. At various times, these teachers were brought to the Learning Resource Center at the Board of Cooperative Educational Services, Erie County District 1, for the time required to complete the work on each unit. Their task began with writing the objectives for the units.

Writing Unit Objectives

Teachers who were to participate in the project were given a short orientation, introducing them to the overall design of the units. An integral phase of this orientation was instruction in writing objectives as desired student behaviors. This phase was quite successful, judged by the quality and quantity of behavioral objectives which were ultimately written.

Three basic reasons were cited for specifying objectives as terminal behaviors for students. The first reason was that with behavioral objectives the student can easily interpret what is expected of himself. This can greatly assist instruction. Second, objectives stated in terms of observable behavior easily lend themselves to evaluation of pupil progress in achieving these outcomes. Third, behaviorally stated objectives make the selection of content, activities, and materials for achieving these outcomes considerably easier than trying to specify learning experiences for goals that are not clearly understood.

Two alternative methods were described for writing objectives. Either method was considered acceptable for specifying desired student outcomes for the unit. All objectives, however, began with the word "to" with the precedent, "The student should be able," implied. The first alternative, then, was to follow the first word with a term which indicated a specific behavior (i.e., to list, to point, to select, to describe), and to complete the statement with whatever response was desired. For example: "To list the seven natural wonders of the world," or "To select the seven natural wonders of the world from several given alternatives."

The second method of writing objectives was used in order to satisfy the natural desire to use such terms as "understand, appreciate, value, and learn." Where words such as these were used, the objective had to contain the performance criteria which would be used as indicators of successful achievement of the objective. For example: "To understand the significance of the Bill of Rights by listing the rights which are commonly practiced in our country which are not commonly practiced in Cuba," or "To show appreciation for the plight of the minority groups in America by selecting a minority group and comparing their living conditions with those of a majority group in America." These performance criteria may or may not be acceptable to all users of the units, but they do indicate the behavior which can be expected as a result of using the unit.

The total number of such objectives for each unit varies depending upon the nature and scope of the unit. The smallest number of objectives is forty-seven while the largest number exceeds two hundred for an individual unit.

Content

Educators have been known, at times, to confuse content of instruction with objectives of instruction. Having carefully spelled out the behaviors which could be achieved in the unit, the project teachers readily accepted the definition of content as "the facts and information about the subject which were relevant to the particular unit." This definition seemed to help create an attitude toward content that, in order to be worthwhile, the content had to be information which was useful in helping the student achieve an objective of the unit. Also, that the content which was written is not useful alone; the objectives are necessary to specify what is to be done with the content of a unit. Specialists in the respective subjects were available to the teachers to assist them and to assure the accuracy and completeness of the content portion of the unit.

Instructional Activities

Activities for the units are classified under nine different headings. Activities were written which were introductory for large groups, small groups, and individuals; developmental for large and small groups, and individuals; and culminating for large and small groups, and individuals.

Introductory activities are those which are designed to motivate the student and establish the necessary requisites for the desired behavior changes. Developmental activities are those which are designed to actually create the desired changes in student behavior. Culminating activities are those which are designed as reinforcers of the desired behavioral outcomes. Large group, small group, and individual activities should be self-explanatory.

Teachers constructing the units were encouraged to list as many of these different kinds of activities as possible. All of the activities listed were selected on either empirical or intuitive evidence that they would contribute to the achievement of one or more of the objectives of the units (part of the overall plan is to eventually test these suggestions). This procedure tended to allow for much creativity in designing instructional activities and resulted in a storehouse of suggestions for teaching each unit.

Identifying Materials

Similar to the manner in which activities were specified, all the possible instructional materials for the unit were written down in bibliographic notation. These, again, were specified because there was empirical or intuitive evidence that they would be useful in helping students achieve some objective of the unit.

This task was an extremely difficult one to accomplish. Unfortunately, most instructional materials are designed and constructed with little regard for any desired behavioral outcomes.

One possible outcome of projects such as this may ultimately be that producers of materials will give credence to desired terminal behaviors as specified by educators. Back to the point, considerable effort was necessary to analyze materials for the possible outcomes which they could be expected to help students achieve. Nevertheless, each unit consists of many suggested materials (no less than eighty) which otherwise might pass without notice by the average classroom teacher.

Evaluating Pupil Achievement

The final component of the units is the suggested means for evaluating student success in achieving selected objectives. The project teachers had to identify a number of possible procedures for evaluating any or all objectives. An interesting facet of this task was that most of the teachers had formerly been accustomed to using only paper-pencil tests of achievement. The search for other means of evaluation was quite en-lightening to many of them.

A listing of the specified evaluation devices is not feasible in this space. A unit could, conceivably, have more evaluation devices than objectives, assuming that each objective could have more than one appropriate means of evaluation. This never actually occurred, although each unit contains more suggestions for evaluation than could normally be found in any other source.

Coding Components

Once written, the units had to be coded so as to produce the desired printout for the teachers using the units. Three separate "sets" of vari-ables were used in coding the components of each unit. These variables, already mentioned, are the objectives, learner characteristics, and pro-fessional concerns.

Coding to Objectives

One sheet used for coding contained only blank spaces at top and numerals from one to two hundred fifty. This sheet was used to code components, except objectives, to the unit objectives. The blank space at top was used to record each item of each component of the units. The numerals referred to the list of objectives for any given unit. With the item recorded at the top of the sheet, then, the item could be coded for the objectives to which it related by circling the respective numerals.

Coding to Learner Characteristics

Another sheet used to code the units contained blank spaces at top and also an abbreviated reference to fifteen categories of learner charac-teristics broken into one hundred twenty-two separate classifications (i.e., social class: lower level, upper lower, lower middle, upper middle, lower upper, upper upper). This sheet also contained references to six categories of professional concern broken into fifty-three separate classifications (i.e., group activity: large group, small group, individual).

Each item of each component of the units was recorded on the top of one of these coding sheets. Then, by circling the appropriate classifica-tions, the items were coded for the classification to which they related. For example, a book could be coded for reading level, interest areas, and other relevant characteristics as well as professional concerns.

Computer Printouts

The unit, written and coded, is stored on magnetic computer tape for transfer to disk when retrieval is desired. By following specified procedures, any teacher can have access to the fifteen units which are now completed.

The first procedure is for the prospective user to select the objectives which he wishes his students to achieve from the total list for any unit. The teacher may, if he wishes, do this cooperatively with the students, allowing for teacher-pupil planning. He selects those objectives he desires for the total class and, then, for the individual students.

Secondly, the prospective user indicates the characteristics, on a printed form, which match the characteristics of each student in the class. At the same time, the teacher will be able to make any professional decision he wishes which is provided for in the coding of the units.

Using this data as input, the computer performs the necessary information retrieval. An objective at a time, the computer scans the unit and retrieves all the content, large and small group activities, materials and evaluation devices related to the objective. This is done for each objective for the total class and the result is a printed curriculum guide for the class consisting of the objectives chosen for this purpose.

Then, for each student, the computer again matches the content, activities, materials, and evaluation devices to each objective and also to the characteristics of each particular student. The printout is an "individually tailored curriculum guide," with necessary components listed under each objective. The individualized portion differs from the total class portion in that the items now are matched against the data on each student as well as against the chosen objectives.

The printouts, called Resource Guides, allow considerable latitude for the user. Even when matching items against objectives, learner characteristics, and professional decisions, the guides usually offer enough suggestions that the teacher must still make a final selection. This step usually involves further planning between teacher and student, apparently a worthy pursuit in itself.

Implications for Planning

Future plans for work with computer based resource units are based primarily on implications resulting from experiences to date. This refers to a total of four to five years of planning and constructing the original units, producing computer programs capable of rapid information retrieval, testing and trying out of six units for a total of about one hundred fifty applications, and four carefully controlled experimental studies. These future plans call for a two-phased approach with other possibilities to follow. The initial two phases are the development of more units and research on the existing ones.

Development of More Computer Units

Although this project is believed to represent the largest stockpile of resource plans for teaching and learning, an obvious need exists to greatly expand what already exists. An ultimate aim is to have units on every conceivable topic, comprehensive enough to serve any student in any locality and on any level of achievement. This is a dream which may be years and years away.

Research on Existing Units

Research on units which are being used in classrooms must be conducted continuously. One form of research comes from obtaining systematic feedback from teachers who use the units. Evidence obtained in this way not only serves to test the validity of the units but also provides valuable information for improving and updating the units. This information will be obtained by providing users with a form designed to allow suggestions about objectives, content, activities, materials, or evaluation devices for the units. Where teachers have ideas for additions to the units, these specific suggestions are also desired.

REFERENCES

1. William H. Bristow & David A. Abramson (Eds.) Curriculum Planning and Development, *Review of Educational Research, 36,* No. 3, June, 1966.
2. James E. Eisele & Robert S. Harnack. Improving Teacher Decision-Making and Individualization of Instruction. *The Quarterly, 18,* No. 4, May, 1967, p. 8.
3. James B. Macdonald, Dan W. Anderson & Frank B. May (Eds.) *Strategies of Curriculum Development.* Columbus: Charles E. Merrill Books, Inc., 1965, p. 107.

Part VI

Additional Media

Bern, H. A. *et al*. Reply to Questions About Systems. *Audiovisual Instruction, 10,* May, 1965, pp. 366-370.

Carpenter, C. R. A Constructive Critique of Educational Technology. *AV Communication Review, 16,* Spring, 1968, pp. 16-24.

Carter, Launor F. The Systems Approach to Education: Mystique and Reality. *Educational Technology, 9,* April, 1969, pp. 22-31.

Churchman, C. West. On the Design of Educational Systems. *Audiovisual Instruction, 10,* May, 1965, pp. 361-365.

Corrigan, Robert E. Developing and Validating Instructional Materials Through the Instructional-System Approach. *Systems Approaches to Curriculum and Instruction in the Open-Door College.* B. Lamar Johnson (Ed.) Los Angeles, California: School of Education, University of California, Los Angeles, 1967, pp. 37-44.

Csanyi, Attila P. Determining Objectives: A Behavior Systems Approach. *NSPI Journal, 7,* February, 1968, pp. 16-18.

Decker, Edward H. The Systems Approach: A New Educational Technique. *The Science Teacher, 35,* November, 1968, pp. 26-27.

Deterline, William A. Educational Systems. *Technology and Innovation in Education.* New York: Frederick A. Praeger, Publishers, 1968, pp. 51-56.

Educational Technology, 8, January 15, 1968, see entire issue: pp. 1-20.

Gagné, Robert M. Learning Decisions in Education. *The Conditions of Learning.* New York: Holt, Rinehart and Winston, Inc., 1965, pp. 237-266.

Geisert, Paul. A Computer Model for the Slow Student. *The Science Teacher, 35,* March, 1968, pp. 13-17.

Glaser, Robert & James H. Reynolds. Instructional Objectives and Programmed Instruction: A Case Study. *Defining Educational Objectives.* C. M. Lindvall (Ed.) Pittsburgh, Pennsylvania: University of Pittsburgh Press, 1964, pp. 47-76.

Goldberg, Albert L. First Steps in the Systems Approach. *Audiovisual Instruction, 10,* May, 1965, pp. 382-383.

A Guide for Wiley Authors in the Preparation of Auto-Instructional Programs. New York: John Wiley & Sons, Inc., 1967, 14 pp.

Gurau, Peter K. Data Processing in a Continuous Progress Program. *Educational Technology, 8,* May 15, 1968, pp. 5-12.

Hunter, Madeline. The Clinical Management of Learning. *The Elementary School Journal, 68,* November, 1967, pp. 63-67.

Kapfer, Philip G. An Instructional Management Strategy for Individualized Learning. *Phi Delta Kappan, 49,* January, 1968, pp. 260-263.

Lange, Phil C. Technology, Learning and Instruction. *Audiovisual Instruction, 13,* March, 1968, pp. 226-231.

Loughary, John W. Instructional Systems—Magic or Method? *Educational Leadership, 25,* May, 1968, pp. 730-734.

Lysaught, Jerome P. But the Dear Knows Who I'll Marry . . . *Educational Technology, 7,* November 30, 1967, pp. 1-8.

Markle, Susan M. & Philip W. Tiemann. *Programming Is A Process: An Introduction to Instructional Technology.* Chicago: Office of Instructional Resources at the University of Illinois at Chicago Circle, and Tiemann Associates, 1968. A 32-minute, 16mm. color film and audiotape/color filmstrip.

Michael, Jack L., Carole S. Waina & Robert L. Baker. *Managing Classroom Contingencies.* Inglewood, California: Southwest Regional Laboratory for Educational Research and Development, 1968, 50 pp.

See also other materials in the SWRL series (Part I).

Mowrer, Donald E.. The Language of Behavioral Engineering. *Educational Technology, 9,* July, 1969, pp. 34-36.

Nachtigal, Paul. A Computer Approach: Individualizing Instructional Experiences. *Educational Technology, 7,* July 30, 1967, pp. 8-11.

Persselin, Leo E. Systems Implications for Secondary Education. *Journal of Secondary Education, 44,* April, 1969, pp. 159-166.

Pfeiffer, John. *New Look At Education: Systems Analysis in our Schools and Colleges.* Poughkeepsie, New York: Odyssey Press, 1968, 162 pp.

Prescott, Frank J. An Instructional Systems Approach. *Educational Technology, 5,* March 15, 1965, pp. 14-18.

Rath, Gustave J. Preparing Auto-Instructional Programs. *Educational Technology, 5,* January 15, 1965, pp. 1-21.

Ruark, Henry C. Editorial: That Does Not Compute! *Educational Screen and Audiovisual Guide, 46,* November, 1967, pp. 18-19.

Stewart, Donald K. *A Learning Systems Concept as Applied to Courses in Education and Training.* College Station, Texas: Center for the Creative Application of Technology to Education, undated, 74 pp. (Mimeo.)

————. The Learning Systems Approach to Instruction and the Changing Role of the Educator. *Educational Media in Vocational and Technical Education: A Report of a National Seminar,* Calvin J. Cotrell & Edward F. Hauck (Eds.) Columbus, Ohio: The Center for Research and Leadership Development in Vocational and Technical Education, The Ohio State University, 1967, pp. 63-78.

Tanzman, Jack. AV and Behavioral Objectives. *School Management, 13,* December, 1969, p. 70.

Part VII

Behavioral Objectives and the Curriculum Evaluator

What is the function of goal specification in the evaluation procedure? A variety of answers to this question are provided in Part VII. Sorenson, in the initial article, compares the evaluator's role implied in the absolutistic position on evaluation to the role required by the behavioral approach. The final two articles, by Walbesser, provide a type of before-and-after view of the behavioral approach to evaluation, particularly as it compares to the content approach.

In defining the responsibilities of the educational evaluator, Sorenson reviews several tenets of the "absolutistic" position on evaluation. Sorenson finds this view unacceptable for several reasons, and provides an alternate set of assumptions upon which to base the role of the evaluator. He believes that the statement of goals in descriptive language is of central importance in effective evaluation.

A New Role in Education: the Evaluator*

GARTH SORENSON

With the increase of federal funds for education, a new professional is emerging—the evaluator. He is somewhat different from the expert in tests and measurements and in research design usually found working on a college faculty. Rather, he is a person who spends part or all of his working hours at research and development activities, thinking about and planning the evaluation of educational processes. Because his role is a new one on the educational scene, his functions and his relationship to other educational experts need to be more clearly defined. It is the aim of this article to present some ideas about that role.

Two papers on evaluation, one by Scriven (1965) and one by Stake (1966), contain a number of assertions and implicit assumptions about the evaluator's role which deserve examination. Among them are the following:

1. Scriven would assign evaluators the task of determining the effectiveness of instructional programs. But more than that, he would have them evaluate the goals of these programs as well. It is not enough for

*Reprinted from UCLA-CSEIP *Evaluation Comment, 1,* January, 1968, pp. 1-4, by permission of the publisher and the author.

the evaluator to find out whether the teacher of mathematics or English or physical education has taught the students what he intended to teach them. The evaluator must also decide, Scriven believes, whether the specific course content was appropriate and worthwhile; for, as Scriven sees it, the evaluator is the person best qualified to judge.

2. Scriven holds that the relative goodness of different educational goals is to be determined by applying a set of absolute standards which will somehow be obvious to the evaluator. Apparently, Scriven doubts that it is possible for intelligent, informed, and well-intentioned people seriously to disagree about what should be taught, for he asserts that arguments over criteria turn out to be mainly "disputes about what is to be counted as good, rather than arguments about the straightforward 'facts of the situation,' i.e., about what is in fact good."

3. Continuing his argument, Scriven implies that without absolute standards, evaluation is in fact probably impossible. "The process of relativism has not only led to overtolerance for over-restrictive goals, it has led to incompetent evaluation of the extent to which these have been achieved . . ."

4. Stake seems to imply that since absolute standards exist, it is not necessary to take the individual teacher's or the individual school's goals into account. He seems to believe that such standards should be applied even if they relate only slightly or not at all to the local school's resources and goals. "It should be noted that it is not the educator's privilege to rule out the study of a variable by saying, "That is not one of our objectives.' "

5. Both Scriven and Stake believe that it is possible and perhaps desirable to appraise teaching and other instructional programs independently of their effects on the students. Stake says, "The educational evaluator should not list goals only in terms of anticipated student behavior. To evaluate an educational program, emphasis must be given to what teaching as well as what learning is intended . . ." and, "It is not wrong to teach a willing educator about behavioral objectives—they may facilitate his work. It is wrong to insist on them. . . ." Scriven further comments that ". . . pressure on a writer (curriculum maker) to formulate his goals, to keep to them, and to express them in testable terms, may enormously alter his product in ways that are certainly not always desirable."

6. It may be inferred that Scriven believes that teachers who feel threatened by evaluators holding such absolute values should be ignored or at least discounted. "A little toughening of the moral fibre is required if we are not to shirk the social responsibilities of the educational branch of our culture."

7. While it appears that he endorses most of Scriven's assertions,

Stake would qualify at least one of them. If an individual evaluator were less than fully qualified, Stake would substitute a team of specialists as the appropriate determiners of educational goals and practices. The team would consist of experts in "instructional technology . . . psychometric testing and scaling . . . research design and analysis . . . the dissemination of information . . . (and perhaps) a social anthropologist." He does not include historians, philosophers, businessmen, labor leaders, legal experts, or even non-behavioral scientists.

To be sure, the assertions listed above do not constitute a summary of what Scriven and Stake have said in their papers. Nevertheless, it appears that they represent, at least roughly, some of the beliefs of Scriven and Stake and a point of view resembling that of a number of writers on public education.

In spite of the fact that a number of brilliant and famous men support a position similar to that just described, I believe that if evaluators generally were to take an absolutist position, a number of unfortunate consequences would follow.

For one thing, teachers would be unwilling to cooperate and work with these evaluators. An evaluator who insists on evaluating in terms of his own goals while ignoring what the school people are trying to do, and who criticizes them and the school for failing to do what they had not intended to do in the first place would certainly be viewed as threatening. It can be safely predicted that teachers who feel threatened will resist and will devote their time and energies to defending old practices rather than to examining and improving them.

A second unfortunate consequence would be that evaluators would not get the support they need from powerful groups in the community who have a legitimate interest in what goes on in the school. Evaluation requires large amounts of time, money, and other commodities that evaluators cannot get without a good deal of public support—especially if they already have alienated the teachers and school administrators. Many of the individuals and groups in this country whose support is needed believe that the schools were invented to serve the needs of society and ultimately are answerable to the taxpayers, or at least to some one other than professional evaluators.

These individuals and groups do not always agree with one another about how the schools can best serve society, but they do agree that the schools are not autonomous. Many of these individuals—for example, Paul Goodman, Robert Hutchins, Sidney Hook, James Conant, John Goodlad, Roald Campbell, Ralph Tyler, Clark Kerr, Admiral Rickover, Harold Taylor, Paul Woodring, Jerome Bruner, David Ausubel, Myron Lieberman, Lawrence Cremin, and Benjamin Bloom, to name only a few, as well as many groups—have given a good deal of thought and study to questions about the goals and methods of education. They are likely to regard individuals whose main qualification for the prescribing of educational goals is that they are experts in psychometry, research design, or social anthropology, but who are ignorant of the philosophical and political issues in education, as naive, arrogant, parochial, and, therefore, unworthy of assistance.

A third possible consequence—an evaluation program based upon the absolutistic assumption that "good" educational programs exist independent of persons and their preferences and independent of what students learn—is bound to fail. Its results are certain to be inconclusive and meaningless.

An analogy can be found in the attempts to evaluate teacher effectiveness. After surveying the results of half a century of research, investigators like Anderson and Hunka (1963) and Turner and Fattu (1960) have concluded that research in this area has been unproductive and has reached a dead end because of problems encountered in developing suitable criterion variables. In statistical terms, the variables lack reliability. It is my contention that the reason for the failure to develop usable criterion variables is a basic error in the way in which the researchers conceptualized the problem—more specifically in their reliance on an absolute model of teacher effectiveness. Virtually all the investigators assumed either implicitly or explicitly the existence of sets of behaviors that objectively define the teacher—behaviors which exist as an absolute, independent of any particular observer and which would be recognized by an experienced educator when he encountered them, even though he might not be able to verbalize them in advance. Those researchers were failing to recognize and take into account the fact that any two observers are likely to differ in their beliefs about the ideal traits of the good teacher.

Ryans (1960) found that even when two observers were simultaneously watching the same teacher, they did not agree about him in their independent ratings unless they had had considerable training in Ryans' rating system—and sometimes not even then. It was probably his observers' differing notions about the ideal teacher they were observing. Analogously, any two evaluators are likely to disagree about the goals of education and can, therefore, be expected to disagree about the "goodness" of whatever actual method or program they may at a specific time be seeking to evaluate. The point is, there never has been and never will be general agreement on the goals of education any more than there is agreement on the qualifications and characteristics of the ideal teacher. Though particular groups of people will agree on particular goals, we must live with the fact that there is a welter of conflicting ideas on the subject in the society as a whole.

Following is a set of assumptions which may provide a reasonable alternative to those selected from Scriven and Stake.

1. Educational institutions should serve the needs of society and of the individuals who comprise it; these needs are complementary and interdependent.

2. A society's needs can best be defined by the members of that society through discussion, persuasion, and, ultimately, through voting. To insure that the goals of education will correspond with the citizens' views of their needs, the goals should be defined in a process of interaction between professionals and representatives of the society.

3. Every society changes; its needs and values are in a constant state of flux. Because of increases in population, knowledge, and technology, our society is very different from what it was even a decade ago. We now need new classes of workers, e.g., technicians who can build and operate computers. And because, as Gerard Piel (1961) has pointed out, we are no longer a society characterized by scarcity of goods, values based on dearth, such as hard work, thrift, etc., are less salient. Concomitantly, as our needs and values change, we must expect our educational goals to change.

4. Even though many of our values seem to be changing, we continue to prize diversity. Ours is a pluralistic society with different religions, political viewpoints, subcultures, and values. We believe that our heterogeneity makes our society richer, more interesting, and stimulating. What is even more critical, we believe that heterogeneity makes our society viable. To accommodate such a diverse population, we must expect our educational goals and practices to be varied.

5. The goals of our educational institutions are not and never have been limited to purely academic objectives. Most people want the schools to do more than to teach the traditional academic subjects: they want individual and societal objectives included. For example, a century ago, the McGuffey Readers attempted to inculcate moral principles. More recently, James B. Conant (1953) said that the schools should provide a basis for the growth of mutual understanding between the different cultural, religious, and occupational groups in our country. "If the battle of Waterloo was won on the playing fields of Eton, it may well be that the ideological struggle with Communism in the next fifty years will be won on the playing fields of the public high schools of the United States."

6. We can tell if an educational program or teaching method is working only by observing whether hoped-for changes are occurring in the students—while at the same time making certain that damaging changes are not occurring, e.g., learning to hate a particular subject, or learning to believe one cannot learn arithmetic even if he works at it.

We cannot properly evaluate an instructor or a program without assessing the effects, wanted and unwanted, on students. To evaluate a schedule of events within a school, or a series of teacher activities, or any array of teacher characteristics while neglecting the product is to examine intentions without considering consequences.

7. Educational goals must be stated in descriptive rather than in interpretive language. We have learned that it is not useful to define educational goals in the terms formerly used by professional educators and still used by their critics. We know that instead of such high-sounding slogans as "transmitting the cultural heritage," "educating citizens for democracy," and "developing the individual's potential," we must develop objectives defined in terms of changes in pupils' behavior or in the products of student behaviors. We must also be careful that, in rigorously setting behavioral goals, we do not slip into triviality. We must be prepared to defend each behavioral goal in terms of value assumptions and to provide reasons why one particular behavioral goal is better than another. These points do not represent new thinking. They describe a trend, which according to Ralph Tyler (1954, 1956) began about 1935, a trend of which many public school teachers still are unaware. Tyler stated that it is more important to evaluate the educational process than the structure of the school and that it is more important to evaluate the product than the process. I would rephrase this point: the proper way to evaluate both the educational process and the structure of the schools is to find out whether they are in fact producing the hoped-for product.

The function of the professional evaluator should be to help teachers and administrators in a given school to do such things as the following:

1. Define their goals in terms of pupil performance. John McNeil (1966), director of Supervised Teaching at UCLA, and I both have found that many experienced teachers are not able to define their objectives in language which describes observable changes in pupil behavior. It is easy to be critical of such teachers, and it is easy to state educational goals behaviorally—if we limit ourselves to rote learning. For example, "students will be able to name the bones of the body" is a goal stated in behavioral terms. While this goal may be important in some contexts, it is a very limited one. The behavioral definition of higher order goals is much more difficult. At the end of a course, teachers want their students to perform in such a manner as to warrant the inference that the students have learned to "know," "understand," "appreciate," and "think" about what the teacher has tried to teach. Merely to tell teachers that they should state these goals behaviorally is far from sufficient. What would be more helpful would be to show them how, and to invent more sophisticated instruments for them to use.

2. Learn how systematically to discover differences among pupils that require particular kinds of instruction. Teachers need appraisal devices that will do more than reveal differences in what students already have learned. They need instruments that will also reveal barriers to or interferences with learning, among them: (a) misconceptions; (b) particular habits, such as failure to pay attention; (c) certain needs that the child is satisfying at the expense of learning, e.g., need for group approval or sensitivity to peer pressures; and (d) attitudes deriving from class and ethnic background, etc. Some important differences among students are so subtle that, without sophisticated instruments, the child who has not learned to attend to the teacher's instructions may be mistaken for a dull child, or an angry one, or perhaps one with a constitutional impairment.

3. Design and administer evaluation programs. More importantly, professional evaluators should help individual teachers to find out which of their instructional procedures are paying off and which are not. With guidance, it is possible for the teachers themselves to try out and to evaluate alternative instructional methods on the job. For example, Bartlett (1960) demonstrated that when an instructor spent part of his time in algebra class teaching study habits, the students learned more than when he spent the entire time teaching algebra.

Public school people do not need more critics—critics abound. What these educators *do* need is someone to help them find and test alternative solutions to the complex problems they face daily. For the most part, university personnel who have the knowledge to perform the kinds of evaluation functions described above have not been taking their knowledge to the schools. They have been publishing their findings in professional journals, but they have failed to make explicit to teachers the relevance of those findings for the teachers' work. Hopefully, the research and development evaluator will bridge the gap between the laboratory and the field.

REFERENCES

Anderson, C. C. & Hunka, S. M. Teacher Evaluation: Some Problems and a Proposal. *Harvard Educational Review,* 1963, *33,* 1, pp. 74-96.

Barlett, W. H. The Practical Application of Psychological Facts in the Classroom as Demonstrated by Teaching a Specific Study Method to Elementary Algebra Students of the Junior College Level. Unpublished master's thesis, University of California, Los Angeles, 1960.

Conant, J. B. *Education and Liberty.* Cambridge: Harvard University Press, 1953.

Piel, G. *Science in the Cause of Man.* New York: Random House, 1961.

Ryans, D. G. *Characteristics of Teachers.* Washington, D. C.: American Council on Education, 1960.

Scriven, M. *The Methodology of Evaluation.* Bloomington: Indiana University, 1965. (Mimeo.)

Stake, R. E. *The Countenance of Educational Evaluation.* Urbana: University of Illinois, Center for Instructional Research and Curriculum Evaluation, 1966. (Mimeo.)

Tyler, R. W. Modern Aspects of Evaluation. *California Journal of Secondary Education,* 1954, *29,* 410-412.

————. The Curriculum: Then and Now. *Proceedings, 1956. Invitational Conference on Testing Problems.* Princeton, New Jersey: Educational Testing Service, 1957.

The following two articles, both by the same author, are reports on the approach to evaluation taken in the development of the AAAS materials, Science—A Process Approach. *The Walbesser reports cover a span of three years and represent a type of experiential justification of the behavioral position on evaluation. Implications from the reports may be expanded from science to other areas of the curriculum.*

Curriculum Evaluation by Means of Behavioral Objectives*

HENRY H. WALBESSER

The Commission on Science Education of the American Association for the Advancement of Science has undertaken the task of initiating and sponsoring a program to develop instructional materials in elementary science for the early grades. The primary focus of these materials is the construction of a set of activities which have a high probability of shaping those behaviors which reflect the underlying processes of science: that is, those behaviors which are common to all scientific endeavors.

In the development of an experimental science curriculum devoted to the "processes of science," it is obvious that the first step to be taken is the identification of the particular set of processes to be considered. These processes provide the focal point from which the experimental materials are written. The resulting product of the writing efforts is, however, ultimately intended to shape a specific collection of behaviors in students. Hence, an effective evaluation of the resulting materials

*Reprinted from the *Journal of Research in Science Teaching, 1,* 4, 1963, pp. 296-301, by permission of the publisher and the author.

must include a measure or series of measures related to the behaviors which the learners are supposed to acquire as a result of exposure to the experimental curriculum.

The overall strategy of evaluation consists of a three phase attack: the specification of the curriculum objectives as behaviors, the immediate measure of each of these specified behaviors by means of the Check Lists of Competencies, and measures of the behaviors which characterize the processes of science.

The Specification of Behaviors

The first phase of the evaluation began with the first day of writing of the experimental materials. Each of the writers participating in the summer conference was given the charge of specifying precisely what he would expect to *see the child do* or *hear the child say* in order to be satisfied that the child had learned what he intended. This collection of behaviors is identified for each of the exercises and these same behaviors are defined to be the objectives for each of the exercises.

Certainly, one might question the necessity or purpose of such rigid specification of the expected instructional outcomes. The principal justification rests upon the advantage it holds for two groups directly participating in any curriculum experiment: the teacher and the evaluator.

It should be quite apparent that the specification of objectives in behavioral terms provides an immediate and direct vehicle by which to communicate the expected goal of any instructional activity. This is a device by which the individual whose chief responsibility is the shaping of behaviors, the teacher, is informed of the desired outcome of instructional materials. If any hope of success for a given set of activities is to be sustained, then the individuals attempting to use the materials must know the character of what is to be learned. That is, the teacher must be provided with the means by which to recognize whether the terminal goals have been accomplished. Behavioral objectives provide such knowledge.

If a curriculum project claims to have accomplished something, then one of the most fundamental obligations of the experimenter is to present evidence of change or proof of learning. These are basic to a demonstration of accomplishment. But how can such proof be forthcoming unless there is initial agreement upon what the learner will "be able to do" after he has been exposed to the curriculum materials?

The specification of objectives as directly observable human performance also aids in curriculum measurement. An instructional program of any kind, experimental or not, has the goal of establishing a particular set of behaviors. The learner is expected to be able to do something after completing the instruction that he could not do beforehand. In order to determine whether any change has actually occurred, it must be possible to observe, or in a more academic sense to measure, the post-learning behavior. However, if measurement is to be possible, the instructional objectives must be specified in terms of behaviors which are observable. If the desired capability of the learner cannot be specified in such terms, it should be painfully obvious that such a capability cannot be measured. There exists a class of curriculum designers who do not wish to be (as they often contend) "pinned down" to specific behavioral changes. As a direct consequence of this lack of commitment to a behavioral description, they frequently do not specify the performances they expect the learner to accomplish. Even in those rare cases when the specification is made, the objectives are all too often couched in terms of educationally pleasant but meaningless language such as "the child will appreciate" or "the child will be able to deal more effectively with" or "the child will understand better." It is impossible to construct direct measures from such linguistic drivel.

As a result of such inadequate framing of objectives, the task of curriculum evaluation becomes at best a matter left to the collaboration of the curriculum project directors and professional test item writers. The principal criticism of this procedure is that the test development occurs several months after the completion of the instructional materials and within a group that must second-guess the intent of the author of the materials. Such a procedure does not provide the user, the teacher, with a clear set of instructional goals. Furthermore, since such an attitude toward curriculum construction renders any evaluation on objective grounds impossible, it leads to evaluation by "blue ribbon juries." Evaluation of the quality of the content of instructional material by a panel of experts has some measure of justification, but such a strategy cannot hope to ascertain the actual behavioral changes in students exposed to the experimental material—that is, to ascertain the effectiveness of the curriculum.

Therefore, the most significant benefit of curriculum objectives presented as statements of reliably observable behaviors is that it instructs one in precisely what to observe the child doing or saying provided that the materials have been effective. In this way it is possible to evaluate the success or failure of each activity by means of a direct measurement. A logical and necessary refinement of this strategy is to require that each objective contain an indication of what the author of the material considers a minimally acceptable performance. That is, one must account for "how well" or "how much" in addition to "what the child should be able to do or say."

As a result of this first phase of the evaluation, a list of objectives is now available. This list represents the desired behavioral repertoire as specified by the writers who authored the AAAS science materials. The presence or absence of these behaviors in the children exposed to the experimental curriculum represents one significant measure of the success or failure of the curriculum.

Construction of Immediate Behavioral Measures

The second phase of the evaluation strategy is concerned with the actual measure of whether the behaviors specified in each exercise are acquired by the students using these materials. The following individual testing procedure was adopted as a means by which to obtain this measurement. A measure of the behaviors or expected competencies specified in the objectives for each exercise was developed. These measures were defined to be "Check Lists of Competencies" and were constructed in such a manner that each one consisted of two sections. The first section is a description of the stimulus situation to be constructed by the tester together with a series of instructions describing the tasks the child is asked to perform and the range of acceptable responses. The second section of each Check List is a tabular array on which the teacher reports the results obtained from three students. In all cases the learner's performance is reported on a binary scale: yes or no. The three children used in the testing situation are randomly selected for the experimental centers by the AAAS staff. In order to provide for a maximum range of student involvement, a new trio of students is randomly chosen for each month of the academic year.

In order to introduce some measure of reporter independence into the system, two teachers involved in the use of the experimental materials (or a teacher and center coordinator where two teachers are not available) are asked to interchange the testing of students once during each month.

The analysis of the Check List of Competency results includes obtaining measures of association between the children's performance and the teacher dimensions of age, science training, and years of experience. In addition to this, measures of association between the children's performance and their sex and chronological age will also be computed.

As a measure of teacher reaction, a feedback form is also completed by the teacher for each exercise. This instrument is intended to provide measures of planning time and execution time for each exercise, of student reaction to the material as reflected by a four-point rating scale, of minimal student performance as viewed by the teacher and reported as observed behavior, and a sixteen-part measure of the adequacy of the written descriptions for teaching each exercise.

The second phase of the evaluation is intended to collect information on an immediate behavioral level that reflects the extent to which any given set of objectives are accomplished for any given exercise. This analysis, however, does not answer the question of whether the child's behavior has been changed with respect to the scientific processes such as observation, measurement, prediction, and so on. Since it is the expressed intent of this experimental curriculum to provide children with a "better understanding of these scientific processes," it is only reasonable that one is under an obligation to specify the behavioral meaning of the "understanding process" statement, as well as to investigate the validity of this claim. This investigation becomes the focus of the third phase of the evaluation strategy.

The Development of the Process Instrument

In order to initiate this third phase of evaluation, a "process-behavior" instrument is currently being developed and will be administered on a pilot basis at the end of the current academic year. The problem inherent in the development of such an instrument resolves itself with this evaluation design into one of obtaining an appropriate sample of behavioral tasks which are representative of each of the processes included within the curriculum but not restricted to the environment identified in the exercise. In fact, one envisions constructing a scale of tasks for each of the scientific processes which reflects the degree of sophistication present in the behavioral repertoire of the individual for that particular process. The measure of the degree of sophistication might also be considered a measure of horizontal transfer. Again, in the development of such an instrument for children at the K-3 level, there must be a commitment to an individual test instrument for much the same reasons that the Check Lists of Competencies were constructed with this constraint.

The behaviors identified as the objectives for each exercise again serve as the starting point for the process measure. These behaviors are structured into a hierarchy of learning sets which identifies the dependence that exists among them. This procedure is patterned after that developed by Gagné.[1, 2]

In order to obtain a maximum of clarity in the behaviorial description of each learning set, the following operational guides were adopted:

(1) Naming—the child is able to respond accurately with the verbal label to some conceptual category such as color or shape. For example,

he is expected to respond correctly to questions such as "What is the color of this leaf?" or "What is the shape of this figure?"

(2) Identifying—the child is able to respond correctly to the selection of a specific object. One associates an actual physical action of choosing an object or assurance that such action could be taken in the "identifying behavior." For example, he is expected to respond correctly to requests such as "Show me the large block," or "Which square is red?"

(3) Recognizing—the child is able to acknowledge the presence or absence of a specified object when more than one conceptual category is employed. For example, he is expected to respond correctly to requests such as "Which figure is the large, green triangle?" He is also expected to be able to say that object one is whiter, softer, and longer than object two.

(4) Distinguishing—the child is able to respond with more subtle and refined descriminations than when identifying. An objective makes use of the "distinguishing behavior" whenever there is a reasonable chance of the learner confusing two members of a category. For example, one would speak of identifying the green leaf and distinguishing between the maple and elm leaves.

(5) Describing—the child should be able to generate all of the necessary conceptual categories that are relevant to the identification of an object. He should be able to answer the request "Describe this object," by selecting an adequate number of categories so as to guarantee the object's identification. The choice of categories is left solely to the child.

(6) Ordering—the child should be able to arrange any pair of objects from a collection of two or more on the basis of some comparative unit.

It has been contended that placing such severe constraints upon the system of experimental curriculum construction may tend to inhibit the "creativity" of those involved in writing the materials. However, since the proponents of this thesis have as yet presented no experimental evidence to support their claim, it has not affected this strategy for curriculum evaluation.

As an example of the end product which one obtains from the learning set analysis, consider the following levels derived from the set of behaviors presented under the process labeled Observation:

Level 1 (the simplest level): Identifying and naming colors, sizes, shapes, textures, and weights by heft.

Level 2: Distinguishing values of a physical property in comparisons of pairs of objects. The comparisons are made in terms of properties such as heavier, lighter; louder, softer; hotter, colder; harder, softer.

Level 3 (A): Ordering physical properties in relation to a standard: temperature with the use of a thermometer; hardness; weight; size by using volume. *(B):* Identifying and naming changes in physical properties: color, loudness, pitch, brightness, heaviness, size, hardness, change of state.

Level 4 (A): Recognizing various physical characteristics in objects; comparing objects by using several dimensions. *(B):* Recognizing several dimensions of change in physical objects; comparing pairs of events with respect to such changes.

Level 5: Recognizing physical properties in a complex situation involving comparisons and/or descriptions of more than two events.

Level 6: Observing the relations of objects to events and/or the functions of objects in events: magnets are identified because of *what they do* rather than how they appear.

Level 7: Systematic Observation—This involves distinguishing and recognizing objects under conditions in which one or more physical properties is systematically varied.

Although this description contains the seven levels through which each student is expected to proceed, the interrelationships which exist between these learning sets and those generated by the other process categories are not specified. The entire learning set structure has now been constructed for the first four volumes of the AAAS Elementary Science curriculum. However, the size of the learning set hierarchy prohibits its inclusion in this paper, but every effort will be made to make this information available in the next evaluation report. It may be of some interest to observe that this category of Observation leads into the processes labeled Classification (on the basis of physical properties, appearance, and function) and Inference. The Observation process learning sets are interconnected on these first several levels with the processes of Measurement, Numbers, Space/Time, and Communication.

The learning hypothesis which can be tested as a result of this learning set hierarchy is a direct, but powerful, one. If these behaviors are truly ordered in a dependence sequence, then an individual who has acquired all of the behaviors which lead to the level two learning set under Observation should possess a high probability (approximately one) of also possessing the level two behavior; and those individuals who have not acquired the level two behavior possess a high probability of not having acquired one or more of the behaviors of the connected level one learning sets. This relationship is hypothesized to exist between any two consecutive levels in which the higher level learning set is connected in some way to one or more of the adjacent, lower level learning sets. That is, one is able to test a series of predictions concerning the acquisition of the final behavioral goal for any given process. In this way it is possible to obtain a profile for each individual in which he is not compared to a mythical national norm; rather, one assesses an individual in terms of the number of behaviors which are requisite to the performance of the final task that the individual has acquired. For a more detailed discussion of these learning hypotheses see Gagné.[1, 2]

Construction of the Process Instrument

Once this hierarchy is established a series of scaled items reflecting the behavior of the learning set-process are developed. For each scaled set of behaviors, a range of acceptable responses is developed so that the test administrator need not subjectively judge the correctness of the particular response. This strategy for instrument development also enables the test constructors to standardize the testing procedure. It should be apparent from the previous discussion that this instrument is to be administered on an individual basis.

The pilot test for the process instrument will be made at the end of the current academic year with the use of sample subjects from the experimental centers as well as sample subjects from control classes. The revised form of this instrument will then be administered next year on a pre-post test model to experimental and control subjects. This procedure is intended to provide the initial data for standardizing the process instrument.

Thus, the evaluation proceeds directly from what the writer considers success with the experimental materials he has authored to an immediate measurement of the actual success of each exercise in terms of behaviors acquired. The final performance goals of each of these more general process categories are measured by means of a unique individual testing instrument derived from a behavioral analysis of the instructional materials. Observable behavior serves as the foundation upon which the entire evaluation strategy is based.

REFERENCES

1. Gagné, R. M., J. R. Mayor, H. L. Garstens & N. E. Paradise, *Psychological Monographs, 76,* 7, 1962.
2. —— & N. E. Paradise, *Psychological Monographs, 75,* 14, 1961.

Science Curriculum Evaluation: Observations on a Position*

HENRY H. WALBESSER

Two of the fundamental positions concerning the purposes, conduct, and expected outcomes of evaluation, which are currently assumed in the assessment of experimental curriculum materials, are the content position and the behavior position. It is the intention of this paper to point out the differences between these two conceptions of curriculum assessment and to describe the model, based upon the behavior position, which is being used by the AAAS Commission on Science Education in its curriculum project.

Content

It would doubtless be valuable to explore the content position in depth, but it will not be done here. Our chief concern is with the behavior position. We need say only enough about the content position to help distinguish those aspects which are specific to it and those peculiar to the behavior position. In brief—as "content" suggests—those who adopt this view build a curriculum or develop instructional materials as a content-organizing enterprise. They use instructional materials which appeal to a logical, or rational, or historical presentation of a particular discipline or combination of disciplines. Choice of materials is considered in terms of the nature of the items which should be sampled from the content domains and relates to such questions as:

What big ideas from this discipline should be chosen?
What particular topics are fundamental to an understanding of the discipline?
How can certain concepts be best presented?
What particular facts must an individual know if he is to appreciate the significance of this discipline?

*Reprinted from *The Science Teacher, 33,* February, 1966, pp. 34-35, 37-39, by permission of the publisher and the author.

Naturally, in the assessment of the instructional materials developed from such a curriculum orientation, the units of achievement are taken to be content items.

The primary measurement is most often a sequence of content items or content situations, and the measurement is made almost exclusively in terms of paper and pencil performances. Among those who adopt this content position there are some who use subjective "expert" evaluation, particularly among those who contend that the measurement field has not yet achieved the necessary technology so as to be able to provide useful or constructive information about the effects of the curriculum. However, assessment of instructional materials by means of a rigorous research design *is* possible within the content-directed framework.

Behavior Position

The second group of curriculum designers reflect what might be termed the behavior position. The AAAS Commission on Science Education subscribes to this position. The "behavioral" group focuses upon the creation of instructional sequences of material which supposedly assist the learner in the acquisition of a particular collection of behaviors rather than a particular collection of content. Unlike those who favor evaluation of content, the curriculum organization which appeals to a behavioral interpretation approaches the development of instructional materials by asking one question: *What do we want the learner to be able to do after instruction that he was unable to do before instruction?*

Then the curriculum designer proceeds to develop materials related to the answers given to this question.

The existence of each curriculum project is dependent upon being able to demonstrate that it accomplishes something. Whether this accomplishment is content assimilation or performance acquisition is of no real consequence. What is important, however, is the recognition and acceptance of the principle that every curriculum project has the honest and inescapable obligation to supply *objective evidence of accomplishment.* Furthermore, the evidence presented by the project must be able to satisfy the criterion that it was obtained by defensible research procedures and that these procedures can be replicated if someone should desire to do so.

For the behavior-oriented group of curriculum designers, reliably observable performance plays the same role as a content item does for the content-oriented group. As a consequence of the behavior-oriented point of view, the evaluation of a collection of instructional materials becomes the assessment of the presence or absence of specific behaviors or specific sets of behaviors. The accomplishment of these objectives of the instructional materials for the behavior-oriented group is determined by observing the learner performing his specified task and thereby exhibiting the desired behavior. Such an assessment obviously demands that the behaviors under observation be clearly stated, that the criterion for their presence be explicitly stated, and that the conditions under which the evidence of presence or absence is collected be described in such a way that the procedure used to obtain the evidence can be replicated by others. This investigator has adopted the position that the behavioral view of curriculum development possesses advantages sufficiently unique and productive to the design, development, and evaluation of instructional materials so as to make behavioral description of the objectives of instructional materials an unavoidable partner of content selection. The remainder of this paper is an explanation of this position.

Practices for Evaluation

What is the purpose of any collection of instructional materials? One response which has a high probability of acceptance by most, if not all, curriculum designers, is that the purpose of a collection of instructional materials is to effect learning. An appeal to this all-encompassing goal of learning leads one quite naturally to ask two questions: What is to be learned? and, Who is to learn it? The question of who is to learn relates, in this instance, to the population of elementary school children. Upon first consideration, one might argue that "what is to be learned" is exclusively within the domain of content selection. However, this view is soon replaced by the more basic behavioral orientation when one considers that the recognition of whether an individual possesses "knowledge of a particular collection of content" is only possible through some observable response on his part.

Does confinement of statements of what is to be learned to statements of observable performance restrict the nature of the content area or the general character of possible objectives of the curriculum? The constraints imposed by behavioral objectives for curriculum description are amazingly few. Consider, for example, the physicist who might set the goal for his curriculum to be that the student will understand Newton's First Law of Motion. How will the physicist distinguish those students who understand from those students who do not understand? Perhaps someone would wish to contend that the physicist is never certain of when the student understands. This position is indefensible for a writer who intends others to adopt an instructional procedure which will teach "an understanding of that concept." Furthermore, how can any author make a selection of instructional procedures, or decide upon an order, or include or exclude instruction from his discussion if he possesses no indicator of when he has succeeded? How can a writer make any decision under these circumstances? It is quite possible, however, that the physicist may not be able to verbalize the class of learner responses with which he is concerned, but the physicist, nevertheless, does possess them. The problem is merely to help the creator of the instructional sequence verbalize a description of the desired behaviors. From this standpoint one may contend that even the comfortable, ambiguous objectives such as understanding, appreciation, and knowing—so commonplace as objectives for contemporary curriculum projects—are potentially able to yield to a behavioral description.

The content selection and organization made by the writing efforts of the past decade are not under question by this discussion, but rather the lack of evidence to support or describe what these programs accomplish is the focus of attention. What is already available by way of instructional materials is not the central issue either, for this material is part of the past development and should remain part of the past. It is not sensible that one propose taking existing materials and attemping to provide a set of behavioral objectives to describe each program. What is important is that curriculum projects learn from these errors so that current activity improves upon past efforts.

Curriculum designers seldom possess professional interest in the problems associated with the clarification and specification of objectives in terms of a behavioral description. It is the obligation of the behavioral researcher to provide the guidelines which will enable the curriculum writer to make the statements of performance.

How will the project proceed after it has adopted the principle that statements of objectives be statements of observable performance? One procedure is to attempt an adaptation of the Bloom *Taxonomy*.[1] However, lack of specification within, as well as between, Bloom's taxonomic classifications and their relationship to test development rather than instructional development make them somewhat unacceptable for the present purpose. Since the behavioral point of view focuses upon the ability of a learner to perform a specific task, the work of Miller[2] in the area of task analysis, and that of Gagné[3] and Walbesser[4] in the construction and interpretation of behavioral hierarchies, offer an alternative to the Bloom adaptation. It is this alternative strategy which has been adopted by the Commission on Science Education of the American Association for the Advancement of Science in the description and evaluation of the elementary science curriculum, *Science—A Process Approach*. The model of curriculum evaluation developed in this discussion is illustrated by the evaluation program of *Science—A Process Approach*.

Statements of Behavior

Can scientists be persuaded to write behavioral objectives? The experiences with the science curriculum effort of the AAAS Commission on Science Education strongly suggest that the physical, biological, and social scientists can be persuaded to adopt this position, without interfering with their creation of instructional materials for science. The first requirement is a firm commitment on the part of the project decision-making body to have behavioral objectives.

Each instructional segment should clearly state the objectives of instruction—what the child will be able to do or say (observable performance) after instruction with the material that he was unable to do or say before instruction. The objectives must be statements of reliably observable behavior, written by the author of the instructional segment, and stated in terms of observable performances which the scientist feels are necessary as well as sufficient indicators of success.

If this procedure is to be effective, each writer will need to be provided with a description of what is desired by way of statements which are acceptable as behavioral objectives and those statements which are unacceptable. One example of such a description is contained in the subsequent paragraphs. The description is meant to be illustrative of this one effort and nothing more.

Criteria to Be Used in the Construction of Statements of Behavioral Objectives

The statement of objectives should include all of the individual performances one expects the learner to have acquired during the exercise. When conceived as immediately observable performances, these may be thought of as minimal objectives; but, as such, none should be omitted from the statement.

Many authors tend to include some goals such as "increasing understanding," "developing appreciation," and so on. A statement of an objective must be considered unacceptable if it includes this kind of statement. The question to be faced is, what specific things is the learner expected to acquire which can be seen when immediate observations of his performance are made?

A major criterion should be clarity, the avoidance of ambiguity. For example, a statement like this is ambiguous: "The child should be able to recognize that some objects can be folded to produce matching parts, that is, are symmetrical." This statement might mean several different things:

A. The child recognizes symmetrical parts when they are folded to produce matching parts.
B. The child can verbally answer the question about what makes the object symmetrical by saying, "A figure is symmetrical if it can be folded to produce matching parts."
C. The child can demonstrate whether or not a figure is symmetrical by pointing out its matching (or non-matching) parts.

These are not the same things. While the child is unlikely to be able to do C without being able to do A, he could certainly do A without doing C, C without doing B, and B without either A or C.

It is imperative to use words which are as unambiguous as possible. Some examples are:

A. *Identify,* also recognize, distinguish. These mean point to, choose, pick out, or otherwise respond to several stimuli differentially.
B. *Name,* also *state.* These imply that a verbal statement is required. "What color is this ball?" is naming.
C. *Describe.* Means a verbal statement and also that the categories stated are self-generated. "How do you describe this ball?" is describing.
D. *Order,* or *place in sequence.*
E. *Construct, print,* or *draw.*
F. *Demonstrate.* Means that the learner is applying a principle to a specific situation. For example, he may be asked to demonstrate symmetry for a figure by folding or matching halves.

Why the emphasis on performance in words implying behavior? The major reason is to stay away from "mere" verbalization. If one says the child "understands that such and such is true," this might be taken to imply merely that the child can repeat a verbal statement. Much better to have him *identify* something, *construct* something, or *demonstrate* something. Under these circumstances, we know that he "knows."

What does one hope to gain from this procedure? By requesting each author to specify the expected behavioral outcomes for the particular material he has written, we require him to specify what he considers success with this particular piece of instruction. Once this specification is made, any observer—whether he is a scientist, teacher, or interested individual—is able to distinguish those who have successfully achieved the objectives of the exercise from those who have not. Under these circumstances, all that is called for is that individuals making the judgment read the description of the desired performances and then determine whether they are present in the learner being observed.

If a scientist specified the performances one is examining, it can be argued that the scientist should also specify how one goes about the task of determining whether the learner does or does not possess a particular behavior. As an aid to the scientist in the construction of these performance measures, it is helpful to provide him with guidelines which describe the necessary characteristics of such measures.

The guidelines for constructing each of these performance assessments, or competency measures as they are called by the AAAS Commission on Science Education elementary science curriculum project, require that they meet the following criteria:

A. Each objective of the exercise should be represented by at least one task. Hopefully, these tasks should be suggested by the statements of the objectives; but, in any case, behaviors proposed as instructional objectives should be measured.

B. The tasks need to be designed to elicit behaviors of the sort described in the objectives. If an objective calls for the construction of something, the task might begin "Draw a ———." If the learner is being asked to name something, the task might be "What do we call this?"

C. The description accompanying each task should tell the instructor clearly what to do (not just imply it). For example, an accompanying instruction might be: "Place in front of the child a dittoed sheet containing drawings of an equilateral triangle and a circle." Or, "Give the child a meterstick."

D. The kind of performances that are acceptable should be clearly described so that a correct judgment can be made concerning the presence or absence of a particular behavior.

The collection of behavioral objectives for the entire instructional program provides a behavioral map (or bank of descriptions of behavior) which may be used to characterize the entire collection of instructional materials. In short, this totality of behaviors represents a measurable description of what this particular instructional program attempts to accomplish. Such a collection of behaviors is at least one means of providing a lower boundary on what the curriculum is to accomplish.

A behavioral map such as the one provided by these procedures will in turn yield to analysis by behavioral hierarchies such as those of Gagné[2] and Walbesser,[4] thereby providing the vehicle through which to obtain an assessment of the instructional program's effect far beyond that identified by this lower boundary. Assessment of the long-term behavioral acquisition by the children exposed to *Science—A Process Approach* is determined by The Science Process Test or The Science Process Instrument, administered on an annual basis. The Science

Process Test is a performance measure administered individually and based upon the behavioral description provided by the behavioral hierarchies which describe each of the simple science processes. The results of this instrument provide an individual profile of the developmental progress of each child within each of the simple processes. The current version of this instrument, The Science Process Test, covers the kindergarten and first, second, and third grades.

Interest Measurements

Up to this point, the evaluation has concerned itself with assessment within the cognitive domain. One might reasonably ask, what measures should or can be taken of the affective domain? That is, most science curriculum projects are interested in the investigation of the student's attitude toward science as well as the teacher's attitude toward science. The following remarks are directed at the question of student interests. Since the investigation of student interest in science has just been initiated by the *Science—A Process Approach* curriculum, it is only possible to describe the nature of strategies being used.

The first of the three instruments intended to measure the child's interest in science is called the "Extra-School General Information Inventory." The strategy of development calls for the construction of a measure which samples general information from four broad areas: science, fine arts, sports, and literature. The assumption is that the interests of a child will be reflected by his fund of information on topics or in areas to which he is not ordinarily exposed in the formal school environment. Therefore, if the youngster demonstrates that he has a sizeable collection of facts, which are miscellaneous from a standpoint of his formal schooling, but all the facts are science related, then one might reasonably infer that this is a reflection of his reading or activity pursued outside of the classroom—that is, a reflection of his interests. The general information categories which were selected as components for the Inventory are intended to reflect divergent interest areas. By appealing to these rather diverse categories, the science interest is not as visible to the child; that is, the child is not able to guess easily that you are interested in his science interests. With such a less visible indirect measure of interest, one works from the assumption that he has improved his probability of sampling the true interests of the child.

The second form of interest measure which is under development is one in which one employs "duration of looking time" as the measure of interest. Various levels of complexity in pictures depicting several kinds of activities are employed in this procedure. One obtains measures of the length of time which an individual will look at pictures related to four areas: science, fine arts, sports, and literature. The pictures are equated with regard to complexity. The intention is to develop a Looking Time Interest Inventory.

The third interest measure is a Structured Interview of Science Interests in which the interviewer guides the conversation with the child so as to sample the child's recent activities outside of school. It is much too early at this point to decide whether any or all of these interest inventories will be effective with children at this age level. However, they do represent three forms which may be logically supported as possible measures of science interest.

Summary

By way of summary, then, the evaluation begins with the specification of behavioral objectives for each instructional unit, proceeds to assess the success of each instructional unit in terms of measuring the behaviors acquired by each child as set forth in the objectives, and assesses the annual progress of each child in terms of his acquisition of the behaviors identified in the behavioral hierarchies for each of the processes. Finally, the science interests of children exposed to the instructional program may be included within the evaluation design, but by indirect rather than direct measurement.

The case for the behavioral description of a set of instructional materials is not a case against the content-oriented curriculum efforts. Rather, the behavioral view of curriculum is merely a recognition of the fundamental role which behavior and its specification as observable performance must play in a description of what a content-organized curriculum does accomplish. In this context, a content-oriented view of curriculum represents one plausible extension of the behavioral view. The acceptance of the need for the behavioral description of objectives will enable curriculum projects to carry out comparative studies on a basis which does yield to scientific investigation. Hence the benefits to content-oriented curricula would be clarification of the aims of the instructional materials, the existence of a vehicle for assessing the success or failure of the materials, and a technique for conducting comparative studies of curricula as defensible research investigations. Obviously the same benefits are present for behavior-oriented curricula with one additional possibility. Without stretching the point out of all perspective, one could readily imagine the existence of a curriculum development project which first specifies the tasks all learners successful with the curriculum will be able to accomplish, then describes the behavioral sequence in observable performance language so as to identify the behaviors which are prerequisite to the ability to perform each task, and finally develops the instructional materials which would shape the behaviors identified by each entry in the behavioral sequence. The instructional revolution implicit in such a curriculum development project has the potential of reshaping all educational enterprises, since one would finally direct his attention to the potentials of the learner, rather than the appropriateness of content selections.

The importance of a performance-based evaluation to the adoption of an instructional program by the classroom teacher also yields to a most fascinating behavioral assessment. Imagine the impact teachers could have on the curriculum if they demanded behavioral objectives and supporting evidence of accomplishment in terms of acquired behaviors. Why shouldn't every teacher demand statements of the behaviors their students can be expected to acquire as a result of exposure to every instructional program they are asked to use?

References

1. Benjamin S. Bloom. *Taxonomy of Educational Objectives. Handbook I: Cognitive Domain.* New York: David McKay Co., 1956.
2. R. M. Gagné. The Acquisition of Knowledge. *Psychological Review.* 69: 355-356. 1962.
———. *The Conditions of Learning.* New York: Holt, Rinehart and Winston, Inc., 1965.
———. The Implications of Instructional Objectives for Learning. In C. M. Lindvall, Editor. *Defining Educational Objectives.* University of Pittsburgh Press, Pittsburgh, Pennsylvania. 1964.
———. *The Psychological Basis of Science—A Process Approach.* American Association for the Advancement of Science. AAAS Miscellaneous Publication 65-8. 1965.
——— & O. C. Bassler. Study of Retention of Some Topics of Elementary Non-metric Geometry. *Journal of Educational Psychology.* 54:123-131. 1963.
———, J. R. Mayor, H. L. Garstens & N. E. Paradise. Factors in Acquiring Knowledge of a Mathematical Task. *Psychological Monographs.* 76: No. 7 (Whole No. 526). 1962.
——— & Staff, University of Maryland Mathematics Project. Some Factors in Learning Non-metric Geometry. *Society for Research in Child Development.* 30: No. 1, Serial 99. 1965.
3. R. B. Miller. *Handbook on Training and Training Equipment Design.* Wright Air Development Center, Wright-Patterson Air Force Base, Ohio. Technical Report 53-136. 1953.
———. *A Method for Man-Machine Task Analysis.* Wright Air Development Center, Wright-Patterson Air Force Base, Ohio. Technical Report 53-137. 1953.

————. *Some Working Concepts of Systems Analysis.* American Institute for Research, Pittsburgh, Pennsylvania. 1954.

————. *Task and Part-Task Trainers.* Wright Air Development Center, Wright-Patterson Air Force Base, Ohio. Technical Report 60-469; ASTIA No. AD 245652. 1960.

———— & H. P. Van Cott. *The Determination of Knowledge Content for Complex Man-Machine Jobs.* American Institute for Research, Pittsburgh, Pennsylvania. 1955.

4. H. H. Walbesser. Curriculum Evaluation by Means of Behavioral Objectives. *Journal of Research in Science Teaching.* 1:296-301. 1963.

————. *An Evaluation Model and Its Application.* American Association for the Advancement of Science, AAAS Miscellaneous Publication 65-9. 1965.

Part VII

Additional Media

Abramson, David A. Curriculum Research and Evaluation. *Review of Educational Research, 36,* June, 1966, pp. 388-395.

Atkin, J. Myron. Some Evaluation Problems in a Course Content Improvement Project. *Journal of Research in Science Teaching, 1,* 2, 1963, pp. 129-132.

Burns, Richard W. Measuring Objectives and Grading. *Educational Technology, 8,* September 30, 1968, pp. 13-14.

————. Objectives and Content Validity of Tests. *Educational Technology, 8,* December 15, 1968, pp. 17-18.

Carter, Heather L. Testing a Technique for Evaluating Instructional Materials. *The Elementary School Journal, 70,* November, 1969, pp. 99-107.

Chambers, W. M. Testing and Its Relationship to Educational Objectives. *The Journal of General Education, 16,* October, 1964, pp. 246-249.

Consalvo, Robert W. Evaluation and Behavioral Objectives. *The American Biology Teacher, 31,* April, 1969, pp. 230-232.

Flanagan, John C. Evaluating Educational Outcomes. *Science Education, 50,* April, 1966, pp. 248-251.

Gagné, Robert M. Curriculum Research and the Promotion of Learning. *Perspectives of Curriculum Evaluation.* Ralph W. Tyler, Robert M. Gagné & Michael Scriven (Eds.) Chicago: Rand McNally & Company, 1967, pp. 19-38.

Guba, Egon G. The Failure of Educational Evaluation. *Educational Technology, 9,* May, 1969, pp. 29-38.

Lumsdaine, A. A. Assessing the Effectiveness of Instructional Programs. *Teaching Machines and Programmed Learning, II: Data and Directions,* Robert Glaser (Ed.) Washington, D. C.: Department of Audiovisual Instruction, National Education Association, 1965, pp. 267-320.

Maguire, Thomas O. Decisions and Curriculum Objectives: A Methodology for Evaluation. *The Alberta Journal of Educational Research, 15,* March, 1969, pp. 17-30.

————. Value Components of Teachers' Judgments of Educational Objectives. *AV Communication Review, 16,* Spring, 1968, pp. 63-68.

McClelland, David. Measuring Behavioral Objectives in the 1970s. *Technology and Innovation in Education.* New York: Frederick A. Praeger, Publishers, 1968, pp. 46-50.

Popham, W. James. *Educational Criterion Measures.* Inglewood, California: Southwest Regional Laboratory for Educational Research and Development, 1968, 34 pp.

See also other materials in the SWRL series (Part I).

Popham, W. James & Eva L. Baker. *Evaluation.* Los Angeles, California: Vimcet Associates, 1967. Illustrated filmstrip, accompanying audio-taped narration, and instructor's manual, 43 frames, 29 minutes.

See also other materials in the Vimcet series (Part I).

Scriven, Michael. The Methodology of Evaluation. *Perspectives of Curriculum Evaluation.* Ralph W. Tyler, Robert M. Gagné & Michael Scriven (Eds.) Chicago: Rand McNally & Company, 1967, pp. 39-83.

Stake, Robert E. Testing in the Evaluation of Curriculum Development. *Review of Educational Research, 38,* February, 1968, pp. 77-84.

Sullivan, Howard J. Improving Learner Achievement Through Evaluation by Objectives. Inglewood, California: Southwest Regional Laboratory for Educational Research and Development, undated, 38 pp. (Mimeo.)

Walbesser, Henry H. & Heather Carter. Some Methodological Considerations of Curriculum Evaluation Research. *Educational Leadership, 26,* October, 1968, pp. 53-64.

Woodruff, Asahel D. & Janyce L. Taylor. *A Teaching Behavior Code.* Salt Lake City, Utah: The Utah State Board of Education, undated, 54 pp.

Part VIII

Opposing Viewpoints

Few attempts to effect change in society's institutions have met with complete acceptance. No matter how great the potential value of the change or how enthusiastically many people receive it, there are always those who would rather look at the alternatives, at the negative side effects, or at a variety of other things in lieu of the proposed change.

As a matter of fact, these cautioning voices are not only omnipresent, they are necessary and useful. Criticism helps to maintain balance and perspective. It promotes more intelligent handling of the change that finally does occur. And it reinforces rather than undermines the strongest points involved in the change.

Therefore, the articles in Part VIII were selected to fulfill three functions—(1) to provide perspective for the current forces for change being directed toward the curriculum, (2) to represent the type of reservations being voiced concerning the behavioral approach, and (3) to present convincing and articulate responses to such reservations. As such, these ideas deserve careful consideration. Naturally, not all writers whose thoughts are included in this section are concerned with the same problems, nor do they all approach their tasks with equal depth. They are representative, however, of the concerns felt by many educators when faced with the enormous challenges of education in the coming decades.

349

After examining the social and educational context out of which objective-based curriculum development emerged, Kliebard suggests three areas of vulnerability in the behavioral approach. He questions the sources used to define desired behaviors, the feasibility of using behaviors as the primary means of evaluating educational programs, and the possible moral issue involved in stipulating behavioral change as the outcome of instruction. Kliebard urges a crictical re-examination of the dominant concepts and procedures in the curriculum field.

Curricular Objectives and Evaluation: A Reassessment*

HERBERT M. KLIEBARD

One of the most sacrosanct of all our notions in the field of curriculum requires us to begin with a clear and unambiguous statement of objectives in behavioral terms as a prelude to the process of curriculum-making. The justification for this step is simple. In the first place, it permits "learning experiences" to be selected and organized with a particular end (or ends) in view. Secondly, the overt behaviors are supposed to provide a kind of clear-cut standard against which the educational enterprise can be evaluated. When the curricular objectives are not achieved in any significant way, the curriculum planner is then obligated to go back to the drawing board and redesign the curriculum so that the behaviors can be produced more efficiently. The number of steps in this procedure may vary depending on whether one follows Charters or Waples or Tyler, but the essential ingredients in the process

*Reprinted from *The High School Journal, 51,* March, 1968, pp. 241-247, by permission of the publisher and the author.

are basically the same, and they have been the same ever since the field of curriculum emerged as an area of specialization. As a matter of fact, this formula has become so ingrained in our thinking that it has become extremely difficult to examine it critically and to develop alternatives.

It might help us to gain some perspective on this process if we were to go back and examine the social and educational context in which it emerged. The year 1918 was an especially notable one in the field of curriculum. It was the year in which the celebrated *Cardinal Principles of Secondary Education* with its immortal "seven aims" was produced.[1] It was also the year in which Franklin Bobbitt published what is perhaps the first full-length book on curriculum theory, a book entitled simply, *The Curriculum.*[2] In both these important documents, the stamp of the major social doctrine of the period, social efficiency, is apparent. This doctrine, an amalgam of social control and social service,[3] saw education primarily as a way of training the individual for a role in society or, more particularly, to develop within the individual the ability to perform efficiently in various roles. The seven aims of the cardinal principles report, for example, actually constitute a crude set of categories of life activity. Within the categories of health, command of fundamental processes (a kind of afterthought),[4] worthy home membership, vocation, civil education, worthy use of leisure, and ethical character one can set forth virtually all of the activities that men perform. The quality of one's education can then be judged by the efficiency with which he is trained to perform those activities. Bobbitt was quite specific on this point: "The first step in modern curriculum-making is to formulate a statement of activities which constitute a proper quality of human living. These are the objectives."[5] Although later curriculum revision groups and individuals redistributed life's activities into six or ten or four categories instead of seven, the basic principle remained the same: the scope of the curriculum was defined by virtually the full range of man's activities and the standard of excellence was their efficient performance.

Bobbitt's *The Curriculum* and more particularly his *How to Make a Curriculum* formalized and extended this doctrine. In the first volume, Bobbitt set forth the nature of the task: "Our profession is confronted with the huge practical task of defining innumerable specific objectives; and then of determining the countless pupil experiences that must be induced by way of bringing the children to attain the objectives."[6] Such an emphasis on the priority of educational objectives and their clear-cut stipulation was not common in earlier writings on the curriculum. Bobbitt was probably influenced in this direction by Thorndike's theory of identical elements, a rather pessimistic view of how knowledge gained in one situation transfers to another, and by an overreaction on the part of educationists to the theories of mental discipline that had held sway before the turn of the century. The idea that the curriculum should be directed toward "training the mind" or developing "habits of thought" or anything so vague as that was repugnant to the new breed of professional educators that was gaining increasing prominence in the 1920's.

By 1924, with the massive curriculum reform project in Los Angeles behind him, Bobbitt was ready to undertake the task he had set. He began by designating ten major areas of human activity, areas which actually recapitulate with minor modifications the areas set forth in the aims of the cardinal principles report. Carrying forth his earlier dictum that "Human life, however varied, consists in the performance of specific activities" and that "Education that prepares for life is one that prepares definitely and adequately for these specific activities,"[7] Bobbitt undertook the specification of those activities *as* educational objectives. By setting out the range of man's adult activity in detail, he hoped to introduce a measure of practicality and scientific objectivity into the uncertainty and speculation that surrounded the question of the purposes of schooling.

The logical problems associated with such a procedure may seem formidable to the modern reader, but this did not keep many later curriculum theorists from accepting most of the basic procedures outlined by Bobbitt. One critic, Boyd Bode, argued cogently against the notion that one could somehow "derive" statements of value from empirical evidence about the world or society or man's activities in society. "No scientific analysis known to man," he insisted, "can determine the desirability or the need of anything."[8] Bobbitt also faced problems relating to the degree of comprehensiveness that could be achieved using a procedure requiring minute specific objectives. Why, for example, is "ability to protect the home from fire" a stated objective and not ability to protect the home from flood, vandalism, tornadoes, hurricanes, and other exigencies? Bobbitt attempted to meet this problem by subjecting his lists of objectives to the approval of "some twenty-seven hundred well-trained and experienced adults,"[9] hardly a rational solution. Furthermore, although Bobbitt and his followers continually emphasized specificity when stating educational objectives, there was a great deal of latitude in the generality with which objectives were stated by Bobbitt. Under Bobbitt's category, Parental Responsibilities, for example, we find something so general as "The mental, moral, and social qualities necessary for parenthood of proper character,"[10] whereas under the rubric of Maintenance of Physical Efficiency we find a detailed listing of objectives which includes "Ability to care for the teeth; Ability to care for the eyes; Ability to care for the nose, ear and throat; Ability to care for the skin; Ability to keep the heart and blood vessels in normal working condition; Ability to care for the hair and scalp; Ability to care for the nails; and Ability to care for the feet," as well as "Ability to control sex-functions in the interests of physical and social well-being." [11] In point of fact, if one were to seriously embark on a program of stating objectives with such scope and in such detail, the list would literally be endless.

Bobbitt himself was to modify his views sharply by the late twenties and early thirties, but the idea that educational objectives must be specific, detailed, "scientifically" drawn from life activities, and determined in advance of all other curriculum planning was to become immutably infused into the curriculum literature. The first issue of the *Review of Educational Research,* for example, an issue devoted to the curriculum, clearly subscribed to this ideology.[12] So did the great bulk of writing on curriculum from the 1930's on. A few refinements, however, were added here and there. Perhaps the one that received the most attention and enthusiasm on the part of curriculum specialists was the notion that educational objectives ought to be stated in behavioral terms, an idea that received a great deal of impetus through the work of the Eight-Year Study. One of the volumes to arise out of that study states as its first assumption, "It was assumed that education is a process which seeks to change the behavior patterns of human beings"; it then goes on to state as its second assumption "that the kinds of changes in behavior patterns in human beings which the school seeks to bring about are its educational objectives." The third assumption, naturally enough, is that an "educational program is appraised by finding out how far the objectives of the program are actually being realized." [13] A successful curriculum, then, is one which changes the behavior of human beings along certain specified lines.

The "assumptions" stated above had existed in the literature on curriculum in a variety of forms although they were more commonly referred to as "steps" in curriculum planning or "principles" of curriculum development. After 1950, this approach was frequently called a "rationale," or more specifically, the "Tyler rationale."

Tyler built his rationale around four major questions:
1. What educational purposes should the school seek to attain?
2. What educational experiences can be provided that are likely to attain these purposes?
3. How can these educational experiences be effectively organized?
4. How can we determine whether these purposes are being attained? [14]

Tyler's contribution was to weave together the most persistent strands in the curriculum literature and to present them in a coherent and easily understood form along with a strong plea for educational objectives to be stated in behavioral terms. In time Tyler's syllabus for his course, *Basic Principles of Curriculum and Instruction* (a descendent of the curriculum course that Bobbitt taught at the University of Chicago) has become a kind of semi-official doctrine in the field of curriculum.

Support for Tyler's strong emphasis on behavioral objectives came in the form of Will French's study, *Behavioral Goals of General Education in High School*. Apart from this behavioral emphasis, however, French's pattern of curriculum development differs very little from that set by Bobbitt in the Los Angeles project thirty-five years before. The scope is still as wide as all of man's activities and these activities once identified in a precise and specific form become transformed into educational objectives. French even employed a Committee of Reviewers to screen the educational objectives in much the same way that Bobbitt did except that French's group comprised only forty-one whereas Bobbitt had 2,700. Among French's "Illustrative Behaviors" indicating the achievement of the goal called "Is increasingly self directive in care of his health," we find some that overlap with Bobbitt's list. Included, for example, is "Initiates, or cooperates in, practices leading to the correction of physical defects; such as poor vision, poor hearing, or poor teeth. Has regular examinations." [15] On the other hand, some "behaviors" are included by French which probably never occurred to Bobbitt such as "Wears (if a girl) with growing self-assurance appropriate foundation garments and clothing properly styled for the maturing figure." [16]

* * *

I am not prepared here to mount a full-scale attack on one of the most venerable of our precepts in the area of curricular objectives and evaluation, but I shall try to indicate briefly three points at which I think the notion of behavioral objectives as the ultimate criterion of success in teaching is most vulnerable. The first of these points relates to the source of these behaviors. The second considers the question of practicality and whether it is even feasible to consider manifest behaviors as the primary source of data for evaluating educational programs. A final point concerns a possible moral issue that may be involved when behavior is stipulated as the outcome of instruction.

It should be clear at the outset that given the desirability of certain kinds of outcomes, a behavior or the ability to perform a given operation is the most obvious way to evaluate. If, for example, our objective is that a pupil know how to do quadratic equations, the most obvious way to test for the achievement of that objective is to have him solve a few. But major difficulties arise when we want to use *votes in primary elections* as a behavioral criterion for a course in American history or *covers sneezes with a handkerchief* as an outcome of a unit on germ theory. One key difference seems to be whether the stipulated objective is external to the field of study or intrinsic to it. When we draw behaviors from the limitless realm of human activity as did Bobbitt and his heirs rather than looking for objectives within the classroom process itself, we put an unbearable strain on the whole educational enterprise. Thus when various behaviors putatively associated with effective citizenship are imposed as the objectives of a course in American history, we are likely to achieve the overt citizenship behaviors we seek only at the sacrifice of the habits of thought or the ways of inquiring that might be legitimately associated with the study of history.

Involved in the notion of behavioral goals also is a certain naiveté about the effects and consequences of instruction. Teaching is most immediately directed toward creating a condition of knowing on the parts of those being taught. When teaching is successful and those being taught know something more than they knew before, this can conceivably create a disposition to behave in certain ways under certain circumstances. But we might as well recognize that those circumstances may never occur or that the behavior will manifest itself in such subtle ways or at such a deferred point in time that it is fruitless from a practical point of view to regard behavioral change as the principle criterion of success in evaluating the achievement of educational outcomes. It also seems naive to assume that the relationship between educational experiences and changes in behavior is so clear and so well-established that we can assume a cause-and-effect relationship between particular events in the classroom and remote behavior on the part of those being taught.

Finally, from a moral point of view, the emphasis on behavioral goals, despite all of the protestations to the contrary, still borders on brainwashing or at least indoctrination rather than education. We begin with some notion of how we want a person to behave and then we try to manipulate him and his environment so as to get him to behave as we want him to. The usual counter-argument here is either that this process is somehow performed democratically (an argument I just do not understand) or that it is carried out with a good end in view rather than an evil one. Again, it seems to me that the stigma of indoctrination is not removed even when we manipulate people with such fine ends in view as world peace or clean fingernails. Creating automatons, even when they are programmed to perform good deeds, just seems incompatible with teaching or education as we have come to use these terms.

The whole question of educational objectives, not just our longstanding insistence that they be stated behaviorally, deserves much more inquiry and reassessment than we have given in the past and certainly more than has been given here. Our unfortunate tendency in the field of curriculum has been to accept uncritically many of the formulations and procedures that were developed when the field was in its infancy and then merely to bewail the intransigence of those who have not recognized their wisdom. If we are to grow and prosper intellectually as a field of study, we have to begin to examine more critically the hallowed concepts and procedures we have inherited from our forbears, beginning, perhaps, with the highly crucial concept of curricular objectives. This would include their sources, how they are formulated and stated, and what actual role they have, if any, in the planning of curricula and in guiding teaching.

References

1. Commission on the Reorganization of Secondary Education. *The Cardinal Principles of Secondary Education.* Washington: Government Printing Office, 1918.
2. Franklin Bobbitt. *The Curriculum.* Boston: Houghton Mifflin Co., 1918.
3. Edward A. Krug. *The Shaping of the American High School.* New York: Harper & Row, 1964, pp. 249-283.
4. *Ibid.,* pp. 384-385.
5. National Society for the Study of Education. *The Foundations and Technique of Curriculum-Construction.* Twenty-Sixth Yearbook, Part II. Bloomington: Public School Publishing Co., 1927, p. 49.
6. Bobbitt, *op. cit.,* p. 282.
7. *Ibid.,* p. 42.
8. Boyd H. Bode. *Modern Educational Theories.* New York: The Macmillan Co., 1927, pp. 80-81.
9. Franklin Bobbitt. *How to Make a Curriculum.* Boston: Houghton Mifflin Co., 1924, p. 10.
10. *Ibid.,* p. 26.
11. *Ibid.,* p. 14.
12. L. Thomas Hopkins. Curriculum Making: General. *Review of Educational Research, 1,* January, 1931, pp. 5-8.
13. Eugene R. Smith and Ralph W. Tyler. *Appraising and Recording Student Progress.* New York: Harper & Brothers, 1942, pp. 11-12.
14. Ralph W. Tyler. *Basic Principles of Curriculum and Instruction.* Chicago: The University of Chicago Press, 1950, pp. 1-2.
15. Will French. *Behavioral Goals of General Education in High School.* New York: Russell Sage Foundation, 1957, p. 118.
16. *Ibid.*

Eisner points out that arguing against precise educational objectives seems to be like arguing for irrationality—hardly a comfortable position in today's world. After citing events from the history of the behavioral movement, the author details four aspects of the specification of objectives which he feels actually hamper effective education. He supports his opinions, in part, by observing that "in large measure the construction of curriculum and the judgment of its consequences are artful tasks," not all of which are reducible, in Eisner's view, to precision and specificity.

Educational Objectives: Help or Hindrance?*

ELLIOT W. EISNER

If one were to rank the various beliefs or assumptions in the field of curriculum that are thought most secure, the belief in the need for clarity and specificity in stating educational objectives would surely rank among the highest.[1] Educational objectives, it is argued, need to be clearly specified for at least three reasons: first, because they provide the goals toward which the curriculum is aimed; second, because once clearly stated they facilitate the selection and organization of content; third, because when specified in both behavioral and content terms they make it possible to evaluate the outcomes of the curriculum.

It is difficult to argue with a rational approach to curriculum develop-

*Reprinted from *The School Review*, 75, Autumn, 1967, pp. 250-260, by permission of the publisher and the author. Also in the Autumn 1967 issue of *The School Review* are comments on Eisner's article by Ebel, Hastings, and Payne. These comments are followed by a final response by Eisner, all of which provide additional depth and focus to the article reprinted above.

ment—who would choose irrationality? And, if one is to build curriculum in a rational way, the clarity of premise, end or starting point, would appear paramount. But I want to argue in this paper that educational objectives clearly and specifically stated can hamper as well as help the ends of instruction and that an unexamined belief in curriculum as in other domains of human activity can easily become dogma which in fact may hinder the very functions the concept was originally designed to serve.

When and where did beliefs concerning the importance of educational objectives in curriculum development emerge? Who has formulated and argued their importance? What effect has this belief had upon curriculum construction? If we examine the past briefly for data necessary for answering these questions, it appears that the belief in the usefulness of clear and specific educational objectives emerged around the turn of the century with the birth of the scientific movement in education.

Before this movement gained strength, faculty psychologists viewed the brain as consisting of a variety of intellectual faculties. These faculties, they held, could be strengthened if exercised in appropriate ways with particular subject matters. Once strengthened, the faculties could be used in any area of human activity to which they were applicable. Thus, if the important faculties could be identified and if methods of strengthening them developed, the school could concentrate on this task and expect general intellectual excellence as a result.

This general theoretical view of mind had been accepted for several decades by the time Thorndike, Judd, and later Watson began, through their work, to chip away the foundations upon which it rested. Thorndike's work especially demonstrated the specificity of transfer. He argued theoretically that transfer of learning occurred if and only if elements in one situation were identical with elements in the other. His empirical work supported his theoretical views, and the enormous stature he enjoyed in education as well as in psychology influenced educators to approach curriculum development in ways consonant with his views. One of those who was caught up in the scientific movement in education was Franklin Bobbitt, often thought of as the father of curriculum theory. In 1918 Bobbitt published a signal work titled simply, *The Curriculum*.[2] In it he argued that educational theory is not so difficult to construct as commonly held and that curriculum theory is logically derivable from educational theory. Bobbitt wrote in 1918:

> The central theory is simple. Human life, however varied, consists in its performance of specific activities. Education that prepares for life is one that prepares definitely and adequately for these specific activities. However numerous and diverse they may be for any social class, they can be discovered. This

requires that one go out into the world of affairs and discover
the particulars of which these affairs consist. These will show
the abilities, habits, appreciations, and forms of knowledge that
men need. These will be the objectives of the curriculum. They
will be numerous, definite, and particularized. The curriculum
will then be that series of experiences which childhood and
youth must have by way of attaining those objectives.[3]

In *The Curriculum,* Bobbitt approached curriculum development
scientifically and theoretically: study life carefully to identify needed
skills, divide these skills into specific units, organize these units into
experiences, and provide these experiences to children. Six years later,
in his second book, *How To Make a Curriculum,*[4] Bobbitt operationalized
his theoretical assertions and demonstrated how curriculum components—especially educational objectives—were to be formulated. In this
book Bobbitt listed nine areas in which educational objectives are to
be specified. In these nine areas he listed 160 major educational objectives which run the gamut from "Ability to use language in all ways
required for proper and effective participation in community life" to
"Ability to entertain one's friends, and to respond to entertainment by
one's friends."[5]

Bobbitt was not alone in his belief in the importance of formulating
objectives clearly and specifically. Pendleton, for example, listed 1,581
social objectives for English, Guiler listed more than 300 for arithmetic
in grades 1–6, and Billings prescribed 888 generalizations which were
important for the social studies.

If Thorndike was right, if transfer was limited, it seemed reasonable
to encourage the teacher to teach for particular outcomes and to construct curriculums only after specific objectives had been identified.

In retrospect it is not difficult to understand why this movement in
curriculum collapsed under its own weight by the early 1930's. Teachers
could not manage fifty highly specified objectives, let alone hundreds.
And, in addition, the new view of the child, not as a complex machine but
as a growing organism who ought to participate in planning his own educational program, did not mesh well with the theoretical views held
earlier.[6]

But, as we all know, the Progressive movement too began its decline
in the forties, and by the middle fifties, as a formal organization at least,
it was dead.

By the late forties and during the fifties, curriculum specialists again
began to remind us of the importance of specific educational objectives
and began to lay down guidelines for their formulation. Rationales for
constructing curriculums developed by Ralph Tyler[7] and Virgil Herrick[8]
again placed great importance on the specificity of objectives. George

Barton[9] identified philosophic domains which could be used to select objectives. Benjamin Bloom and his colleagues[10] operationalized theoretical assertions by building a taxonomy of educational objectives in the cognitive domain; and in 1964, Krathwohl, Bloom, and Masia[11] did the same for the affective domain. Many able people for many years have spent a great deal of time and effort in identifying methods and providing prescriptions for the formulation of educational objectives, so much so that the statement "Educational objectives should be stated in behavioral terms" has been elevated—or lowered—to almost slogan status in curriculum circles. Yet, despite these efforts, teachers seem not to take educational objectives seriously—at least as they are prescribed from above. And when teachers plan curriculum guides, their efforts, first to identify overall educational aims, then specify school objectives, then identify educational objectives for specific subject matters, appear to be more like exercises to be gone through than serious efforts to build tools for curriculum planning. If educational objectives were really useful tools, teachers, I submit, would use them. If they do not, perhaps it is not because there is something wrong with the teachers but because there might be something wrong with the theory.

As I view the situation, there are several limitations to theory in curriculum regarding the functions educational objectives are to perform. These limitations I would like to identify.

Educational objectives are typically derived from curriculum theory, which assumes that it is possible to predict with a fair degree of accuracy what the outcomes of instruction will be. In a general way this is possible. If you set about to teach a student algebra, there is no reason to assume he will learn to construct sonnets instead. Yet, the outcomes of instruction are far too numerous and complex for educational objectives to encompass. The amount, type, and quality of learning that occur in a classroom, especially when there is interaction among students, are only in small part predictable. The changes in pace, tempo, and goals that experienced teachers employ when necessary and appropriate for maintaining classroom organization are dynamic rather than mechanistic in character. Elementary school teachers, for example, are often sensitive to the changing interests of the children they teach, and frequently attempt to capitalize on these interests, "milking them" as it were for what is educationally valuable.[12] The teacher uses the moment in a situation that is better described as kaleidoscopic than stable. In the very process of teaching and discussing, unexpected opportunities emerge for making a valuable point, for demonstrating an interesting idea, and for teaching a significant concept. The first point I wish to make, therefore, is that the dynamic and complex process of instruction yields outcomes far too numerous to be specified in behavioral and content terms in advance.

A second limitation of theory concerning educational objectives is its failure to recognize the constraints various subject matters place upon objectives. The point here is brief. In some subject areas, such as mathematics, languages, and the sciences, it is possible to specify with great precision the particular operation or behavior the student is to perform after instruction. In other subject areas, especially the arts, such specification is frequently not possible, and when possible may not be desirable. In a class in mathematics or spelling, uniformity in response is desirable, at least insofar as it indicates that students are able to perform a particular operation adequately, that is, in accordance with accepted procedures. Effective instruction in such areas enables students to function with minimum error in these fields. In the arts and in subject matters where, for example, novel or creative responses are desired, the particular behaviors to be developed cannot easily be identified. Here curriculum and instruction should yield behaviors and products which are unpredictable. The end achieved ought to be something of a surprise to both teacher and pupil. While it could be argued that one might formulate an educational objective which specified novelty, originality, or creativeness as the desired outcome, the particular referents for these terms cannot be specified in advance; one must judge after the fact whether the product produced or the behavior displayed belongs in the "novel" class. This is a much different procedure than is determining whether or not a particular word has been spelled correctly or a specific performance, that is, jumping a 3-foot hurdle, has been attained. Thus, the second point is that theory concerning educational objectives has not taken into account the particular relationship that holds between the subject matter being taught and the degree to which educational objectives can be predicted and specified. This, I suppose, is in part due to the fact that few curriculum specialists have high degrees of intimacy with a wide variety of subject matters and thus are unable to alter their general theoretical views to suit the demands that particular subject matters make.

The third point I wish to make deals with the belief that objectives stated in behavioral and content terms can be used as criteria by which to measure the outcomes of curriculum and instruction. Educational objectives provide, it is argued, the standard against which achievement is to be measured. Both taxonomies are built upon this assumption since their primary function is to demonstrate how objectives can be used to frame test items appropriate for evaluation. The assumption that objectives can be used as standards by which to measure achievement fails, I think, to distinguish adequately between the application of a standard and the making of a judgment. Not all—perhaps not even most—outcomes of curriculum and instruction are amenable to measurement. The application of a standard requires that some arbitrary and socially defined quantity be designated by which other qualities can be compared. By virtue of socially defined rules of grammar, syntax, and logic, for example, it is possible to quantitatively compare and measure error in discursive or mathematical statements. Some fields of activity, especially those which are qualitative in character, have no comparable rules and hence are less amenable to quantitative assessment. It is here that evaluation must be made, not primarily by applying a socially defined standard, but by making a human qualitative judgment. One can specify, for example, that a student shall be expected to know how to extract a square root correctly and in an unambiguous way, and through the application of a standard, determine whether this end has been achieved. But it is only in a metaphoric sense that one can measure the extent to which a student has been able to produce an aesthetic object or an expressive narrative. Here standards are unapplicable; here judgment is required. The making of a judgment in distinction to the application of a standard implies that valued qualities are not merely socially defined and arbitrary in character. The judgment by which a critic determines the value of a poem, novel, or play is not achieved merely by applying standards already known to the particular product being judged; it requires that the critic—or teacher—view the product with respect to the unique properties it displays and then, in relation to his experience and sensibilities, judge its value in terms which are incapable of being reduced to quantity or rule.

This point was aptly discussed by John Dewey in his chapter on "Perception and Criticism" in *Art as Experience*.[13] Dewey was concerned with the problem of identifying the means and ends of criticism and has this to say about its proper function:

> The function of criticism is the reeducation of perception of works of art; it is an auxiliary process, a difficult process, of learning to see and hear. The conception that its business is to appraise, to judge in the legal and moral sense, arrests the perception of those who are influenced by the criticism that assumes this task.[14]

Of the distinction that Dewey makes between application of a standard and the making of a critical judgment, he writes:

> There are three characteristics of a standard. It is a particular physical thing existing under specifiable conditions; it is *not* a value. The yard is a yard-stick, and the meter is a bar deposited in Paris. In the second place, standards are measures of things, of lengths, weights, capacities. The things measured

are not values, although it is of great social value to be able to measure them, since the properties of things in the way of size, volume, weight, are important for commercial exchange. Finally, as standards of measure, standards define things with respect to *quantity*. To be able to measure quantities is a great aid to further judgments, but it is not a mode of judgment. The standard, being an external and public thing, is applied *physically*. The yard-stick is physically laid down upon things to determine their length.[15]

And I would add that what is most educationally valuable is the development of that mode of curiosity, inventiveness, and insight that is capable of being described only in metaphoric or poetic terms. Indeed, the image of the educated man that has been held in highest esteem for the longest period of time in Western civilization is one which is not amenable to standard measurement. Thus, the third point I wish to make is that curriculum theory which views educational objectives as standards by which to measure educational achievement overlooks those modes of achievement incapable of measurement.

The final point I wish to make deals with the function of educational objectives in curriculum construction.

The rational approach to curriculum development not only emphasizes the importance of specificity in the formulation of educational objectives but also implies when not stated explicitly that educational objectives be stated prior to the formulation of curriculum activities. At first view, this seems to be a reasonable way to proceed with curriculum construction: one should know where he is headed before embarking on a trip. Yet, while the procedure of first identifying objectives before proceeding to identify activities is logically defensible, it is not necessarily the most psychologically efficient way to proceed. One can, and teachers often do, identify activities that seem useful, appropriate, or rich in educational opportunities, and from a consideration of what can be done in class, identify the objectives or possible consequences of using these activities. MacDonald argues this point cogently when he writes:

Let us look, for example, at the problem of objectives. Objectives are viewed as directives in the rational approach. They are identified prior to the instruction or action and used to provide a basis for a screen for appropriate activities.

There is another view, however, which has both scholarly and experiential referents. This view would state that our objectives are only known to us in any complete sense after the completion of our act of instruction. No matter what we thought we were attempting to do, we can only know what we wanted to accomplish after the fact. Objectives by this rationale are heuristic devices which initiate consequences which become altered in the flow of instruction.

In the final analysis, it could be argued, the teacher in actuality asks a fundamentally different question from "What am I trying to accomplish?" The teacher asks "What am I going to do?" and out of the doing comes accomplishment.[16]

Theory in curriculum has not adequately distinguished between logical adequacy in determining the relationship of means to ends when examining the curriculum as a *product* and the psychological processes that may usefully be employed in building curriculums. The method of forming creative insights in curriculum development, as in the sciences and arts, is as yet not logically prescribable. The ways in which curriculums can be usefully and efficiently developed constitute an empirical problem; imposing logical requirements upon the process because they are desirable for assessing the product is, to my mind, an error. Thus, the final point I wish to make is that educational objectives need not precede the selection and organization of content. The means through which imaginative curriculums can be built is as open-ended as the means through which scientific and artistic inventions occur. Curriculum theory needs to allow for a variety of processes to be employed in the construction of curriculums.

I have argued in this paper that curriculum theory, as it pertains to educational objectives, has had four significant limitations. First, it has not sufficiently emphasized the extent to which the prediction of educational outcomes cannot be made with accuracy. Second, it has not discussed the ways in which the subject matter affects precision in stating educational objectives. Third, it has confused the use of educational objectives as a standard for measurement when in some areas it can be used only as a criterion for judgment. Fourth, it has not distinguished between the logical requirement of relating means to ends in the curriculum as a product and the psychological conditions useful for constructing curriculums.

If the arguments I have formulated about the limitations of curriculum theory concerning educational objectives have merit, one might ask: What are their educational consequences? First, it seems to me that they suggest that in large measure the construction of curriculum and the judgment of its consequences are artful tasks. The methods of curriculum development are, in principle if not in practice, no different from the making of art—be it the art of painting or the art of science. The identification of the factors in the potentially useful educational activity and the organization or construction of sequence in curriculum are in principle amenable to an infinite number of combinations. The variable teacher, student, and class group require artful blending for the educationally valuable to result.

Second, I am impressed with Dewey's view of the functions of criticism—to heighten one's perception of the art object—and believe it has implications for curriculum theroy. If the child is viewed as an art product and the teacher as a critic, one task of the teacher would be to reveal the qualities of the child to himself and to others. In addition, the teacher as critic would appraise the changes occurring in the child. But because the teacher's task includes more than criticism, he would also be responsible, in part, for the improvement of the work of art. In short, in both the construction of educational means (the curriculum) and the appraisal of its consequences, the teacher would become an artist, for criticism itself when carried to its height is an art. This, it seems to me, is a dimension to which curriculum theory will someday have to speak.

REFERENCES

1. This is a slightly expanded version of a paper presented at the annual meeting of the American Educational Research Association, Chicago, February, 1966.
2. Franklin Bobbitt. *The Curriculum.* Boston: Houghton Mifflin Co., 1918.
3. *Ibid.,* p. 42.
4. Franklin Bobbitt. *How To Make a Curriculum.* Boston: Houghton Mifflin Co., 1924.
5. *Ibid.,* pp. 11-29.
6. For a good example of this view of the child and curriculum development, see *The Changing Curriculum, Tenth Yearbook,* Department of Supervisors and Directors of Instruction, National Education Association and Society for Curriculum Study. New York: Appleton-Century-Crofts Co., 1937.
7. Ralph W. Tyler. *Basic Principles of Curriculum and Instruction.* Chicago: University of Chicago Press, 1951.
8. Virgil E. Herrick. The Concept of Curriculum Design. *Toward Improved Curriculum Theory.* Eds. Virgil E. Herrick & Ralph W. Tyler. Supplementary Educational Monographs, No. 71, Chicago: University of Chicago Press, 1950, pp. 37-50.
9. George E. Barton, Jr. Educational Objectives: Improvement of Curriculum Theory about Their Determination. *Ibid.,* pp. 26-35.
10. Benjamin Bloom *et al. Taxonomy of Educational Objectives, Handbook I: The Cognitive Domain.* New York: David McKay Co., 1956.
11. David Krathwohl, Benjamin Bloom & Bertram Masia. *Taxonomy of Educational Objectives, Handbook II: The Affective Domain.* New York: David McKay Co., 1964.
12. For an excellent paper describing educational objectives as they are viewed and used by elementary school teachers, see Philip W. Jackson and

Elizabeth Belford, Educational Objectives and the Joys of Teaching. *School Review, 73,* 1965, pp. 267-91.

13. John Dewey. *Art as Experience.* New York: Minton, Balch & Co., 1934.
14. *Ibid.,* p. 324.
15. *Ibid.,* p. 307.
16. James B. MacDonald. Myths about Instruction. *Educational Leadership, 22,* 7, May, 1965, pp. 613-14.

Atkin acknowledges the current high level of acceptance of behavioral objectives as an effective working tool. At the same time, however, he also suggests several areas of concern. He believes that behavioral objectives tend to cause oversimplification of curricular outcomes, that certain types of innovations are hampered by the early application of the behavioral approach, and that questions concerning instructional priorities and educational values are sometimes overlooked. Examples are taken from the field of science, but are also applicable to other fields of study. Atkin's appeal for "fresh perspectives" emphasizes the need for continuing debate on the behavioral approach.*

Behavioral Objectives in Curriculum Design: A Cautionary Note**

J. MYRON ATKIN

In certain influential circles, anyone who confesses to reservations about the use of behaviorally stated objectives for curriculum planning runs the risk of being labeled as the type of individual who would attack the virtues of motherhood. Bumper stickers have appeared at my own

*Responses to the Atkin article appeared in *The Science Teacher* in November 1968 and January 1969. The latter, by Gideonse, is reprinted following this paper.
**Reprinted from *The Science Teacher, 35,* May, 1968, pp. 27-30, by permission of the publisher and the author.

institution, and probably at yours, reading, STAMP OUT NON-BEHAVIORAL OBJECTIVES. I trust that the person who prepared the stickers had humor as his primary aim; nevertheless the crusade for specificity of educational outcomes has become intense and evangelical. The worthiness of this particular approach has come to be accepted as self-evident by ardent proponents, proponents who sometimes sound like the true believers who cluster about a new social or religious movement.

Behavioral objectives enthusiasts are warmly endorsed and embraced by the systems and operations analysis advocates, most educational technologists, the cost-benefit economists, the planning-programming-budgeting system stylists, and many others. In fact, the behavioral objectives people are now near the center of curriculum decision making. Make no mistake; they have replaced the academicians and the general curriculum theorists—especially in the new electronically based education industries and in governmental planning agencies. The engineering model for educational research and development represents a forceful tide today. Those who have a few doubts about the effects of the tide had better be prepared to be considered uninitiated and naive, if not slightly addlepated and antiquarian.

To utilize the techniques for long-term planning and rational decision making that have been developed with such apparent success in the Department of Defense, and that are now being applied to a range of domestic and civilian problems, it is essential that hard data be secured. Otherwise these modes for developmental work and planning are severely limited. Fuzzy and tentative statements of possible achievement and questions of conflict with respect to underlying values are not compatible with the new instructional systems management approaches—at least not with the present state of the art. In fact, delineating instructional objectives in terms of identifiable pupil behaviors or performances seems essential for assessing the output of the current educational system. Presently accepted wisdom does not seem to admit an alternative.

There are overwhelmingly useful purposes served by attempting to identify educational goals in non-ambiguous terms. To plan rationally for a growing educational system, and to continue to justify relatively high public expenditures for education, it seems that we do need a firmer basis for making assessments and decisions than now exists. Current attention to specification of curriculum objectives in terms of pupil performance represents an attempt to provide direction for collection of data that will result in more informed choice among competing alternatives.

Efforts to identify educational outcomes in behavioral terms also provide a fertile ground for coping with interesting research problems and challenging technical puzzles. A world of educational research opens to the investigator when he has reliable measures of educational output (even when their validity for educational purposes is low). Pressures from researchers are difficult to resist since they do carry influence in the educational community, particularly in academic settings and in educational development laboratories.

Hence, I am not unmindful of some of the possible benefits to be derived from attempts to rationalize our decision making processes through the use of behaviorally stated objectives. Schools need a basis for informed choice. And the care and feeding of educational researchers is a central part of my job at Illinois. However, many of the enthusiasts have given insufficient attention to underlying assumptions and broad questions of educational policy. I intend in this brief paper to highlight a few of these issues in the hope that the exercise might be productive of further and deeper discussion.

Several reservations about the use of behaviorally stated objectives for curriculum design will be catalogued here. But perhaps the fundamental problem, as I see it, lies in the easy assumption that we either know or can readily identify the educational objectives for which we strive, and thereafter the educational outcomes that result from our programs. One contention basic to my argument is that we presently are making progress toward thousands of goals in any existing educational program, progress of which we are perhaps dimly aware, can articulate only with great difficulty, and that contributes toward goals which are incompletely stated (or unrecognized), but which are often worthy.

For example, a child who is learning about mealworm behavior by blowing against the animal through a straw is probably learning much more than how this insect responds to a gentle stream of warm air. Let's assume for the moment that we can specify "behaviorally" all that he might learn about mealworm *behavior* (an arduous and never-ending task). In addition, in this "simple" activity, he is probably finding out something about the interaction of objects, forces, humane treatment of animals, his own ability to manipulate the environment, structural characteristics of the larval form of certain insects, equilibrium, the results of doing an experiment at the suggestion of the teacher, the rewards of independent experimentation, the judgment of the curriculum developers in suggesting that children engage in such an exercise, possible uses of a plastic straw, and the length of time for which one individual might be engaged in a learning activity and still display a high degree of interest. I am sure there are many additional learnings, literally too numerous to mention in fewer than eight or ten pages. When any piece of curriculum is used with real people, there are important learning outcomes that cannot have been anticipated when the objectives were formulated. And of the relatively few outcomes that can be identified at all, a smaller number still are translatable readily in terms of student behavior. There is a possibility the cumulative side effects are at least as important as the intended main effects.

Multiply learning outcomes from the mealworm activity by all the various curriculum elements we attempt to build into a school day. Then multiply this by the number of days in a school year, and you have some indication of the oversimplification that *always* occurs when curriculum intents or outcomes are articulated in any form that is considered manageable.

If my argument has validity to this point, the possible implications are potentially dangerous. If identification of all worthwhile outcomes in behavioral terms comes to be commonly accepted and expected, then it is inevitable that, over time, the curriculum will tend to emphasize those elements which have been thus identified. Important outcomes which are detected only with great difficulty and which are translated only rarely into behavioral terms tend to atrophy. They disappear from the curriculum because we spend all the time allotted to us in teaching explicitly for the more readily specifiable learnings to which we have been directed.

We have a rough analogy in the use of tests. Prestigious examinations that are widely accepted and broadly used, such as the New York State Regents examinations, tend over time to determine the curriculum. Whether or not these examinations indeed measure all outcomes that are worth achieving, the curriculum regresses toward the objectives reflected by the test items. Delineation of lists of behavioral objectives, like broadly used testing programs, may admirably serve the educational researcher because it gives him indices of gross achievement as well as detail of particular achievement; it may also provide input for cost-benefit analysts and governmental planners at all levels because it gives them hard data with which to work; but the program in the schools may be affected detrimentally by the gradual disappearance of worthwhile learning activities for which we have not succeeded in establishing a one-to-one correspondence between curriculum elements and rather difficult-to-measure educational results.

Among the learning activities most readily lost are those that are long term and private in effect and those for which a single course provides only a small increment. If even that increment cannot be identified, it tends to lose out in the teacher's priority scheme, because it is competing with other objectives which have been elaborately stated and to which he has been alerted. But I will get to the question of priority of objectives a bit later.

The second point I would like to develop relates to the effect of demands for behavioral specification on innovation. My claim here is that certain types of innovation, highly desirable ones, are hampered and frustrated by early demands for behavioral statements of objectives.

Let's focus on the curriculum reform movement of the past 15 years, the movement initiated by Max Beberman in 1952 when he began to design a mathematics program in order that the high school curriculum would reflect concepts central to modern mathematics. We have now seen curriculum development efforts, with this basic flavor, in many science fields, the social sciences, English, aesthetics, etc. When one talks with the initiators of such projects, particularly at the beginning of their efforts, one finds that they do not begin by talking about the manner in which they would like to change pupils' behavior. Rather they are dissatisfied with existing curricula in their respective subject fields, and they want to build something new. If pressed, they might indicate that existing programs stress concepts considered trivial by those who practice the discipline. They might also say that the curriculum poorly reflects styles of intellectual inquiry in the various fields. Press them further, and they might say that they want to build a new program that more accurately displays the "essence" of history, or physics, or economics, or whatever. Or a program that better transmits a comprehension of the elaborate and elegant interconnections among various concepts within the discipline.

If they are asked at an early stage just how they want pupils to behave differently, they are likely to look quite blank. Academicians in the various cognate fields do not speak the language of short-term or long-term behavioral change, as do many psychologists. In fact, if a hard-driving behaviorist attempts to force the issue and succeeds, one finds that the disciplinarians can come up with a list of behavioral goals that looks like a caricature of the subject field in question. (Witness the AAAS elementary-school science program directed toward teaching "process.")

Further, early articulation of behavioral objectives by the curriculum developer inevitably tends to limit the range of his exploration. He becomes committed to designing programs that achieve these goals. Thus if specific objectives in behavioral terms are identified early, there tends to be a limiting element built into the new curriculum. The innovator is less alert to potentially productive tangents.

The effective curriculum developer typically begins with *general* objectives. He then refines the program through a series of successive approximations. He doesn't start with a blueprint, and he isn't in much of a hurry to get his ideas represented by a blueprint.

A situation is created in the newer curriculum design procedures based on behaviorally stated objectives in which scholars who do not talk a behavioral-change language are expected to describe their goals at a time when the intricate intellectual subtleties of their work may not be clear, even in the disciplinary language with which they are familiar. At the other end, the educational evaluator, the behavioral specifier, typically has very little understanding of the curriculum that is being designed—understanding with respect to the new view of the subject field that it affords. It is too much to expect that the behavioral analyst, or anyone else, recognize the shadings of meaning in various evolving economic theories, the complex applications of the intricacies of wave motion, or the richness of nuance reflected in a Stravinsky composition.

Yet despite this two-culture problem—finding a match between the behavioral analysts and the disciplinary scholars—we still find that an expectation is being created for early behavioral identification of essential outcomes.

(Individuals who are concerned with producing hard data reflecting educational outputs would run less risk of dampening innovation if they were to enter the curriculum development scene in a more unobtrusive fashion—and later—than is sometimes the case. The curriculum developer goes into the classroom with only a poorly articulated view of the changes he wants to make. Then he begins working with children to see what he can do. He revises. He develops new ideas. He continually modifies as he develops. *After* he has produced a program that seems pleasing, it might then be a productive exercise for the behavioral analyst to attempt with the curriculum developer to identify *some* of the ways in which children seem to be behaving differently. If this approach is taken, I would caution, however, that observers be alert for long-term as well as short-term effects, subtle as well as obvious inputs.)

A third basic point to be emphasized relates to the question of instructional priorities, mentioned earlier. I think I have indicated that there is a vast library of goals that represent possible outcomes for any instructional program. A key educational task, and a task that is well handled by the effective teacher, is that of relating educational goals to the situation at hand—as well as relating the situation at hand to educational goals. It is impractical to pursue all goals thoroughly. And it does make a difference *when* you try to teach something. Considerable educational potential is lost when certain concepts are taught didactically. Let's assume that some third-grade teacher considers it important to develop concepts related to sportsmanship. It would be a rather naive teacher who decided that she would undertake this task at 1:40 P.M. on Friday of next week. The experienced teacher has always realized that learnings related to such an area must be stressed in an appropriate context, and the context often cannot be planned.

Perhaps there is no problem in accepting this view with respect to a concept like sportsmanship, but I submit that a similar case can be made for a range of crucial cognitive outcomes that are basic to various subject matter fields. I use science for my examples because I know more about this field than about others. But equilibrium, successive approximation, symmetry, entropy, and conservation are pervasive ideas with a broad range of application. These ideas are taught with the richest meaning only when they are emphasized repeatedly in appropriate and varied contexts. Many of these contexts arise in classroom situations that are unplanned, but that have powerful potential. It is detrimental to learning not to capitalize on the opportune moments for effectively teaching one idea or another. Riveting the teacher's attention to a few behavioral goals provides him with blinders that may limit his range. Directing him to hundreds of goals leads to confusing, mechanical pedagogic style and loss of spontaneity.

A final point to be made in this paper relates to values, and it deals with a primary flaw in the composition of much educational research. It is difficult to resist the assumption that those attributes which we can measure are the elements which we consider most important. This point relates to my first, but I feel that it is essential to emphasize the problem. The behavioral analyst seems to assume that for an objective to be worthwhile, we must have methods of observing progress. But worthwhile goals come first, not our methods for assessing progress toward these goals. Goals are derived from our needs and from our philosophies. They are not and should not be derived primarily from our measures. It borders on the irresponsible for those who exhort us to state objectives in behavioral terms to avoid the issue of determining worth. Inevitably there is an implication of worth behind any act of measurement. What the educational community poorly realizes at the moment is that behavioral goals may or may not be worthwhile. They are articulated from among the vast library of goals because they are stated relatively easily. Again, let's not assume that what we can presently measure necessarily represents our most important activity.

I hope that in this paper I have increased rather than decreased the possibilities for constructive discourse about the use of behavioral objectives for curriculum design. The issues here represent a few of the basic questions that seem crucial enough to be examined in an open forum that admits the possibility of fresh perspectives. Too much of the debate related to the use of behavioral objectives has been conducted in an argumentative style that characterizes discussions of fundamental religious views among adherents who are poorly informed. A constructive effort might be centered on identification of those issues which seem to be amenable to resolution by empirical means and those which do not. At any rate, I feel confident that efforts of the next few years will better inform us about the positive as well as negative potential inherent in a view of curriculum design that places the identification of behavioral objectives at the core.

In a response directed toward the preceding article by Atkin, Gideonse poses and answers several critical questions concerning behavioral objectives in curriculum building. In support of the behavioral approach, Gideonse asserts that behavioral objectives will (1) help assess the value of curriculum development activities before they are begun, (2) serve as guides to the curriculum development process, and (3) provide minimum standards for assessing the completed product.

Behavioral Objectives: Continuing the Dialogue*

Hendrik D. Gideonse

In an article in *The Science Teacher,* J. Myron Atkin twice stated the hope that his paper might be productive of further and deeper discussion.[1] As Atkin himself knows, there are many who apparently do not understand the significance of the positions which are being offered about behavioral objectives or, what is even more serious, who, knowing, choose not to play the game squarely.

Atkin is certainly correct. Much more needs to be said about behavioral objectives and what is and is not being claimed for them. Therefore, I, too, would like to try to contribute positively to the dialogue and thereby perhaps move it a little further along.

Atkins speaks from a long and exciting tradition of curriculum building at Illinois. It is an important base upon which to stand, but there are other vantage points from which to conduct the argument. Consider instead the following questions as a starting point:

*Reprinted from *The Science Teacher, 36,* January, 1969, pp. 51-54, by permission of the publisher and the author.

1. What *should* we mean by the phrase "behavioral objectives"?
2. What criteria (or whose?) *should* we employ in our attempt to better the practices, processes, materials, and organizational forms by which we carry out instruction *and* (note the conjunction!) education? Which should we think about before we begin, which should we think about as we proceed, and which should we apply after we have completed an effort? Whose criteria of "better" do we accept?
3. Do we know enough (not everything, now, but enough) about learning, cognitive development, motivation, and so on to build instructional systems of greater effectiveness than the ones we currently use in our schools?
4. What conclusions, if any, should we draw from the fact that the kind of curriculum building which Atkin describes in his article (including the kind which the engineers, as Atkin calls them, are interested in doing) costs millions of dollars? How should we ask for results? How do we determine accountability? How do we judge whom and what to support?

As a planner of educational research and development and as one who believes that the research and development we do today in education helps to invent the futures for education for our children and our children's children, I think the above issues are of critical importance.

What Should We Mean By Behavioral Objectives?

The phrase itself is something of a misnomer. What we *should* mean by behavioral objectives is not so much the *ends* that we are trying to achieve through schooling as the performance indices that *we would accept as evidence* that we have achieved, or had a reasonable hope of achieving over time, the objectives toward which given curricular or extracurricular experiences were aimed. The behaviors may be ends in themselves, or they may be simply indicators that certain knowledge or skills deemed desirable by those who set the objectives for schooling in education inhere in the learner as a consequence of his exposure to the curriculum or technique.

The above statement represents a deliberate limitation of the concept. It says, in effect, that the behavior identified is not necessarily the objective in itself. It implies that it is necessary to ask what relation the sought-for behavior has to educational objectives. It also implies that behaviors produced through instruction bear complex relationships to the broader, more philosophical goals of education. All of this, I think, is clearly in step with Atkin's own views.

But it implies even more. What it says is that educators and scholars, curriculum developers (in Atkin's sense) and engineers (in mine), teachers and school board members need to pay much more explicit attention to exactly what they hope they are achieving and how they are assessing what they are achieving. In short, I think that the idea of behavioral indicators of progress suggested above can lead us to much more explicit and justifiable formulations for what we do with school children and why we do it, what we intend through curriculum development, and how we evaluate whether our intentions are indeed being met.

One of the outcomes of such an analysis, I would think, would be much more careful attention to the specific outcomes that schools as a *minimum* ought to secure for all the children who attend. Can there be any real debate, for example, over stipulating the behavioral outcome that a child be able to demonstrate the ability to distinguish the letters of the alphabet, a minimum vocabulary of 10,000 words and a working knowledge of their usage, and the ability to understand numbers and the logic which governs their use? Is it unreasonable in this day of rapid technological growth to ask that a child exploring the concepts of science should, on completion of the experience offered to him, be able to demonstrate some minimum competencies with respect to the ways in which science proceeds and the ways in which it can and does affect our lives?

What criteria (or whose) should we employ in our attempt to better the practices, processes, materials, and organizational forms by which we carry out instruction and *education? Which should we think about before we begin, which should we think about as we proceed, and which should we apply after we have completed an effort? Whose criteria of "better" do we accept?*

The end of my answer to the first question leads nicely into the problem of criterion measures, whether it be in regard to the reasons for the selection of particular curricular experiences for children or for the evaluation of traditional, "under construction," or newly developed curricular offerings. The notion of specifying certain outcomes for all of the society's young *as a minimum* standard of educational output has long been an implied philosophical underpinning of American schooling. Its birth can be found in the Massachusetts Bay Colony, its most vigorous expression during the period of common school reform in the 1830's and 1840's, and its most recent revolutionary reformulation in an article by James Coleman in *Harvard Educational Review*[2] proffering the view that equality of educational opportunity means some notion of the equality of *results*.

Certainly as a minimum we should be able to expect that schools— and curricula—would produce certain specifiable outcomes in terms of learner behavior. The consequence of specifying outcomes in such a manner and relating them to explicit instructional or curricular experiences, is to cause us to distinguish between those elements of schooling—call them instruction, if you will—which we engage in because we *know* that certain behaviors will change or develop in meaningful ways as a consequence of having undergone them, and those experiences—call them education—we provide children and young people because we *believe* it is important for pupils to undergo them and because we *hope* that certain generalized outcomes sometime in the future will result.

The distinction just noted is why I stressed the conjunction between "instruction" and "education" in the second question. There are certain things we do because we *know* what will happen as a consequence; there are others that we do because we *hope* that there will be favorable and productive outcomes. I take the job of the curriculum developer and professional educator to be continually expanding our proficiency with the former so that more and more time is opened up for the latter.

But there is another aspect of criterion measures dealing with the idea of *who* is choosing what *kinds* of objectives. Many of the curriculum projects Atkin describes were initiated, directed, and staffed by highly competent specialists from the academic disciplines. But, the question must be asked: On what grounds should the nation accept the academic disciplines as the most suitable structures within which curricular objectives should be chosen? The question appears particularly acute in view of the growing interdisciplinary approaches to the problems confronting mankind and the fact that even basic research in the sciences proceeds now in many cases on an interdisciplinary basis (although not without the lament of the university advocates of strong discipline-oriented departments). In view of the rapid rate at which knowledge advances, what should school curricula look like? Moreover, what about the 60 to 80 percent of the students who won't be going on to complete college? Why should *their* curricula be organized around academic disciplines? Can't we, with all our ingenuity, teach in ways which don't depend upon the disciplines for their rigor, but rather on more fundamental cognitive and affective skills and competencies, perhaps along the lines of the taxonomies developed in the Bloom, Krathwohl, *et al.* volumes? [3]

These challenges boil down to one essential question: Who should set the objectives for curriculum development, anyway? Should it be the academicians alone, or in concert with educators, or in concert with the lay public (which is responsible for education in this country), or, heresy of heresies, in concert with the young, who after all will live in and with the future we have invented for them?

Subsequent to the problem of criterion measures in relation to objectives, there remains the problem of how the developer will know or be able to tell whether his product in fact constitutes an improvement. What obligation, for example, does the developer have for saying what is wrong with current practice or materials and how he hopes to improve them? What kinds of reasonable guarantees ought we to ask for—in advance—that the developer does indeed have in mind the kinds of criteria which will help him build materials and techniques which, because those criteria exist to provide the developer with standards for his formative evaluation, have a much higher probability of constituting an "improvement"? Of what good is it, to give still other examples, to have materials whose logical structure and content sophistication meet the substantive expectations of the scholar, if they are unteachable in current school settings, or if they do not produce any measurable changes in students' behavior that are different from current outcomes, or if they do not accomplish, or give promise of accomplishing, other possible objectives sought for the materials, such as in the examples of PSSC and Project Physics, halting declining enrollments in the subject matter area in question? The answer, of course, is that they might still be good, but in order to determine that, we must know on what basis that good is being claimed and what evidence there is that such good has been or is likely to be achieved.

Do we know enough (not everything, now, but enough) about learning, cognitive development, motivation, and so on to build instructional systems of greater effectiveness than the ones we currently use in our schools?

Curriculum development as one might come to understand it on the basis of Atkin's article would seem to be a highly empirical business. According to Atkin the developer begins with only a general set of objectives, moves through a series of successive approximations (although Atkin says nothing about *what* criteria are used to move the approximations in *which* direction), and certainly does not proceed in terms of any blueprint. The developer, he continues, begins with "only a poorly articulated view of the changes he wants to make. Then he begins working with children to see what he can do. He revises. He develops new ideas. He continually modifies as he develops." And finally he may produce something, says Atkin, which he finds "pleasing."

There is much that I find troublesome about that description of curriculum building. Perhaps the most serious problem stems from Atkin's implicit conclusion of what we know about learning—know, that is, in the same sense that a scientist knows chemistry, or biology, or physics. He implies we know rather little about learning and, further, that because of this deficiency, we need to proceed in development largely on a trial-and-error basis.

I don't believe that this conclusion is valid. I think we know a considerable amount about the nature of learning, cognitive growth, and motivation, and even a little about affective processes. And what is absolutely certain is that we know far more than we are currently able to implement in actual instructional settings precisely because we have not yet gone through the kind of engineering to which Atkin refers. We know, for example, that children learn at different rates and that they have different cognitive styles. We know certain things about increasing motivation in children. But how many curricula have been seriously engineered on that research base? Very few indeed, and it is to this end that the stress on the "engineering" approach to building of curriculum is being made.

It is simply not necessary (and certainly not very economical) for every mathematician, city planner, physicist, historian, artist, futurist, or geographer to discover for himself the principles of human learning by the highly empirical means of direct contact with children. A knowledge base about human learning exists, and the people who are familiar with it need to be brought together with those familiar with the content area (scholars), with those familiar with the ways in which schools operate (teachers and administrators), and with those knowledgeable about the ingenious uses to which the new media can be put.

When I assert that it is not necessary for scholars in substantive fields to learn, themselves, about the dynamics of human learning, I am certainly not saying that development should proceed independently of trial on real students. Quite to the contrary, the trial and revision methodology is essential to good development. But unless one has some notion *in advance* of the end objectives or some notion of performance indicators the developers would accept as progress toward their objectives, there is no basis for knowing what direction the revision should take.[4] The presence of learners, therefore, is an essential precondition for the establishment of the feedback loop which is so characteristic of the development process in all fields.

This view of development, however, is based on the involvement of diverse groups of people from the very beginning of the process. It is not a question of *when* certain people should be involved during the course of a three- or five-year development effort, but *how* they can be meaningfully and productively brought together at the outset to insure, to the highest degree possible, that what comes out of the development effort will be useful, significant, workable, and installable improvement. In short, development is not the responsibility of substantive scholars alone, but also of cognitive, developmental, and behavioral psychologists, teachers and other appropriate instructional personnel, and media specialists, all operating as part of an engineering team.

What conclusions, if any, should we draw from the fact that the kind of curriculum building which Atkin describes in his article (including the kind which the engineers, as Atkin calls them, are interested in doing) costs millions of dollars? How should we ask for results? How do we determine accountability? How de we judge whom and what to support?

The position I would take on this question should be clear. It would be extremely hard to justify the allocation of large sums of money to curriculum developers if the only criterion that they offer is that they would work until they have something that "pleases" them. No congressman, no superintendent, no taxpayer, and no Bureau of the Budget examiner would be happy with that state of affairs. While pleasure does arise from the contemplation of elegance, curriculum is developed for practical reasons having to do with the functions of schools, the responsibilities of educational professionals, and the social and technological requirements which schools are asked and expected to meet.

The move toward greater specification of anticipated or sought-after outcomes stems not only from the requirements of development as a process, but also from the character of the support which is necessary for development. It is expensive; so expensive that it is clearly beyond the reach of individual school systems and even states. Furthermore, the magnitude of the expense, even if it comes from the federal treasury, is still so large as to mandate some caution in regard to its allocation. And that caution should find expression in the form of statements about the intended outcomes of given projects in terms which will (1) allow adequate evaluation of those projects before funding to insure that they serve the highest priority national, state, and local requirements and (2) provide the basis for the kinds of anticipated performance specifications—or the means for deriving them—which will insure that adequate feedback and formative evaluation procedures can be brought to bear during the life of the project.

I cannot conclude this brief discussion about behavioral objectives without complimenting Atkin on his clear statement of two extremely important points which are often left begging in much of the discussion about behavioral objectives. First, he points out that the total effects of instructional program and curricular offerings are *always* much broader than the outcomes which are specifically being sought. That is an important point to keep squarely before us whether we are writing behavioral objectives or performance specifications or muddling through. It should be central to our thinking about curriculum and instruction, whether one adopts the view Atkin proposes or the one indicated here.

Second, in pointing out that there are certain kinds of learning which, for want of a better term, might be called synergetic (those would be learnings that are greater than the sums of the individual learnings, difficult to identify, dependent in some measure on factors beyond the school's control, and, therefore, out of the reach of the behavioral objective domain), Atkin again calls our attention to the importance of distinguishing between evidence of progress and goal achievement, the importance of learnings which transcend individual courses of study, and the importance of distinguishing the identification of educational goals from the specification of instructional objectives.

In summary, I have tried to describe the development of behavioral objectives as the generation of criterion measures which will help us assess whether the curriculum development activity has value before it has begun, which will serve as effective (albeit modifiable) guides to the curriculum development process, and which will provide us with at least *minimum* standards by which the efficiency and effectiveness of the completed product can be assessed. The idea of behavioral objectives is more than a frame of mind; it is in that sense, I think, that Atkin sees it as being espoused by its opponents today as the core of curriculum design. I would accept his terminology with the stipulation that its importance as the core be exactly analogous to the core of a nuclear reactor; it is necessary but certainly not sufficient for any of the functions which nuclear reactors are supposed to perform.

REFERENCES

1. J. Myron Atkin. Behavioral Objectives in Curriculum Design: A Cautionary Note. *The Science Teacher, 35,* May 1968, pp. 27-30.
2. James Coleman. The Concept of Equality of Educational Opportunity. *Harvard Educational Review, 38,* Winter, 1968, pp. 7-22.
3. Benjamin S. Bloom. *Taxonomy of Educational Objectives. The Classification of Educational Goals, Handbook I: Cognitive Domain.* New York: David McKay Co., 1956. David R. Krathwohl, Benjamin S. Bloom & Bertram D. Masia. *Taxonomy of Educational Objectives. The Classification of Educational Goals, Handbook II: Affective Domain.* David McKay Co., Inc., New York, 1964.
4. This is probably the key point in the whole debate. The principal value of the behavioral objectivists to my mind is their press to force more careful delineation of the criteria to be used to judge whether or not the product developed really is—or is going to be—an improvement.

Tiemann reviews familiar criticisms of the behavioral approach, particularly the notion that behavioral objectives tend to be trivial and unrelated in nature. He suggests avoiding triviality both in objectives and in resulting evaluative criteria by carefully analyzing the broad objectives of an area of study prior to deriving specific desired behaviors. He urges greater guidance for teachers and other instructional designers in the important skills related to the analysis of content and behavior.

Analysis and the Derivation of Valid Objectives*

PHILIP W. TIEMANN

Nasty words like "B.O.'s" (Oettinger, 1968) and "industrial production model" (Travers, 1968) are touted about by educators observing instructional technology's insistence upon behavioral objectives and the resulting impact on the practicing teacher. A behavioral objective is a trivial objective, the critics claim. The industrial production model treats the learner like just so much raw material—a pliable lump of clay—to be molded into a specified shape rigidly circumscribed by the trivial objectives and to be stamped into shape by the drop-forge of behavioral technology. Originality and creativity are foresaken. The learner fails to learn *how* to learn and faces a narrowed life squeezed into a pre-shaped vocational mold.

Is such criticism irresponsible or irrational? I think not. Practitioners of instructional technology will benefit from a look beyond the nasty words to the important intent of these critics.

*Reprinted from the *NSPI Journal, 8,* July, 1969, pp. 16-18, by permission of the publisher and the author.

Several years ago, Atkin (1963) observed that an insistence upon behavioral objectives tended to focus attention on the trivial. He was concerned with skills students appear to need in order to engage in effective inquiry in any scientific discipiine. As examples of such cross-curricular skills, he listed comprehension of such concepts as "randomness," "proportionality," "successive approximation," and "discreteness."

Similarly, there are desirable outcomes of formal education which are not limited to occupational clusters such as scientific inquiry but, in all probability, extend across all disciplines. One such goal might be to prepare an individual to be a self-evaluator. Evaluation judgments must shift gradually from the standards imposed by others to one's own standards (Tiemann, 1967).

Travers (1968) suggested proper evaluation of learning to be analogous to evaluation of "the mutations produced in genetic material through radiation. One cannot predict what new mutations will be produced by radiation, but there is an expectancy that there will be mutations and there are criteria that can be applied to the evaluation of any that occur."

Other critics seem to agree that criteria must be established in order to evaluate the effect of instruction. We must specify what we *mean* by such broad goals as "creative originality," "proportionality," and "self-evaluation." As we develop the criteria for such non-trivial goals, we find ourselves generating objective statements which—indeed— become quite specific if, in fact, they are to serve their function as criteria.

The apparent characteristic of the model our critics would have us apply is not the absence of specific behavioral objectives. It is the manner by which such objectives are arrived at—in that they must serve to define overall goals.

It is my belief that a more general acceptance of instructional technology by our critics is limited by our lack of skill in developing specific criteria serving to define meaningful goals and not by something inherent in the specific statement of the criteria themselves. Travers recognized this deficiency when he indicated his preference for student performance on a specific task as an acceptable alternative to behavioral objectives. He then noted the difficulty of extrapolating from performance on one sample task to the universe and the difficulty of defining the universe.

But what is meant by "lack of skill" in developing objectives derived from worthwhile goals? The problem is really one of analysis of the universe of those behaviors which we might consider to be acceptable evidence that a student is, for example, a competent self-evaluator. However, there doesn't seem to be any shortage of individuals who are able to state trivial objectives. Of course, trivial objectives are understandable when individuals first struggle to specify measurable objectives in instructional technology workshops.

In 1967, we* conducted a workshop for instructional television people in Dade County, Florida. The staff of the ITV facility invested six full days which we began with the film *Programming is a Process* (Markle & Tiemann, 1967). Three teams of ITV teachers, producer-directors, and graphics support personnel actually developed, tried, revised, and tried again various short sequences of televised instruction with real live student subjects who were prospective eleventh-graders.

The team assignment for the second day was to develop an objective for a short sequence which that team would program on videotape. One of the teams, the language arts group, finally decided to work on this objective:

"Given several passages from the *House of Seven Gables* and *The Scarlet Letter* by Hawthorne, the student will be able to identify in each at least one element which signifies superstitions or fears of colonial times."

To an extent, the objective fulfills Mager's (1962) three criteria. It describes the conditions—the givens, i.e., given a paragraph by Hawthorne from either of the two novels listed. The objective suggests a standard, i.e., the student must recognize one element. And it describes what it is the student must do. The student must recognize an instance of reference to something that was fearful or superstitious in colonial times. The TV instructors in the group—two English teachers—intended to confront the student with a typical analysis task of a high school language arts course.

The English teachers began the second morning by trying out a few of the Hawthorne passages. One teacher read a few sentences and looked expectantly to other members of the team. Amid generally blank looks were a couple of reluctant volunteers. This procedure was repeated a few times. Gradually it became apparent to the English teachers that something was wrong. As "naive students," the other team members faced a problem. The problem is common to much meaningful verbal learning and can be considered in the general as well as the specific case.

Specifically, the student must recognize a reference to an instance of fear or superstition existing in colonial times. In the abstract, this might be called an "instance of X." To the student reading a passage, each sentence, phrase, or even an isolated word represents a possible "instance

---

*"We" were a team of instructional technologists sponsored by the National Project for Improvement of Televised Instruction, a project of the National Association of Educational Broadcasters. Members included George Hall of NPITI, Lark Daniel, Susan Markle, and Philip Tiemann.

of X." With each possibility, the student faces a choice-point. Is it or isn't it an instance of X? Analysis of the problem facing the student forces us to ask, "What must the student be able to do in order to demonstrate the (called for) behavior?" Well, the student must classify each possibility as either an instance or non-instance of X.

Basically, there are two ways to help the student to do this. We can require the student to memorize the universe of instances of X. Or we can give the student some means by which to make the decision—some conceptual scheme that enables the student to make a reasonably reliable choice at each point.

One scheme, which the team decided upon, was to provide the student with several categories of "instances of X." Of the several categories suggested, physical deformity was assumed to be most obvious to prospective students, so it was sequenced first. But given a possible instance of reference to physical deformity, the student is still faced with the same choice. How is he taught to recognize instances of physical deformity? The task is one of learning a concept, that is, the student must recognize instances and non-instances of reference to physical deformity. Stated another way, he must learn to recognize members of a set and to distinguish between members and non-members.

Students learn concepts by responding to sufficient examples and non-examples until they can demonstrate a reliable level of generalization—responding to any new member of the class with the label "physical deformity"—and a parallel level of discrimination, that is, not responding to new non-members of the class with the class label (Englemann, 1969; Markle & Tiemann, 1969; Mechner, 1967).

Such categories as "physical deformity," while useful in organizing the discipline, may often be selected as a matter of convenience. While the categories may foster student learning by enabling mastery of a complex level within the hierarchy, they only serve this purpose if they are comprehensible to the student. This is an additional problem. Hierarchical levels of the structured disciplines of physical science and mathematics are operational, e.g., chemists agree that a certain set of examples constitutes a given category. When we analyze one of the less-structured disciplines of social science or humanities, we must make certain that the hierarchy we construct also possesses such operational worth.

Thus having decided upon the category "physical deformity," the two English teachers proceeded to test whether or not it was operational. From the same paragraph, they selected examples independently and then compared selections. Then they tried from the other direction by testing each other with passages from Hawthorne. The procedure was followed to build five categories for use in the teaching sequence that would eventually be videotaped and tried in first draft form.

Having analyzed instances of reference to colonial superstition and fear, we could ask, "Does the objective possess any validity? Is it worth teaching?" Mager (1968) suggested the "Hey, Dad!" test at this point. Picture a student saying, "Hey, Dad! Know what I'm learning in school? Let me show you how I can recognize instances of reference to colonial superstition and fear!" Dad's response could be "So what!" By Mager's test, we recognize that we might be dealing with a trivial objective.

But the objective may be related logically to other objectives, that is, it may be part of a hierarchy. The English teachers really weren't interested in this single objective alone. Many teachers would want to deal with such an objective in a way that students would acquire the analysis skill and, as a result of experiencing success in applying the skill, actually enjoy applying it to Hawthorne.

A further aim should be for the student to apply the analysis skill to writings by other authors—Poe, for example. Learning sequences should be designed to provide for such transfer. Similarly, related analysis skills covered by other objectives—recognition of instances of concepts A and B—should also be acquired and in a way that students enjoy voluntarily applying them. Concepts A and B could be higher levels of concept X. They could relate colonial times to current literature, requiring students to identify up-to-date superstitions and fears. Once acquired, a set of analysis skills so defined might constitute partial evidence of "literary appreciation."

The student would demonstrate a variety of related analysis skills which he would enjoy applying, that is, he would seek out opportunities to employ and refine many of these skills. Note that people seldom apply all such skills. People indicate preferences. Some appreciate literature but particularly prefer 19th century Romantics. Others attend symphonies regularly but never seem to develop a keen interest in opera, although they may know many scores and friends will vow that they "appreciate" opera. Appreciation, as defined in this manner, would seem to depend upon an interaction between the way in which instruction is presented and the manner in which objectives are derived.

With the best of intentions, we may pursue behavioral objectives—one after another—as though students were required to accumulate unrelated skills like threading so many beads on a string. However, to the extent that behavioral objectives are derived from an analysis of relatively broad objectives, they can serve as valid criteria which enable our students to avoid trivia.

Our enthusiasm to have instructors attend to observable behavior may have oversold the case of the behavioral objective. We've taught teachers to recognize one when they see one, but have given little attention to the relationships which must exist between objectives in order to make any of the objectives valid.

Well-intentioned technologists, some apparently obsessed with the need for "action verbs," have convinced many teachers that "to understand" and "to appreciate" are bad words. Workshop experiences indicate that teachers are delighted when told there is nothing wrong with such terms. These terms are just broad goals which need to be further defined. We must restore such terms to dignity. Not only are they our best starting point, but we must never lose sight of these overall goals during the analysis process.

Development of effective materials requires analysis skills furnished either by the subject matter expert or by supporting personnel. Those of us who are charged with the responsibility of providing such service in support of instruction experience a three-fold set of frustrations.

First, instructors may not know the subject in sufficient depth to analyze what it is they are attempting to teach. Second, instructors— when they are quite competent in their field—usually are on their way to bigger and better things and can afford little time to "improve" their current teaching. Finally, in some cases, instructors have no subject matter; that is, they have precious little to say, but are highly respected by their academic peers for saying it in a very precious way.

But, in any case, teachers may be expected to continue to deal with trivial objectives and to continue to apply trivial evaluative criteria to students who are required to accumulate sets of unrelated skills until such time when we stop admonishing them to state "B.O.'s" and start providing them with guidance in the content and behavior analysis skills which are the foundation of instructional technology.

References

Atkin, J. M. Some Evaluation Problems in a Course Content Improvement Project. *Journal of Research in Science Teaching, I,* 129-132, 1963.

Englemann, S. *Conceptual Learning.* San Rafael, Calif.: Dimensions Press, 1969.

Mager, R. F. *Preparing Instructional Objectives.* San Francisco: Fearon, 1962.

————. The Hey Dad Test. Presentation to the NSPI Annual Convention. San Antonio, April, 1968.

Markle, Susan M. & Tiemann, P. W. *Programming Is A Process: An Introduction to Instructional Technology.* (16mm film, with accompanying viewer handout). Chicago: Office of Instructional Resources, University of Illinois at Chicago Circle, 1967.

————. *Really Understanding Concepts.* (Audiotape-slide, with accompanying program book.) Chicago, Tiemann Associates, 1969.

Mechner, F. Behavioral Analysis and Instructional Sequencing. In *Programmed Instruction, Part II: 66th Yearbook of the NSSE.* (Edited by P. C. Lange) Chicago: University of Chicago Press, 1967.

Oettinger, A. G. The Myths of Educational Technology. *Saturday Review,* May 18, 1968.

Tiemann, P. W. Outcomes in a Televised College Economics Course with Variable Student Knowledge of Objectives. Unpublished Ph.D. dissertation. Urbana, University of Illinois, 1967.

Travers, R. M. W. Models of Education and their Implications for the Conduct of Evaluation Studies. Presentation to the AERA Annual Meeting. Chicago, February, 1968.

Popham presents eleven of the usual reasons advanced against the efficacy of the behavioral approach, and subsequently points out the fallaciousness of each of the reasons. In so doing, he builds a strong case for precisely stated goals. Among the recommendations which evolve is the suggestion that national catalogs of behavioral objectives in all fields at all grade levels be prepared.

Probing the Validity of Arguments Against Behavioral Goals*

W. James Popham

Within the last few years a rather intense debate has developed in the field of curriculum and instruction regarding the merits of stating instructional objectives in terms of measurable learner behaviors. Because I am thoroughly committed, both rationally and viscerally, to the proposition that instructional goals should be stated behaviorally, I view this debate with some ambivalence. On the one hand, it is probably desirable to have a dialogue of this sort among specialists in our field. We get to know each other better—between attacks. We test the respective worth of opposing positions. Yet, as a partisan in the controversy, I would prefer unanimous support of the position to which I subscribe. You see, the other people are wrong. Adhering to a philosophic tenet that error is evil, I hate to see my friends wallowing in sin.

Moreover, their particular form of sin is more dangerous than some of the time-honored perversions of civilized societies. For example, it will

*Paper originally presented at the annual meeting of the American Educational Research Association, Chicago, Illinois, February 9, 1968, printed by permission of the author.

probably harm more people than the most exotic forms of pornography. I believe that those who discourage educators from precisely explicating their instructional objectives are often permitting, if not promoting, the same kind of unclear thinking that has led in part to the generally abysmal quality of instruction in this country.

In the remainder of this paper I shall examine eleven reasons given by my colleagues in opposition to objectives stated in terms of measurable learner behaviors. I believe each of these reasons is, for the most part, invalid. There may be minor elements of truth in some; after all, the most vile pornographer must occasionally use a few clean words. In essence, however, none of these reasons should be considered strong enough to deter educators from specifying all of their instructional goals in the precise form advocated by the "good guys" in this argument. I shall not attempt to develop any arguments in favor of precisely stated goals, for these are treated elsewhere.* My only concern will be with the dubious validity of each of the following reasons often advanced against the behavioral approach.

Reason one: Trivial learner behaviors are the easiest to operationalize, hence the really important outcomes of education will be underemphasized.

This particular objection to the use of precise goals is frequently voiced by educators who have recently become acquainted with the procedures for stating explicit, behavioral objectives. Since even behavioral objectives enthusiasts admit that the easiest kinds of pupil behaviors to operationalize are usually the most pedestrian, it is not surprising to find so many examples of behavioral objectives which deal with the picayune. In spite of its overall beneficial influence, the programmed booklet by Robert Mager (1962) dealing with the preparation of instructional objectives has probably suggested to many that precise objectives are usually trivial. Almost all of Mager's examples deal with cognitive behaviors which, according to Bloom's taxonomy, would be identified at the very lowest level.

Contrary to the objection raised in reason one, however, the truth is that explicit objectives make it far *easier* for educators to attend to *important* instructional outcomes. To illustrate, if you were to ask a social science teacher what his objectives were for his government class and he responded as follows, "I want to make my students better citizens

---

*Popham, W. James, *Educational Objectives,* Vimcet Associates, Los Angeles, 1966; Popham, W. James, *Selecting Appropriate Educational Objectives,* Vimcet Associates, Los Angeles, 1967.

so that they can function effectively in our nation's dynamic democracy," you would probably find little reason to fault him. His objective sounds so profound and eminently worthwhile that few could criticize it. Yet, beneath such a facade of profundity, many teachers really are aiming at extremely trivial kinds of pupil behavior changes. How often, for example, do we find "good citizenship" measured by a trifling true-false test. Now, if we'd asked for the teacher's objectives in operational terms and had discovered that, indeed, all the teacher was attempting to do was promote the learner's achievement on a true-false test, we might have rejected the aim as being unimportant. But this is possible *only* with the precision of explicitly stated goals.

In other words, there is the danger that because of their ready translation to operational statements, teachers will tend to identify too many trivial behaviors as goals. But the very fact that we can make these behaviors explicit permits the teacher and his colleagues to scrutinize them carefully and thus eliminate them as unworthy of our educational efforts. Instead of encouraging unimportant outcomes in education, the use of explicit instructional objectives makes it possible to identify and reject those objectives which are unimportant.

Reason two: Prespecification of explicit goals prevents the teacher from taking advantage of instructional opportunities unexpectedly occurring in the classroom.

When one specifies explicit *ends* for an instructional program there is no necessary implication that the *means* to achieve those ends are also specified. Serendipity in the classroom is always welcome but, and here is the important point, *it should always be justified in terms of its contribution to the learner's attainment of worthwhile objectives.* Too often teachers may believe they are capitalizing on unexpected instructional opportunities in the classroom, whereas measurement of pupil growth toward any defensible criterion would demonstrate that what has happened is merely ephemeral entertainment for the pupils, temporary diversion, or some other irrelevant classroom event.

Prespecification of explicit goals does not prevent the teacher from taking advantage of unexpectedly occurring instructional opportunities in the classroom, it only tends to make the teacher justify these spontaneous learning activities in terms of worthwhile instructional ends. There are undoubtedly gifted teachers who can capitalize magnificently on the most unexpected classroom events. These teacher should not be restricted from doing so. But the teacher who prefers to probe instructional periphery, just for the sake of its spontaneity, should be deterred by the prespecification of explicit goals.

Reason three: Besides pupil behavior changes, there are other types of educational outcomes which are important, such as changes in parental attitudes, the professional staff, community values, etc.

There are undoubtedly some fairly strong philosophic considerations associated with this particular reason. It seems reasonable that there are desirable changes to be made in our society which might be undertaken by the schools. Certainly, we would like to bring about desirable modifications in such realms as the attitudes of parents. But, as a number of educational philosophers have reminded us, the schools cannot be all things to all segments of society. It seems that the primary responsibility of the schools should be to educate effectively the youth of the society. And to the extent that this is so, all modifications of parental attitudes, professional staff attitudes, etc., should be weighed in terms of a later measurable impact on the learner himself. For example, the school administrator who tells us that he wishes to bring about new kinds of attitudes on the part of his teachers should ultimately have to demonstrate that these modified attitudes result in some kind of desirable learner changes. To stop at merely modifying the behavior of teachers, without demonstrating further effects upon the learner, would be insufficient.

So while we can see that there are other types of important social outcomes to bring about, it seems that the school's primary responsibility is to its pupils. Hence, all modifications in personnel or external agencies should be justified in terms of their contribution toward the promotion of desired pupil behavior changes.

Reason four: Measurability implies behavior which can be objectively, mechanistically measured, hence there must be something dehumanizing about the approach.

This fourth reason is drawn from a long history of resistance to measurement on the grounds that it must, of necessity, reduce human learners to quantifiable bits of data. This resistance probably is most strong regarding earlier forms of measurement which were almost exclusively examination-based, and were frequently multiple-choice test measures at that. But a broadened conception of evaluation suggests that there are diverse and extremely sophisticated ways of securing qualitative as well as quantitative indices of learner performance.

One is constantly amazed to note the incredible agreement among a group of judges assigned to evaluate the complicated gyrations of skilled springboard divers in the televised reports of national aquatic championships. One of these athletes will perform an exotic, twisting dive and a few seconds after he has hit the water five or more judges raise cards reflecting their independent evaluations which can range from 0 to 10. The five ratings very frequently run as follows: 7.8, 7.6, 7.7, 7.8, and 7.5. The possibility of reliably judging something as qualitatively complicated as a springboard dive does suggest that our measurement procedures do not have to be based on a theory of reductionism. It is currently possible to assess many complicated human behaviors in a refined fashion. Developmental work is underway in those areas where we now must rely on primitive measures.

Reason five: It is somehow undemocratic to plan in advance precisely how the learner should behave after instruction.

This particular reason was raised a few years ago in a professional journal (Arnstine, 1964) suggesting that the programmed instruction movement was basically undemocratic because it spelled out in advance how the learner was supposed to behave after instruction. A brilliant refutation (Komisar and McClellan, 1965) appeared several months later in which the rebutting authors responded that instruction is by its very nature undemocratic and to imply that freewheeling democracy is always present in the classroom would be untruthful. Teachers generally have an idea of how they wish learners to behave, and they promote these goals with more or less efficiency. Society knows what it wants its young to become, perhaps not with the precision that we would desire, but certainly in general. And if the schools were allowing students to "democratically" deviate from societally-mandated goals, one can be sure that the institutions would cease to receive society's approbation and support.

Reason six: That isn't really the way teaching is; teachers rarely specify their goals in terms of measurable learner behaviors; so let's set realistic expectations of teachers.

Jackson (1966) recently offered this argument. He observed that teachers just don't specify their objectives in terms of measurable learner behavior and implied that, since this is the way the real world is, we ought to recognize it and live with it. Perhaps.

There is obviously a difference between identifying the status quo and applauding it. Most of us would readily concede that few teachers specify their instructional aims in terms of measurable learner behaviors; *but they ought to.* What we have to do is to mount a widespread campaign to modify this aspect of teacher behavior. Instructors must begin to identify their instructional intentions in terms of measurable learner behaviors. The way teaching really is at the moment just isn't good enough.

Reason seven: In certain subject areas, e.g., fine arts and the humanities, it is more difficult to identify measurable pupil behaviors.

Sure it's tough. Yet, because it is difficult in certain subject fields to identify measurable pupil behaviors, those subject specialists should not be allowed to escape this responsibility. Teachers in the fields of art and music often claim that it is next to impossible to identify acceptable works of art in precise terms—but they do it all the time. In instance after instance the art teacher does make a judgment regarding the acceptability of pupil-produced artwork. What the art teacher is reluctant to do is put his evaluative criteria on the line. He has such criteria. He must have, to make his judgments. But he is loath to describe them in terms that anyone can see.

Any English teacher, for example, will tell you how difficult it is to make a valid judgment of a pupil's essay response. Yet criteria lurk whenever this teacher does make a judgment, and these criteria must be made explicit. No one who really understands education has ever argued that instruction is a simple task. It is even more difficult in such areas as the arts and humanities. As a noted art educator observed several years ago, art educators must quickly get to the business of specifying "tentative, but clearly defined criteria" by which they can judge their learners' artistic efforts (Munro, 1960).

Reason eight: While loose general statements of objectives may appear worthwhile to an outsider, if most educational goals were stated precisely, they would be revealed as generally innocuous.

This eighth reason contains a great deal of potential threat for school people. The unfortunate truth is that much of what is going on in the schools today is indefensible. Merely to reveal the nature of some behavior changes we are bringing about in our schools would be embarrassing. As long as general objectives are the rule, our goals may appear worthwhile to external observers. But once we start to describe precisely what kinds of changes we are bringing about in the learner, there is the danger that the public will reject our intentions as unworthy. Yet, if what we are doing is trivial, educators would know it and those who support the educational institution should also know it. To the extent that we are achieving innocuous behavior changes in learners, we are guilty. We must abandon the ploy of "obfuscation by generality" and make clear exactly what we are doing. Then we are obliged to defend our choices.

Reason nine: Measurability implies accountability; teachers might be judged on their ability to produce results in learners rather than on the many bases now used as indices of competence.

This is a particularly threatening reason and serves to produce much teacher resistence to precisely stated objectives. It doesn't take too much insight on the part of the teacher to realize that if objectives are specified in terms of measurable learner behavior, there exists the possibility that the instructor will have to become *accountable* for securing such behavior changes. Teachers might actually be judged on their ability to bring about desirable changes in learners. They should be.

But a teacher should not be judged on the particular instructional *means* he uses to bring about desirable *ends*. At present many teachers are judged adversely simply because the instructional procedures they use do not coincide with those once used by an evaluator when "he was a teacher." In other words, if I'm a supervisor who has had considerable success with open-ended discussion, I may tend to view with disfavor any teachers who cleave to more directive methods. Yet, if the teacher using the more direct methods can secure learner behavior changes which are desirable, I have no right to judge that teacher as inadequate. The possibility of assessing instructional competence in terms of the teacher's ability to bring about specified behavior changes in learners brings with it far more assets than liabilities to the teacher. He will no longer be judged on the idiosyncratic whim of visiting supervisors. Rather, he can amass evidence that, in terms of his pupils' actual attainments, he is able to teach efficiently.

Even though this is a striking departure from the current state of affairs, and a departure that may be threatening to the less competent, the educator must promote this kind of accountability rather than the maze of folklore and mysticism which exists at the moment regarding teacher evaluation.

Reason ten: It is far more difficult to generate such precise objectives than to talk about objectives in our customarily vague terms.

Here is a very significant objection to the development of precise goals. Teachers are, for the most part, far too busy to spend the necessary hours in stating their objectives and measurement procedures with the kind of precision implied by this discussion. It is said that we are soon nearing a time when we will have more teachers than jobs. This is the time to reduce the teacher's load to the point where he can become a professional decision-maker rather than a custodian. We must reduce public school teaching loads to those of college professors. This is the time when we must give the teacher immense help in specifying his objectives. Perhaps we should *give* him objectives from which to choose, rather than force him to generate his own. Many of the federal dollars currently being used to support education would be better spent on agencies which would produce alternative behavioral objectives for all fields at all grade levels. At any rate, the difficulty of the task should not preclude its accomplishment. We can recognize how hard the job is and still allocate the necessary resources to do it.

Reason eleven: In evaluating the worth of instructional schemes it is often the unanticipated results which are really important, but pre-specified goals may make the evaluator inattentive to the unforeseen.

Some fear that if we cleave to behaviorally stated objectives which must be specified prior to designing an instructional program, we will overlook certain outcomes of the program which were not anticipated yet which may be extremely important. They point out that some of the relatively recent "new curricula" in the sciences have had the unanticipated effect of sharply reducing pupil enrollments in those fields. In view of the possibility of such outcomes, both unexpectedly good and bad, it is suggested that we really ought not spell out objectives in advance, but should evaluate the adequacy of the instructional program after it has been implemented.

Such reasoning, while compelling at first glance, weakens under close scrutiny. In the first place, really dramatic unanticipated outcomes cannot be overlooked by curriculum evaluators. They certainly should not be. We would judge an instructional sequence not only by whether it attains its prespecified objectives, but also by any unforeseen consequences it produces. But what can you tell the would-be curriculum evaluator regarding this problem? "Keep your eyes open," doesn't seem to pack the desired punch. Yet, it's about all you can say. For if there is reason to believe that a particular outcome may result from an instructional sequence, it should be built into the set of objectives for the sequence. To illustrate, if the curriculum designers fear that certain negative attitudes will be acquired by the learner as he interacts with an instructional sequence, then behavioral objectives can be devised which reveal whether the instructional sequence has effectively counteracted this affective outcome. It is probably always a good idea, for example, to identify behavioral indices of the pupil's "subject-approaching tendencies." We don't want to teach youngsters how to perform mathematical exercises, for example, and to learn to hate math in the process.

Yet, it is indefensible to let an awareness of the importance of unanticipated outcomes in evaluating instructional programs lead one to the rejection of rigorous pre-planning of instructional objectives. Such objectives should be the primary, but not exclusive, focus in evaluating instruction.

While these eleven reasons are not exhaustive, they represent most of the arguments used to resist the implementation of precise instructional objectives. In spite of the very favorable overall reaction to explicit objectives during the past five to ten years, a small collection of dissident educators has arisen to oppose the quest for goal specificity. The trouble with criticisms of precise objectives isn't that they are completely without foundation. As conceded earlier, there are probably elements of truth in all of them. Yet, when we are attempting to promote the widescale adoption of precision in the classroom, there is the danger that many instructors will use the comments and objections of these few critics as an excuse from thinking clearly about their goals. Any risks we run by moving to behavioral goals are miniscule in contrast with our current state of confusion regarding instructional intentions. The objections against behaviorally stated goals are not strong enough. To secure a dramatic increase in instructional effectiveness we must abandon our customary practices of goal-stating and turn to a framework of precision.

References

Arnstine, D. G. The Language and Values of Programmed Instruction: Part 2. *The Educational Forum, 28,* 1964.

Jackson, P. W. The Way Teaching Is. Washington, D.C.: National Education Association, 1966.

Komisar, P. B. & McClellan, J. E. Professor Arnstine and Programmed Instruction. *The Educational Forum, 29,* 1965.

Mager, R. F. *Preparing Objectives for Programmed Instruction.* San Francisco: Fearon, 1962.

Munro, T. The Creative Arts in American Education. *The Interrelation of the Arts in Secondary Education.* Cambridge: Harvard University Press, 1960.

Part VIII

Additional Media

Arnstine, Donald G. The Language and Values of Programmed Instruction:
Part One. *The Educational Forum, 28,* January, 1964, pp. 219-226.
————. The Language and Values of Programmed Instruction: Part II. *The Educational Forum, 28,* March 1964, pp. 337-346.
Baker, Robert L. The Educational Objectives Controversy. Paper presented
at the annual meeting of the American Educational Research Association,
Chicago, Illinois, February 9, 1968, 7 pp. (Mimeo.)
Dyer, Henry S. Discovery and Development of Educational Goals. *The Bulletin of the National Association of Secondary School Principals, 51,* March, 1967, pp. 1-14.
Ebel, Robert L. Some Comments. *The School Review, 75,* Autumn, 1967,
pp. 261-266.
Eisner, Elliot W. A Response to My Critics. *The School Review, 75,* Autumn, 1967, pp. 277-282.
————. Instructional and Expressive Educational Objectives: Their Formulation and Use in Curriculum. *Instructional Objectives.* Chicago: Rand McNally & Company, 1969, pp. 1-18.
Evans, James. Behavioral Objectives Are No Damn Good. *Technology and Innovation in Education.* New York: Frederick A. Praeger, Publishers, 1968, pp. 41-45.
French, Will, *et al. Behavioral Goals of General Education in High School.* New York: Russell Sage Foundation, 1957, 247 pp.
Gagné, Robert M. Educational Objectives and Human Performance. *Learning and the Educational Process.* John D. Krumboltz (Ed.) Chicago, Illinois: Rand McNally & Company, 1965, pp. 1-24.
Haberman, Martin. Behavioral Objectives: Bandwagon or Breakthrough. *The Journal of Teacher Education, 19,* Spring, 1968, pp. 91-94.
Hastings, J. Thomas. Some Comments. *The School Review, 75,* Autumn, 1967, pp. 267-271.

Kearney, Nolan C. *Elementary School Objectives.* New York: Russell Sage Foundation, 1953, 189 pp.

Koepke, Charles A., III. Reply to Atkin on Behavioral Objectives. *The Science Teacher, 35,* November, 1968, pp. 12, 14.

Komisar, B. Paul & James E. McClellan. Professor Arnstine and Programmed Instruction. *The Educational Forum, 29,* May, 1965, pp. 467-475.

Lindvall, C. M. Some Background to Present Practices. *Defining Educational Objectives: A Report of the Regional Commission on Educational Coordination and the Learning Research and Development Center.* C. M. Lindvall (Ed.) Pittsburgh, Pennsylvania: University of Pittsburgh Press, 1964, pp. 3-4.

Nelson, Gerald E. Of Myths and Strawmen: A Reply to Stansfield. *Educational Technology, 9,* October, 1969, pp. 103-104.

Ojemann, Ralph H. Should Educational Objectives Be Stated in Behavioral Terms? *The Elementary School Journal, 68,* February, 1968, pp. 223-231.

————. Should Educational Objectives Be Stated in Behavioral Terms?— Part II. *The Elementary School Journal, 69,* February, 1969, pp. 229-235.

Payne, Arlene. Some Comments. *The School Review, 75,* Autumn, 1967, pp. 272-277.

Popham, W. James & Eva L. Baker. Measuring Teachers' Attitudes Toward Behavioral Objectives. *The Journal of Educational Research, 60,* July-August, 1967, pp. 453-455.

Raths, James D. Specificity as a Threat to Curriculum Reform. Paper presented at the annual meeting of the American Educational Research Association, Chicago, Illinois, February 9, 1968, 5 pp. (Mimeo.)

Shettel, Harry H. Objectives, 'Ours' and 'Theirs.' *NSPI Journal, 3,* May, 1964, pp. 12-14.

Stansfield, David. The Educational Technology Myth. *Educational Technology, 9,* July, 1969, pp. 52-54.

Thompson, Merritt M. The Levels of Objectives in Education. *Harvard Educational Review, 8,* May, 1943, pp. 196-211.

Tyler, Ralph W. The Curriculum—Then and Now. *The Elementary School Journal, 57,* April, 1957, pp. 364-374.

Wagschall, Peter H. Performance vs. Experience-Based Curricula. *The High School Journal, 52,* May, 1969, pp. 466-471.